THE
UNITED STATES
IN
WORLD AFFAIRS
1964

THE
UNITED STATES
IN
WORLD AFFAIRS
1964

BY JULES DAVIDS

Published for the
COUNCIL ON FOREIGN RELATIONS
by
HARPER & ROW, *Publishers*
NEW YORK *and* EVANSTON

1965

The Council on Foreign Relations is a non-profit institution devoted to the study of political, economic, and strategic problems as related to American foreign policy. It takes no stand, expressed or implied, on American policy.

The authors of books published under the auspices of the Council are responsible for their statements of fact and expressions of opinion. The Council is responsible only for determining that they should be presented to the public.

For a list of Council publications see pages 384–386.

PREFACE

THIS BOOK continues the series of annual survey volumes initiated by the Council on Foreign Relations in 1931 and interrupted only by the war years 1941–1944. Like its predecessors, its purpose is to present a concise, descriptive, and interpretive account of major events and developments of the year that affect U.S. foreign policy.

In his Preface to the volume for 1947–1948, John C. Campbell commented: "One problem which remained at the center of American thought and action in the field of foreign policy was that of adjusting to the realities of living in the same world with the Soviet Union. Another was that of helping to establish a functioning world economic system which would give this country some prospect of future prosperity and peace." Despite the fact that the world scene had altered markedly in the span of almost two decades, these two goals continued to be of major concern to the United States.

In 1964, the United States with its thriving Western allies— a contrast to 1947–1948—still faced the task of establishing a better functioning world economic system, one that would provide for a freer flow of trade among industrial nations and a balance between them and the developing countries. Like the years which saw the launching of the Marshall Plan and the Point Four program, 1964 witnessed the opening of the Kennedy Round and the meeting of the United Nations Conference on Trade and Development, both of which pointed to significant changes in the international community. The problem of how to deal with the Communist world, though now it was a very different sort of world from Stalin's, was still central in American thought and action. While major issues remained unresolved, most Americans by the mid-1960's had learned to adjust to the realities of living in the same world with the Soviet Union. The question posed more particularly in 1964 was whether and how the United States could live in the same world with Communist China.

During the year the main theater of the cold war was not in Europe but in Asia. The removal of Nikita S. Khrushchev as Soviet Premier, to be sure, created new uncertainties; troublesome also were the situations in Cyprus and in the Congo, the disputes in the Middle East, the crisis in the United Nations, the anti-American riots that flared up in Panama, and the controversies between the United States and Castro's Cuba. Still the most threatening developments occurred in Asia. Peking's militancy and its successful test explosion of a nuclear device marked a new phase in the conflict over Southeast Asia. Determined to "hold the line" against the spread of Asian Communism, America's military involvement in South Vietnam's struggle against the Vietcong increased steadily during the year, especially after the Gulf of Tonkin episodes. But the problems in Southeast Asia were not limited to Vietnam; the entire region was in ferment. In addition to the growing prestige and influence of Communist China, the depth of the challenge to the West in Asia was indicated by President Sukarno's assault on Malaysia and Indonesia's withdrawal from the United Nations.

Although crises dominated the headlines, the United States continued to try to build up the strength of the free world, to restore the cohesion of the Atlantic alliance, and to make more effective the Alliance for Progress in the Western Hemisphere. The "pause" in the cold war in Europe and the loosening of ties in the Soviet bloc offered an opportunity to establish a closer relationship with some of the countries of Eastern Europe. Above all, the United States persisted in its efforts to foster a peaceful and healthful world society by its support of international organizations and by helping underdeveloped nations cope with their numerous and difficult problems.

Collating and organizing the vast body of material and documentation relating to international affairs while history is in motion has many pitfalls. Since this book is concerned with the immediate present, and the author is dependent upon selected official documents released for publication and journalistic information, this survey cannot be definitive. It is intended to provide a helpful reference, and by comprehensively reviewing the main developments in international affairs, to aid in the understanding of the key foreign policy issues of 1964. Many available documents used as the basis for this book will be found in the companion volume, *Documents on American Foreign Relations, 1964.*

The author appreciates the help he received from many sources. Georgetown University graciously granted him a year's leave of absence to work on this book. The cordiality and warmth of all the staff members of the Council on Foreign Relations made the experience of being with the Council a memorable one. The numerous off-the-record talks at the Council by world leaders and by scholars and specialists in the field of international relations were both stimulating and profitable. John C. Campbell, Senior Research Fellow, and David W. MacEachron, Director of Program, read the entire manuscript. Their advice and constructive criticism were invaluable. William Diebold, Jr., Senior Research Fellow, contributed materially to sections on international economic policies. Comments from members of the Committee on Studies were most useful. The author is grateful for the suggestions and encouragement he received from Henry M. Wriston, Caryl P. Haskins, Byron Dexter, Hamilton Fish Armstrong, Joseph E. Johnson, and Alfred C. Neal. Special thanks are owed to Elaine P. Adam who guided the manuscript through its various stages and meticulously handled countless details; to Robert W. Valkenier for his expert editorial assistance; to E. D. Weldon for preparing the maps; and to Grace Darling, Production and Promotion Manager. Help was also provided by Donald Wasson, Librarian, Janet Rigney, Assistant Librarian, the courteous and efficient Council library staff, as well as Alice E. Fine and Joseph Cucolo.

Acknowledgment is extended to the Department of State with gratitude for the comments made on the manuscript by many officials, and especially for the help provided by John F. King, Public Affairs Adviser for European Affairs. Jack H. Newman, a close friend and Treasury Department representative who attended the National War College class of 1964–1965, read the entire manuscript and offered many astute observations. Valuable suggestions were also provided by others. Although help was obtained from many directions, the author assumes personal responsibility for all the statements contained in the book.

JULES DAVIDS

April 1965

CONTENTS

MAPS

THE
UNITED STATES
IN
WORLD AFFAIRS
1964

[1]

CHAPTER ONE
THE TORCH IS PASSED

AMERICA'S MOOD was sober and quiet. Six weeks had passed since John F. Kennedy had been assassinated and Lyndon Baines Johnson had assumed the presidency. These were weeks of difficult adjustment, but President Johnson recognized that his first great problem lay in assuring the nation and the world that there would be, as he phrased it, "continuity in transition." With speed and energy, he proceeded to demonstrate that the United States had a vigorous new Chief Executive. "The ideas and ideals which he [Mr. Kennedy] so nobly represented," President Johnson declared in his first address to Congress on November 27, 1963, "must and will be translated into effective action." [1]

Mr. Johnson set a fast pace of activity. While his initial policies, domestic and foreign, reflected an extension of the Kennedy program, their tone and style quickly assumed the imprint of the new President's personality. Above all, he stressed that he intended to be "President of all the people," and "to make our people aware that they share a fundamental unity of interest and purpose and belief."

No major international crises darkened the horizon immediately following Mr. Kennedy's assassination, but the momentary pause soon ended. The Johnson administration entered a new year of great turmoil. Crises erupted in Cyprus, in Panama, in South Vietnam, and in Africa. Cracks widened in the Atlantic alliance. Controversy deepened over the creation of a NATO multilateral force (M.L.F.), over Western trade with Cuba and

with the Soviet Union and Eastern European countries, and over
the policies being followed by President Charles de Gaulle.
French recognition of Communist China, the British Labor
party's political victory, the deposition of Premier Nikita S.
Khrushchev, and Peking's explosion of a nuclear device marked
some of the significant developments. The United States also
became deeply involved in the Kennedy Round of tariff negotiations, the U.N. Conference on Trade and Development, and
the financial impasse at the United Nations. And again the
balance of payments proved troublesome.

Difficulties posed by a changing world order were immense.
In certain respects many problems differed in nature from those
of previous years. The Soviet-American "confrontation" in the
Cuban missile crisis of 1962 seemed in retrospect to have been
a real turning point. More than any other event, it had confirmed the belief that hostilities among the nuclear powers would
assure their mutual destruction. Under the umbrella of "nuclear
peace," attention turned to more immediate problems of national
life, and latent tensions came increasingly to the surface both
within societies and between them. The United States, while
trying to deal with critical and ever-changing problems abroad,
was, no less than other nations, swept along by revolutionary
change at home.

Although some Americans nostalgically recalled the days when
the burdens of world leadership were seemingly not so great
and problems not so complex, President Johnson made clear
that if anything was certain, it was that the nation could never
again safely retreat from its responsibilities. "You must know,
and we must realize," he warned, "that we will be involved in
the world for the rest of our history. We must accustom ourselves
to working for liberty in the community of nations as we have
pursued it in our community of States. . . . There is no turning
from a course which will require wisdom and much endurance
so long as the name of America still sounds in this land and
around the world." [2]

1. THE JOHNSON ERA TAKES SHAPE

Historians looking back on America's role in the year 1964 will probably take note of four significant developments. First, they will perhaps point to some shift of emphasis in public policy from national security to domestic social and economic problems. Since the end of World War II the great preoccupation of the United States had centered on thwarting Communist expansion, and this had led to a progressive involvement in the affairs of Europe, the Middle East, Asia, Latin America, and Africa. While this goal continued to be fundamental in the mid-1960's, certain changes in emphasis became discernible. For one thing, there was a tendency to view the challenge more in political and economic, rather than military, terms. In addition, as the sharp polarization of the cold war steadily diffused on both sides of the dividing line, attention focused more directly on what might be called the "human situation" in individual countries, as well as in world society. The United States, of course, could not disengage itself from crisis situations in which American interests were vitally involved. Nevertheless, there was a strong pull within the country to reduce America's international commitments so that greater efforts could be directed to neglected domestic tasks.

Second, the loosening of ties in blocs and alliances encouraged states to strive for greater independent action. Whether this development, especially manifest in both Western and Eastern Europe, as well as in the "third world," was merely temporary could not be determined. What was evident was that a new spirit seemed to be emerging, one which was reflected in a stronger will on the part of lesser powers to assert the unencumbered prerogatives of sovereignty. As Roberto Ducci, an Italian diplomat, astutely commented, "Big Brother has ceased to be feared because of his bigness, or to be loved because of his brotherhood. Die-hard capitalism and intransigent Communism are both becoming obsolete and out of fashion. All this presages something new—for something has to fill the void which will be created." [3]

A third striking feature was the great importance attached to the so-called third world in the design of American foreign policy. During 1964 the United States came to recognize—even more strongly than it had in the past—that while most of the newly independent states and developing countries were individually weak, collectively they could and would exert increasing influence in world affairs. Besides accounting for the greater part of the world's population, these nations provided needed commodities for the American economy and markets for its products, and a number of them controlled geographic areas of strategic significance. They had gained a strong position in the United Nations. Their future and their freedom constituted vital interests of the United States. In recognition of these facts, as Under-Secretary of State George W. Ball pointed out, the United States "felt it necessary to extend its protective military shield to embrace large areas of the world left undefended by the disappearance of colonial power," and undertook, at the same time, "the equally necessary task of providing the new nations with technical and economic assistance to help them raise their standards of living." [4] The consequence was a vast extension of American responsibility. By the mid-1960's a central problem for the United States was to determine how this responsibility could be shared with its allies, and how the resources of the Atlantic world could be harnessed to help the underdeveloped countries become viable and remain independent.

Finally, the year brought to the forefront the dilemma created, on the one hand, by the inclination in some countries toward the untrammeled exercise of sovereignty, and on the other, by the tendencies toward the growing interdependence among nations. Advances in science and technology, the growth of industrial and military power, the population explosion, and the development of rapid communications emphasized the need for world-wide cooperation. They underscored the necessity of achieving a durable and effective relationship in the Atlantic community, so important not only for security reasons, but also for creating a cohesive world society.

A striking evidence of change could be observed in the nation's mood. Every public opinion poll had shown that a large majority of the electorate wanted to find an honorable way back from the nuclear precipice. By 1964 most Americans no longer felt nuclear war to be inevitable. Believing that peace was possible, they favored pushing negotiations to the limit in order to ease world tensions; but willingness to negotiate did not imply willingness to make unilateral concessions or to neglect the means of defense. The chances were reasonably good, in the opinion of many, that some positive steps could be taken through negotiations with the Communists.[5] Although less worried about the imminent threat of a nuclear war, Americans were perturbed by problems at home: the rise in crime and teenage violence, urban sprawl, inadequate schools, and racial problems, to mention only a few that weighed heavily upon the country.

Cannily expressing the nation's mood, President Johnson in his first State of the Union message on January 8, 1964,[6] set the tone and direction of his administration's policies in calling for an attack on domestic problems. The President placed top priority on three issues—civil rights, a tax cut, and a "poverty package." It was imperative that "not some but all racial discrimination" be abolished. "Today Americans of all races stand side by side in Berlin and Vietnam," Mr. Johnson declared. "They died side by side in Korea. Surely they can work and eat and travel side by side in their own country." He strongly recommended a far-reaching tax reduction that would add $11 billion to "the private spending stream to create new jobs and new markets in every area of this land." And Mr. Johnson urged that a concerted effort be made on the local, state, and national levels to deal with the poverty that still blighted one-fifth of the nation.

In foreign affairs, President Johnson pledged continued efforts to maintain America's military strength, to seek the control and eventual abolition of arms, to work for an expanded food-for-peace program, to assure the nation's preeminence in the peaceful exploration of outer space, to expand world trade, to strive to correct the imbalance of international payments, to close the economic "gap" between developed and developing nations, to become "better neighbors with the free states of the Americas," and to strengthen "our Atlantic and Pacific partnerships, maintain our alliances, and make the United Nations a more effective instrument for national independence and international order." These were expected generalities. They did not indicate any new lines of policy or what the approach would be to specific questions.

The President's speech drew a mixed reaction in the nation. Some saw it not only as an outline of a program, but as an election platform, shrewdly prepared with an eye to the presidential campaign. James Reston commented that the President's remarks seemed to have a "Franklin Delano Hoover twist" with its emphasis on "the forgotten Forgotten Man, and flashes of Roosevelt in a three-inch Hoover collar." Several journalists suggested that the President seemed to be offering a "bargain basement Utopia." But many Americans were inclined to agree with Walter Lippmann who thought that the speech fully displayed Mr. Johnson's gifts, and disclosed that he was "just about the shrewdest practical politician that the country had known in this generation." Those were talents that had great promise of success at home and should also prove useful in facing the many challenges abroad.

During the year the distinctions between the Kennedy and Johnson administrations became more and more apparent. Complaints were voiced that Mr. Johnson had taken such Kennedy programs as the war on poverty and labeled them his own. The President's folksy style, at times, met with criticism. However, his boundless confidence in his intuitive judgments about what men would or would not do, his enormous energy, his tireless, almost nagging persistence in following things through were greatly admired. Mr. Johnson's finger-tip sensitivity to Congress proved to be far more effective in many respects than the relations of his three predecessors with the Hill. Most Republican members conceded, as minority leader Charles A. Halleck said, that the President "knows the score up here." To maintain good relations with his former colleagues, Mr. Johnson consulted with them frequently and invited every member of Congress to at least two White House social functions. Conservative congressmen of both parties were won over by the President's pledge to get "a dollar's worth from a dollar spent," by his efforts to cut governmental expenses, and by his instructions to eliminate "nonessential military installations," though here he was bound to tread on some congressional toes. The President established a close rapport not only with Congress, but with the business and labor communities—a remarkable political feat. Whether he would be able to count on strong congressional and public support for his foreign policies, however, remained a question.

For President Johnson, a fundamental challenge in America's domestic life lay in the opportunity to move "upward to the Great Society." Late in May, speaking at the University of Michigan, the President defined the "Great Society" as one "where every child can find knowledge to enrich his mind and enlarge his talents," where creation would be honored "for its own sake and for what it adds to the understanding of the race," and where men would be more concerned "with the quality of their goals than the quantity of their goods." It would be a society where "the marvelous products of our labor" would be matched by the "meaning of our lives." [7] During the year, he set up numerous task forces—composed of labor, business, government, and academic leaders—to explore new approaches to the problems relating to automation, conservation, the expansion of schools, the rebuilding of cities, the use of leisure time, as well as to the federal-state relationship and the reorganization of the executive branch of government.

While the American people, on the whole, were content with the direction of Mr. Johnson's policies—their support was dramatically shown in the President's victory in the November elections, which he won by the biggest popular margin in American history (61 per cent) and an electoral vote majority second only to Franklin D. Roosevelt's in 1936—they were uneasy about the growing deterioration of the situation in South Vietnam, and the explosive political forces in underdeveloped countries, especially in Africa. The proliferation of nuclear weapons and the menace of Communist China created an undercurrent of apprehension. With trust in the nation's powerful military capability, however, they seemingly were developing the will to seek small gains for peace, despite the frustrations of coping with a turbulent world.

2. CONGRESS SETS "A YEAR WITHOUT PRECEDENT"

The pause in the cold war coupled with increasing internal pressures and tensions were, in part, responsible for directing President Johnson's attention to the tasks of mitigating racial strife and strengthening the economy. Although the President seemed to set a higher priority on domestic issues, this did not signify any withdrawal from the international arena. On the contrary, it was a tangible recognition that the well-being of the United States was vitally related to America's leadership in the world.

Congress, under President Johnson's constant prodding, passed some impressive legislation. With a few important exceptions, much of the program outlined by President Kennedy in his two years and ten months in office was enacted into law. Not only did Congress take steps to spur the nation's growth and economic activity, but it dramatically endorsed the civil rights bill, adopted an antipoverty bill, and approved a foreign aid bill that was remarkably close to the administration's request. On August 19 the President declared in his salute to the 88th Congress, "This has been a year without precedent in the history of relations between the Executive and Legislative branches of our Government. This session has enacted more major legislation, met more national needs, disposed of more national issues than any other session of this century or the last." [8]

President Johnson achieved his first legislative triumph when he pried out of the Senate Finance Committee the bill to reduce individual and corporate taxes by $11 billion. The tax cut fulfilled its promise as a spur to economic growth. By the end of the year the dollar value of all goods and services in the country climbed to an estimated $624 billion, an increase of some $40 billion over the gross national product of 1963. The American economy represented fundamental power, without parallel or precedent in history.

The capstone to the achievements of the 88th Congress was clearly the enactment of the Civil Rights Act. For months the Senate debated the crucial issues involved in the law. Behind it stood a decade of mounting racial tensions, started mainly by efforts to implement the 1954 Supreme Court decision on school integration. In the 1960 campaign President Kennedy had espoused a strong and effective civil rights program. During his first two years in office he had tried to deal with the problems of racial relations through administrative action and through the courts; but when this approach failed, he shifted his ground in 1963 and turned to Congress for legislative action. President Johnson, upon assuming office, made the passage of a civil rights bill his key target—for "no memorial oration or eulogy could more eloquently honor President Kennedy's memory."

The bill was signed into law on July 2 [9] after an historic struggle which included the first successful use of cloture in support of civil rights legislation in the Senate. Although the Civil Rights Act of 1964 represented a milestone, the American Negroes' struggle for equality was by no means ended; the problem of breaking down the barriers of prejudice, ignorance, and intolerance remained. Nevertheless, adoption of the civil rights law demonstrated to all other nations, as Adlai E. Stevenson, the U.S. Ambassador to the United Nations, cogently pointed out, the capacity of the United States to deal with "the gut issue of the modern world. . . . We add to our stature in all things because we have added to the quality of our own life." [10]

Perhaps the most striking evidence of President Johnson's ability to deal with Congress was his success in obtaining the foreign aid funds he requested. At the end of 1963 the foreign aid program, never very popular with Congress, received some of the most severe cutbacks and crippling restrictions in seventeen years in the Senate. Seeking to placate Congress and deflect an incipient "revolt," Mr. Johnson appointed an eight-man committee, headed by Under-Secretary Ball, to explore "all possible means to achieve economies and efficiencies" in the administration of the foreign aid program. Although the Ball committee considered a major overhaul of the program's administrative structure (possibly integrating the Agency for International Development [AID] within the State Department or scattering its functions among six or seven other departments and agencies), President Johnson rejected this approach. In its final recommendations the committee made no drastic proposals for change, but its review and ratification of reforms already initiated by AID helped to ease congressional pressure.

President Johnson managed to win over Congress by adopting a new strategy. For one thing, in the foreign aid message submitted to Congress in March, he asked for only $3.4 billion for foreign assistance.[11] This sum, which was $1.1 billion less than President Kennedy's 1963 request, was the lowest administration proposal since the United States started financing Europe's postwar reconstruction. But he made it clear that this was a "barebones" figure, representing cuts already made by the administration. During the following months, Mr. Johnson personally directed the battle for its approval. Principal opposition, as in the past, came from Representative Otto E. Passman, chairman of the House Appropriation Subcommittee on Foreign Operations. Declaring that he was not buying the President's "bare-bones" argument, he called for an additional reduction of some $500 million. "There's an asking price and a settling price. That's the asking price." Arguing that the foreign aid program had become vastly overextended, he declared, "It cries out for correction. It cries out for control." But for the first time in his ten years as chairman, the subcommittee refused to go along with his proposals for drastic cuts and accepted for the most part the administration's bill. Late in September, Congress approved a $3.3 billion program of economic and military aid.[12] Although the administration adroitly managed to maneuver around Representative Passman, it suffered a setback in its efforts to extend assistance to Eastern European countries. Through an amendment in the Food-for-Peace program, Poland and Yugoslavia, as well as other potential beneficiaries, were required to pay for surplus farm products in dollars rather than in their own currencies.

Congress, of course, did not give President Johnson everything that he wanted. There were some major disappointments, an outstanding one being the failure to secure health care for the aged to be financed through Social Security. Nevertheless, the record of accomplishment was considerable. In terms of its achievements, it was undoubtedly the most productive Congress since President Roosevelt's first term.

3. PROBLEMS IN FOREIGN AFFAIRS

While Congress was so largely occupied with domestic issues, the Johnson administration also had to deal with the many foreign policy problems it inherited. In international affairs the President appeared to lack the sureness of "touch" that he demonstrated on the domestic front. Much more so than President Kennedy, Mr. Johnson tended to place a heavier burden of responsibility on Secretary of State Dean Rusk and Defense Secretary Robert S. McNamara. A tendency to drift could be discerned on certain critical political and strategic problems, but it was perhaps more strikingly disclosed in connection with international economic policies.

At the beginning of the year there was general agreement among experts that 1964 would see a substantial advance over the improvement shown in 1963 in the nation's balance of payments. Until autumn that prediction seemed to be accurate, but then a combination of events reversed the situation and the last quarter registered a deficit as great as that of the first three, combined. As a result, the deficit in regular transactions for 1964 was $3.05 billion, only a little less than that of 1963. If some special transactions were taken into account, such as the advance repayment of debt by foreign governments in 1963, the 1964 deficit was a bit larger than that of the previous year.

The situation was particularly disappointing because there had been a substantial improvement in the United States' foreign trade position during the year.[13] Exports rose faster than imports so that the commercial export surplus increased to $3.7 billion from $2.3 billion in 1963. Government spending abroad for foreign aid and military purposes was cut. While returns on past investments reached record heights, the outflow of new private funds rose by a little more than $2 billion. Inevitably, old questions were reopened. Was the administration trying to get by with palliatives? Should it raise interest rates in spite of its worries about the impact on the domestic economy? Ought the tax already levied on new foreign securities be extended to bank loans and perhaps other kinds of borrowing? Should direct private investment abroad be restrained? Should the government discourage Americans from travelling and spending so much overseas? Was there anything more that could be done to reduce American military spending outside the country?

Even more complicated questions arose about the international position of the dollar. International cooperation seemed to be working well. In the spring the United States had played a key part in helping Italy deal with its payments difficulties and in raising a large international fund in November. The United States lost much less gold in 1964 than the year before, but the foreign demand for gold resulting from the 1964 deficit was bound to make itself felt in early 1965. At the annual meeting of the International Monetary Fund (I.M.F.) and the International Bank for Reconstruction and Development (I.B.R.D.) in Tokyo in September, the French Finance Minister, Valéry Giscard d'Estaing, had made a speech that was interpreted by some as an attack on the dollar and the pound, while others saw his proposals for a new kind of international reserve arrangement as reasonable suggestions worth discussing along with the other ideas under active international consideration. However, it was recognized that if France or other governments that held large amounts of dollars decided to hasten the process by asking the United States for larger amounts of gold, then another test of the international monetary system, as well as of American policies, might occur.

Among other continuing problems the most difficult was that pertaining to relations with President de Gaulle. Here the dif-

ferences between the United States and France over the structure
of Europe, over the M.L.F. and the sharing of nuclear weapons,
and over the nature and function of the Atlantic alliance sharpened during the year. Until the November election, signs pointed
to a showdown with de Gaulle, the consequences of which might
have gravely jeopardized the NATO system and the European
Union movement. Although a head-on collision was avoided, the
Johnson administration was still faced with the task of restoring
the cohesion of the North Atlantic alliance.

4. THE PRESIDENTIAL CONTEST

American politics, and America's foreign relations for that
matter, are bound to be marked with uncertainty in a presidential
election year. Little or no doubt existed that President Johnson
would be the Democratic candidate. Speculation, and excitement, centered on the struggle between moderates and conservatives for the Republican nomination. The American elections of
1964, nevertheless, aroused far more concern both in the United
States and throughout the world than ever before.

Since World War II both Democrats and Republicans had
generally upheld the principle of bipartisanship in foreign affairs;
for the most part they agreed on fundamentals though disagree-
ing on details. But Senator Barry M. Goldwater, who captured
the Republican party's nomination as leader of its conservative
right-wing faction, brusquely broke with this tradition. He bluntly
challenged the basic policies that guided America's relations with
the Communist world in the cold war and that had shaped the
nation's social and economic life since Franklin D. Roosevelt's
administrations. The Arizona Senator rallied behind him those
Americans who, as he asserted, wanted "a choice, not an echo."
But his candidacy badly split the Republican party and created
much internal discord.

The Republican party spelled out its "across-the-board" attack
on foreign and domestic policies in a platform drafted by Goldwater supporters.[14] Specifically, it criticized the Johnson administration's conduct of foreign affairs for seeking an accommoda-

tion with Communism without adequate safeguards and compensating gains for freedom, for permitting an erosion of the NATO alliance, and for creating discord and distrust among NATO members by failing to develop an adequate nuclear policy. The thought that there were different kinds of Communists—Soviet, Chinese, Cuban, or some other variety—was rejected. Trade with Communist countries was firmly opposed lest it enhance their power and influence. Such trade, the "Goldwater platform" stated, could only be justified "if it would diminish their power." At the same time the Republican party reaffirmed its commitment to seek the "eventual liberation" of the Communist-dominated nations of Eastern Europe, Asia, and Latin America. Although the reference to "liberation" was not different from statements in previous Republican party platforms, Senator Goldwater's presentation of his position created the impression that he would militantly pursue this objective. In his speech accepting the nomination on July 16, he declared: "The Republican cause demands that we brand Communism as the principal disturber of peace in the world today. . . . We must make clear that until its goals of conquest are absolutely renounced and its relations with all nations tempered, Communism and the governments it now controls are enemies of every man on earth who is or wants to be free." [15]

Most Americans generally agreed with the view that the Communist powers were a threat to freedom in the world. Under the Kennedy and Johnson administrations, the United States had maintained its efforts to check Communist advances carried out by open attacks and subversion. However, largely as a result of changed conditions that arose after the Cuban missile crisis, Washington's approach in dealing with Communist countries was partially modified. In particular, the United States began to encourage trends toward independent action on the part of Eastern European countries, and to search for agreements and understandings to settle or blunt dangerous disputes between the West and the Soviet Union. Senator Goldwater disagreed sharply with this approach. He was convinced that the Communist system had to be destroyed or the United States would be destroyed.

The Republican candidate also apparently believed that Communist advances could be rolled back by astutely playing the game of "brinkmanship," and that "total victory" in the cold war could be achieved by forceful diplomacy.

Senator Goldwater's earnestness in expressing his intention to use the presidency for militant resistance to Communism and for leading Americans as "missionaries of freedom" aroused concern. There was widespread fear that a Republican victory would increase the danger of a nuclear holocaust. Although few Europeans seriously believed that Senator Goldwater would win the election, a great many were disturbed over the nomination of a man who repudiated so many of the fundamental doctrines of American foreign policy. It was taken as proof that the political climate in America was not completely sound, and it tended to strengthen the Gaullist argument that the United States could not be relied on indefinitely to protect Europe and that Europe should therefore control its own nuclear defense and destiny.

During the campaign the foreign policy issue that stirred the greatest controversy was the question of the control of nuclear weapons. Indeed, this problem was the most sensitive and critical in the NATO alliance, as well as the most complex. Basically, Senator Goldwater stressed three points: that steps should be taken to strengthen and revitalize the NATO alliance, which the Republican party felt was "indispensable for the prevention of war and the protection of freedom"; that NATO should be provided with a stockpile of small tactical nuclear weapons—"what may truly be called and ultimately will be called *conventional* weapons"; and third, that some measure of control over these weapons should be delegated to the NATO Supreme Allied Commander in Europe who, under certain contingencies, could be authorized to use them immediately on his own authority. Senator Goldwater's case was based on two assumptions: that the erosion of the NATO alliance stemmed chiefly from uncertainty that prevailed in Europe about America's commitment to the defense of the Continent and its general will to fight; and that the West was vulnerable to a surprise Soviet attack launched against the NATO powers.

In October a Republican task force, headed by Neil H. Mc-
Elroy, a former Secretary of Defense, charged in a report that
the Johnson administration was responsible for the distrust of the
United States that existed among the NATO allies, chiefly because it had "overextended" the President's personal control of
nuclear weapons. The task force's report especially criticized the
fact that "electronic locks" on nuclear weapons made their prompt
use difficult. These electro-mechanical locks, called "Permissive
Action Links," rendered nuclear bombs impotent until a secret
combination was flashed by the President. Because of the President's absolute control over the Permissive Action Links, it said,
NATO nations were no longer confident that the United States
would respond quickly enough in repelling a surprise Soviet
assault on Western Europe. To allay misgivings, the report suggested that the President delegate to the NATO Supreme Commander sufficient authority to use tactical nuclear weapons
"under predetermined circumstances" without having to consult
the President. Moreover, the President should assure the American people of the nation's ability to respond to an atomic attack
immediately, even in the event that the President should die or
be disabled.

The Johnson administration disagreed completely with the
views expressed in the report. It flatly denied that the confidence of NATO allies had been shaken by the President's personal control over nuclear weapons, or that Europeans wanted
the NATO Supreme Commander to have the authority to fire
tactical nuclear arms. In his campaign speeches Mr. Johnson
strongly emphasized the importance of keeping this control and
custody in the hands of the President alone, at least until such
time as proper and effective arrangements for the sharing of
nuclear responsibility could be worked out. In its effort to increase
Atlantic unity the United States had been discussing with its
European allies the problem of sharing nuclear weapons control;
but all the proposals contemplated keeping the decision for their
use in the hands of the civilian heads of government, not the
military. Defense Secretary McNamara ridiculed the idea that
any nuclear arms could be considered "conventional." "The aver-

age tactical weapon in Europe has a yield five times the bomb that was dropped on Hiroshima," he said. "I simply leave it to you to decide whether you think power of that kind should be placed at the disposal of anyone other than the President." [16]

Although Senator Goldwater argued that the responsible use of power through military force was the key to a "rational solution" that would end the cold war without nuclear destruction or a Communist takeover,[17] the campaign quickly drifted away from a discussion of the specific issues and centered on the question as to which candidate was best fitted to exercise responsible judgment on how to use America's awesome military power, and on how to reduce world tensions so that it would never have to be used. In their attack the Democrats concentrated on Senator Goldwater's temperament. They pictured him as "rash," "trigger-happy," and a man "who shoots from the hip," and warned he was governed by "primitive passions." They ridiculed his expressed concern for the unity of NATO, charging that the one thing that really frightened the Europeans and would break the alliance apart was the possibility of Senator Goldwater's election. President Johnson dwelt heavily on peace and preparedness, on "prudence" and "responsibility." He assured the nation on September 16 that his administration had "taken every step man can devise to insure that neither a madman nor a malfunction could ever trigger nuclear war." [18]

Abroad, the President's landslide victory on November 3 was almost universally welcomed with relief. Mr. Johnson accepted it as an expression of the American people's desire to maintain peace, and as a mandate to follow a prudent course and to work for unity within the nation.

CHAPTER TWO

THE ATLANTIC ALLIANCE IN THE MID-SIXTIES

BY THE MID-1960's the United States and the Soviet Union had to face the fact that they could no longer determine the future design of Europe or exercise a controlling influence in the affairs of developing nations. In his Dag Hammarskjold Memorial Lecture on January 10, Secretary Rusk spoke of the passing of the "cobweb syndrome," by which he meant "the illusion that one nation or bloc of nations could, by coercion, weave the world into a single pattern directed from a single center of power . . ." And, "That other illusion, the bipolar theory, of a world divided permanently between two overwhelming centers of power with most other nations clustered about them, is fading too. The reality of a world of great diversity with many centers of power and influence is coming into better focus." [1]

Three episodes in recent years have had much to do with creating the climate in which Western Europe, especially France, began to assert greater independence of action. First, the Suez crisis of 1956 had placed a heavy strain on the Atlantic alliance and led to a lessening of confidence in Washington. By its strong disapproval of the Anglo-French-Israeli intervention in Egypt the United States indicated that outside the area defined in the NATO treaty it would not necessarily support its major European allies, although they considered their vital interests to be at stake. Second, the Soviet Union's launching of Sputnik I in October 1957 persuaded Western Europe that Moscow had the capability of acquiring operational intercontinental ballistic missiles in the not-too-distant future. The prospective effect, it was feared, would be to neutralize America's nuclear deterrent. Pressures therefore built up for the creation of a nuclear deterrent capability that would not be entirely dependent upon the decision of American policy-makers. Third, the Cuban missile affair in 1962 increased Europe's apprehension about Washington's policies. Although Western Europe supported President Kennedy's action in seeking the removal of Soviet nuclear weapons from Cuba, doubts were nevertheless raised about America's *unilateral* response—a response that could have thrust the world into an atomic holocaust if the crisis had not been so effectively managed by the late President. Further uneasiness arose the following year when Europeans discovered that a *rapprochement* between the United States and the U.S.S.R., in effect, had developed without a voice on the Continent being heard.

In January 1963 President de Gaulle, who had already taken minor steps to reduce France's role in NATO, dramatically struck the first major blow at America's European policies. His brusque veto of Britain's entry into the Common Market and his rejection of the Nassau agreement on nuclear weapons marked a significant turning point in relations between the United States and Western Europe. In his celebrated press conference [2] de Gaulle implied that France would follow an emphatically *French* policy in Europe and toward Communist countries. In so doing, he called on Europe to affirm a declaration of diplomatic independence. A year later de Gaulle extended his independent policy to Asia when he announced France's recognition of Communist China. At his news conference on January 31, he explained the reasons which impelled France to recognize Peking, and he made clear his intention to support a policy of "neutralization" in Southeast Asia and to expand French influence in Latin America and Africa.[3] Although none of the other states within the European Economic Community supported de Gaulle's frontal assault on Washington's leadership, no effective effort was made to counter the French leader's stand. An immediate consequence, however, was that the forward momentum of the Common Market was stalled.

Stresses and strains were not uncommon in the Atlantic alliance's fifteen-year history. As with most traditional alliances, cooperation was readily forthcoming when dangers were great; but when threats receded, national self-interest quickly encroached upon the larger community interest. But in 1964, even more so than in the past, the Atlantic alliance seemed to be threatened by apathy and disintegration. Several issues, in particular, caused pessimism among those who were devoted supporters of NATO. Difficult problems were created by France's reluctance to cooperate militarily and politically; pressures for organizational changes, however, arose not only in Paris, but also in Bonn and other NATO capitals. West Germany especially thought the time had come for it to enjoy increased representation in NATO councils commensurate with its contributions to the alliance's defense system. An overriding concern was that of nuclear-sharing within the alliance, which Washington sought to meet by its proposal for the creation of a multilateral force. The dispute between Greece and Turkey over Cyprus, in addition, threatened to undermine the alliance and to damage seriously the Western position in the Mediterranean. These problems raised fundamental questions relating to the future structure of Europe and the Atlantic community.

5. NATO DILEMMAS

France had been the keystone in NATO's arch from its inception. To President de Gaulle, the French role within the Western defense system continued to be important, but he drew a distinction between the North Atlantic Treaty *Organization* and the *alliance* which its members had formed. In General de Gaulle's view the alliance remained vital, whereas the organization had become obsolete. Although security requirements still made American support necessary the changed political environment, combined with Western Europe's increased strength, he felt, made NATO's imbalanced structure out of date. Specifically, de Gaulle was convinced that the European states could no longer tolerate a situation in which they were wholly involved in NATO's defense structure while the United States and, to a lesser extent, Britain dominated the command system. He therefore argued that it was essential to revise the organization to bring it into line with the existing, much more complex, condition that now prevailed.

The United States, of course, refused to concede that the alliance and the organization through which it acted were less essential or less desirable than they had been in previous years. Washington considered NATO much more than a collective military pact, looking upon it as a steppingstone to the creation of an Atlantic partnership in which a gradual accommodation would bind the United States and Europe to common, long-term political goals. Though the risks of another war had diminished, Washington maintained that since the threat of Communist totalitarianism remained, a genuine *détente* did not exist. Hence, the need for unity within the Atlantic alliance was as imperative as ever. For these reasons Washington deeply resented what it suspected were French efforts to split the alliance into two camps or factions, the so-called Anglo-Saxons and the Continentals. On April 3, the occasion of NATO's fifteenth anniversary, President Johnson strongly asserted, "We find no contradiction between national self-respect and interdependent mutual reliance. We are eager to share with the new Europe at every level of power and responsibility." [4]

But there were several complications to developing a growing partnership with Europe, not the least of them being de Gaulle's insistence on maintaining France's independence of action, as he defined it. The French President's policies posed a basic dilemma for the United States. On the one hand, Washington desired to expand the responsibility of the NATO alliance so that it could cope with the threat of Communist encroachment on the European continent and, at the same time, deal with the problems of developing nations in Asia, Africa, and the Western Hemisphere, without, however, diluting America's own responsibilities in those areas. On the other hand, the United States was convinced that in order to share in the tasks of world-wide responsibility, it would be necessary for Europe to achieve political unity. Only when this had been accomplished, Under-Secretary Ball remarked, would Europe be able to command resources adequate to the requirements of the age and play an effective role of leadership in the modern world, contributing to "the building and maintenance of a free and stable world." [5] Many Europeans, including leaders in both the Italian and German governments, shared this view. But de Gaulle refused to accept the concept of an Atlantic partnership, partly because he feared that in a "United States of Europe" French national interests would be submerged, and partly because he felt that changed world conditions had provided an opportunity for nations to assert a greater freedom of action, which the dangerous cold-war atmosphere of the past had so largely circumscribed.

French reluctance in 1964 to cooperate militarily and politically in strengthening the Atlantic alliance was demonstrated in a variety of ways: in the demand that NATO should be revised in order to increase the military responsibility of European members, thereby establishing more fully France's independence from the United States; in de Gaulle's withdrawal of French naval officers from NATO commands; and in France's unwillingness to contribute troops to a NATO peace-keeping force in Cyprus.

Early in 1964 President de Gaulle directed his attention toward seeking a change in NATO's system of military integration, and perhaps ending it before the North Atlantic treaty came up for review and renewal in 1969. He objected specifically to the fact that under the integrated command an American as Supreme Commander directed the operations of French forces in Germany. French criticism of the integrated command was further linked to the question of Europe's defense. The North Atlantic treaty stipulated that an attack on any of the alliance's fifteen members would be considered an attack on all. President de Gaulle did not doubt that the United States would fight if an alliance member was attacked. What he was uncertain about was whether Washington would react immediately with nuclear weapons. While recognizing that neither France nor the countries of Western Europe could defend themselves successfully against the Soviet Union, he did feel that Europe should provide its own nuclear defense in cooperation with the United States. Moreover, de Gaulle wanted Europe to provide this defense by means of national nuclear forces, although he did not specifically favor such a force for Germany. Only with an independent nuclear force and under an independent national command, the French President thought, could a nation be led to make sacrifices necessary for maintaining a modern military establishment.

More explicitly, the French found fault with the NATO command structure on three counts. First, the Standing Group, composed of representatives of the chiefs of staff of the United States, Britain, and France, sat in Washington, separated by the Atlantic Ocean from the operational command vested in the Supreme Allied Commander. Second, the command structure failed to give West Germany and Italy a voice in alliance decisions commensurate with their contributions. Third, more authority, the French felt, should be given to Europeans in the use of both nuclear and conventional weapons. Arguing that the NATO integrated command system set up by General Dwight D. Eisenhower in 1950 to meet a Soviet attack in Europe was outdated, the French called for a new system of coordinated planning among allied military establishments, whereby each would be responsible for the defense of its own national territory.

Washington agreed on the need for continually adapting the Atlantic pact to a changing environment. As Secretary Rusk remarked early in the year, "When NATO was set up, we had a virtual atomic monopoly and the Soviets had massive conventional superiority. Since then the Soviets have achieved an atomic arsenal and NATO has gained in both conventional and nuclear strength. This makes it even more important that NATO have a force structure capable of deterring, or coping with, a wide range of possibilities—that it should be able to respond with the force appropriate to each threat." [6]

While the United States urged the buildup of a unified force structure, France pushed in the opposite direction. Late in April de Gaulle withdrew French naval officers from the North Atlantic alliance commands in the Mediterranean and the English channel, a step which completed the process of establishing the operational independence of the French navy. Although Washington felt that this action was not particularly important in itself— France had already withdrawn its Mediterranean fleet from NATO command in 1959, and four years later had pulled out its Atlantic ships as well—it was interpreted as an effort to weaken the system of integrated defenses, and as a slap at NATO, especially since it came only two weeks before the annual NATO foreign ministers' meeting at The Hague on May 12–14.[7]

Many feared that at the Council meeting France would launch a frontal attack on the alliance, but the expected crisis did not occur. Belgian Foreign Minister Paul-Henri Spaak challenged France to propose the exact changes it wanted in the alliance. Although the French Foreign Minister, Maurice Couve de Murville, asserted France's strong opposition to the NATO command system, he did not make any specific proposals. He merely stressed that military efficiency had to be reconciled with political considerations and that greater attention should be paid to consultation, particularly on matters of national interest.

The French attack fizzled. The alliance, in fact, found itself in a stronger position than had been expected. France's suggestions for altering the system of integrated military command were too vague, and its failure to take the initiative in offering specific proposals in this and other spheres of alliance activities tended to reduce its influence. When none of the other fourteen members came to its support, France found itself isolated in its stand. French criticism nevertheless had a twofold result. It evoked a strong emotional response of loyalty to NATO among the members and prodded them into considering the need for revisions in the organization's structure.

Washington warned against "tinkering" with the Atlantic pact. Under-Secretary Ball, in a speech of May 7, stressed that progress would come only by achieving a greater cohesion in the relations among NATO members. "NATO should not be regarded as an end in itself," he said. "It should be thought of as one of the pillars in a more comprehensive Atlantic partnership—an Atlantic relationship we must achieve in due course if we are to gain that ultimate goal of which Woodrow Wilson spoke with such prophetic passion—the 'universal dominion of right by such a concert of free peoples as shall bring peace and safety to all nations and make the world itself at last free.' " [8]

6. STRATEGIC PARTNERSHIP OR MULTILATERAL FORCE?

Basically, the United States did not regard the weaknesses in the Atlantic alliance system in terms of its organizational problems. Much more fundamental, in its view, was the question of developing improved ways and means for managing the nuclear deterrent. There seemed to be three broad alternatives whereby this goal could be attained: to retain an exclusive American responsibility, while strengthening nuclear consultation within the alliance; to share operational responsibility more widely on a national basis; or to provide for multilateral sharing which would be consistent with the concepts of European integration and Atlantic partnership.[9] Overarching these alternatives was the problem of how to reconcile the desire of some NATO members to participate in the ownership and control of the deterrent with the objective of avoiding the dangers of nuclear proliferation.

In grappling with this dilemma the United States had set forth over the years several proposals for the establishment of a multilateral force. The issue first came to the forefront in the late 1950's when Europe began to chafe under the American nuclear monopoly. At the Heads of Government conference held in Paris on December 16–19, 1957, the question of nuclear sharing was explored, and a decision was made to "establish stocks of nuclear warheads, which will be readily available for the defence of the Alliance in case of need." [10] A great many hundreds of tactical nuclear weapons have since been deployed to allied forces in Europe under this so-called NATO Atomic Stockpile. The weapons are held under a "two-key" system: the delivery systems (e.g., the missiles) are under the national ownership and manning of the allied country (e.g., Germany) which bought them; the warheads are under the dual control of the allied country and the United States. In other words, the consent of both that country and the United States is required before the missile with its nuclear warhead can be fired.

Two years later, General Lauris Norstad, then NATO's Supreme Allied Commander in Europe, proposed a formula for giving NATO its own land-based medium-range missiles controlled by this same "two-key" system in order to counterbalance the large force of Soviet medium-range missiles aimed at Western European targets. In 1960, however, the Eisenhower administration decided that placing strategic-range missiles under national manning and ownership would be divisive for the West and troublesome for East-West relations. In December 1959 Secretary of State Christian A. Herter had suggested the possibility of committing to NATO a number of Polaris submarines operated by Americans. At the NATO Council meeting of December 1960 he made a more formal offer, but accompanied it with a further proposal to meet General Norstad's MRBM requirement by means of a seaborne missile force manned by mixed, multinational crews. Thus, MRBM's would be deployed to allied forces without the political disadvantages of placing them under national manning and ownership. Secretary Herter did not specify whether these sea-based missiles would be placed on surface ships or submarines. The proposal was put forward in general terms so as not to bind the hands of the Kennedy administration that was assuming office in January. The United States declared, in brief, that it was ready both to commit its Polaris submarines to NATO command and to work with other members of the alliance in building up a multilateral seaborne force of medium-range ballistic missiles, which would be jointly owned and operated by allies under NATO command.[11]

After a thorough study of NATO policy by former Secretary of State Dean Acheson and after reviewing the matter himself, President Kennedy decided to endorse this concept. In an important address to the Canadian Parliament on May 17, 1961, the late President declared that the United States planned to commit "five—and subsequently still more—Polaris atomic-missile submarines" to NATO. "Beyond this," Mr. Kennedy added, "we look to the possibility of eventually establishing a NATO seaborne force, which would be truly multilateral in ownership and control, if this should be desired and found feasible by our allies once NATO's nonnuclear goals have been achieved." [12] This was the origin of the multilateral force or M.L.F., with the purpose of providing an enlarged role for Europe in the ownership, operation, and control of strategic nuclear power. Since the United States already possessed an awesome nuclear capability, the most important advantage of the M.L.F. was clearly political. Major NATO participants would play a key role in M.L.F. planning. Equally important, they would exercise control over a force far larger and more effective than any which they could create individually by independent national effort. The M.L.F. was thus seen as a program that could curb the proliferation of nuclear weapons.

A key problem centered on the sharing of controls—both between the United States and the European participants, and among the European powers themselves. In the first phase of establishing the M.L.F., the United States insisted on retaining a veto in the final decision on the use of nuclear missiles. Washington deemed the veto power essential. No indication existed that Congress would be willing to hand over to any other country the means to unleash nuclear missiles independently of the United States. But the United States also indicated that European control, especially as Europe moved toward unity, would not be precluded. This was, however, a long-term prospect. In the meantime, the question of how the European nations would share in control, whether by giving each of the major European countries a veto or by some form of majority voting, remained to be determined.

Following a meeting in April 1964 with his principal advisers, including Thomas K. Finletter, Ambassador to NATO, President Johnson gave his full support to the M.L.F. proposal. The project suddenly developed a perceptible new vigor during the spring, although it met with a variable response in Europe. France, with its strongly nationalistic policy in acquiring nuclear capability, opposed the idea from the beginning, as had been expected. Britain was cautious and the British Labor party openly attacked

the plan, indicating that it would join only if the M.L.F. proved
to be the only way to prevent a German national program. Moderate political leaders in Bonn—both in the government and in
the Socialist party—supported the M.L.F., since it acknowledged
the importance of giving West Germany a voice in allied nuclear
matters. Three of the four coalition parties in the Italian government also supported the M.L.F., but the Nenni Socialists were
reserved. There was more opposition to the proposal in Belgium.

The prospect of German access to strategic weapons was at
the heart of much of the apprehension and dissension within the
Atlantic alliance. There was little question that the German
Federal Republic wanted a bigger role in NATO, and the problem was how to respond to that desire. Early in March 1964
Bonn pressed for an increase in the membership of the NATO
Standing Group from three to four. Tactfully, however, it suggested that the proposed new member represent "some other
nation." West Germany's claim for a stronger position was recognized as having merit—particularly since it contributed twelve
divisions to NATO's ground forces as against France's two.
Nevertheless, the pressure to increase German influence aroused
fears on the part of other European powers. It also created great
agitation in Moscow, which looked upon the M.L.F. as the first
move to put a German finger on NATO's strategic trigger. The
Russians refused to accept Western assurances that the M.L.F.
would, in fact, circumscribe West Germany's access to nuclear
control, as compared with its *national* role under the existing
"two-key" arrangement. The Soviet Union argued the possibility
that West Germany, under the cover of NATO, might secure
nuclear weapons and then (perhaps in conjunction with a Western coalition) seek to blackmail Eastern Europe for the recovery
of its 1937 frontiers.

While some West Germans would have preferred land-based
MRBM's, Bonn strongly supported the M.L.F.—as Washington
did—because it offered a means of tying the United States closer
to Europe and of adding strategic weapons to the NATO armory.
Bonn's unequivocal support of the M.L.F. abetted the misgivings
of Britain and France. Although they had believed since the

1950's that a Germany integrated into Western Europe would be less of a threat to European peace than a Germany left outside to build its own power in its own way and for its own national aims, they remained unconvinced that the M.L.F. was the best instrument for the purpose.

It was partly a recognition of West Germany's increasing strength and influence that led some European powers, however grudgingly, to give some support to the M.L.F. plan. For over a year, a working group in Paris, with a military subcommittee in the Pentagon and a legal subcommittee in Munich, concentrated on devising a feasible scheme for consideration by the various governments.

In June, a demonstration ship, the *Biddle*, with a training crew of mixed nationalities was put into operation at Norfolk, Virginia. Of more than 300 men assigned to the vessel, about 50 per cent were Americans and the remainder West Germans, Britons, Greeks, Italians, Turks, and Dutch. Eventually, it was anticipated, a multilateral mixed-manned force of twenty-five missile-bearing surface warships would be built in about three and one-half years, and put into operation two years later. Total cost for construction and operation over a five-year period was put at about $3 billion. The M.L.F. plan called for the cost to be apportioned among the participating nations with the United States and West Germany providing the major share.

A further step in sharing control of the nuclear deterrent was taken on June 30 when President Johnson asked for congressional approval to permit the United States to provide NATO with more information about the use of nuclear weapons.[13] The new atomic information agreement between the United States and NATO, superseding that of 1955, was intended to allow the American government for the first time to share with "NATO and its member states" information related to "the development of delivery systems" for atomic weapons.[14] This information was needed to permit the allies to make effective use of the tactical nuclear delivery systems provided under the "two-key" system. The new agreement did not permit the European allies to obtain any design information or nuclear parts that would help them build an atom bomb. The great cost of research and development for delivery systems had been one of the major barriers to the proliferation of national nuclear forces.

Despite the strong advocacy of the M.L.F. on the part of the United States and West Germany and some support in Italy and the Netherlands, much skepticism and opposition continued to be voiced by many Europeans, and its fate remained uncertain. Opponents maintained that the M.L.F. merely provided the *form* of nuclear participation without its *substance*, and at heavy expense. European and American critics contended that it could not be justified on military grounds since it would not add appreciably to the American nuclear deterrent. Moreover, rather than prevent the diffusion of nuclear weapons, it was feared that the M.L.F. might well accelerate it. "The danger in the multilateral force," one critic pointed out, "is that those who want effective control over their nuclear destiny will not long remain content with the projected arrangements, while those who go along for such motives as pleasing us, defying France, or keeping an eye on Germany will soon grow tired of the expense and will search for other options." [15] Cynics referred to the proposal as a "multilateral farce."

In June Britain proposed that the Paris working group which had been studying the establishment of the U.S.-sponsored mixed-manned fleet also consider a land-based aircraft and Pershing missile force as a supplement to a smaller M.L.F. fleet. Such a mixture, the British argued, might offer a more suitable focus for joint European-American financing and control than the seaborne fleet alone. The Paris working group referred the British proposal to a military sub-group for study, while the European countries which had been studying the M.L.F. reacted coolly to the British suggestion. The Germans, in particular, pointed out that since they were already getting strike aircraft and Pershing missiles as nuclear delivery systems under the "two-key" arrangement, their enthusiasm for buying even more of those weapons under the M.L.F. was limited. Moreover, the British proposal for shorter-range systems did not meet two of the sources of European interest in the M.L.F., namely, the desire to have MRBM's deployed to Europe to counter Soviet missiles and to have a role in ownership and manning of *strategic*-range weapons. In Washington, the concept of eventually adding other weapons systems to the M.L.F. was considered an interesting one, but there was concern over the timing.

It was hoped that the creation of a multilateral force would be undertaken by the end of the year or soon thereafter. Bonn wanted to dispose of the matter before the West German elections, scheduled to be held in 1965; and Washington, concerned over possible Gaullist pressures on Bonn to follow a less desirable nuclear policy, agreed that prompt action was needed as a rallying point for the growth of a more organic system of alliance cooperation to halt the process of gradual fragmentation. The question was whether a decision could be reached on the British proposals within this time limit.

The British insisted that the land-based weapons would cost less than the proposed nuclear surface fleet. Furthermore, they said, instead of having to wait some five years for the surface ships to be built and become operational, the land-based M.L.F. could be created more quickly by training mixed national teams for weapons already in existence. The British made it clear late in July that their proposals were a prerequisite for their joining any mixed-manned force. The plan was not a sudden improvisation; careful consideration had evidently been given to finding a way in which Britain could achieve a parity with Germany. Slated to have only a 10 per cent share in the seaborne force, and thus only a relatively minor participation, Great Britain found it necessary to persuade the allies to cut down the size of the seaborne force and extend the M.L.F. plan to aircraft and missiles in Europe, to which it was a major contributor. Ambassador Finletter, however, insisted in September that the M.L.F. plan must include missile-bearing surface warships as the essence of the force. "As goes this fleet, so may go the defense of the West, and our efforts to prevent war." He warned that an unsuccessful outcome on negotiations for a multilateral force could seriously affect the survival of the Atlantic alliance as an effective guarantee of peace.[16]

7. DE GAULLE PROVOKES WASHINGTON AND BONN

An unquestionably remarkable achievement of the 1950's was the development of Franco-German reconciliation, a goal that had been one of the lifelong ambitions of former German Chancellor Konrad Adenauer. "If the European peoples continue to make their policies on the basis of the past," he had once said, "Europe will go down and become only a historical memory." Only if Western Europe were united and made politically, economically, and militarily strong, would it be possible, Adenauer believed, to find an acceptable solution to the German problem with the Soviet Union. Thus, he had sought, on the one hand, to remove past Franco-German bitterness and, on the other, to support vigorously the movement for European integration. The first objective was obtained, in part, with the settlement of the Saar issue in 1955 and with the signing of the Franco-German Treaty of Friendship in January 1963. The second was advanced by Germany's participation in NATO, and by the creation of the European Economic Community and its sister institutions.

Adenauer failed to take two matters into account: the virulence of de Gaulle's nationalistic policies and the persistence in France of fear and enmity toward Germany. An advocate of close relations with Germany, General de Gaulle, like Adenauer, made much of the Treaty of Friendship. Yet French nationalism, especially as de Gaulle conceived it, was concerned not merely with jealously safeguarding national interests, but also with asserting French leadership on the Continent and expanding French influence throughout the world. France's foreign policies, already in conflict with those of the United States, soon collided with the policies of West Germany.

In the autumn of 1963, after Adenauer retired, the creator of West Germany's economic "miracle," Ludwig Erhard, succeeded to the chancellorship. He soon found himself caught between Paris and Washington, as both the Treaty of Friendship and United States support were vitally important to the German

Federal Republic. Dr. Erhard sought to maintain, as firmly as he could, cooperation with France, for without this cooperation there could be no European union. At the same time, he believed it was essential to continue a close relationship with the United States, for without American support the security of West Germany (as well as Europe) would be gravely endangered. Chancellor Erhard refused to regard the situation as one confronting Bonn with the need to choose. Nevertheless, it appeared to Washington that General de Gaulle was pressing for a decision: either a Europe of fatherlands on French terms, or an Atlantic alliance dominated by the "Anglo-Saxons."

The French President called into question not only the basis of the Atlantic alliance, but also the value of Western negotiations with the Soviet Union and the West's relations with the developing countries and Communist China. De Gaulle's policies, it was evident, were designed to further France's role as an independent and influential force in international affairs. His over-all objective, as one observer pointed out, was to make certain that "his beloved France will never be merely one of a group of European nations and that Europe's destinies will be in her own hands and not in those of Americans." [17] De Gaulle opposed the process of integration within the Atlantic alliance and insisted that its structure should be one in which governments cooperated politically and were mutually responsive to any aggressive threats against it. He believed, above all, that France must assert itself in the councils of the West—and to gain this end he insisted on making France, regardless of cost, an independent nuclear power.

On January 27 Paris recognized Communist China. The move was not unexpected, but its timing was a source of great embarrassment to the United States, given its heavy military commitment in Southeast Asia. It was immediately interpreted as a direct rebuff to American policies. In addition to the possible damaging effect on the U.S. position in South Vietnam, Washington was concerned that France's recognition would increase Afro-Asian pressures for Peking's admission into the United Nations. More immediately, the United States was disturbed about the impact the action might have on allied unity, already strained over a number of other issues. Although forty-eight countries had recognized the Chinese Communist regime and forty-two maintained diplomatic relations with it—among these being four NATO members: Britain, Norway, Denmark, and the Netherlands—the French decision was the first on the part of a major Western nation since the Korean War.

Four days later at his news conference, General de Gaulle explained the reasons for French recognition of Peking. From his remarks, trade and commercial benefits appeared to be only a minor consideration. More important, it seemed, was his desire to reestablish French influence in Southeast Asia, as he reiterated a proposal, advanced the previous summer, for the neutralization of the Indochinese peninsula. The French leader especially urged the establishment of an international guarantee, in co-operation with Communist China, that would free the region from any kind of foreign intervention. Thus de Gaulle said: "In Asia there is no political reality . . . that does not interest or concern China. On this Continent, there is no imaginable peace or war without her being implicated and it is inconceivable to suppose that it is possible ever to conclude a neutrality treaty concerning the states of Southeast Asia, to which we French show a very special and cordial attention, without China's being a party to it." [18]

The steady erosion both in Franco-American and Franco-German relations became evident during 1964 in Washington's cool reception to the French diplomatic intrusion in Southeast Asia, in President de Gaulle's visits to Latin American republics, and in Chancellor Erhard's disappointment over the lack of "motion" in the European union movement. In July President de Gaulle bluntly suggested that the United States, the Soviet Union, Communist China, and France agree to get out and stay out of the Indochinese peninsula so that the fighting in South Vietnam and Laos could be brought to an end. He declared that West Germany was at fault for the absence of a French-German policy for European unity, largely because Bonn refused to believe that "this policy [for Europe] should be European and independent." Although de Gaulle asserted that the Atlantic alliance had to be maintained so long as the Soviet threat persisted, he stressed again France's goal of ending its subordination to the United States in alliance affairs. "A European Europe," he insisted, "means that it exists by itself for itself, in other words in the midst of the world it has its own policy." The General went on to warn that if the drift continued in Franco-German relations, it could result in a possible "breakup" of the Common Market.[19]

Bonn was greatly perturbed by de Gaulle's remarks and annoyed at the implication that its relationship to the United States was one of "subordination." Smaller nations in the Common Market, for their part, were angered at what they considered clear evidence that France was interested in unity only if it was based on the Gaullist concept of an alliance of sovereign states dominated by the most powerful countries, France and Germany. By the end of the year, however, much of the tension generated by de Gaulle was eased when agreement was reached in the Common Market on agricultural prices. (Section 12.)

8. WEST GERMANY: FRANCO-GERMAN AND EAST-WEST RELATIONS

A major factor that underlay the crisis in the Atlantic alliance stemmed from President de Gaulle's unsuccessful efforts to counterbalance West Germany's growing power. During the 1960's the German Federal Republic began to emerge as the foremost economic and military power in Western Europe. Its military establishment had grown rapidly in strength, and by 1964 the German army had become the backbone of the NATO ground forces. As a result of de Gaulle's steady withdrawal from NATO and doubt concerning the scale of British participation, the alliance's structure on the Continent seemed, in fact, to be developing into an American-German partnership. This situation greatly perturbed the French leader. While de Gaulle pressed for the elimination of America's influence in Europe, Chancellor Erhard strongly believed that none of West Germany's main goals could be obtained without the wholehearted support of the United

States. He defined these objectives as the reunification of Germany, the security of the Federal Republic, and European union.

Convinced that a new attack had to be made by the allies on Germany's key problem, namely, reunification, the West German Chancellor urged that an imaginative new approach to this problem be developed. In December 1963 Bonn had endorsed a West Berlin-East German agreement on Christmas visits. At the beginning of the new year a feeling arose that a break might occur in the seemingly irreconcilable positions between the East and West. Some hopeful signs were seen in the dramatic economic, political, and psychological changes that were occurring within the Communist camp. It was even thought that a relaxation might take place in East Germany comparable to what was going on in Hungary, Czechoslovakia, and Poland. Bonn came to the conclusion that the climate would perhaps be ripe for a "step-by-step" approach to reunification (such as had initially been proposed by Mr. Herter and later embodied in a Western "package" plan in 1962) that would accord with present-day realities.

A parallel change of attitude toward East-West developments was also noted in the United States. Since 1947 American policy had accommodated itself to the fact of a divided Germany—with East Germany remaining in the Soviet orbit, and the Federal Republic integrated into a Western European system—though it remained committed to an eventual reunification. Conditions in the 1950's definitely seemed to dictate the continued existence of a divided Germany, especially after the East German uprising of 1953 and the Hungarian Revolution of 1956 had been ruthlessly crushed by the Soviet Union while the United States stood by as a spectator. But after the "hot-line" agreement and the signing of the limited test-ban treaty,[20] and after the ending of Russian jamming of the Voice of America broadcasts and the start of trade talks in 1963, Washington began to feel hopeful that there might be a way out of the reunification impasse. Rather than try to solve issues head-on, it was thought that they could be approached indirectly. Bonn was thus encouraged to seek new contacts and trade partners in Eastern Europe. Through such mutually beneficial ties, the United States believed, the Iron Curtain and the Berlin Wall could perhaps be breached. New agreements might then be concluded to stabilize the West's position in Berlin, to open up access to East German territory, and to bind the two parts of Germany more closely together so that reunification might ultimately be achieved. Commenting on the decisive change in Europe that had taken place Walter Lippmann wrote: "If we compare 1964 with 1954, we see first that this postwar 'Europe' was merely Western Europe with Western Germany, whereas increasingly today the idea of 'Europe' is tending to include the old Soviet satellites in Eastern Europe and the Soviet Union itself as a power in the Western world." [21]

During January the problem of negotiating a new and more liberal pass agreement posed a dilemma for West Berlin and the Federal Republic. On the one hand, the arrangement offered an opportunity to reestablish contacts between East and West Berlin; on the other, it was seen by some elements in West Germany as a clever maneuver whereby Moscow hoped to obtain *de facto* recognition of East Germany. When the East Germans proposed a renewal of the Christmas agreement for the Easter period, Bonn decided to reject it, since the language of the agreement seemed to accord too much status to East Germany. On September 8 East Germany announced its willingness to let elderly persons visit relatives in West Germany and West Berlin. This was the first time that Communist Germany suggested the resumption of travel of any kind from the East to the West sector since the Berlin Wall was erected in August 1961. Two weeks later, on September 23, the West German cabinet unanimously approved a new agreement—after several changes in language were made—allowing West Berliners to visit their relatives in East Berlin. This agreement permitted visits for several days during the periods of October 19 through November 15, Christmas and New Year, Easter and Whitsunday (Pentecost).

By spring Chancellor Erhard's policies took a clearer shape. First, he favored a policy of "flexibility" in German relations with the U.S.S.R. This contrasted sharply with former Chancellor Adenauer's aversion toward any East-West talks with the Soviet Union—an attitude which he had shared with General de Gaulle. Second, Erhard strongly espoused an Atlantic policy, based on American leadership, as fundamental to European security. Although Franco-German reconciliation was held to be highly important, the Chancellor did not feel that it should override cooperation with all of Germany's allies. Third, he vigorously supported German self-determination in free elections, without resort to the use of force. Pending a final peace settlement, he upheld the "legitimacy" of Germany's claim to the borders that existed as of December 31, 1937. Thus, he implicitly rejected the annexation of territories beyond the Oder-Neisse line by Poland and Russia. Finally, Dr. Erhard favored an "opening to the East," without, however, repudiating the Hallstein Doctrine of breaking relations with any country (other than the U.S.S.R.) that recognized the East German regime, and encouraged trade missions and trade agreements with the Eastern European countries.

Bonn continued to exert pressure on its Western allies to take up with the Soviet Union the issue of German reunification. It urged the United States, Britain, and France to put forward and endorse a new proposal. But there were doubts that Moscow would accept a revamped Western "package" plan. The allies, moreover, feared that a reopening of the German question could upset the relative tranquility in relations between the West and the Soviet Union. Nevertheless, despite these misgivings, the NATO Council at its spring meeting agreed to charge an American, British, French, and West German ambassadorial group in Washington with the responsibility for studying the German suggestion. Declaring that no solution had yet been found for the problems of Germany and Berlin, the communiqué issued on May 14 "reaffirmed that a just and peaceful solution" could be reached "only on the basis of the right of self-determination." It further said that "every suitable opportunity should be taken to bring nearer to realization the wish of the German people for reunification in freedom, and thereby ensure an enduring peace in Central Europe." [22]

The following month, Chancellor Erhard made a trip to Canada and the United States. While in Ottawa the information that a treaty of "friendship and mutual assistance" was about to be concluded between East Germany and the Soviet Union was relayed to him by the Department of State. Moscow had taken the precaution of notifying the Johnson administration in advance, giving assurances that the agreement would in no way create a new international crisis. The Soviet move caught Washington, no less than Dr. Erhard, by surprise. Premier Khrushchev had evidently decided to act quickly to anticipate any step the West might take; on June 12 the Soviet Union signed a twenty-year treaty of friendship and cooperation with the "German Democratic Republic." [23] With the apparent purpose of bolstering the prestige of the Ulbricht regime at home and abroad, the treaty gave East Germany the same status as all other members of the Communist bloc in relations with Moscow. It pledged that the two signatories would give each other "immediate assistance" in the event of military aggression, and stressed that the borders of East Germany were "inviolable." The heart of the treaty was the provision stating that German reunification could be achieved only through negotiation on an equal basis between the "two sovereign German states."

The Soviet-East German agreement naturally occupied the discussions of President Johnson and the German Chancellor in Washington on June 12, and both could detect some encouraging signs in its conclusion. From Washington's point of view, in fact, the treaty seemed to suggest several reassuring prospects. Moscow's prior notification of the signing of the treaty showed how greatly the climate of the cold war had changed. (The treaty seemed to lay for the time being the specter of a separate Soviet peace treaty signed with East Germany alone.) More particularly, there was nothing in the agreement indicating any intent on the part of the Russians to give East Germans control over access to Berlin.

Chancellor Erhard was nevertheless well aware of the damaging effect the treaty could have on West Germany's foreign policy. In his talks with President Johnson, he especially emphasized the need to reopen the reunification issue. A joint communiqué underlined the point that so long as Germany remained divided, Europe could not achieve stability. The two leaders declared further that "no unilateral move by the Soviet Union [such as the signing of the Soviet-East Germany treaty] could in any way affect the rights of the three Western Powers or modify the obligations and responsibilities of the Soviet Union with respect to Germany and Berlin." [24]

President Johnson told Chancellor Erhard, however, that while the United States was still committed to the importance of reunification, it intended to seek a relaxation of tension between East and West by all possible means, even though each step might of itself not necessarily represent progress toward reunification. Mr. Johnson indicated that Western policy had to take into account the security of Europe as a whole, and particularly stressed the importance of improving relations with the Communist countries of Eastern Europe. West German leaders were concerned that the "central" question of reunification would recede in importance in the thinking of Washington policymakers. Fear was expressed that the progressive accumulation of limited agreements between the United States and the Soviet Union could lead eventually to Western acceptance of a "two-Germanys" theory. For this reason, Erhard insisted on including in the communiqué a restatement of America's commitment to reunification through free elections. But in return he had to agree to two policies which the Johnson administration considered important. The Chancellor pledged that he would not negotiate any trade agreements or establish trade missions with Peking, and he promised to support American efforts in South Vietnam. When Erhard returned to Germany, he frankly acknowledged that there had been a change in atmosphere since his previous talks with President Johnson in December 1963—a change from the "family feeling" of the Texas ranch to a "brisk and businesslike" relationship.

As for positive steps on reopening the question of German reunification, the action taken was perhaps not as strong as Chancellor Erhard would have preferred. The United States, Britain, and France on June 26 issued a "firm declaration" in which they denounced the Soviet-East German agreement and affirmed their conviction that it was another effort to perpetuate a divided Germany, thereby obstructing a peaceful settlement of Europe's problems. The statement also reiterated their commitment to Germany's reunification on the basis of self-determination through free elections. Such a settlement, they asserted, "should be sought as soon as possible." [25]

In the meantime, differences between Bonn and Paris increased. Early in July President de Gaulle and eight ministers flew to Bonn for a two-day semiannual meeting held under the Franco-German Treaty of Friendship. An effort was made to obtain West German support for the Gaullist concept of a six-nation confederation. The French hoped to secure an agreement setting up a special Franco-German committee to draw up a blueprint for European political unity. But Chancellor Erhard shied away from the French proposal, which some of the smaller Common Market countries regarded as a move toward Franco-German hegemony in the European community. Although outwardly a spirit of harmony prevailed, the meeting disclosed a widening rift between Paris and Bonn.

The 88-year-old Adenauer, bitterly disappointed over the deterioration of Franco-German collaboration, which he considered the greatest achievement of his "era," declared that only by binding the ties more tightly together could a force be built against the spread of Communism. Dr. Erhard, however, maintained that "a Europe that consists of two states is not the Europe that the [German] Federal Government has in mind. Close cooperation between France and the Federal Republic is a condition for the creation of Europe. But it is not an end in itself." [26] He thus emphatically rejected the building of Europe's structure on the foundation of a Bonn-Paris axis. The German Chancellor further remarked that it was necessary to have the courage not to clutch at a superficial solution "which does not serve the common interest in the end, which does not serve to unite us but to divide us."

Although rebuffing the French plan, Dr. Erhard promised to submit new proposals on ways to overcome the deadlock in efforts toward European unity. He made it clear that Germany needed the support of all its allies, but particularly of the United States, and frankly said, "We are more dependent on our allies than a sovereign nation would normally be." It became increasingly evident that while France equated its "independence" with its ability to act outside the Atlantic alliance—and often contrary to the interests of allied unity—the West Germans recognized the necessity of integrating themselves more closely into the alliance in order to further their own interests. Whereas President de Gaulle was convinced that the time had arrived to let go of Uncle Sam's coattails, Bonn believed that this should be done by strengthening Europe's influence within the Atlantic alliance. The Germans neither wanted to see Europe as a third force nor wished to contest American world leadership on which the Continent's security depended. Their major desire was to work within the framework of Europe and Atlantic cooperation.

9. THE M.L.F. IS STALLED

The debate over the M.L.F. reached a critical stage during the fall. Among the several reasons for this development were the increasing pressures of the United States to reach a decision on the issue before the end of the year; the growing impatience of West Germany, which favored the creation of a NATO multilateral force; the change of government in Britain; and the antagonistic attitude of President de Gaulle.

A crucial factor vitally affecting the M.L.F. project was Britain's position. For the most part, the Conservative government had been equivocal about the proposal. The Labor party, however, had adamantly opposed both a NATO multilateral force and the acquisition of American Polaris missiles for a fleet of four British nuclear submarines, and in the election campaign party leaders had gone even further in proposing to give up

Britain's independent nuclear deterrent. On October 15 Labor defeated the Conservatives by the slim margin of four seats in the 630-member House of Commons, and Mr. Harold Wilson became Prime Minister. The victory, which brought the Labor party back into power after thirteen years in the opposition, foreshadowed immediate and important changes in British policies.

Not only did the new Labor government have to make urgent decisions on the future of British nuclear weapons, but it also faced a grim financial situation that had become ominous in recent months. Ever since World War I when Britain's unique position as the world's creditor and financier was destroyed, it had found itself periodically grappling with monetary problems; after World War II these crises became chronic. Unable except at intervals to earn enough from its foreign sales, investments, and invisibles to match its payments abroad, the country's annual balance-of-payments deficits had increased alarmingly. In 1964 these deficits climbed to a record total of some $2 billion. Prime Minister Wilson adopted drastic measures to remedy the problem. A straight 15 per cent surtax on imports was levied on everything except food and raw materials, and tax incentives were extended at home to stimulate exports. To help Britain meet its financial crisis, the world's financial powers agreed on November 7 to extend $3 billion in aid through the International Monetary Fund and bilaterally.

The straitened financial situation posed a serious dilemma for the British, which was reflected in the M.L.F. issue. The question was how Britain could maintain its power and influence within the NATO structure without being required to bear any additional expense. In an effort to fulfill his promise to abandon Britain's independent nuclear deterrent and, at the same time, retain its power position, Prime Minister Wilson suggested modifying the M.L.F. proposal to provide for an allied force that would include Britain's Polaris submarines and strategic bombers. A force that included these arms might not only strengthen Britain's role but also reduce the relative weight of West Germany's contribution.

During the weeks following the general election, Britain's new leaders worked on a plan for a reorganization of the Western military alliance to cope with the whole range of problems of sharing control of nuclear weapons. Although details were not officially disclosed, the British scheme appeared to have a two-fold purpose. First, the British apparently hoped to increase substantially allied participation in the formulation of America's global military policy. They suggested the desirability of establishing an advisory group consisting of the three Western nuclear powers as well as Germany and possibly Italy, with one other rotating member drawn from the smaller members of the alliance. This group would sit in Washington and would presumably be composed of special representatives of cabinet rank. It would be concerned not only with the NATO area but with the whole world, and with planning for American conventional as well as nuclear forces. While the plan in some ways resembled an enlarged version of President de Gaulle's 1958 proposal for a three-power allied directorate, it did not go so far as to seek a veto on American decision. Its purpose was primarily to involve the advisory group in American strategic and contingency planning, targeting, and crisis control so that the United States would be clearly and directly informed of the views of other participating countries before making decisions.

The second purpose of the British scheme involved the idea of establishing a separate NATO nuclear command to consist of a force of surface ships—greatly reduced from the number originally proposed by the United States—as well as all of NATO's existing medium-range weapons in Europe and Britain's V-bombers and Polaris submarines. A separate nuclear force thus constituted would make Britain the biggest contributor after the United States. For this enlarged NATO force, the United Kingdom suggested a double veto—one for the United States alone and the other for the European countries collectively. The European veto might be based on either a simple majority vote or on a weighted system, depending on the size of each member's contribution to the force. From Britain's point of view the creation of an advisory group seemed to be of more importance than the establishment of a separate NATO nuclear command. Because of the complexities involved in working out a satisfactory solution to the problems of nuclear power and command, the British leaders stressed that since no emergency existed, more time should be devoted to their consideration.

Despite the exploratory nature of the British proposals and the coolness of the U.S. response, President de Gaulle, fearing that the M.L.F. would be established and that it would link Europe—particularly Britain and West Germany—more closely to the United States, intensified his hostility toward the project. He indicated that European political and economic unity was incompatible with participation in the mixed-manned crew force. France was especially incensed by Chancellor Erhard's hint in early October that West Germany would consider going along with the United States on the M.L.F. even if other European countries refused to do so—an idea which Washington immediately repudiated. But French suspicions were not allayed, particularly since the United States was pressing for definite commitments and seemed determined to establish a multilateral force.

On November 3 Couve de Murville warned that going ahead with the M.L.F. would "cause a division within NATO." Two days later, Premier Georges Pompidou declared that any accord between the United States and West Germany on a nuclear fleet would lead to a denunciation of the Franco-German treaty of cooperation. Although he denied that France was considering withdrawing from NATO, he bluntly asserted that "its organization, its present strategy do not satisfy us, either for the defense of the West, of Europe or of France." [27] The French Premier intimated that drastic action would be taken against NATO unless the M.L.F. idea was abandoned. Charging that it was directed politically "more or less against France," M. Pompidou said that the suggested multilateral force would not only hurt European unity, but also provoke some countries, including the Soviet Union. These were the sharpest attacks yet made publicly by French officials.

The crisis in the NATO alliance worsened during November,

as the United States indicated its willingness to consider the British proposals, and Britain and West Germany explored the possibility of agreement. On November 14 Washington and Bonn announced a far-reaching military accord. A communiqué stressed "the close and continuing German-American military relations"; both countries reaffirmed their support of the M.L.F., urging that the concept be implemented "as soon as possible after the requisite political decisions have been made." [28] The agreement clearly underlined the American determination to continue to play a major role on the European continent with West Germany as an active partner, despite French opposition. Confident of obtaining an agreement on the M.L.F., Washington seemed fully prepared to risk any possible retaliation against the NATO structure on the part of President de Gaulle. Prime Minister Wilson, at the same time, warned France that its "nostalgic delusions" could endanger the Western alliance. Categorically rejecting "any idea of a separate European deterrent," he said such a course could only result in dividing NATO, in prompting America's reappraisal of its attitude toward Europe, and in taking a "grave step in the proliferation of nuclear weapons."

Delays in reaching agreement stemmed not only from French opposition, but also from the failure of Britain and West Germany to reconcile their own views. Mr. Wilson was skeptical about the M.L.F. in the form presented by the United States; on November 23 he told the House of Commons that the force of Polaris-armed surface vessels would add "nothing to Western strength, is likely to cause a dissipation of effort within the alliance, and may add to the difficulties of East-West agreement." Bonn, for its part, had grave doubts about the merits of the British proposals, especially the setting up of a separate command within NATO over an enlarged M.L.F. West Germany believed that Britain could obtain an equal voice far more simply by combining its Polaris submarines which were under construction with the M.L.F. and keeping the nuclear fleet under the authority of the NATO Supreme Commander in Europe.

Meanwhile, President de Gaulle increased pressure on West

Germany by threatening to cease to "participate" in the Common Market if Bonn did not agree on a uniform grain price. The attack on West Germany's agricultural policy was then linked to the M.L.F. He flatly declared that the proposed creation of a multilateral force within NATO was an American, not a European, concept of defense. In effect, the French leader offered Bonn the choice between entry into the M.L.F. and close relations with the United States or cooperation with France toward the attainment of European unity, presumably along Gaullist lines. Former Chancellor Adenauer warned at the same time of the possibility of a Paris-Moscow axis if Germany continued to turn its back on France. The Bonn government thus found itself in a tight squeeze. Disappointed at British criticism of the M.L.F. and uncertain about the direction of U.S. policy, Chancellor Erhard decided to "trim his sails." On November 27, in an important policy speech, he announced that an agreement on grain prices would be forthcoming "immediately," thus indicating his willingness to compromise with France. No strong reaffirmation was made of recent German pledges to move full steam ahead with the M.L.F.

Late in November President Johnson began to veer away from a rigid position on the M.L.F. At a press conference in the front yard of the LBJ ranch, he said that the United States would not be "adamant" in its attitude. "The ultimate essentials of the defense of the Atlantic community are the firmness and mutual trust of the United States and Europe." He saw "no safe future for ourselves and none for any other Atlantic nation in a policy of narrow national self-interest." [29] In a subsequent speech the President stressed that the Western alliance was not in the midst of crisis but of change. He indicated, however, that control over nuclear weapons, the major issue dividing the NATO countries, had to be solved. Alluding to the Coal and Steel Community, the integration of Germany into NATO, and the Common Market, Mr. Johnson observed that "every important period of progress" was marked by the same kind of discussion and debate as had arisen over the M.L.F. "To change patterns of thought or the shape of institutions is never very easy." Despite the difficulties, the President did not suggest abandoning America's commitment to the M.L.F. On the contrary, he urged America's allies to move ahead. "Those of us who are ready to proceed in common ventures must decide to go forward—always with due deliberation, with due respect for the interests of others and with an open door for those who may join later." Emphasizing that Americans did "not seek to have our way, but to find a common way," the President made it clear that the United States would "never insist on unanimity." [30]

On December 7–9, the long-awaited talks between Prime Minister Wilson and President Johnson were held in Washington. The joint communiqué indicated little. The two leaders agreed on the objective of seeking arrangements for the allied control of nuclear weapons "which best meet the legitimate interests of all members of the Alliance, while maintaining existing safeguards on the use of nuclear weapons, and preventing their further proliferation." [31]

It was apparent that both the M.L.F. and the British counterproposals were discussed at length, but there was no indication that either scheme was endorsed. The communiqué also stressed the need for sharing defense burdens more equitably among the countries of the free world, reflecting Britain's need to reduce defense costs in order to improve its balance-of-payments position. No firm decisions seemed to have been reached, but significantly Prime Minister Wilson remarked at a news conference after his meetings with the President that there was "a total identity of views" between the two countries on "the objectives we have set to guide our respective approaches to our allies and friends."

By the end of the year the problem of the Atlantic alliance became more sharply defined. Fundamentally, it was how to draw its members, particularly Britain, France, West Germany, and Italy, into a concert that would also work with the United States. As Walter Lippmann pointed out, "Nothing less will do. A 'European' concert which isolates itself from the United States is impossible and indeed inconceivable. An 'Atlantic' agreement which does not include France will disrupt the Atlantic Alliance." [32] But the problem was more easily stated than resolved. Implied in the question of European defense—whether it was to be dependent or independent of the United States, and whether it was to be national or integrated—was the larger, and more crucial, issue of the future structure of Europe.

As the NATO foreign ministers assembled in Paris for the annual ministerial Council meeting on December 15–17, the expectation was strong that a showdown would take place. Despite French forebodings, Secretary Rusk declared on his arrival that the United States remained fully committed to the security of the North Atlantic alliance. America, he said, was also equally insistent on maintaining its "rights and obligations" in Europe to which it had fallen heir as a result of World War II.[33] The United States hoped that the quarrel within the alliance over the M.L.F. would be confined to private talks. But this proved to be impossible. More than any other issue, it dominated the Council sessions. Foreign Minister Couve de Murville—Belgium, Norway, and Denmark also voiced their own opposition to the project—reiterated French objections to the M.L.F. and urged that it be dropped. He underscored the point that no meaningful negotiations could be undertaken with the Soviet Union on the reunification of Germany if Bonn were given a share in the control of strategic nuclear weapons through participation in the M.L.F. Mr. Rusk, however, warned that the force should not be downgraded, declaring that the proposal had been made in good faith by the United States in response to European requests, and appealed for more consultation among the NATO members and for greater integration of Western defense—a suggestion which the French Foreign Minister did not consider fruitful.

On December 16 Defense Secretary McNamara forcefully presented to the NATO Council the military and political reasons for European reliance on American nuclear protection. Discussing the extent of the U.S. nuclear commitment, he reported that 40 per cent of the United States stockpile in 1964 was either in West Germany or allocated to the defense of Europe. More than 800 intercontinental ballistic missiles, more than 300

Polaris missiles, and hundreds of B-52 and medium-range bombers with an intercontinental nuclear capacity had been placed "at the service of NATO." In answer to French doubts about the American commitment to defend Europe in case of attack, the Defense Secretary emphatically asserted that the United States could not make a distinction between a nuclear threat to Europe and one to America, and it would not permit the loss of Western Europe in a "limited" nuclear war. He made it clear that American nuclear power was targeted to defend the United States *and* Europe, not the United States *or* Europe.[34]

Secretary McNamara's report to the Council evidently impressed President de Gaulle. For the first time, he began to move slowly but perceptibly toward a more accommodating position in his relations with the United States. In talks with Mr. Rusk, he agreed on the importance of halting the spread of nuclear weapons, and accepted in principle an offer to coordinate the targets of France's new nuclear-armed force and America's Strategic Air Command. This move reflected the assurances given by President Johnson and Secretary Rusk that the United States was not seeking to isolate France in the Western alliance. The decision to share intelligence and coordinate the designation of possible targets went far toward contributing to a changed spirit within the alliance. The basic differences between the French and American concepts on European unity and defense remained; it was, however, apparent that President Johnson had decided on a path of reasoned argument rather than pressure in dealing with America's allies.

The December Council meeting marked a significant turning point.[35] The long-expected collision between the U.S. and France did not materialize, mainly because Washington indicated that the M.L.F. proposal was not unalterable. Secretary Rusk's call for "fresh thinking" on the force and President Johnson's willingness to consider modifications in the M.L.F. to meet the Western allies' needs and desires opened a new phase in the effort to create a collective Atlantic nuclear force. One concrete result of the Paris meeting was a decision by the United States, Britain, West Germany, Italy, and the Netherlands to

meet in January for further discussions on the problems connected with the formation of the force. The change in the
American attitude did not mean abandonment of the multilateral force. It did mean that Washington had decided to shift
to its European allies the major part of the responsibility for
finding a solution.

A high-level policy memorandum, signed by President Johnson on December 17, indicated that the United States would
neither approve any defense plan that was unacceptable to
both Britain and West Germany, nor agree to any program not
discussed in advance and in detail with France. To encourage
the maximum unity of Europe, the memorandum said that no
"pressure tactics" were to be used on allies, no "special arrangements" would be made with any single ally, no "deadlines"
would be fixed for acceptance of U.S. proposals, and no plan
would be approved that did not leave the door open for any
ally to join in the defense of the Atlantic community at any
time in the future.[36] The President made it clear that there
must be consultation with France before an agreement was
concluded, but French acceptance was not made a condition
to any agreement that might be finally reached. Moreover, he
insisted, that the door be left open for France to join, if it so
desired.

As the year came to an end there was less talk about the
NATO alliance splitting up. The United States was still determined to halt the proliferation of nuclear weapons, and, at the
same time, it sought to satisfy the desires of nonnuclear allies
to participate in nuclear strategy. Although it was not prepared
to abandon the M.L.F., thus inviting dangerous alternatives
in Europe, it was willing to consider modifications and alternative solutions, as well as to pursue a more flexible course
toward improving relations with France. President Johnson emphasized that the fundamental task for the new year would be
to seek to reunite the NATO members and restore the cohesion
of the Western alliance.

CHAPTER THREE
CONFLICT AND TENSIONS WITHIN
THE WESTERN COMMUNITY

GRAND STRATEGY and the future structure of Europe were not the only problems facing the United States. Within the Western community national interests were sharply at odds, and one particularly troublesome conflict festered on. Above all, there were complex economic issues to negotiate in order to spur the development and prosperity of the free world.

Especially acute was the situation in Cyprus. Unfortunately, the bloody feud that flared up during the year was much more than a quarrel between the local Greek and Turkish Cypriotes on the island, since it jeopardized world peace and imperiled a wide range of Western interests. As a result of the concerted efforts of many nations, the turbulence on the island was contained; but the search for a solution to the difficulties continued to be elusive. While tensions within Canada were by no measure as explosive as those in Cyprus, the demands of French Canadians in Quebec for greater autonomy remained another source of potential trouble.

A momentous development of the year was the effort of the Western community to seek an adjustment of economic relations and the lowering of tariff barriers in the so-called Kennedy Round of negotiations. While progress was painfully slow, a number of important hurdles were overcome. As President Johnson said, the need was great "to build a partnership for progress among the free-world industrial nations and then between them and the developing nations." [1] But far more than a general desire or good will was necessary to cope with the tough and complicated problems that stood in the way of that goal.

10. CYPRUS CRISIS

Late in December 1963 communal fighting erupted in Cyprus. For months Greek and Turkish Cypriotes had been importing arms and organizing civilian militias of their own. Only a spark was needed to set fire to the mounting fears and hatreds. On the night of December 21 a Greek Cypriote policeman stopped a Turkish Cypriote in a street in Nicosia. A crowd gathered and heated words were exchanged. Someone started shooting. Before passions cooled, two Turkish Cypriotes lay dead. During the next five days clashes broke out in Nicosia's narrow streets, and fighting soon spread to other communities. Four months later, about 40,000 local Greeks and 10,000 Turks were under arms. Fortifications were put up everywhere; dozens of villages were placed under siege; and shooting and killing occurred daily.

The Cyprus conflict threatened to involve Greece and Turkey in war, to cripple the NATO alliance, and to bring the Soviet Union into a sensitive area. Unexpectedly, a crisis had flared up, with the potential of precipitating a dangerous confrontation between East and West. Although not a party to the dispute, the United States was deeply concerned with maintaining peace and the solidarity of NATO and with making sure that Cyprus would not become a Mediterranean Cuba.

Although the origin of trouble in Cyprus was in large part internal, the interests of Greece and Turkey were but one step removed. Three sources of conflict can be singled out. First, the Greek Cypriotes, who outnumbered the Turkish minority by four to one in the island's population of some 550,000, claimed that the 1960 constitution gave the Turks a disproportionately large role in the affairs of the island republic. The Greek majority especially resented the fact that nothing of importance affecting foreign policy, defense, internal security, and taxation, among other things, could be done without the consent of the Turkish minority. When Archbishop Makarios became the first President of Cyprus, he made no secret of his intention to scrap the constitution since he and the Greek majority considered it unworkable. The Turkish Cypriotes, suspicious of the Archbishop, used their veto power to block vital income tax and customs legislation and, in general, paralyzed government administration. Makarios proceeded to collect taxes and customs without waiting for the enabling legislation, but he was so angered that he drafted thirteen constitutional amendments which practically abrogated all Turkish privileges. In November 1963 he demanded that they be accepted. The Turks brusquely rejected them. When the shooting started a month later, the Turkish Cypriotes believed that this was a planned attack, the beginning of a concerted effort to wipe out their communities.

A second problem stemmed from two treaties, initialled in February 1959.[2] The first was a Treaty of Guarantee whereby Britain, Greece, and Turkey endorsed the independence and territorial integrity of Cyprus, and obtained the right to act together or singly to prevent the island's annexation or partition. The second—a Treaty of Alliance—provided for cooperation by Cyprus, Greece, and Turkey to defend the island against aggression. It also permitted the stationing of Greek and Turkish troops on the island, and allowed Britain to retain sovereignty over two sizable military enclaves. The British had insisted on their right to maintain bases in Cyprus to guard their interests in the Middle East, to protect the southern flank of NATO, and to have a base of operation to come to the defense, if need be, of Turkey and of Greece. Archbishop Makarios regarded the alliance treaty as an infringement on his country's independence, and he sought, in particular, to oust the Turkish and British forces.

The third focal point of tension lay in the conflicts of interest between Greece and Turkey over Cyprus. Greece was as deeply committed to support Greek-speaking Cypriotes as Turkey was to protect the Turkish minority. But beyond strong emotional ties, there existed Greece's desire to further the cause of *enosis* or union with Greece, and Turkey's support of *taksim* or parti-

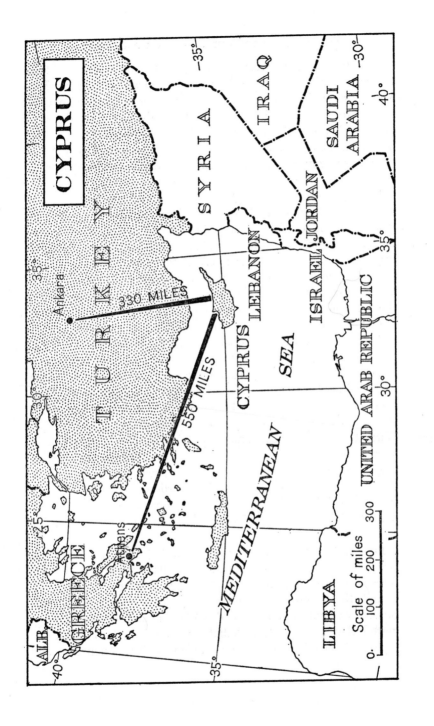

tion of the island between the local Turks and Greeks. Within Cyprus, Greek Cypriotes clearly favored *enosis*. But Archbishop Makarios, while espousing the principle of self-determination, tended to champion the maintenance of the island's independence, with political power vested in the Greek Cypriotes. The Turks, on the other hand, were convinced that unless their rights were absolutely protected, the only possible solution was partition.

President Makarios brought the crisis to a head when he announced on January 1 his intention to abrogate the treaties of guarantee and of alliance. Britain, declaring that these agreements could not be rescinded unilaterally, quickly took steps to bring the Greek and Turkish Cypriote leaders around a conference table in London. Reluctantly, Archbishop Makarios and Vice-President Dr. Fazil Kutchuk, a Turkish Cypriote, agreed to the London talks. Meanwhile, more than 2,500 British soldiers were dispatched to the island to maintain order.

The London conference opened formally on January 15, but it was immediately evident that the outcome would not be successful. As the meeting tottered on the verge of collapse, Britain appealed to Washington to send troops to the island. At the same time, France, Italy, and West Germany were asked if they would join a selective force in Cyprus that would represent NATO. With its military forces almost stretched to the breaking point because of the commitment to Malaysia and the dispatch of troops to put down rebellions in East Africa, England indicated that it would not be able to carry the burden of patrolling Cyprus for long. While the United States was considering a British proposal for a NATO force, Turkey and Greece girded for possible war.

President Johnson cautiously supported a joint American-British proposal which recommended placing an international force of at least 10,000 troops in Cyprus to keep the peace. Although the troops were intended to be drawn from NATO nations, it was not to be an official NATO mission. It was also suggested that an impartial mediator be appointed to break the diplomatic deadlock in London. This move, it was hoped, would forestall Greek or Turkish intervention, allow tempers to subside, and make possible a political settlement without involving the United Nations. Although accepted by Greece and Turkey, the plan was summarily rejected by Makarios. The Archbishop feared that a force provided by NATO powers might lead to a settlement favorable to Turkey, particularly since Turkey was of greater strategic importance to the Atlantic alliance than was Greece. President Makarios insisted that the force be placed under the United Nations with a guarantee that the territorial integrity of Cyprus would be respected.

On February 7 Premier Khrushchev warned other powers not to "interfere" in the internal affairs of Cyprus. He called on the U.N. Security Council to safeguard the island's independence, charging that there was a "serious danger of aggression against Cyprus." Any effort to encroach on the sovereignty of Cyprus, Khrushchev declared, would present "a serious danger to world peace and could become the source of international complications fraught with grave consequences for the peoples." [3] The Soviet Union, of course, had long sought to establish a position of power in the eastern Mediterranean. The Cyprus issue provided an opportunity for the U.S.S.R. to inject itself into the middle of a NATO dispute and, if the crisis should continue on the island, to bolster Communist strength—which was strong in the Greek labor unions—and push a left-wing bid for governmental control.

By February the American-British compromise peace proposal collapsed. France's refusal to join in a NATO peace-keeping operation, lack of cooperation on the part of other members, and Greek and Turkish Cypriote opposition led to the shelving of the plan. On February 15 Britain unexpectedly requested an early meeting of the U.N. Security Council. Washington and London had strongly opposed bringing the Soviet Union into the Cyprus picture through the United Nations, but by now they feared that without U.N. intervention the situation would get out of hand. Secretary-General U Thant proposed the creation of a U.N. peace-keeping force and the appointment of a mediator, and a lively discussion ensued during the next two weeks. Ambassador Stevenson stressed the "critically urgent" need for a peace-keeping force. "The world," he said, "cannot stand by as an idle and silent witness to the fire that is consuming Cyprus and could spread so rapidly." The immediate task of the United Nations was to restore peace and stop the bloodshed. "Time," he declared, "is wasting." [4] On March 4 the Security Council unanimously approved a resolution providing for ·a United Nations peace-keeping force for Cyprus, and the appointment by Secretary-General Thant of a mediator "for the purpose of promoting a peaceful solution and an agreed settlement of the problem confronting Cyprus." [5] But the task of ending the fighting was made difficult, since the consent of both the Greek and Turkish Cypriotes had to be obtained before the troops of the United Nations could be used for almost any purpose. The United Nations forces were apparently called upon chiefly to act as observers. Although the Security Council evidently thought that both sides could be talked into a truce and a peace settlement, this assumption ignored the hatreds and prejudices that had built up so fiercely on the island.

During mid-March, before the U.N. troops arrived, the Cyprus crisis was pushed to the edge of a widespread war. On March 11 the uneasy truce was broken. Two days later Turkey warned Greek Cypriote leaders that it would intervene in Cyprus unless the killing of Turkish Cypriotes stopped. This ultimatum was rejected. As troops boarded ships at Turkish ports, Greek troops were put to sea to head off a possible invasion. At the same time, Archbishop Makarios terminated the treaty of alliance. But Turkey declared that the Cypriote President's action was worthless, since there was no provision in the treaty for its cancellation or abrogation "by Makarios or anyone else."

In the meantime, the dispatch of U.N. troops was delayed because of the problem of financing the operation. Under the terms of the March 4 resolution, expenses were to be borne by the nations providing troops and by Cyprus. Secretary-General Thant estimated that the total cost for three months would be $6 million. On March 11 the United States and Britain agreed to contribute half the money required. Initially, Washington had offered to supply an airlift, but had refused to make a monetary contribution. Although the money was raised and the United Nations was spared the ignominy of impotence, the haggling and delay highlighted a perilous weakness in carrying out U.N. peace-keeping obligations. A Canadian advance party arrived on Cyprus March 14, and by the end of the month some 7,000 U.N. troops began operations. The situation was brought under a measure of control, and on April 6 a cease-fire was arranged between the warring Greek and Turkish Cypriote communities in western Cyprus.

Maintaining the cease-fire proved to be virtually an impossible task. Turkish Cypriotes refused to lay down their arms, since they feared that if they did so, the Greeks would exterminate them. No Turk on the island was prepared to trust U.N. peace-keeping forces to prevent this. Local Greeks, for their part, were greatly worried about the imminent danger of a massive invasion from the Turkish mainland. While the United Nations sought, in effect, to restore the situation to the "normal conditions" before the Christmas riots, pending the negotiations for a political settlement, the Greek and Turkish Cypriotes preferred to go on fighting until a "final solution" was obtained.

The acid test in the Cyprus crisis, of course, was finding an acceptable political solution to end the strife. Archbishop Makarios and Greek Premier George Papandreou declared in April that the only permanent and just answer to the explosive Cyprus problem was self-determination under the aegis of the United Nations. They called for international guarantees to protect the security and well-being of the island's Turkish minority, and a referendum to give the Cypriote people the opportunity to determine whether they wished to remain an independent state or to be united with Greece. Turkey, fearing the revival of enosis, insisted that the best solution would be a federated Cyprus republic in which the island would be divided into two states.

Attempting to break the impasse, President Johnson invited Turkish Premier Ismet Inönü and Premier Papandreou to the White House. Each leader was seen separately. The President was especially concerned to impress upon them that a war between their countries over Cyprus was "unthinkable." Mr. John-

son's venture into personal diplomacy to encourage direct negotiations was far from successful. After two days of talks, June
22–23, the President and Premier Inönü issued a communiqué
which merely stated that they had stressed the validity of the
1959 treaties that had led to the island's independence. The
meetings produced nothing resembling a formula which might
solve the crisis in Cyprus.[6] The communiqué issued by President
Johnson and Premier Papandreou at the end of their two-day
visit, June 24–25, was even less conclusive.[7] Premier Papandreou's
reaction to the U.S.-Turkish communiqué was made known in a
press conference held immediately following his meeting with
President Johnson. The Premier felt that Washington had taken a
position hostile to Greece in recognizing the validity of the 1959
treaties. Although the Greek government had not formally denounced the treaties, it argued that the realities of the Cyprus
situation had rendered them invalid. The fate of Cyprus, Mr.
Papandreou said, could be solved only under the United Nations and through "democratic" procedures, such as a referendum.

U.N. mediator, Ambassador Sakari S. Tuomioja of Finland,
tried to work out a political settlement for the deteriorating Cyprus situation. Preparations had been made in the spring for a
meeting early in July at Geneva with Turkish and Greek representatives. With the approval of Ambassador Tuomioja, as well
as of Greece and Turkey, President Johnson sent Mr. Acheson
to help in these negotiations. Discussions were expected to be
long and difficult.

The explosiveness of the situation was increased during the
summer by the military buildup of Greece and Turkey on the
island, by the Archbishop's "flirting" with the Soviet Union and
Egypt, and by the breakdown of the Geneva talks.

Greece and Turkey secretly began to land troops on the island
from small boats, thus augmenting the levels that each country
had tacitly agreed to maintain when the United Nations consented to send a peace-keeping force. While the military buildup
took place, General George Grivas, a hero to local Greeks for his
leadership of the underground war against Britain and against
the Turkish Cypriotes during the four years preceding independ-

ence, arrived in Cyprus. The former Greek guerrilla commander quickly established himself as co-leader with Archbishop Makarios. The two were diametrically opposed in many ways, their personal and political rivalry going back to the terrorist struggle against the British. Backed by a small, fanatical right-wing group that opposed the Archbishop, Grivas' presence stirred up not only the embers of *enosis*, but also an internal struggle for political power. Bitterly anti-Communist, the Greek General was determined that Cyprus, under President Makarios, would not be seduced by Soviet arms into becoming a Mediterranean Cuba.

General Grivas embarked on a campaign to secure the union of Cyprus with Greece. He stressed particularly that a reconciliation should be effected among the Greek Cypriote political factions, as well as between the Greeks and Turks, declaring that unconditional self-determination should be obtained as soon as possible. At the same time, Makarios took steps to halt the clandestine arrivals of Turkish soldiers on the island. A blockade by sea was imposed on the Tylliria region along the northwest coast, where the smuggling of Turkish arms and men had been going on for some time. Confirming the military buildup, Secretary-General Thant appealed to all parties to reverse the "perilous trend" before a major clash occurred. The situation was further exacerbated by the decision to expel the Greeks living in Turkey. In March Turkey unilaterally abrogated a treaty of thirty-four years' standing which had guaranteed minority rights. About 1,000 Greeks were forced to leave the country during the following months. Partly in retaliation, Cyprus barred a shipload of Red Cross food and medicine to besieged Turkish Cypriotes and threatened to cut off their water supply as well.

A showdown came early in August. Four Turkish jet fighters, identified as U.S.-made Sabre jets, on August 7 attacked the northwestern coastal town of Polis on Cyprus. The next day Turkish planes fired rockets and machine guns at Greek Cypriote villages. They also hit military forces that were moving toward a Turkish Cypriote strip in the northwest. Premier Inönü ordered the "police action" ostensibly to stop Greek Cypriote advances in the Tylliria Promontory area. It was emphasized that the military intervention was strictly limited, and had been decided upon because the U.N. peace force had failed to halt three days of fighting in the region. With the Mediterranean threatened with war, the U.N. Security Council held an emergency session on August 8–9. Turkey charged the Greek Cypriote community with trying to seize the government by force; Cyprus appealed to the Security Council "to put an end to the armed Turkish aggression" against the island's population and the "indiscriminate slaughter of its civilian population." At the same time, Premier Papandreou sent a message to President Makarios urging him to cease hostilities. Greek forces, significantly, were not ordered into action.

On August 9 Turkey struck again with an air raid, inflicting some 300 casualties. Archbishop Makarios warned that unless the raids ended by 6:00 P.M. local time, Greek Cypriotes would launch full-scale indiscriminate attacks against Turkish Cypriote villages. Turkey replied that Makarios would have to stop all military operations in Cyprus before it would agree to halt the air assaults. Meanwhile, Turkey withdrew its air units and bases from NATO's command to use them in its national interest in the Cyprus crisis.

In an atmosphere charged with war-like tensions, the eleven-member Security Council adopted a resolution by a vote of 9-0 with two abstentions (the Soviet Union and Czechoslovakia), which authorized the Council's President to make "an urgent appeal" to Turkey to halt instantly her "bombardment and the use of military force of any kind against Cyprus," and directed Cyprus "to order the armed forces under its control to cease firing immediately." All parties were called upon to agree immediately to a cease-fire, and to cooperate with the U.N. commander to restore "peace and security." [8] President Makarios replied that Cyprus would agree to a cease-fire. Turkey also consented to end its "limited police action," which Premier Inönü declared had been undertaken "with the sole purpose of stopping the Greek Cypriote armed attacks . . . and to protect the lives of innocent Turks."

The prompt response to the U.N. resolution eased the threat of war; but danger remained. Although halting the air bombardments, Turkey asserted that it would not cease "reconnaissance and warning flights" over Cyprus until President Makarios recalled Greek Cypriote forces in the island's northwest area back to positions they had occupied on August 5. The Archbishop, however, stubbornly held his ground. "We shall not give in," he said, "we shall not be broken, we shall not surrender." Makarios flatly announced that Cyprus would continue the struggle either by itself or "with others," intimating that he would seek help from the Soviet Union, and from friendly Arab states. Moscow, of course, was sympathetic to the Greek Cypriote cause, but Premier Khrushchev showed little inclination to become directly involved in the crisis. He was much too preoccupied with the Soviet-Chinese dispute, as well as with agricultural and administrative problems, to plunge into the eastern Mediterranean controversy in a way that would disrupt his relations with the United States.

Nevertheless, the Archbishop's flirtation with the Soviet Union elicited an offer of aid to Cyprus on August 24. Moscow proposed to extend $30 million in economic credits on condition that the Archbishop would continue to insist on self-determination, and demilitarize the island as far as NATO was concerned. Five days later Makarios secretly met President Gamal Abdel Nasser of Egypt. Besides securing Egypt's help in providing arms—Cairo had allegedly been supplying Cyprus with pistols, rifles, machine guns and hand grenades for two or three years—it was believed that the Archbishop was anxious to obtain Nasser's influence in getting the Afro-Asian countries to support the Cypriote cause in the United Nations. Nasser's opposition to foreign bases (the Egyptian leader still resented the fact that Cyprus had been used as a British staging area during the Suez Canal crisis in 1956) and his desire to see the Atlantic alliance's influence reduced in the eastern Mediterranean seemed to be chiefly responsible for his support of Makarios.

Late in July, at the U.N.-sponsored Geneva meetings, Dean Acheson put forward a compromise plan, which stressed, among other ideas, four points: (1) the union of Cyprus with Greece—*enosis;* (2) Turkey's renunciation of its right of intervention under the 1959 treaty; (3) protection of the Turkish Cypriote community; and (4) compensation for Turkey. Besides recognizing the predominant rights of the Greek majority, it was thought that *enosis* would remove a besetting problem for Greece, as well as Turkey, namely, the danger that the island might fall under Communist control. Should Cyprus become an integral part of Greece, Turkey's right of intervention would, of course, no longer be valid. A guarantee by several outside powers would assure the protection of the Turkish Cypriote minority. And it seemed more likely that the local Turks would fare better under Greek sovereignty. Compensation, it was suggested, might be effected by ceding to Turkey the tiny Greek Dodecanese Island of Kastellorizo, and by making payments to Turkish Cypriotes who wanted to leave Cyprus and settle abroad. Other proposals touched on such ideas as establishing a NATO base that would be jointly administered by Greece and Turkey, and forming two cantons under Turkish Cypriote administration. In the final analysis, Mr. Acheson's wide-ranging suggestions for settlement of the Cyprus dispute appeared to point to the dissolution of the Makarios regime.

Greece and Turkey seemed amenable to the Acheson "plan," but they were unable to overcome the opposition of Makarios, who bitterly denounced it. The delicacy of the situation was underlined by the Archbishop's wooing of Russia and the Arab states. Premier Papandreou desperately sought to deflect Makarios' moves in this direction, while at the same time taking every precaution to prevent an open rupture between Athens and Nicosia. Under the circumstances Greece found it impossible to accept fully the formulas advanced by the United States.

In the meantime, new tensions arose in Cyprus. On August 27 a critical issue developed when Makarios refused to permit the Turkish government to rotate half of its 650 regular army troops based on the island. Adequate food and other supplies were also prohibited from reaching Turkish Cypriote civilians. Frustration among the Turks was suddenly focused against the United States and the Soviet Union, who were believed to be supporting the Greek Cypriotes in their dispute with the Turkish community.

For four days during August 27-30 riots raged in Ankara, Istanbul, and the Aegean port city of Izmir. The Turks were especially infuriated by a letter which President Johnson sent to Premier Inönü that apparently contained a warning that American aid might be stopped if Turkey continued to use American-supplied war equipment in its conflict over the Cyprus issue.

The possibility that a new attack might occur over the Turkish troop rotation issue created considerable anxiety. The United States, Britain, and Secretary-General Thant persuaded Turkey to postpone "for a short time" the replacement of part of its military forces in Cyprus, and, as a result, the storm subsided. On September 12 Makarios agreed to allow food supplies to reach besieged Turkish Cypriotes. Three days later, without committing himself on the island's political future, he unexpectedly offered a peace plan for Cyprus, and agreed to lift the economic blockade of Turkish Cypriote areas, remove fortifications, declare a general amnesty, and give financial help to displaced local Turks.

In the meantime the U.N. mediation efforts in Geneva reached a complete deadlock, and Dean Acheson returned to Washington early in September. Although his compromise settlement plan failed to win full approval from either Greece or Turkey in the seven weeks of talks, he felt that much progress had been made in removing the differences between Greece and Turkey. He did not disguise his opinion that Archbishop Makarios was a serious stumbling block to a permanent solution to the Cyprus problem. The situation, Mr. Acheson indicated, remained in a highly precarious state because of the inflamed emotions among the Greek and Turkish Cypriotes. "It's like trying to solve a problem in a powder magazine," he said, "with all the powder barrels open and everyone throwing cigarettes around. You could easily blow yourself up." [9]

Although no solution to the Cyprus problem was in sight, the United Nations continued its efforts to contain the conflict between local Greek and Turkish Cypriotes and to prevent the outbreak of war between Greece and Turkey. On September 25 the Security Council voted unanimously to retain U.N. peace-keeping forces on the island for three more months, until December

26.[10] Mr. Thant had requested broadened powers both for the Secretary-General and the U.N. force, but the Soviet Union and France insisted that the peace-keeping operation had to continue to be financed exclusively by voluntary contributions. They made it clear, as they had in the past, that they would not contribute any money for the peace-keeping force on Cyprus. Thus the operation was maintained in strict accordance with the March 4 Security Council resolution under which it had been established.

After the Security Council's vote extending the U.N. mandate, Secretary-General Thant announced that arrangements had been made to place the Turkish army contingent on Cyprus under U.N. control—which would allow the rotation of one-third of the forces—and to permit the United Nations to assume control over a disputed and strategic highway from Nicosia to Kyrenia that had been closed to Greek Cypriotes since the crisis on the island erupted. Turkey, however, reserved the right to withdraw its contingent from U.N. command if the security of Turkish Cypriotes was threatened. The danger of renewed fighting was lessened, but these favorable developments were somewhat overshadowed when, on September 30, the Greek Cypriot government signed an agreement with the U.S.S.R. to receive Russian arms. A communiqué declared that an accord had been reached "on practical measures of assistance that the Soviet Union will render to the Republic of Cyprus for safeguarding her freedom and territorial integrity." [11]

As the year drew to a close, the outlook for Cyprus remained uncertain. On December 18 the Security Council again voted to continue the U.N. peace-keeping force for still another three months, until March 26, 1965.[12] Precious time was thus gained for seeking a political solution. But in Turkey frustration deepened. The Turkish government seemed especially disheartened by Washington's attitude toward Cyprus and insistence that Turkey not intervene directly in the dispute to impose a settlement. A feeling became increasingly strong that the United States had not adequately helped the Turkish people in the Cyprus quarrel, and as a result they were losing out. Signs thus pointed to a

cooling of Turkish-U.S. relations and the adoption of a more independent Turkish policy.

11. CANADA'S QUIET REVOLUTION

Another member of the Atlantic community affected by tensions and strife was Canada, normally a quiet country. Fortunately, its trouble held no threat of international conflict. Prime
Minister Lester B. Pearson's most pressing problems centered on
domestic troubles with Quebec, quarrels precipitated by a new
flag design, and the working out of changes in the Canadian
constitution. In contrast to the storms that raged within Canada,
its relations with the United States showed considerable improvement over the recent past. After several years of negotiations, a
protocol to the 1961 United States-Canadian treaty for the joint
development of a multimillion-dollar hydroelectric power and
flood control project for the Columbia River basin in the Pacific
northwest was signed on January 22 at the White House.[13]

The Columbia River treaty, ratified on September 16,[14] represented a significant step by the two countries in fostering a peaceful partnership. Initially negotiated in 1961, the delay in concluding the treaty had been caused by disputes between the
Canadian government and British Columbia and between the
United States and Canada over financial arrangements and the
conditions under which Canada would provide flood control services to the United States. Only after long and difficult negotiations were these problems resolved to the satisfaction of all
parties.

By far the most serious problem that Canada had to deal with
was the upsurge of French Canadian nationalism in recent years.
Quebec, the largest of Canada's provinces in size and second to
Ontario in population, was not playing a national role commensurate with the changes that were taking place. Since World
War II it had been transforming its static agrarian society, largely
intent upon preserving its language and Roman Catholic religion,
into a society modernizing under the impact of industrialism and
increased prosperity. The pivot of social and political power was

shifted from Quebec's rural population to its new urban, middle class. Accompanied by an intensification of nationalism, this "quiet revolution" led to demands for establishing the province as a separate nation. At the start of the year, Quebec's secession from the Canadian confederation no longer was viewed as a remote contingency; it was seen as a distinct possibility if the province's demands for greater autonomy were not satisfied.

Like Cyprus, the Quebec problem was heavily loaded with emotional factors, for French Canadians had been resentful of their English-speaking neighbors ever since the British conquest in 1763. While a very small group of fanatical extremists insisted on complete independence—by armed revolt, if necessary —most nationalists in Quebec simply wanted sufficient autonomy for the province to run its own affairs, retaining only loose ties with the federal government. Ottawa's powers, they felt, should be restricted to administering Canadian defense, foreign policy, and currency. Financially, they wanted for Quebec a larger share of the public revenues collected in the province; politically, a revision of the Canadian federal structure so that they would have a greater voice in Canada's affairs; and culturally, official status for the French language equal to that of English in the life of the country.

To satisfy the aspirations of the French Canadians, Prime Minister Pearson went far toward recognizing their special status within the Canadian confederation. Thus he appointed nine French Canadians, a record number, to his twenty-six-member cabinet, and they held the powerful ministries for justice and external affairs. A new federal, social-security-type pension plan was modified to guarantee Quebec's participation—it permitted the provinces that wished to do so to administer their own provincial pension plans. In addition, a Royal Commission on Biculturalism was appointed. Besides these and other concessions, Mr. Pearson, largely as a gesture of good will toward French Canada, practically demanded the adoption of a new flag that would be Canada's own. During his election campaign in 1963 he had promised that this would be done, for French Canadians had objected to the existing flag, the "unofficial" Red Ensign of the

British merchant marine with the Union Jack in the upper left-hand corner. After long and heated debates and one rejected design, the Canadian Parliament adopted a new flag—a banner with a red vertical stripe at each end and a single red maple leaf on a white center. At the end of the year all that was necessary was for Queen Elizabeth to proclaim it as the official emblem for Canada.

But the flag issue did not placate Quebec's nationalists or separatists. Most of the French Canadians had been unenthusiastic, if not indifferent, to Mr. Pearson's proposal; they felt that the change was much too little and too late. The flag controversy merely disclosed how great the gulf was between English and French Canada.[15] The depth of French animosity was evident in the chilly reception which Quebec accorded to Queen Elizabeth when she visited Canada in October to commemorate events a century ago that led to Canada's independence. In expressing the views of the British government, the Queen showed sympathy for moderate French Canadian demands for a changed role within the Canadian confederation. "A dynamic state should not fear to reassess its political philosophy," she said. "That an agreement worked out a hundred years ago does not necessarily meet all the needs of the present should not be surprising."[16] Although endorsing a bicultural Canada, Queen Elizabeth strongly defended the concepts of constitutional monarchy. In contrast to the cold reception she received in Quebec, the Queen was warmly welcomed and cheered by a tremendous, flag-waving crowd at Ottawa.

In trying to forge the French and English communities into a unified nation Mr. Pearson also took steps to "bring home" the Canadian constitution. Since Canada's constitution had originally been written as part of the British North American Act of 1867, amendments could be obtained only by vote of the British Parliament. This procedure was simply a formality, but it was regarded as a symbol of Canada's subservience to England. On September 2 the Prime Minister met with the premiers of Canada's ten provinces to get rid of what he called an "anomalous, archaic, and somewhat humiliating" requirement. Agreement was reached in principle on a proposed formula for enacting amendments without the formality of British assent. It declared that matters affecting the division of powers between federal and provincial governments, education, and minority rights would require the unanimous consent of the provinces; but amendments of a general nature would need the approval of only seven of the ten provinces, provided the seven represented half of Canada's population. This formula was unanimously approved on October 14 at a federal-provincial conference. Described as a "milestone in the evolution of Canada's government," a communiqué announced that when the formula became law, "our Constitution will have become for the first time in the history of Canada, truly and wholly Canadian." [17] By the end of the year it was evident that a majority of moderate opinion on the part of both the French and English Canadians had concluded that significant changes were necessary to prevent the breakup of the confederation. Although as yet there was not complete agreement on what these changes should be, the probability of compromise appeared far more promising than it had been previously.

As Canada groped to establish a secure and sound basis for unity, the Liberal government was making an effort to foster a more harmonious relationship with the United States. At the January meeting held at the White House between President Johnson and Prime Minister Pearson, it was decided to set up a senior-level "working group" to study "the practicability" of formulating "acceptable principles" so that "divergences in economic and other policies" would be avoided. For this purpose, the two governments appointed Livingston Merchant for the United States and Arnold Heeney for Canada—two former ambassadors with long experience in Canadian-American relations. Once a common set of principles was agreed upon, it was expected that many points of friction would, in time, be eliminated. An encouraging sign was the fact that conditions were restored which permitted shipping to move freely on the great waterways between Canada and the United States. While a final settlement was not reached in an interunion dispute over shipping on the

Great Lakes, the violence that had occurred in 1963 did not erupt again.[18]

The questions of greatest complexity and difficulty continued to be found in commercial and economic relations. Canada was still deeply disturbed over what it regarded as America's unduly protectionist tariff policies, strongly believing that its serious balance-of-payments problem could be improved only by increasing its exports to the United States. Because of the disproportionate flow in trade relations, Canada found itself faced with a constantly accumulating deficit in its over-all balance of payments with the United States. Over the past ten years these deficits totalled $10 billion, or an average of $1 billion annually.

On April 25 Under-Secretary Ball, in a frank and hard-hitting speech, examined the key problem of economic interdependence between the United States and Canada.[19] "Difficulties necessarily arise," he said, "when the anxiety to avoid economic interdependence leads to policies that are discriminatory and inequitable." One way in which this problem could be overcome, Mr. Ball suggested, lay in the possibility of developing the North American continent as a single market. Since the tastes of the American and Canadian people were sufficiently similar to permit standardization and specialization of production, he urged the two countries to profit by Western Europe's experience and consider whether a "common market" might not be possible so that North America's resources could be more efficiently developed. Mr. Ball did not feel that the creation of an economic union, despite Canadian misgivings, would necessarily lead to a loss of political independence. "For better or worse, natural trends will lead in the direction of greater economic interdependence. . . . Canada will become increasingly important to the United States and the United States to Canada." Significantly, *Maclean's* magazine in its June 6 issue published the results of a Canadian public opinion survey on whether Canada should join the United States, or whether an economic union short of a merger should be established. Twenty-nine per cent of the Canadian people, it reported, favored political union, a surprisingly large proportion. But even more surprising was that on the question of economic union 65 per cent of the Canadians voted yes. The latter percentage was still higher among the unemployed (79 per cent), Quebec (78 per cent), students (78 per cent), and the Maritime Provinces (75 per cent).[20]

Much more aware of their increasing interdependence with the United States, Canadians, however, were irked that so many Americans knew so little about Canada and tended to take them for granted. Since the volume of their bilateral trade was the largest between any two nations in the world, they felt that more attention should be given by each country to the importance of promoting the economic growth of the other. Canada's special problem, as Mr. Pearson pointed out, was that its economy was "so closely geared to the much larger economy of the United States" that it inevitably was more deeply influenced "by trends south of the border than is the case of any other country."[21] One of the promising developments during the year was the progress made in undertaking joint studies and consultations on the principles of cooperation and the problems of particular industries, such as the automotive industry. Encouragingly, both the United States and Canada demonstrated an increased awareness of the need to follow economic policies that would adequately take account of the interests of the other.

12. THE KENNEDY ROUND

No less difficult of resolution than the conflict in Cyprus or the tensions in Canada were the efforts of the Western community to liberalize world trade—a task of a much different order. In 1962 President Kennedy had launched a vigorous campaign to remove trade barriers and had succeeded in persuading Congress to adopt the Trade Expansion Act.[22] This law granted the President the broadest tariff-cutting powers and negotiating authority the nation had ever accorded its Chief Executive. It marked the high point of three decades of effort—going back to the Reciprocal Trade Agreements Act of 1934—in which the United States had sought to encourage the development of a multilateral system of economic cooperation. While the purpose of the Trade Expansion Act was chiefly to foster greater growth at home, to stimulate U.S. and world trade, and to strengthen the Atlantic partnership, its specific aim had been to make sure that the new and enlarged market of the European Economic Community would be open, not closed, to the products of the United States and the rest of the world.

The Trade Expansion Act set the stage for negotiations on tariff reductions, which became popularly known as the Kennedy Round. Formal meetings were scheduled to open in Geneva early in May 1964. Strictly speaking, this was the sixth round of international trade negotiations under the auspices of the General Agreement on Tariffs and Trade (GATT). Originally subscribed to by twenty-three countries in 1947, GATT had grown into a substantial institution, including more than sixty nations. Although previous GATT conferences—in 1947, 1949, 1950–51, 1956, and 1960–61—had been mainly hard bargaining sessions, the Kennedy Round was intended to be something quite different, and far more ambitious than anything attempted before. Optimistically, it was hoped that new ground would be broken in developing methods to effect tariff-cutting among the industrialized countries, on handling the unresolved problem of agricultural trade, and on finding ways to cope with the trade problems of developing countries. For more than a year "preliminary" discussions were undertaken to find common formulas to deal with these matters.

These negotiations, as might be expected, were highly complex. Moreover, it was recognized that the Kennedy Round could have a profound effect not only on economic but also on power relationships. Since the consequences could be far-reaching, the great powers naturally approached the task of reordering trade patterns with caution. From America's point of view the political implications of the Kennedy Round were as important —if not more so—as the trade problems raised. Its failure, as Secretary Rusk pointed out, would signify that "the industrial nations were unready to abandon the economic parochialism that was so costly to us all in the past" and, equally important, would be interpreted as "a break of faith with the emerging nations of the world." [23]

The underlying difficulties in the negotiations grouped themselves in the three areas where, it was hoped, new ground would be broken. The first touched on tariff-cutting for industrial products. The Trade Expansion Act gave the President the authority over a five-year period to reduce by as much as 50 per cent U.S. tariff duties, as of July 1962, with only a limited number of exceptions. Where a duty was no greater than 5 per cent, the President could abolish it completely. A major aim of the Trade Expansion Act was to put an end to customary item-by-item tariff bargaining. It sought instead to obtain an "across-the-board" or linear reduction of tariffs pertaining to specific categories of products. The Common Market countries balked at a straight, across-the-board 50 per cent reduction of tariffs on industrial goods, especially since it would still leave many U.S. tariffs so high as to be seriously protective, while almost nine-tenths of their duties would be cut to 10 per cent or less. At the May 1963 GATT ministerial meeting it was decided that these "disparities" should be dealt with by a special automatic rule. [24] Seeking to work out an equitable arrangement in tariff-cutting, the European Economic Community in December 1963 tried to identify these disparities—nearly 1,200 items were singled out—and it suggested criteria for exempting them from across-the-board reductions. It proposed that these items, or "exceptions," should be subject to bilateral negotiations with the countries concerned. The United States largely accepted the E.E.C. recommendation, but it stressed that the exceptions should be reduced to a bare minimum. It strongly preferred, however, spelling out the criteria for exceptions in an automatic rule, rather than negotiating on them bilaterally. Between January and May efforts were made to work out a compromise, but until the opening of the Kennedy Round, the problem remained unresolved.

Even more difficult was the issue of agricultural products. The agricultural problem was compounded by conflicts in policy between France and West Germany over the level at which unified grain prices in the Common Market should be set. Paris desired low prices to counter inflation and to get France's fair share of the market; Bonn, high prices to protect Germany's high-cost farmers. In July 1963 President de Gaulle had warned West Germany and the other E.E.C. countries that unless "essential agreements in agriculture" were reached by the end of the year, "the Common Market may disappear." In December the European Economic Community just barely managed to survive this worst storm since its founding in 1957. A broad agreement was reached at the ministers' meeting in Brussels about a week before the January 1 deadline. Although common prices for wheat and feed grains—the most troublesome issues in the long, drawn-out conference—were shelved, common prices and policies were arrived at for rice, beef, and dairy products.

Attempting to break the French-German deadlock on farm policy, Sicco L. Mansholt, Vice-President of the Common Market's Executive Commission, proposed a plan in December 1963 to establish unified grain prices that would fall between the French and German levels. Owing primarily to German resistance, this proposal did not win the necessary unanimous support of the E.E.C. Council of Ministers. For the Kennedy Round Dr. Mansholt also set forth a plan which called for measuring and freezing levels of support and protection for all agricultural products, in the importing and exporting nations alike. This plan was adopted by the Council of Ministers and became the mandate for its negotiators.

The United States found the Mansholt plan for the Kennedy Round negotiations unsatisfactory. On March 31 Mr. Herter, President Johnson's Special Representative for Trade Negotiations, declared that it was "neither acceptable nor workable." Washington officials pointed out that, at best, the plan would not lead to any liberalization of agricultural trade, which the GATT ministerial meeting had declared in May 1963 to be a goal of the Kennedy Round. Some aspects of the plan, it was felt, might even open the way to further restrictions. Moreover, the United States held that the spectrum of agricultural products was too wide for such an "across-the-board" approach. Instead it proposed that agricultural products be dealt with on a pragmatic basis,

ranging from the negotiation of international commodity agreements for such basic products as grains and meat to straightfor-
ward tariff-cutting for highly processed products, such as canned
fruits and vegetables. At the same time Washington made it clear
that it would not enter into any final agreement unless some
significant progress was made toward trade liberalization in agricultural as well as industrial products. "We are willing to offer
our free-world friends access to American markets, but we expect and we must have access to their markets also," President
Johnson said on April 21. "That applies to our agricultural as well
as our industrial exports." [25]

A third aspect of the negotiations related to reducing trade
barriers to the exports of developing countries, and to eliminating nontariff restrictions, such as quotas, exchange controls, and
other devices that limited the flow of trade. The United States
believed that it was essential not only to strengthen the economic
and trade ties of the industrial countries, but also to open their
markets to all of the less developed nations, without discrimination. Washington was well aware that trade alone was not the
answer to stimulating economic growth. As Assistant Secretary
for Economic Affairs G. Griffith Johnson pointed out: "They [the
developing countries] must themselves provide the necessary
conditions for development, the political and social climate, the
advancement of education from the most elementary to the most
technical, the institutions, the monetary stability, the incentives,
the plans, and the energy to advance." [26] To be sure, trade expansion was vital to the improvement of economic conditions.
Any circumscribing of the export possibilities of poorer nations
inevitably reduced their development prospects. The problem of
reconciling the needs of underdeveloped countries with the over-
all objective of trade liberalization was not easily resolved. That
it was of major concern to the developing nations was abundantly
evident in the United Nations Conference on Trade and Development, held in Geneva simultaneously with the Kennedy Round
negotiations. (Section 48)

The opening sessions of the sixth round of GATT trade negotiations, attended by some sixty ministers, were held on May

4–6. Speaking for the United States, Mr. Herter lamented the procrastination and lack of progress that had been made in the preparatory talks. Only conditional agreement had been reached on "special rules" pertaining to disparities; a formula still had not been determined. "We have, unfortunately, made little progress on agriculture," said the American representative. "We have not yet come to grips with the problem of nontariff barriers." Although considerable achievements had been made on rules and procedures relating to less developed countries, much more needed to be done.[27] It was clear that the negotiations were going to be difficult and protracted. The ministers decided to postpone any formal bargaining session until all countries had prepared their "exceptions lists"—those trade items which they wanted to exempt from across-the-board tariff cuts. Later it was agreed that these should be submitted by November 16, a date set after both the American and British elections to avoid any political embarrassment.

During the following months, the progress of the negotiations, especially in resolving the agricultural issue, was painfully slow. Both the United States and France—but for different reasons— exerted pressure for an agreement on the ground rules to negotiate trade in farm products. Washington insisted that tariff policies affecting agriculture had to be negotiated simultaneously with those on industrial goods, and it indicated that it would withhold its exceptions list if the Common Market countries did not straighten out their differences. Bonn, however, continued to offer resistance. Chancellor Erhard, facing an election in 1965 and fearing that he would alienate the farm bloc if West Germany's agricultural prices were reduced, pressed for a postponement of any action. Late in October, the French government threatened to "cease to participate in the European Economic Community" unless the agricultural market was organized.

As the November 16 deadline approached, a crisis of major proportions within the Western community seemed to be coming to a head. The possibility loomed of a complete breakdown of the Kennedy Round. However, on November 3, the day of the presidential election, the United States took a major step toward checking this damaging trend. It dropped its insistence that the European countries had to agree on an agricultural tariff policy before depositing their exceptions lists. A week later Bonn undertook to work out a compromise on grain prices, the chief stumbling block in reaching an agreement with France on agricultural policy. On November 11 France announced its willingness to resume discussions in the Kennedy Round without waiting for a settlement of its dispute with Bonn. Thus, after a year and a half of haggling over rules and procedures, the Kennedy Round finally turned to hard bargaining over tariff cuts.

Seventeen key trading nations submitted their exceptions lists at Geneva on November 16. These contained the industrial products which each country wanted excluded—either in whole or in part—from consideration for 50 per cent "across-the-board" tariff cuts. Although the lists remained secret (proposals were submitted in sealed envelopes), the products involved were expected to include steel, oil, textiles, chemicals, machinery, industrial commodities, and consumer items. Critical to the negotiations were the exceptions lists of the European Economic Community, the United States, Britain, and Japan. The Common Market listed about 19 per cent of all its dutiable imports (excluding steel); the United States about 8 per cent (excluding crude oil); Britain about 4.7 per cent; and Japan about 9 per cent. On the whole, the exemptions appeared modest and workable, although numerous specific problems would have to be resolved.

As the year came to a close the prospect that the Kennedy Round would be successful brightened considerably. Early in December West Germany conditionally agreed to reduce its grain prices to a uniform Common Market level by July 1, 1967. The plan called for both the Bonn government and the European Economic Community to compensate West German farmers for losses suffered as a result of lower prices. Bonn would spend $280 million, to be spread over three years in diminishing annual payments, and the European Economic Community agreed to provide $175 million annually from the time the common grain prices went into effect until the end of the Common Market's transition period in 1970. The breakthrough on agricultural policy was a historic landmark. Not only did it indicate that the Common Market movement was virtually irreversible, but it opened the promise of more fruitful progress toward the political union of the E.E.C. countries, a goal which the United States had long favored.

CHAPTER FOUR
A PAUSE IN THE COLD WAR

A DEFINITE AND CONTINUING EFFORT toward relaxing East-West tensions became discernible during the year. Dangerous political issues remained, such as the future of Berlin and Germany, Southeast Asia, Cuba, and control of nuclear weapons, but Washington and Moscow proceeded cautiously on these issues. Unquestionably, the event that came as the greatest surprise was the sudden deposing of Premier Nikita S. Khrushchev in mid-October. As 1964 drew to a close, the reasons for his ouster were still a matter of great speculation, although it was evident that the action reflected serious dissatisfaction with the manner in which the Soviet leader had handled domestic affairs—particularly his agricultural and economic policies—and relations between the Soviet Union and Communist China.

At the beginning of the year no one suspected that the Khrushchev era would end so precipitately. Recent years had seen significant changes in the Communist world; the intensification of the Sino-Soviet quarrel, the loosening of ties in the Soviet bloc, and the weakening of Soviet leadership in the world Communist movement had posed formidable problems for Moscow. But until the day that he was replaced Khrushchev seemed to be in full control of the situation and the Kremlin hierarchy. His departure from the world scene did not appreciably change the relationship between the West and the Soviet Union, since the policy of "peaceful coexistence" was affirmed by his successors. Encouraged by the climate of relaxation during the year, the

West had sought to probe such questions as: Could an accommodation with the Soviet Union ultimately be achieved? And, in the light of changing conditions, how should the West deal with the Communist world? The answers proposed to these and other questions continued to be sources of great controversy, not only in the United States but in Europe as well.

Although Washington viewed world developments as favorable on the whole to the West, it did not believe that the cold war had come to an end. As Secretary Rusk put it, "We . . . are under no illusions as to the designs of the Communists against us and the entire free world. No one needs to tell us that the Communist menace is deadly serious, that the Communists seek their goals through varied means, that deception is a standard element in their tactics, that they move easily from the direct attack to the indirect, or to combination of the two." The Secretary of State was fully aware that by their official doctrine Moscow and Peking were committed to world revolution, and he made it clear that the United States intended to play its part in checking and reversing Communist imperialism. Noting new trends in recent years, however, Mr. Rusk said that "the Communist world is no longer a single flock of sheep following blindly behind one leader." The Eastern European countries were "increasingly, although in varying degree," beginning to assert their own policies. There were "signs—small but varied and persistent signs—of yearnings for more individual freedom." An effort should be made, the Secretary felt, "to encourage evolution . . . toward national independence and open societies." This development could best be promoted Mr. Rusk pointed out, "by adjusting our policies to the differing behavior of different Communist states—or to the changing behavior of the same state." [1]

In responding to changes in the Communist world, the United States also took steps to reduce the dangers of a major war. In this respect, it recognized that the policy of "containment" was not enough. Thus, the Johnson administration continued the late President Kennedy's efforts at concentrating on limited areas where agreements with the Soviet Union might be possible and progress toward cooperation could be achieved. Washington also

drew a distinction between the Soviet Union and the Eastern
European countries, on the one hand, and Communist China, on
the other. Evidence indicated that Moscow would not risk its
national interests to promote world revolution, whereas Peking
seemed willing to promote aggressions. Given these tendencies,
President Johnson indicated that he preferred Soviet realism
to Chinese militancy.

The United States groped toward developing a more flexible
response to the Communist challenge in the 1960's than had been
the case during the previous decade. In his significant speech at
American University on June 10, 1963, President Kennedy had
suggested the need for a reexamination of American attitudes
"as individuals and as a nation" toward the possibilities of peace
and the course of the cold war, a suggestion taken up by the
Johnson administration.[2] An attempt to further the "reexamination" was made by Arkansas Senator J. W. Fulbright in his celebrated address of March 25.[3] Urging the American people to
adapt themselves to a complex and changing world, to shed old
moralistic "myths," and to dare think "unthinkable things," the
Democratic Senator asserted that Moscow's repudiation of
"total victory" strategies, along with America's nuclear superiority, had ushered in a new age. Communist hostility to the free
world, Fulbright said, appeared in his view to be less significant
than the great variations that existed among the Communist nations. "Only if we recognize these variations," he declared,
"ranging from China, which poses immediate threats to the free
world, to Poland and Yugoslavia, which pose none, can we hope
to act effectively upon the bloc and to turn its internal differences to our own advantage and to the advantage of those bloc
countries which wish to maximize their independence." Senator
Fulbright was speaking for himself, not for the administration,
and on some points the differences were marked, but on this
theme of Communist diversity and its implications there was no
disagreement.

While the United States sought new foreign policy approaches, so, too, did the Western European countries. As the
cold war thawed, external pressures that had bound the free

nations together for their mutual protection no longer seemed so great. Each nation began to feel free to pursue its own national interests. Thus, Britain, France, and other Western European countries moved toward major new economic agreements with the Soviet Union; France recognized Communist China and indicated that it would support Peking's admission to the United Nations; and West Germany expanded its trade relations with Eastern European nations and had even sought to establish economic ties with Peking. Questions arose within the free world on a wide range of problems, but most fundamentally on the whole meaning of the changes in the Communist world.

13. WATCHFUL COEXISTENCE

Both President Johnson and Premier Khrushchev started the new year by embarking on "peace-probe" offensives. Mr. Johnson announced that the United States would make every effort to maintain an atmosphere of good will, and in his New Year's message the Soviet leader urged a policy of "mutual example." [4] The prospect of a "pause" in the cold war was as welcome to the President, because it offered the opportunity to focus attention on neglected domestic problems, as it was to the Soviet Premier, because it provided him with a chance to improve Russian economic performance. The new President talked about taking small steps on the long journey to international accommodation. Echoing this sentiment, Premier Khrushchev declared that the limited nuclear test-ban treaty had been a "good beginning." It showed, he said, that it was possible for governments to co-operate and resolve urgent international problems. A most vital task, both leaders asserted, was to learn to live together in peace. "No feat of physical science," Mr. Johnson remarked, "can compare to the feat of political science which brings a just peace on earth."

Seeking to capitalize on the new climate, Moscow attempted to seize the initiative in the "peace offensive." In a propaganda move of large proportions, the Soviet Union at the turn of the year announced a detailed proposal for the renunciation of force

in all territorial disputes.[5] Designed to prevent countries from
resorting to force in order to change existing "state frontiers,"
the Kremlin asked all nations to sign a formal agreement to
repudiate the use of force "for whatever political, economic,
strategic, frontier or any other considerations"—thus virtually
ruling out war. But a number of exceptions and qualifications
were set forth. For example, the Soviet Union, in effect, sanc-
tioned the right of people under colonial rule to use force in
their struggle to achieve independence, since peaceful means
were not always adequate. Moscow also drew a distinction between ordinary territorial disputes among states and the demands of newly independent countries for areas which were
"theirs by right," but which were still under foreign occupation.
In addition, it called for the removal of foreign troops from
Germany, Korea, and Vietnam—the post-World War II divisions
of these countries, the Soviet Union maintained was "associated
to a certain degree with the territorial question"—and for letting
their people seek unification by peaceful means. Demands of
"revanchist circles" in West Germany for a revision of postwar
territorial settlements, however, were ruled out. Except for
these qualifications, all other territorial disputes, Moscow declared, should be settled by negotiation. The new agreement
would confirm and strengthen the United Nations Charter, which
already bound its members to settle disputes by peaceful means,
and would be "an expression of good will and determination
of states firmly to abide by [its] principles."

The reaction to the Soviet Union's message, on the whole, was
mild. Although Moscow's note was ably written and moderately
phrased, its purpose quite obviously was directed toward serving
the U.S.S.R.'s self-interest, and not toward presenting a practical
program to further world peace. An acceptance of Khrushchev's
proposals would, in effect, have resulted in sanctioning all Communist territorial acquisitions, past or present, and would also
have disregarded the basic Communist tactic of trying to impose
change by a combination of force and subversion. Western
powers could not help but recall the Kellogg-Briand Pact, signed
in 1928 by more than sixty nations, which demonstrated during

the interwar years the futility of a paper pledge to renounce the use of force as an instrument of policy without any proper enforcement mechanism to back it up.

In his reply to the Soviet letter on January 18, President Johnson urged building on "areas of agreement" instead of rehashing "well-known disagreements." He outlined an American program which he believed was much "broader and stronger" than that of the Soviet Union to prevent the use of force for the solution of territorial disputes. In particular, the President stressed the need to strengthen the machinery and methods for peaceful settlement, especially the peace-keeping operations of the United Nations.[6] No one disputed the general proposition that territorial issues should be settled peacefully. But how to solve these problems peacefully challenged and eluded the ingenuity of the world's statesmen.

So, too, was the problem of securing a workable accommodation between the East and West. More than mere words were necessary to bridge the political and ideological chasm that divided them. Each side stood on a watchful alert, carefully safeguarding national interests and probing for weaknesses on the other side. The sensitivity of the situation was disclosed in the shooting down of American planes over East Germany, and in the firing on an American vessel making a wheat shipment to a Soviet port.

On January 29 the relative calm in the cold war was suddenly interrupted when a Soviet aircraft shot down an unarmed American jet training plane over East Germany. Washington charged that the attack was a "careless and inexcusably brutal act of violence against an unarmed aircraft" that had accidentally strayed across East Germany's border, and had caused "the needless death of three officers."[7] Anxiety mounted over whether this incident would seriously damage efforts to develop a Moscow-Washington *rapprochement*. Acknowledging that a U.S. Air Force jet trainer had been shot down, Moscow explained that the plane had failed to react first to signals and then to warning shots. As a result, a Soviet fighter took "measures provided for by instructions concerning the protection of air space." Although strong protests were made, the episode was viewed as an "isolated incident," caused by a trigger-happy Russian.

But no sooner had the excitement died down when a U.S. reconnaissance bomber, straying across the East German frontier, was shot down on March 10. Three crew members bailed out and were captured by the Russians. Moscow declared that the flight was a "premeditated provocation." The wreckage uncovered "reconnaissance equipment for aerial photography and radio-technical intelligence," demonstrating that the plane had penetrated East German territory for the purpose of carrying out military reconnaissance. The Soviet Union declared that it could not accept Washington's explanation that these planes were accidentally straying from their course, especially since they appeared "precisely in those areas in which United States intelligence has a particular interest." [8]

Denying that the reconnaissance bomber was on a spying mission, Washington informed Moscow that it "expected" the three American airmen to be returned "without delay." But no action was taken. Prospects of a major crisis loomed as rumors spread that the crew members might be put on trial unless the United States made a public admission that it had ordered them to fly over East German territory. There were also hints that the men might be turned over to the East German government in an attempt to force Washington to negotiate with and grant recognition to the "German Democratic Republic." Secretary Rusk called in Soviet Ambassador Anatoly F. Dobrynin on March 19 and demanded the prompt release of the three fliers. Mr. Rusk warned that other issues in Soviet-American relations were at stake. He conceded the difficulty of his contention that navigational errors had twice led American planes to stray into East Germany. However, he told the ambassador that it would be an even greater mistake for the Soviet Union to ignore the facts and to manufacture evidence of aerial espionage. The bomber had taken off from a French base and, according to Washington's version, was simply on a two-and-one-half-hour routine "navigational training mission." The plane was unarmed and did not carry bombs or weapons of any sort. It had instructions to go no closer than seventy miles from the East German border. But, according to an Air Force official, "They were about 120 miles off course—a tremendous error."[9] Fortunately, the Soviet Union made no attempt to capitalize on this incident for propaganda or other purposes. Three days after Mr. Rusk's meeting with Ambassador Dobrynin one of the airmen who had been injured was turned over to American authorities; a week later the two other Air Force officers were returned to West Germany after the United States expressed regret for their "violation of East German air space."

Another ugly incident occurred on July 15 when a Soviet patrol vessel fired three shells across the bow of an American wheat ship when it sailed from a Black Sea port in a dispute over unloading charges. There were no injuries or damage, but the American ship captain was forced to pay a $55-fine before being allowed to proceed. Protesting the action, Washington said that the Soviet authorities may have been "within strictly legal rights" under international law. But it noted that the methods employed "were excessive and clearly outside the norms of acceptable behavior."[10]

In contrast to similar incidents in the past, a significant aspect of these altercations was the relatively amicable manner in which they were quickly settled. Neither Washington nor Moscow desired to jeopardize the possibilities for expanding areas of cooperation. Late in February agreement was finally reached to extend the cultural exchange program that had expired on December 31, 1963.[11] Part of the delay had been caused by the repercussions of the arrest and subsequent release in Moscow of Yale Professor Frederick C. Barghoorn in 1963. On June 1 the United States and the Soviet Union signed an important consular convention in Moscow, the first bilateral treaty that had ever been negotiated between the two countries. Subject to Senate ratification, the thirty-article treaty was designed to promote commercial and cultural relations and to provide new protection for citizens of each country in the territory of the other. With the Barghoorn case still fresh in mind, President Johnson expressed his pleasure at the clause that required the

Soviet Union to give prompt notice of the detention of American citizens and to permit American officials access to them.[12] Although the United States and the U.S.S.R. had never had a consular agreement, they had exchanged consulates under the Roosevelt-Litvinov agreement of 1933 whereby the United States and the Soviet Union established formal diplomatic relations. Fifteen years later the American consulate at Vladivostok and the Soviet consulates at New York, San Francisco, and Los Angeles, had been closed as a result of the deterioration of relations in the postwar period.

Other areas in which the United States and the Soviet Union continued their efforts at cooperation included the working out of a charter for a Moscow-New York air route; the expansion of scientific cooperation in space matters to cover biology and medicine; and the establishment of a joint program to explore methods for desalination. A preliminary accord was reached early in June at Geneva on scientific cooperation in space problems, and on November 18 a formal agreement was concluded to cooperate in desalination research, including the use of atomic energy in an economically feasible process.[13]

East-West relations underwent the hazard of a possible turn for the worse when the world learned on October 16 that Premier Khrushchev had been deprived of political power. In a matter of fact way, Moscow announced that he had been replaced by Leonid I. Brezhnev as First Secretary of the Communist party, and by Aleksei N. Kosygin as Premier.[14] Although taken aback by the news the United States did not expect any major change in the Soviet policy of "peaceful coexistence." Reporting to the nation two days later on the change in Soviet leadership, President Johnson observed that Brezhnev and Kosygin were "the same men that he [Khrushchev] picked for leadership. These men carried on the administration of the Soviet Government when he was absent from the Soviet capital, and that was nearly half the time he was in power." Mr. Johnson declared that the new Soviet government had informed him officially that it "plans no change in basic foreign policy." [15]

While Moscow attributed Khrushchev's removal to reasons

of health, this explanation met with skepticism. Among the
factors responsible for the Soviet Premier's fall, evident from
later statements and *Pravda* editorials, were the extent of the
deterioriation in Sino-Soviet relations and the unwillingness of
the Soviet hierarchy to accept his insistence on a showdown conference of world Communist parties in December; his tendency
to deal with major questions on his own initiative, of which his
proposed visit to West German Chancellor Erhard was singled
out as a flagrant example; and especially the opposition which
had developed among Soviet leaders against Khrushchev's constant reorganization of the economy, his revision of the Communist party's economic functions, and his periodic shifting of
priorities. Only two weeks before his removal, he had called for
a new and major change in Soviet agricultural policy. The Soviet
Premier's failure to consult his colleagues, his erratic behavior
and "harebrained schemes," to use *Pravda's* term, in addition
to the decline of Soviet influence within the Communist world,
also seemed to have contributed to his removal.

In the West a great deal of attention focused on how the
removal was effected. Especially noted was the indifference
or apathy of the Russian people. Former Ambassador to the
Soviet Union George F. Kennan, however, observed that it had
been plain for some time that Premier Khrushchev's position
had not really corresponded to that of "the supreme dictator and
arbiter" as he was "so often pictured in the West." [16] Although
the details of the ouster were, of course, not revealed, bits of
evidence as pieced together indicated that the decision was
made by the Presidium of the Communist party's Central Committee—the highest decision-making body in the Soviet Union.
Exactly when it was reached is not known, but it is clear that
it was not spontaneous. On October 13, Khrushchev reportedly
attended an eight-hour Presidium meeting where he was permitted to defend himself orally. When the Soviet Premier had
previously been voted out by the Presidium in 1957, he had
been able to overrule the verdict by obtaining the majority
support of the full Central Committee. But this time, the Committee, meeting on October 14, refused to reverse the Presid-

ium's decision. Mikhail A. Suslov, the Soviet expert on ideology, led the attack against Khrushchev and accused him of everything from nepotism and agricultural mismanagement to bungled relations with foreign Communist parties. After a half-dozen speakers rose to attack him, the Soviet Premier apparently acknowledged defeat and accepted the majority vote. Late in October, a list of twenty-nine charges evidently leveled against Khrushchev at the plenary Central Committee meeting were circulated to Communist parties in other countries. The former Soviet Premier was accused, among other things, of errors in policy on China, Cuba, and Suez, of provoking a "crisis" in Soviet agriculture and committing major errors in economic planning, and of "undignified" behavior for a Communist leader.[17]

Following Khrushchev's downfall, the new Soviet leadership promptly cancelled projected plans that had been made by the former Premier for a trip to West Germany, the only instance in which a change in Soviet foreign policy with respect to the West was apparent. Absorbed in the tasks of reorganizing the country's agricultural and industrial management, of coping with the Sino-Soviet dispute, and of redefining the role of the Communist party and government in Soviet society, the new leadership, at the end of the year, appeared to be holding off from any new initiatives on the world scene.

14. DEBATE ON EAST-WEST TRADE

The easing of international tensions and the huge Soviet wheat imports necessitated by the Russian agricultural crisis in 1963 heightened interest in East-West trade. By the end of 1963 much of the non-Communist world, including the United States, was engaged in a reappraisal of policies on trade with Eastern European nations. The most dramatic development, of course, was Russia's purchase of $500 million of Canadian wheat, and its large supplemental purchases from the United States and other Western nations. Khrushchev's announcement in December 1963 of a seven-year program to expand the chemical industry, involving an investment of $46 billion to build 200 new chemical plants, modernize 500 others, and obtain necessary equipment, also acted as a stimulus. In effect, the Soviet Premier notified the West that he was in the market to buy whole complexes of chemical plants that would be paid for "according to commercial conditions," i.e., on long-term credits of ten, fifteen, or twenty years.

The Soviet leader's bid for long-term Western credits opened up a year of controversy. Washington had vigorously opposed any such grants. In November 1963 Under-Secretary Ball and Special Adviser on Soviet Affairs Llewellyn E. Thompson traveled to Western Europe to urge the adoption of a uniform allied policy of refusing long-term credits and extending only five-year credits, which the Western industrial nations had informally agreed upon. But Britain, whose economy was vitally dependent on foreign trade, said no to Washington's call to limit credits to five years on permissible trade. The United States became apprehensive that if Britain broke ranks and provided the long-term credits, there would be a rush among all the Western European nations to compete for the trade with the Soviet bloc.

Early in 1964, debate in the West on expanding trade relations with the Soviet Union and Eastern European countries reached a high pitch. The United States argued that the denial of long-term credits to the Soviet Union would compel the Kremlin to divert money from military spending and space programs to consumer needs. This, in turn, would incline the Russians to negotiate more seriously on ways to reduce East-West tensions. The British contended that, on the contrary, the Soviet Union had a fixed level of military spending and would not cut into this sum to divert it to consumer spending. To deny the Soviet Union long-term credits, the British maintained, would cause the Kremlin to return to a more rigid Stalinist line of reducing production for consumers and tightening controls to keep its citizens in line. The long-run effect on East-West relations would be the exact opposite of that desired by both London and Washington. The United States countered that extending long-term credits would be giving what could be

described as "economic assistance" to the Communist bloc; the
West would be using capital resources needed for underdeveloped nations, and Western creditor nations would become tied
to Soviet trade for repayment of the loans just as Nazi Germany
had tied its creditors to it in the 1930's. The British disagreed
on all counts, taking the position that a "fat" Communist was
preferable to a "lean" one. They were perfectly ready, they
declared, to take justifiable commercial risks in transactions with
the Soviet Union.

The issue on East-West trade relations came to the forefront
in a meeting between President Johnson and Prime Minister
Sir Alec Douglas-Home at the White House, February 12–13.
The President argued strongly against Britain's willingness to
extend twelve-and fifteen-year credits to Moscow to promote
the sale of chemical and other plants, and against the United
Kingdom's sale of industrial products to Cuba. Although he
understood American concern, the Prime Minister said that British tradition and opinion were opposed to all boycotts and trade
discrimination.[18]

Despite Washington's opposition, Western industrial countries pushed ahead with trade expansion to the Soviet bloc. In
February a four-year trade accord was signed between Italy
and the Soviet Union; France and Poland entered into a commercial agreement; and Japan concluded an agreement which
provided for a substantial increase over 1963 in its trade with
the Soviet Union. At the same time, a British banking con-
sortium indicated that it was ready to grant more than $200
million in long-term credits to the Soviet Union to finance the
construction of a British-made polyester fiber plant. It marked
the first time that the British government was prepared to guarantee long-term credits of seven to fifteen years to the Soviet
Union.

While signs in England and on the Continent pointed to
enlarged trade relations with Communist countries, a reverse
trend was manifest in the United States. During February,
leaders of the A.F.L.-C.I.O. maritime unions called on President
Johnson to halt the sale of American wheat to Russia. Instructions

were issued to union members in all Atlantic and Gulf ports to suspend the loading of wheat. It was "superficial and stupid" for the United States to forbid trade with Cuba, the unions maintained, while Americans helped to feed the Soviet Union. Although the action of the unions reflected a distaste for any commercial deals with the Communist bloc, what seemed to bother the leaders even more was the failure of the Johnson administration to live up to its promise to transport half of the grain in American ships, thus providing more jobs for American seamen. It was only with great difficulty that this problem was straightened out.

But other indications in the United States seemed to point to the adoption of a more flexible policy on East-West trade relations. "We are now at the stage," Secretary of Commerce Luther H. Hodges said on March 10, "where we could go a long way toward normalizing trade relations" with the Soviet Union.[19] The main barrier to such a change, he acknowledged, was the "political feeling" in the country that could be overcome only by "more education." American policy, as it stood, was "schizophrenic," Secretary Hodges thought. Senator Fulbright suggested that it might be the United States, which had exerted so much effort to convince its allies to change their views, that was "out of step" concerning trade policies with Communist nations.

Speaking on East-West trade before the Senate Foreign Relations Committee on March 13, Secretary Rusk explained the diversified United States policy toward trade with different Communist countries. He made two points: (1) "trade with Communist countries should not be conducted purely on the basis of commercial considerations and as though there were no political and military issues dividing East and West"; and (2) the policy "must be flexibly adapted and flexibly applied on the basis of political, military and economic realities." Members of the Senate Foreign Relations Committee questioned the Secretary of State's view that the United States should "respond" with increased trade to the "signs of change" and "some liberalization" in such satellite countries as Poland and

Yugoslavia, since trade with them could undermine the chances of their eventual freedom from Communist control by helping to "legitimatize" their regimes.

As Secretary Rusk saw the problem, America's trade policy toward Communist nations was an integral part of its over-all policy toward international Communism. The objectives of this policy were: "a. To prevent the Communists from extending their domain, and to make it costly, dangerous, and futile for them to try to do so; b. To achieve agreements or understandings which could reduce the dangers of a devastating war; and c. To encourage trends within the Communist world making for an evolution toward greater national independence, peaceful cooperation, and open societies." Policies, Mr. Rusk said, had to be adjusted to the differing behavior of Communist states if these objectives were to be promoted. "Under some circumstances," he explained, "we may *deny* trade, in order to influence Communist economic, military, and political decisions and capabilities in our interest. Under other circumstances, we may *encourage* trade for the same purposes." Differences with allies, he observed, stemmed largely from basic differences in economic interests. Most of the European countries, he pointed out, being far more dependent on trade than the United States, had close economic ties with Eastern Europe. Although some of the European allies argued that economic denial did not weaken Soviet power, but rather slowed down the trends toward moderation in Communist policy, Mr. Rusk dismissed the idea that a well-fed Communist would have a greater stake in the *status quo* and therefore would be less adventurous, less aggressive, and more friendly to the West. "Whether the Soviet standard of living improves," he said emphatically, "depends primarily on policies, both internal and external, of the Soviet Government." [20]

Nevertheless, the United States failed not only in obtaining the support of its European allies on long-term credits to the Soviet Union, but also in maintaining a boycott of Cuba. Early in January Britain had weakened the American economic blockade of Cuba by permitting the negotiation of a multimillion dollar sale of 450 buses to the Castro government. In April a

Soviet delegation arrived in London and negotiated a new five-year trade agreement on consumer goods. These official negotiations were separate from the more important deals that were being worked out by British chemical firms to sell plants to the Soviet Union on long-term credits. These companies eventually hoped to sell up to $250 million worth of fertilizer, synthetic fiber, plastics and other chemical engineering machinery to the Russians.

As Western Europe and Britain pressed their trade offensive, the United States began to change the emphasis in its policy position. On April 25 President Johnson said that he welcomed all proposals for more trade with Communist countries.[21] With Britain on the verge of breaking ranks by extending long-term credits to Moscow, a strong feeling arose in business circles that Washington should seek a share of the trade that would be generated. The U.S. government, on its part, favored contacts with Hungary, Rumania, and other Soviet bloc countries to encourage their drift away from Soviet influence. A wise course for the country to follow, the *New York Times* suggested editorially on April 27, was "to re-examine its entire trade policy toward the Communist world in the light of present world conditions and present national needs." Such a reexamination, it was thought, would lead to the conclusion "that a substantial liberalization of American policy in this area will serve the nation's political and economic interests far better than does the obsolete existing attitude."

At the annual convention of the U.S. Chamber of Commerce, a resolution was adopted on April 29 which urged the American government to cut back the list of items barred from sale to the Soviet Union and other European Communist nations. It called for a level of trade in that area equal to that of the European allies. Representing a major policy change in the organization, this resolution on East-West trade was the first offered by a major business group that went beyond generalities to specific policy recommendations. Increasingly, the feeling developed that the United States was accomplishing little by its restrictive trade policies to Communist countries except to deny orders to

American business and jobs to American workers. But equally strong was the attitude that the United States should not help the Soviet Union strengthen its economy.

British businessmen effected a major breakthrough in East-West trade relations on September 7 when the biggest single contract in British-Soviet trade history was signed. This called for the building of a polyester fiber plant at a cost of $84 million. In addition, the Russians indicated that they would buy $140 million worth of capital goods and technical information, mostly in the field of agricultural chemicals, such as fertilizers and pesticides. Just a week earlier, Moscow and Tokyo had concluded an agreement whereby the Japanese government was to guarantee an eight-year, $10 million loan for the purchase of fertilizer production equipment. The British deal provided for long-term loans, some extended for fifteen years. Up to 80 per cent of the total amount—or $67.2 million—was covered by a British bank, with the British government's approval. Thus Moscow definitely appeared to have broken the "time barrier" which the United States had sought to impose.

The move was also seen as an effort on the part of British Conservatives to prop up Britain's sagging exports and to steal a march on the Labor opposition, which favored more trade with Russia. The United States promptly made known its displeasure with, and disapproval of, the transaction. But, significantly, Washington's reaction was mild in comparison with the uproar that had greeted the British bus sales to Cuba in January. Britain, moreover, stressed the fact that although it was willing to grant long-term credits for nonstrategic economic development projects, it would continue to abide by the ban on the sale of strategic materials to the U.S.S.R.

15. LOOSENING TIES IN THE SOVIET BLOC

As in the Atlantic alliance, a process of fragmentation was under way in the Soviet bloc during the 1960's. A trend toward greater autonomy in the relations of Eastern European countries with the Soviet Union appeared, as they exhibited a growing

EASTERN EUROPE

0   100   200   300   MILES

FINLAND

Helsinki

Leningrad

NORWAY

Oslo

SWEDEN

Stockholm

ESTONIA

BALTIC

LATVIA

SEA

LITHUANIA

U. S. S. R.

DENMARK

Copenhagen

Kiev

EAST

Berlin

GERMANY

POLAND

Warsaw

WEST

Bonn

GERMANY

Prague

CZECHOSLOVAKIA

Vienna

Budapest

AUSTRIA

HUNGARY

Bern

SWITZ.

RUMANIA

Bucharest

Belgrade

YUGOSLAVIA

BULGARIA

Sofia

BLACK SEA

ITALY

Istanbul

Rome

Tirana

ALBANIA

TURKEY

MEDITERRANEAN

GREECE

Athens

SEA

spirit of national independence, a greater responsiveness to public opinion, and a desire to establish closer ties with non-Communist countries. Poland had led the way ever since 1956. By 1963, Rumania, Hungary, and Czechoslovakia were also asserting themselves.

A complex of many reasons underlay this "movement" to acquire a greater freedom of action. More immediately, the trend arose from a combination of frustration and disillusion. Agricultural failures, industrial difficulties, and an inabilility to develop intrabloc trade and economic coordination produced a restive climate which was abetted by the sharp contrast in living conditions between the East and West. The Sino-Soviet dispute contributed new opportunities for the "loosening" of ties in the Soviet bloc in Europe. So, too, did the U.S.S.R.'s policy of improving (to some extent) its relations with the United States, thereby setting an example for East European countries to follow. Action truly independent of Soviet authority, however, seemed highly unlikely unless there was a fundamental transformation of the Soviet system—a development that few in the West believed would occur in the foreseeable future.

Like the West, the Soviet Union sought to effect the economic integration of its sphere in Europe. Rumania took the lead in opposing this development. Its trade with the West, which had more than doubled over a five-year period, was estimated to comprise about one-third its total trade by 1963. Increasingly the Rumanians insisted, contrary to Moscow's plans, on concentrating on industrial development and adapting their trade policies to their own design. A turning point came in 1962–63 when Moscow displayed its lack of enthusiasm for the building of a giant metal combine at Galati, the key prestige project in Rumania's industrialization program. Russia delayed its deliveries. Rumania consequently turned to Western firms for help. When Rumania openly took a position of neutrality as the Soviet Union's quarrel with the Chinese intensified, the Rumanian leaders not only challenged Khrushchev's "grand design," but also insisted on pursuing policies in their own national interest.

Meanwhile, in a growing emphasis on nationalism, Rumania

quietly began to eliminate elements of Russian social and cultural influence. Late in 1963 the Maxim Gorky Institute of Russian Language and Literature was incorporated into Bucharest University as part of the Slavic language department. The compulsory study of Russian was ended, and in other ways Russian cultural penetration was reduced. Gheorghe Gheorghiu-Dej, who headed the Rumanian regime as President, did not, however, oppose his giant neighbor on every count. His government remained committed to virtually all the foreign policy goals of Moscow. Moreover, there was no substantial liberalization at home, and Rumania's system of centralized state control still closely resembled that of the Soviet Union.

Insisting upon the complete independence of every Communist party and country to determine its own affairs without outside intervention, a 12,000-word Rumanian statement issued on April 26 dealt at length with the Soviet-Chinese ideological dispute. It vigorously defended Rumania's economic position, declaring that the attempt to impose supranational control in the Council for Mutual Economic Assistance (Comecon) was "not in keeping with the principles that underlay the relations between Socialist countries . . . The sovereignty of the Socialist state requires that it hold in its hand all the levers for managing economic and social life." The document further affirmed that there was not and could not be a "parent" party and a "son" party, "parties that are 'superior' and parties that are 'subordinate'; rather there is the great family of communist and workers parties which have equal rights." [22] During the following months a polemical dispute with serious economic and political implications waxed strongly as Bucharest and Moscow made charges and countercharges in radio broadcasts.

The United States closely followed the fundamental changes that were taking place. Most significant, from Washington's point of view, was the fact that Eastern Europe was emerging from its isolation from the West. This was seen on many fronts: in the substantial increase in trade between Soviet bloc countries and Western nations, in the encouragement of tourism, and in in the development of exchanges with the West in cultural and other fields. The Johnson administration strongly favored extending material aid, expanding exchange programs, and encouraging trade in nonstrategic goods. "We believe that Europe cannot enjoy a full measure of security and prosperity until the Eastern European countries are drawn back into their historical relationship with the rest of Europe," Under-Secretary W. Averell Harriman declared. "We share with our friends in Western Europe the desire to see this inevitable transformation. They are in a position to influence the Eastern European countries at close range toward that goal by their policies. It is essential, therefore, for the United States to work with them in facilitating this process." [23]

Encouraged by events, the United States sought practical results when it opened talks on May 18 with a Rumanian delegation in Washington on trade and other issues. Foundations were laid for increasing trade cooperation. Agreement was reached early in June to allow Rumania to purchase "most commodities" in the United States without the need for individual export licenses. Rumania was also granted licenses to buy a number of industrial installations. In addition, the United States, like many Western European countries, raised the status of its legation in Rumania to that of an embassy. [24]

Speaking on May 23 at a dedication ceremony for the George C. Marshall Research Library at Lexington, Virginia, President Johnson made a major statement on America's attitude toward Eastern Europe. [25] He expressed the hope that America would carry on the vision of the Marshall Plan by strengthening "the ability of every European people to select and shape its own society." Eastern European countries, Mr. Johnson said, were beginning to reassert their identity, and he urged the United States to continue "to build bridges across the gulf which has divided us"—bridges of increased trade, of ideas, of visitors, and of humanitarian aid. Four reasons, the President said, motivated the American purpose: "First, to open new relationships to countries seeking increased independence yet unable to risk isolation. Second, to open the minds of a new generation to the values and the visions of the Western civilization from which they come and to which they belong. Third, to give freer play to the powerful forces of legitimate national pride—the strongest barrier to the ambition of any country to dominate another. Fourth, to demonstrate that identity of interest and the prospects of progress for Eastern Europe lie in a wider relationship with the West."

President Johnson's speech attempted to define American goals realistically, as well as the means with which to achieve them. For some years American policy had been gradually moving toward such a position. It marked a response to changed conditions and a definite advance over the policies of "containment"—which had appeared to imply that Eastern Europe was beyond the perimeter of American influence—and of "liberation," espoused but not accomplished by the Eisenhower administration. Because of continuous pressures within the Communist area, there was "no longer a single Iron Curtain," Mr. Johnson observed. There were many, and each differed "in strength and thickness—in the light that can pass through it and the hopes that can prosper behind it."

In the United States, opinion remained sharply divided on the whole question of "polycentrism" and the appropriate policies for the West.[26] At issue were three basic problems: (1) whether the trend should be encouraged; (2) if so, within what limits should this be done; and (3) how should it be effected. East-West trade was one subject immediately at hand for the study of new policies, and it was quite evident that the problems were not merely economic but also political.

Nevertheless, the Rumanian-American agreement was viewed as a major step toward President Johnson's announced goal of building "bridges" to link the United States with Eastern Europe. The new agreement aimed not only at helping Rumania to build up its industrial capabilities and to stimulate the economy, but also at providing some of the financial means to do so. Privately extended credits to buy substantial amounts of American machinery were to be guaranteed by the United States through the Export-Import Bank. Perhaps more significantly, the trade agreement with Rumania was looked upon as an opening wedge that could weaken the Soviet Union's hold on its other "satellites."

During the summer the Soviet Union, on its part, turned to the gentler approach of persuasion and compromise in dealing with the Rumanians. A top-level Rumanian delegation, headed by Premier Ion Gheorghe Maurer, was most hospitably received in Moscow, July 6–14. More important was the fact that Russia agreed to make concessions with respect to Rumania's desire for greater economic independence. Earlier plans for the economic integration of Eastern Europe were not pushed, and greater stress was placed on "voluntary" bilateral cooperation. But these overtures, as well as others, failed to win Rumanian support for Moscow's China policy, nor did they deter Rumanian leaders from undertaking new trade negotiations with Western European countries and with Communist China. In July Rumania agreed to extend scientific and technical help to China in return for industrial and consumer goods. Agreement was also reached at the end of the month with Paris on negotiating a long-term commercial exchange, and a basis for cooperation on technical matters was established. Other delegations were sent to West Germany, Italy, and Austria in an effort to strengthen economic relations with the West.

Khrushchev's downfall in October brought to the fore the key question of whether the gradual loosening of ties between the U.S.S.R. and the East European Communist countries would be continued or whether the new regime would attempt to restore the bloc unity of the Stalin period. That it would be impossible to return to past patterns of subservience became immediately evident. With the exception of the Albanians, none of the East Europeans expressed enthusiasm over Khrushchev's ouster. The independent reaction on the part of the individual countries reflected the basic political change in Soviet relations that had occurred in recent years. Western analysts, assessing the consequences of Khrushchev's removal, were convinced that Communist ideology would play a declining role in the future and that the trend toward ever greater diversity in national policy would persist. On October 26 the new Soviet regime made it clear that the autonomy achieved during Khrushchev's tenure of office would not be reversed. It declared that it would work for unity on the basis of equality and sovereignty, and rather than curb the movement toward greater freedom of action, it would seek to enlarge it. By the end of the year, it thus became apparent that the iron grip with which Moscow had once held Eastern Europe in the Stalin era was gone.

16. DISARMAMENT STALEMATE

Major agreement in 1963 on the "hot line" direct communications link between Washington and Moscow, the limited nuclear test-ban treaty, and the prohibition of nuclear weapons in space awakened hopes that the momentum for peace could be nudged along. Psychologically, the climate was favorable. As preparations were made for the resumption of meetings of the Eighteen-Nation Committee on Disarmament in January—they had begun March 1962 at Geneva—the feeling arose for the first time that the talks might not be futile. Both the United States and the Soviet Union appeared to be genuinely intent on finding additional areas for agreement to maintain a relaxed atmosphere. To demonstrate that America was ready to act with deeds, and not merely resort to words, President Johnson announced in his State of the Union message that the United States would cut back its production of enriched uranium for nuclear weapons by 25 per cent and close four plutonium piles. He called on the Soviet Union to do the same.[27] Although no startling breakthrough was anticipated on disarmament during the year, Washington was optimistic that certain arms limitations might be effected without formal agreements. President Kennedy's efforts to achieve results through "reciprocal understanding" had been encouraging, and it was thought that further progress might be obtained by working for peripheral rather than major accords.

Two extended sessions on disarmament negotiations were held during the year, the first from January 21 to April 28 and the second from June 9 to September 17. The United States set forth five key issues at the opening meeting: (1) the prohibition of the threat or use of force, directly or indirectly, to change boundaries or to extend control over territory by displacing established authorities; (2) a "verified" agreement on halting the production of fissionable materials "for weapons use"; (3) a "verified freeze" on "strategic nuclear offensive and defensive vehicles"; (4) reduction of the danger of war by accident, miscalculation or surprise attack; and (5) halting the spread of nuclear weapons to nations that did not possess them.[28]

On January 28 the Soviet Union presented its nine-point list of measures to curb the arms race and ease international tension. This was essentially a reiteration of points made again and again in Soviet propaganda. Among other things, it called for the withdrawal of "all foreign troops from all foreign territories," especially in Europe; the reduction of armed forces and military budgets; a nonaggression treaty between NATO and Warsaw Pact countries; the creation of nuclear-free zones, particularly in Central Europe; the physical destruction of bombers; and the extension of the partial ban on nuclear tests to include underground tests without, however, any "special controls." [29]

The two lists did not actually overlap. Each was designed to fit the strategic doctrine of the country proposing it. Three items, however, were given primary attention: the proposal for a "verified freeze" on nuclear delivery vehicles; the destruction of bomber aircraft; and the creation of a nuclear-free zone in Europe.

President Johnson's proposal for a "verified freeze" on the numbers and types of vehicles—mainly long-range bombers and missiles—for the delivery of strategic nuclear weapons sought to break new ground. The idea had been implicit in the first stage of a disarmament plan the United States had submitted in April 1962.[30] But Washington now offered to negotiate on it separately. For the first time, it opened the way for East-West action on perhaps the single most critical issue in arms control. Danger of all-out nuclear war hinged not so much on the possession of nuclear warheads, as on the delivery systems that could carry them to targets. By 1955 both the United States and the Soviet Union recognized that nuclear warheads had become so small, numerous, and easily concealed that it was impossible to establish effective control over their possession. But delivery systems were still of such size and complexity that inspection remained feasible, *provided* an agreement could be reached to limit numbers and types. While a "balance of terror" clearly inhibited both the East and the West from starting a major war, dangerous instabilities nevertheless continued. In particular, a nuclear war could still occur as a result of a technological breakthrough, such as the perfection of an anti-missile weapons system that might tempt a would-be aggressor to launch a first-strike attack; or it could arise by accident or miscalculation. The "verified freeze" on nuclear delivery systems tried to come to grips with all of these problems, but most especially it aimed at checking the arms race in the missile field.

The United States carefully spelled out the control measures necessary in establishing a "freeze" on offensive and defensive strategic weapons. These envisaged, first, the placing of missile plants and testing sites under international control; second, allowing an agreed number of strategic bombers and missiles to be retained; and third, prohibiting the development of any "significantly new type" of delivery vehicle. Thus, the "verified freeze" implied that both sides would agree to an upper limit on the number of delivery vehicles; no improvement would be made on either the range or performance of missiles or planes; and some form of inspection would be accepted.

Soviet delegate Semyon K. Tsarapkin charged that the proposed "verified freeze" would legalize espionage without reducing armaments. He put forward the shopworn Soviet argument that verification would enable a potential aggressor to collect enough information to launch a sudden blow. On March 2 Foreign Minister Andrei A. Gromyko, condemning all of the Western disarmament proposals, dismissed President Johnson's idea for a "freeze" as "propaganda." [31]

In a surprise move, India, on March 24, urged the West to accept "in principle" the Soviet suggestion for a massive destruction of missiles as the first stage of disarmament. A detailed examination of the Russian plan, the Indian delegate said, might lead to a "narrowing of the gap between the two sides." [32] The British objected, declaring that Moscow's proposal did not permit a balanced approach to arms reduction such as had been offered in the American disarmament plan, which provided for a 30 per cent first-stage reduction in all major categories of weapons. The Soviet Union, moreover, refused to give any details on the numbers and types of missiles that would be retained, nor would it consent to any inspection arrangements to guard against cheating. As a result, both the United States and the United Kingdom rejected India's plea.

Seeking to break the deadlock at the Geneva conference, President Johnson on April 20 suddenly announced that the United States was reducing its production of enriched uranium by 15 per cent beyond the reduction made in January, to a total cutback of 40 per cent during the next four years. In a simultaneous declaration from Moscow, Premier Khrushchev pledged to discontinue construction of two big new reactors for producing plutonium, to reduce "substantially" the production of U-235 for nuclear weapons during the next several years, and to allocate more fissionable materials for peaceful uses. [33] Prime Minister Douglas-Home quickly associated his country with the actions taken by Washington and Moscow and told the House of Commons that Britain's production of plutonium was "being gradually terminated." Actually, the parallel moves on the part of Washington and Moscow had little effect on the ability of either power to wage nuclear war. After nearly two decades of producing enriched uranium and plutonium, both powers had more than enough of the materials to meet their weapons requirements. The reduction, therefore, appeared to have primarily a psychological significance as a follow-up to the nuclear test-ban treaty and the American-Soviet agreement not to put nuclear weapons into outer space.

Arguing that a "verified freeze" would increase rather than lessen international tension, Moscow proposed instead the destruction of "all bombers of all countries," and an agreement among all nations to slash simultaneously their military expenditures by 10 to 15 per cent. The United States promptly asserted that the destruction of *all* bombers of *all* countries was utterly unrealistic and impossible. France's participation, it was pointed out, would be necessary, and the bomber was the cornerstone of President de Gaulle's independent nuclear striking force. No prospect existed that the French leader, who had boycotted the disarmament conferences, would consider the Soviet proposal. Western spokesmen also emphasized that it was possible to reduce a budget while hiding increased expenditures for such items as weapons research and development.

The disarmament stalemate was underlined by the debate that arose over a new Polish plan to create a nuclear-free zone in Central Europe. First outlined in a speech by Communist party leader Wladyslaw Gomulka on December 28, 1963, it was elaborated upon and made public as a memorandum on March 5.[34] The "Gomulka Plan" differed from the familiar proposal first presented by Polish Foreign Minister Adam Rapacki in 1957 that had been the subject of great controversy ever since. Whereas the "Rapacki Plan" had aimed at the *removal* of all nuclear arms from Central Europe, Gomulka's new initiative was confined to a more modest first step. It proposed that they be frozen at their present levels, "irrespective of the means of their employment and delivery." It specified that the freeze should apply to the same territories that were included in the Rapacki Plan—Poland, Czechoslovakia, and East and West Germany, including their "territorial waters and airspace." The area, Poland suggested, might be enlarged by "the accession of other European states." The Gomulka Plan also provided that nations maintaining armed forces in the area, including the United States and the Soviet Union, "would undertake obligations not to produce, not to introduce or import, not to transfer to other parties in the area or to accept from other parties in the area," nuclear or thermonuclear weapons. It urged the establishment of an "appropriate system of supervision and safeguards" against possible violations of the freeze, and recommended that controls be exercised by mixed commissions composed of representatives of the Warsaw Pact and NATO.

The West's reaction to the Gomulka Plan was, on the whole, negative. Although the United States and Britain expressed interest in the contents of the proposal, they foresaw many difficulties. Not the least of these was the fact that West Germany strongly objected to being a part of the regional grouping suggested by Poland for arms control. Not only was it discriminatory, Bonn declared, but it ignored the need for the reunification of Germany. The major criticism of the Gomulka Plan on strategic grounds was that although it established a nuclear freeze in Central Europe, the Soviet Union still retained its powerful nuclear missiles aimed at targets in NATO countries. The new proposal clearly appeared to have political objectives, for it seemed to be directed, among other things, at enhancing the position of East Germany and at restricting West Germany's military development. It was quite evident that a great fear existed in Eastern Europe over the possibility that West Germany might acquire an independent control of nuclear weapons. The Gomulka Plan sought to eliminate the slightest chance that this might occur.[35]

The first session of the Eighteen-Nation conference adjourned on April 28 without achieving any tangible results. Basic issues relating to inspection and verification, as well as the question of the priorities in measures to advance disarmament, persisted. Some of the optimism that prevailed earlier in the year was deflated. But in view of the complexity of the problems that underlay arms control and disarmament measures, any progress was bound to be slow. When meetings resumed on June 9, President Johnson, noting the reductions in the production of fissionable material for nuclear weapons by both the United States and the Soviet Union, called for a redoubling of efforts to achieve "effective control of arms." [36]

Deputy Foreign Minister Valerian A. Zorin headed the Soviet Union's delegation to the second session. He brought no surprises, but he did help to break a two-year procedural deadlock. Agreement was reached on June 18 between the United States and the Soviet Union on an order of priorities for discussion of arms control and disarmament proposals. For the next four weeks, certain days were fixed to discuss an American plan to halt the output of fissionable materials, the Soviet plan for a 10 to 15 per cent cut in arms budgets, and the proposals of the two countries to halt the spread of nuclear weapons. The Soviet Union's willingness to take up one specific proposal at a time was viewed as part of Moscow's effort to dramatize the relaxed relations with the United States. Despite this agreement, no advances were made; both countries merely reaffirmed their former positions. Zorin directed himself chiefly to attacking the creation of a NATO multilateral force. He warned the Western powers on July 2 that they would have to make a choice between the M.L.F. project and an agreement to stop the spread of nuclear weapons. Charging that the NATO mixed-manned fleet aimed at "quenching the nuclear thirst of West German revenge seekers," the Soviet official declared that its creation could jeopardize all future disarmament developments. But the United States replied that these arguments were groundless and had as their principal aim the long-standing Soviet goal of disrupting NATO defensive arrangements. Thus, lines were sharply drawn on the issue, with little likelihood that a compromise could be reached. On July 14 the two countries announced their failure to agree on a method for detailed discussions of nuclear disarmament.

Efforts during the following weeks to find a basis for negotiation were all without result. "Sometime, somewhere, it will be necessary for the Soviet Union to join in halting the build-up of nuclear weapons," U.S. delegate William C. Foster said. "We still hope that sometime we shall get a more positive response." [37] Although the second session of the 1964 Geneva meetings, like the first, did not produce any significant accomplishments, President Johnson decided to adopt a public attitude of optimism. He expressed his belief on the eve of the session's adjournment that it had laid the ground work "for the agreements of the future." "The road to peace is not an easy one," he said. "The concrete gains so far achieved required long and diligent effort. So will the accomplishments of tomorrow." [38]

CHAPTER FIVE
SINO-SOVIET CONFLICT AND THE FAR EAST

THE STRUGGLE for power and influence in the Far East in the mid-1960's grew more complicated as the conflict between Peking and Moscow and the dissension between Paris and Washington were superimposed on the longer-standing, implacable contest between the United States and Communist China. The Sino-Soviet rivalry, which first manifested itself in 1956–57 and increased in bitterness over the years, threatened to fragment the Communist world, with momentous implications for the future character of Communist revolution and the cold war.

In some respects, China's bid for a big-power role within the Communist world paralleled President de Gaulle's efforts to assert French independence within the Atlantic alliance. By demonstrating its closer affinity on grounds of color and economic aspiration with Asians, Africans, and Latin Americans and its militant support for "wars of liberation," Peking seemed determined to show that its strategy—not Moscow's—was the correct one for advancing Communist revolution. In short, as Mao Tsetung phrased it, "The East Wind will prevail over the West Wind"—a wind rising in Peking, and not in Moscow.

The French President's recognition of Peking in January challenged Washington on Western strategy in Asia and was a rebuff to American leadership. The United States did not conceal its concern over the breakdown of efforts to isolate Communist China diplomatically and to hold the line against any expansion of trade relations. French diplomatic recognition dramatically enhanced Peking's prestige, and hence its ability to promote aggression in Southeast Asia and to subvert Western interests everywhere. Likewise, it also strengthened Communist China in the contest with the Soviet Union for control of the Communist movement.

The division between Paris and Washington disclosed how antithetical the assessments of Communist objectives could be. Whereas the United States saw Communist China as an aggressive, expansionist power, President de Gaulle seemed convinced that it was entering a period of consolidation. Fundamental conflicts between Peking and the West (as well as between the Soviet Union and China) were, he believed, the result of differences in "national policies," and could best be dealt with by establishing, rather than avoiding, direct contacts. "China's own mass, her value and her present needs, the scope of her future, cause her to reveal herself increasingly to the interests and concerns of the entire world," he said in his January 31 news conference. "It is clear that France must be able to listen to China directly, and also to make herself heard." [1] By recognizing Peking the French leader deliberately sought to bolster China's "independence"—thus widening the breach between the Chinese Communists and Moscow and, hopefully, exposing them more to Western viewpoints. China's energies, he felt, needed to be directed toward constructive purposes.

Washington strongly disagreed with this assessment; to disregard the aggressive intentions of the Chinese Communists would be foolhardy. According to the State Department, Peking's actions attested to its long-run ideological, economic, and territorial ambitions for establishing China's hegemony in Asia and beyond. The United States, of course, could not ignore the fact that a prime Chinese objective was to wipe out American influence in Southeast Asia, Korea, Taiwan, and Japan and to bring all of these regions under Communist control. Nor could the Chinese Communists' efforts to establish themselves at the head of a new international Communist movement, based on Mao's interpretation of Marxist-Leninist orthodoxy, be overlooked—or their attempt to create a loose alliance with the nations of Asia,

Africa, and Latin America in the hope of eradicating all Western, including Russian, influence in these three continents.

Washington was well aware that its attitude toward China also ran great hazards by reason of its "inflexibility." Despite the hatred spewed forth in Peking's propaganda against the United States, President Kennedy, in one of his last press conferences, said that America was not wedded to a policy of hostility toward Communist China. On December 13, 1963, Roger Hilsman, then Assistant Secretary of State for Far Eastern Affairs, declared, ". . . we have no reason to believe that there is a present likelihood that the Communist regime will be overthrown. . . . we pursue today toward Communist China a policy of the open door." [2] In effect, Mr. Hilsman suggested that the United States was prepared to respond to any sign of reasonableness from Peking.

If Washington had indeed sought to effect a modification of the American attitude toward Communist China the groundwork was destroyed by President de Gaulle's announcement of recognition, by the generally unfavorable American reaction to the precipitate and unilateral manner in which this was done, and by Peking's blunt rejection of any overtures Mr. Hilsman's speech might have contained. On February 19 Communist China declared that conditions for improving relations, which the United States suggested, such as abandoning its advocacy of violent revolution or relinquishing its claims to Taiwan, were "preposterous." Peking asserted that as a matter of principle it was "absolutely impossible" to stop helping revolutionary movements and that Washington policy-makers were daydreaming if they thought the Chinese would give up their intention to "liberate Taiwan without fail." [3]

Speaking to the Associated Press convention in New York on April 20, President Johnson replied that ". . . so long as the Communist Chinese pursue conflict and preach violence, there can be and will be no easing of relationships. There are some who prophesy that these policies will change. But America must base its acts on present realities and not on future hopes. It is not we who must reexamine our view of China. It is the Chinese Communists who must reexamine their view of the world." [4]

Contrary to any expectations that the Sino-Soviet rupture might ease the tensions between Washington and Peking, the split weakened the Soviet Union's restraining influence in Asia and brought the United States increasingly into direct confrontation with Communist China. Although Peking carefully avoided triggering any military action, it seemed to feel that by a process of attrition, especially in Laos and Vietnam, the United States position in Asia would eventually be destroyed.

17. STRUGGLE FOR COMMUNIST WORLD LEADERSHIP

Three main policy objectives of Communist China during 1963–64 were to end its political, economic, and diplomatic isolation; to compel Moscow to accept it as an equal partner both in the formulation of Communist strategy and in the advancement of the Communist revolution; and to extend its influence throughout Asia, Africa, and Latin America. The isolation of China had been at the core of American policies since a tight trade embargo had been imposed by the United States at the start of the Korean War in 1950. The signing of the Moscow nuclear test-ban treaty in August 1963 made it apparent that the Soviet Union, for different reasons, was also trying to isolate China.

As the Sino-Soviet quarrel intensified, the substantial economic assistance given to the Chinese by the Russians during the 1950's was progressively reduced until, by 1963, it dwindled to practically nothing. To counter the withdrawal of Russian aid and the effects of the American economic embargo, Peking began to seek new trading partners and new sources of credit in the non-Communist world. In particular, it looked to Britain for aircraft, to Canada and Australia for grain, and to France and Italy for industrial goods. The lure of China's trade proved to be entrancing not only to Western European countries, and especially to Japan, but it was also enticing to Latin American nations as well. As cracks developed in the American trade boycott, Secretary Rusk urged the free world not to do anything that would convince Peking that its militant policy paid dividends. But in view of the U.S.-Soviet wheat transaction and other measures of economic help to Soviet-bloc countries, this appeal brought little favorable response.

In mid-December 1963, Premier Chou En-lai, seeking to end his country's isolation, began a three-month tour of Africa and Asia to cultivate good will and present China's case against the Soviet Union. Wherever he went the Chinese Premier attempted to alter his country's image in the eyes of Africans and Asians by refuting charges that China was a belligerent power and depicting a "peaceable" Communist China. On his tour, the most ambitious public relations trip undertaken by the Chinese Communist regime since it acquired control in 1949, Chou En-lai visited ten African states as well as Albania, Pakistan, and Burma. He met with varying degrees of courtesy and curiosity and, although he did not change either the attitudes or policies of most of the countries he visited, some successes were scored. Five African states—Kenya, Tanganyika, Uganda, Tunisia, and Ethiopia—took steps toward recognizing Peking, although Tunisia declared that it would not break relations with the Chinese Nationalists on Taiwan, and Ethiopia merely limited itself to an assurance of its intention to "normalize relations." Both countries were critical of Peking's refusal to sign the nuclear test-ban treaty. The Chinese Premier obtained only nominal support in his bid for another Afro-Asian conference similar to the one held in 1955 at Bandung, Indonesia. On the whole, however, Chou En-lai succeeded in projecting Communist China into a more influential role in world affairs, and its prestige was greatly elevated by France's recognition.

A second and far more intensive Communist Chinese campaign was its open challenge to Moscow's leadership of the international Communist movement. During 1964, both a theoretical justification for a formal break with the Soviet Union and a proposal to create an independent Communist organization were advanced. On February 4 the relative calm in the "ideological" dispute between the two powers ended when the Chinese levelled a full-scale attack against Soviet policies. This was the seventh statement in the series of bitter exchanges since the U.S.S.R. had published its critical "open letter" on July 14, 1963.[5] In its latest attack, Peking bluntly charged that the Soviet Union's misguided policies confronted the world Communist movement with "an unprecedentedly serious danger of a split." Premier Khrushchev and his associates were denounced as enemies of Communist unity and accused of being "the greatest of all sectarians and splitters known to history." Challenging the Soviet leadership, Peking declared that Moscow, with its majority support among the Communist parties, had abused its power. "We would like to tell them [the Russians] that we do not recognize their majority."

The Chinese flatly asserted that Khrushchev was seeking world domination through collaboration with the United States and that unless Moscow gave up its efforts to establish friendly relations with Washington, no hope was possible for restoring the unity of the international Communist movement. "It is absolutely impermissible," the Chinese declared, "for them to treat enemies as friends and friends as enemies and to ally themselves with the United States imperialists, [and] reactionaries of various countries . . . in a vain pursuit of world domination through United States-Soviet collaboration." Thus the Chinese demanded that the Soviet Union draw a sharp line between "enemies and comrades" and unite with the Communist world in opposition to the United States.

The February 4 blast, Peking's strongest since the Sino-Soviet dispute erupted, shook Moscow. Premier Khrushchev decided to hasten agreement on holding a conference of Communist parties at which the Chinese leadership would be denounced. Although such a conference had been suggested in the fall of 1963 the proposal was shelved when several powerful parties, particularly those in Italy and Poland, opposed a showdown and urged a conciliatory course. As the Soviet leaders had few illusions about reaching an understanding with the Chinese, they were anxious to convince pro-Soviet parties that if a formal break became inevitable, it would be the Chinese, not the Russians, who were responsible.

The Soviet Union was naturally concerned about the effects of a final break with Peking, with its repercussions in Eastern Europe and the disruption it would cause in other Communist parties throughout the world. Beset by agricultural and domestic problems, the U.S.S.R. was reluctant to stir up trouble with the Chinese or anyone else. At a high-level meeting of the Soviet party's Central Committee held on February 14 to review the Chinese situation, it was decided to withhold a lengthy rebuke that had been prepared by Presidium member Mikhail A. Suslov. Urged by the Rumanians, the Soviet leaders agreed instead to make another effort to put an end to the "open polemics," as Khrushchev had proposed in the fall of 1963.

Rumania's efforts to persuade Peking to resume discussions with Moscow collapsed in March. Premier Khrushchev could no longer contain his anger. After delivering a prepared speech on April 1, he told a mass meeting of factory workers in Budapest, "There are people in the world who call themselves Marxist-Leninists and at the same time say there is no need to strive for a better life. According to them only one thing is important—revolution." Scornfully, Khrushchev asked, "What kind of Marxism is this?" If Communism could not give the people what they wanted, he said, it would achieve little. "The important thing," the Soviet leader remarked, "is that we should have more to eat—good goulash—schools, housing, and ballet. How much more do these things give to the enlargement of man's life. It is worth fighting and working for these things." Five days later he again lashed out at the Chinese Communists, ridiculing their claims that they would rely on their own resources for economic development. "Only a complete idiot," the Soviet leader exclaimed, "could pretend to prove that it is easier to build Socialism alone than by using the possibilities and support of the fraternal community of people who had previously taken the road." And, he added, "If our people begin to be better dressed, to have better shoes, to be better fed, to have better houses, better incomes toward the satisfaction of their needs and cultural requirements, that is rebirth. How crazy it is to look on that as degenerate."

While Khrushchev fired these broadsides in Hungary, the

Soviet party assailed Peking not only for trying to split the world's Communist parties, but also for seeking to alienate the Soviet people from the party and its leader. On April 3, *Pravda* published Suslov's February 14 report, which denounced the "erroneous anti-Leninist views" of the Chinese leaders and castigated Peking for its "national arrogance" and for subordinating the Communist movement to its "great-power, egotistical interests." [6] Moscow strongly defended its policies of "peaceful coexistence" and again asserted that a nuclear conflict would be "the greatest tragedy for humanity" and the cause of Communism. It ridiculed the idea that U.S.-Soviet relations were in any way a "conspiracy with the imperialists." The Soviet Union pointed out that China itself was making "feverish" efforts to improve its relations with Britain, France, Japan, West Germany, and Italy, and that this was merely a normal and intrinsic element of the policy of peaceful coexistence. The Suslov report went on to observe that when these efforts were undertaken by the Chinese it was in accord with "revolutionary" policy, but when the Soviet Union did the same thing, it was considered "revisionism" and "treachery." To counter Peking's challenge, Russia called for a meeting of the world's Communist parties.

When Khrushchev returned from his ten-day visit to Hungary, he pledged in a radio-television address that the Soviet Union would strictly respect the equality of all members of the Communist community, large or small. In contrast, the Chinese were seeking a "special role" in the movement and were trying to impose their will on other Communist countries and parties as Stalin had done. By stressing the theme of "equality" within the Soviet bloc, it was evident that the Soviet Premier was making a bid to gain the support of foreign Communist parties for a "resolute rebuff" against Peking.

On April 28, Moscow for the first time challenged the legality of the Chinese party's leadership. Mao Tse-tung was charged with violating the statutes of his party by refusing to convene a party congress. This attack, it was thought, was intended to lay a basis for challenging Peking's right to participate in a future conference. Ten days later, the Chinese emphatically rejected

the Soviet call for an early meeting. "It may require perhaps
four or five years or even longer," Peking said, "to complete
the preparations for such a conference" and warned that if a
conference was convened in the fall, it might result in an open
split within the Communist movement, for which the Soviet
Union would "bear responsibility." [7]

Despite Peking's rebuff, Moscow decided to step up its drive
for convening a conference. The Soviet Union publicly committed itself to a timetable by announcing on August 10 that
invitations had been sent to twenty-five foreign Communist
parties for a preliminary meeting to be held in Moscow on
December 15. At that time, arrangements were to be made for a
full-scale conference of all parties in the summer of 1965. "The
day you convene [this] schismatic meeting," Peking replied, "will
be the day you step into your grave. . . . With fraternal greet-
ings, the Central Committee of the Chinese Communist party." [8]
Thus the rejection of Moscow's call for an international Communist congress finally "formalized" the Sino-Soviet dispute.

18. COMMUNIST CHINA JOINS THE NUCLEAR "CLUB"

For some time, predictions had been made that Communist
China would soon explode its first atomic bomb. On September
29 Secretary Rusk alerted the world that this event "might occur
in the near future." Stressing that the "detonation of a first device" did not mean "a stockpile of nuclear weapons and the
presence of modern delivery systems," he assured the American
people that the United States had "fully anticipated the possibility of Peiping's entry into the nuclear weapons field," and had
taken it into account "in determining our military posture and
our own nuclear weapons program." [9] This statement blunted
the surprise of Peking's announcement on October 16 that Communist China had successfully conducted its first nuclear test,
which, by coincidence, was carried out less than twelve hours
after Khrushchev was ousted from the leadership of the Soviet
party and government.

The Chinese Communists declared that their purpose in de-

veloping nuclear weapons was to strengthen their national defense and to protect the Chinese people "from the danger of the
United States launching a nuclear war." Peking solemnly pledged
that it would "never at any time and under any circumstances
be the first to use nuclear weapons," and made a formal proposal to convene a summit conference of all the countries of the
world to discuss the question of the "complete prohibition and
thorough destruction of nuclear weapons." [10] President Johnson
cautioned the world against overestimating the military significance of the test explosion, which he described as "a tragedy for
the Chinese people who have suffered so much under the
Chinese regime." While it did not serve the cause of peace, the
President saw no reason to fear that it would lead to an immediate danger of war. "The nations of the free world," he
said, "will recognize its limited significance and will persevere in
their determination to preserve their independence." [11]

Although China's possession of an atomic bomb did not suddenly alter the existing balance of world power, the successful
test explosion was clearly a historical landmark, for Western
observers generally agreed that its psychological and political
effects were more important than its military results. The entry
of the first nonwhite nation into the exclusive nuclear club was
expected to enhance greatly China's prestige in the underdeveloped areas of Asia, Africa, and Latin America. Fears were
also expressed that it might encourage other countries to follow
the Chinese example, thus making the proliferation of nuclear
weapons far more difficult to halt. On October 22 Secretary-
General U Thant suggested that the five nuclear powers, including Communist China, might meet in 1965 to discuss a prohibition on all nuclear tests, measures to prevent the spread of
nuclear weapons, and other phases of disarmament. But Washington politely rebuffed Mr. Thant's proposals, and promptly rejected Peking's call for a world summit conference to prohibit
nuclear weapons. "We know from many signs," Secretary Rusk
said, "that they [the Chinese Communists] are not seriously interested in disarmament." [12] State Department officials were con-

vinced that China's request for a meeting of world leaders to discuss the prohibition of nuclear weapons was nothing more than propaganda, a "grandstand play."

Khrushchev's fall and China's explosion of the bomb quickly intruded into the Sino-Soviet dispute. One of the reasons for the Soviet Premier's ouster, it was believed, was a desire of the Soviet hierarchy to deflect a collision with Peking. Although the new Kremlin leadership did not expect to overcome the basic disagreements with the Chinese, it was hopeful that it could put an end to open polemics. Peking, of course, was overjoyed at Khrushchev's removal, which it interpreted as a great triumph in its ideological contest with Moscow, and it greeted the new Soviet leaders warmly. Both the Russian and Chinese leaders appeared eager to soften their conflict, and as a result Premier Chou En-lai arrived in Moscow early in November to participate in the forty-seventh anniversary of the Bolshevik Revolution. This was the Chinese Premier's first visit to the U.S.S.R. since October 1961 when he had angrily walked out of the Twenty-Second Congress of the Soviet Communist party. Top-level private talks held during his visit, however, proved inconclusive. Agreement was apparently reached to postpone the international Communist meeting which Khrushchev had scheduled for December 15, and in which he had invested so much of his personal prestige. But Leonid Brezhnev, the new Soviet party leader, refused to cancel the plans for a future conference. On the contrary, he professed to believe that the need for such a meeting remained as great as ever in order to further the unity and cohesion of the world Communist movement. But unity on whose terms? Shortly after Premier Chou En-lai returned to Peking, the polemics were resumed. Chinese propagandists again returned to practices of the Khrushchev era and castigated the Soviet party on a wide range of national and ideological issues.

As the year drew to a close, no signs were visible that the rift between the two countries had in any way been healed. The Soviet Union's announcement on December 12 that a commission would meet on March 1, 1965, in Moscow to plan a world Communist conference was an implicit admission that the effort to secure a substantial improvement in relations with the Chinese had failed.

19. PEKING SEEKS TO EXTEND ITS INFLUENCE AND POWER

Behind the Sino-Soviet "ideological" dispute, a fundamental power rivalry could be discerned—one that, as Khrushchev admitted, extended into "inter-state relations." [13] On this level the conflicts of interest between Communist China and the U.S.S.R. were world-wide in scope, for Peking had two interrelated goals of expanding its influence and control throughout Asia and of reducing or ending Soviet (and American) influence in Africa and Latin America, as well as in the Far East. In particular, by catering to powerful emotions on racial and economic matters, the Chinese attempted to establish a common bond with the peoples of the underdeveloped countries. A massive propaganda campaign stirred up explosive racist feelings, frustration over continued poverty, and hatred over past Western colonial exploitation. At the same time Peking sent agents all over the world to encourage the creation of pro-Chinese Communist parties and provided funds for newspapers, magazines, and pamphlets in many languages to spread Peking's message.

The conflict of national interests between China and the U.S.S.R. reflected itself in many ways: in the different nature of their societies, in the different stages of their economic development, and, above all, in the rivalry of their power ambitions. It became evident in the mid-1960's that both Premier Khrushchev and Mao Tse-tung basically desired to shape the direction of the international Communist movement in order to serve their respective "national" purposes. It was this fact that was so crucial in the Sino-Soviet dispute and that motivated Peking's drive to win the allegiance of Communist parties throughout the world.

During the year tensions steadily increased over border difficulties. Peking had asserted for some time that parts of Russian territory in Asia, consisting of eastern Siberia, the Maritime Provinces, and at least 500,000 square miles of Central Asia had been carved out of China through a series of "unequal" treaties dating back to 1858. The Chinese did not conceal their wish to recover these regions. From 1954 to 1963, although disturbances and clashes took place along the border, the territorial issue was played down. That it was a point in dispute was first officially disclosed on January 23 by Premier Chou En-lai. In an interview with journalist Edgar Snow, he mentioned the fact that an agreement had been reached with Moscow to hold negotiations on "the Sino-Soviet boundary questions." [14] But differences immediately emerged in deciding upon the matters to be negotiated. Peking demanded that there be a comprehensive review of the frontier disputes, in which the "unequal treaties" would be reexamined. Moscow insisted upon discussing only minor boundary "adjustments." Talks continued, but little was publicly revealed.

The two vast borderlands of Sinkiang and Mongolia were another source of trouble because of rival territorial claims and unrest among Central Asian minorities who were neither Russian nor Chinese. Here, too, the Sino-Soviet ideological dispute was a complicating factor, for the Mongolian People's Republic unequivocally sided with Moscow in the quarrel. Grievances accumulated, and on September 2 Moscow denounced the Chinese Communists for coveting more than half a million square miles of Soviet territory. Mao Tse-tung had reportedly declared, "There are too many places occupied by the Soviet Union." Indicting Russia for its "seizures" of territory following World War II, the Chinese leader noted that in accord with the Yalta agreement the Soviet Union had "under pretext of guaranteeing the independence of Mongolia, actually put that country under its rule," and he intimated that the Russians also had designs on the Sinkiang province. Angrily, Premier Khrushchev declared that the Chinese leader's pronouncements showed how far Peking had gone in its quarrels with the Soviet Union. Mao Tse-tung was "not only claiming this or that part of Soviet territory," but he was "portraying his claims as part of some 'general territorial question.' We are faced with an openly expansionist program with far-reaching pretensions." [15]

In the maze of charges and countercharges, the true situation was difficult to untangle. Unquestionably, the Soviet Union was disturbed at Peking's efforts to squeeze Russia out of Asia, and Moscow had no intention of seeing its influence as an Asian power reduced. Khrushchev pointedly remarked that China's claims were not something that had suddenly appeared. "In 1954, a textbook on modern history was published in the Chinese People's Republic with a map of China showing it as it was in the opinion of its authors, before the First Opium War," he said. "This map included Burma, Vietnam, Korea, Thailand, Malaya, Nepal, Bhutan and Sikkim in China. In the north, the border ran along the Stanovik Mountain range cutting the Maritime Territory from the USSR. In the west, a part of Kirgizia, Tadzhikistan and Kazakhstan up to Lake Balkhash was also included in China. Sakhalin was also shown as Chinese territory. If one is to believe the textbook, all these lands and countries were 'state territory of China' and had been taken away from it." [16]

Conflict over the "territorial question" tended to shift the ground of the Sino-Soviet dispute from an "ideological" to a state level. The deepening of the rift definitely indicated to the West that the struggle for leadership in the international Communist movement was much more than a family squabble.

20. THE "FORMOSA QUESTION"

The Sino-Soviet conflict understandably affected other problems in the Far East, not the least of these being the "Formosa question." Four factors in particular raised fears in Taiwan of a weakening of support for the Chiang Kai-shek regime. First, the Nationalists saw the signing of the nuclear test-ban treaty as a lessening of firm American commitments to cold-war positions. Second, Mr. Hilsman's statement of December 1963,[17] which indicated that the United States might be prepared to change its attitudes toward Communist China if Peking mended its ways, was taken as additional evidence of a tendency to seek some *rapprochement* with the Communist bloc. Third, increased Japanese and Western European trade relations with Communist China bolstered Peking's position to the detriment of Taiwan's interests. Finally, and perhaps most immediately serious of all, President de Gaulle's recognition of Communist China raised the possibility that other countries might follow France's lead, and there was apprehension over the eventual seating of the Peking government in the United Nations.

France's recognition put in question the status of the Nationalist regime. The Nationalists claimed, as the only legitimate government of China, the right to speak for all the people of China. But de Gaulle's action clearly reduced the Generalissimo's pretensions; equally serious was its damaging effect among the 13 million overseas Chinese, the majority of whom lived in Southeast Asia. A great many began to turn to Peking rather than to Taipei. Unquestionably, Chiang Kai-shek's task of pressing for a Nationalist return to the mainland was made far more difficult, and his "sacred mission" seemed like a fading dream.

President de Gaulle tried to avoid coming to grips with the issue of Taiwan's status. In an effort to skirt the problem, the United States urged the Nationalists not to break relations with Paris. Immediately upon the French announcement of recognition of the Peking regime, Chiang Kai-shek contented himself with merely delivering a "vigorous protest" note to Paris. No formal diplomatic break was made, although the Generalissimo reaffirmed the Nationalist government's intention to liberate the mainland and, like Communist China, declared that he was "opposed to any settlement on the thesis of the 'two Chinas.'" Within twenty-four hours after Paris extended recognition, Premier Chou En-lai insisted that France sever its relations with the Formosan government. He declared that once Peking's diplomatic representatives appeared in Paris, "no other man" could "pose as the diplomatic representative of China." General de Gaulle eventually capitulated to this condition and placed the Nationalists in such a humiliating position that they had no alternative except to break diplomatic ties with France—an action taken on February 10. Two weeks later, the French President widened the estrangement when he vetoed Nationalist China's accreditation to the European Common Market.

Early in March, Nationalist China experienced another setback when the United States intimated that because of Formosa's remarkable economic progress, the annual $89 million in aid might be phased out by 1968. Since American economic assistance had already been completely cut off, the United States evidently contemplated the elimination of its military aid program as well. Chiang Kai-shek became worried that American ardor for his cause was definitely on the wane, and he feared that this could spell disaster in the Far East. The United States, however, stood firmly behind its commitment to defend Formosa and kept the U.S. Seventh Fleet in the Formosa Strait.

What perturbed Chiang Kai-shek was not so much the threat of physical attack as the erosion of morale and political support on Taiwan if American interest flagged. Thus, Senator Fulbright's speech of March 25 which assailed the "inflexible policies of long standing" of the United States in Asia alarmed him as a sign of change in U.S. policy. Although strongly opposing American recognition of Communist China and its admission to the United Nations "under present circumstances," Senator Fulbright believed that it was not impossible that in time the relations between the United States and Peking would change, "if not to friendship then perhaps to 'competitive coexistence.'" Echoing some of the sentiments expressed by former Assistant Secretary Hilsman, he said, "We would do well . . . to maintain an 'open door' to the possibility of improved relations with Communist China in the future. For a start we must jar open our minds to certain realities about China, of which the foremost is that there are not really 'two Chinas' but only one, mainland China, and that it is ruled by Communists and likely to remain so for the indefinite future." [18]

Disturbed by these statements, the Generalissimo, in an interview on April 4, stressed that America was and "always will be enemy No. 1" of Peking. "I feel Senator Fulbright is not fully informed of the conditions existing on the mainland of China today," he said. "The Communist regime is built on nothing but brute force. Bayonets keep the people under control. The regime totally lacks popular support. It will never last. It is here today but may be gone tomorrow." The Sino-Soviet split, the Generalissimo thought, had greatly changed the situation in Asia. "It is no longer necessary," he remarked, "for the United States to feel that action to remove the source of all trouble in Asia will touch off a global war. I am certain the Russians will not intervene." [19]

The Nationalist leader was still convinced that discontent was so rife in Communist China that if his forces landed on the mainland they would precipitate an anti-Communist uprising capable of destroying Peking's power. American officials saw no signs of disintegration and pointed out, moreover, that Peking's military forces were four times as large as those of the Nationalists.

Formosa's problems were not only external, but internal. Native-born Formosans outnumbered the Nationalists by five to one, and many were increasingly resentful of Chiang Kai-shek's rule. Dissatisfaction was especially acute over the Nationalist monopoly of top jobs in the government and the repressive measures employed by some Kuomintang officials. Few were interested in the back-to-the-mainland program. The crux of Formosa's dilemma, and of Chiang Kai-shek's also, lay in the fact that the island did not have the capacity to defend itself alone against mainland China. Unless Peking agreed to a separate Formosa state, permanent protection was necessary from the United States or some other strong power or group of powers.

On April 16 Secretary Rusk, who came to Taiwan after attending the annual SEATO meeting in Manila, assured Chiang Kai-shek that no change was contemplated in American policy toward his government or toward Communist China. The United States intended to continue its unwavering support of Nationalist China in maintaining its position against the Peking regime.[20]

Mr. Rusk's visit helped to improve the morale of the Chinese Nationalists. But in May, native Formosans inflicted a severe defeat on the Kuomintang party when Nationalist candidates lost local elections in three major cities and one prefecture. The losses reflected the rising dissatisfaction with Chiang Kai-shek's rule, but they were also related to immediate economic factors. It was feared that the Generalissimo might cut off trade with the Japanese for "moral considerations" because of their efforts to expand their economic ties with Communist China. Since Formosa depended heavily on trade with Japan and many trading companies were owned by native Formosans, such action would be a severe blow to the island's economy. Generally, however, Chiang Kai-shek pursued a conciliatory economic policy that won favor with the local population, and the sweeping land reforms carried out in the 1950's had proved to be most successful. Nevertheless, the unknown quantity in the Formosa equation was not economic, but political, and this centered on Chiang Kai-shek's ability to keep Formosa as the seat of the legitimate government of China.

In this respect, Peking's nuclear test explosion posed a new and ominous problem for the Chinese Nationalists. The Generalissimo regarded it as a psychological victory of the first magnitude for Communist China. Despite Washington's assurances, he questioned whether it would take at least five years for Peking to develop an effective nuclear weapons delivery system. He was inclined to believe that this might be accomplished within two years, and then a landing on the mainland would be impossible without precipitating a nuclear war in the region. To counter the Chinese Communists militarily, the Chiang government apparently asked Washington for the means to bomb Peking's nuclear installations, but the United States showed no interest in the suggestion. Taiwan, nevertheless, was assured that the island would be shielded, regardless of Communist China's nuclear capabilities. Confined by Peking's growing power and Washington's restraint, Chiang Kai-shek could not help but be fearful that the *raison d'être* and legality of the Nationalist government would be undermined. Under no circumstances, however, was he prepared to accept a "two Chinas" policy, which the United States, at least in practice, seemed to favor.

21. UNREST IN SOUTH KOREA

Frustrations in the Republic of Korea were of a different character than those on the island of Formosa. The trouble lay in social, economic, and political instability. Grievances were deep-rooted. The long years of Japanese occupation from 1910 to 1945 had fostered a tradition of civil resistance and had left a spirit of bitterness. World War II and its aftermath resulted in the country's artificial division along the 38th parallel, and led to the creation of two unrealistic states. The Republic of Korea came into being with few trained politicians, and the people were wholly unprepared to function within a democratic system. Then came the Korean War of 1950–53. Cities were shattered, the countryside devastated, and tragedy descended upon almost every family. Despite massive American aid, South Korea was barely able to cope with the enormous tasks of "national reconstruction." Most difficult was the problem of dealing with the enormous obstacles to building up an industrial base in a primarily agricultural state which was one of the most densely populated in the world. Attempts to develop a self-sufficient economy were unsuccessful. By the early 1960's the feeling of despair became so great that it led to the collapse of democratic institutions and the establishment of a military regime.[21]

Internal instability brought renewed pressures on the Korean government to take a fresh and more energetic approach to the question of achieving unification. While most South Koreans favored the long-standing policy of unifying the nation through free, general elections under United Nations supervision, a growing number urged a solution through direct negotiations with North Korea. The sentiment for direct negotiations came as a surprise to the South Korean government. For a long time the merest mention of negotiating with the Communists had been vigorously condemned by the people. However, many students —and their influence was powerful in the country—began to feel that the answer to South Korea's problem could be found only in that way.

The South Korean government firmly opposed any negotiations or contacts with North Korea. Until the Republic of Korea was in a superior position—economically and otherwise—any exchange, it maintained, would be dangerous. To make any overtures now would be most unpropitious. Because of Communist China's increased prestige in Asia, it was feared that whatever compromise could be worked out between North and South Korea would be harmful to the latter—a stand strongly supported by the United States. On January 29, at the end of a visit to Seoul, Secretary Rusk told President Chung Hee Park that America would "continue to stand guard with South Korea against Communist aggression," and he pledged cooperation in the economic, military, and political fields.[22]

But the basic problem remained: How to develop a viable economy? American aid had not been adequate to achieve this goal. In an effort to improve conditions, South Korean leaders had drawn up an ambitious Five-Year Plan for Economic Development, undertaken strenuous efforts to eliminate corruption, and adopted reforms to modernize the nation. Limited successes were achieved. A major stumbling block, however, was the continued failure of the Korean government to establish "normal relations" with Japan, a problem that had remained unsettled ever since the end of Japanese rule. South Korean leaders were eager to obtain an accord in order to start a flow of Japanese goods and funds into the economically shaky country. But negotiations soon reached a deadlock on two issues: the amount of compensation Korea should receive for damages it had suffered as a result of thirty-six years of Japanese occupation, and the question of fishing rights.

Early in 1964 Colonel Kim Chang Pil, who allegedly masterminded the South Korean military coup of 1961 and was second in command to President Park, was sent to Tokyo to break the impasse. Students vehemently denounced the talks, and mass demonstrations in March finally led to Kim's recall. President Park, nevertheless, declared on March 26 in a nationwide broadcast that he would continue negotiations, come what may. But he promised that a settlement would be made "only on terms most favorable to us."

Protests continued to be voiced against Japanese incursions into Korean fishing waters. In the absence of a treaty, a so-called "Peace Line" had been established, extending Korea's territorial waters a minimum of forty miles offshore. Tokyo had long maintained that this "line" could not be recognized legally. But South Korean students demanded that the government not budge on the "Peace Line." They also insisted that South Korean leaders end their "humiliating" diplomacy with Japan, and increase indemnity claims. (Japan had tentatively offered to pay $300 million for "occupation damages.")

Student demonstrations, although directed against Japan and the "normalization" of Korean-Japanese relations, were chiefly an outgrowth of resentment that stemmed from economic difficulties, frustration at the lack of job opportunities, irritation at the corruption and inefficiency of government administration, and dismay at the constantly changing educational policies. The climax to the protest movement came early in June when more than 10,000 student demonstrators overpowered the police in violent clashes around the presidential mansion and other government buildings in Seoul. On June 3 President Park declared martial law to deal with the mob rule that threatened his regime. Seeking to quell the further outbreak of antigovernment demonstrations, he secured Colonel Kim's resignation two days later and ordered all colleges and universities in South Korea closed for the rest of the year. An investigation of the charges of corruption was also begun. Steps were then taken to lift the martial law decree.

By the end of the year tempers had subsided, the political situation became more stabilized, and economic conditions showed some degree of improvement. To start a flow of much-needed economic benefits to his country, President Park again pressed for a settlement of South Korea's long-standing disputes with Japan. With guarded optimism, talks were reopened in Tokyo in December, and hope was expressed for the establishment of diplomatic relations with Japan. Nevertheless, the sources of unrest within South Korea were but partially removed. The yearning for a reunited and free Korea persisted, and the task of developing a viable economy remained.

22. JAPAN: THE QUIET ALLY

Tides of change in world affairs washed Japan's shores. Following World War II, Japan was engrossed in restructuring its society and developing its foreign trade. Its orientation rapidly shifted to the West. This trend was reflected not only in Japan's economic but also in its social life as Western, especially American, patterns were overlaid on its Oriental ways. Caught between the currents of American policy of containing Chinese Communist expansion and strong pressures to establish economic and trade ties with the Asian mainland, Japanese leaders sought to steer a middle course. Content to play a passive role on the international scene, they tried to avoid taking a stand on issues that might generate friction or conflict with other nations.

Before World War II, nearly two-thirds of Japanese exports went to China, Korea, and Formosa. After 1945, however, Japan steadily expanded its markets in the United States and Europe as well as in Latin America and Africa. From 1954 to 1962, Japan's economic growth increased at a phenomenal rate —it was matched only by West Germany's extraordinary "miracle" —and once again Japan became an important world power. The shift in its economic relations was perhaps most strikingly revealed in that by the 1960's the United States was buying about one-third of all Japanese exports, whereas Japan's trade with Communist-bloc countries, including Communist China, totaled 4 per cent.

Despite its changed trade relations, Japan's geography, history, and culture dictated that the country is an intrinsic part of Asia and not the West. Although a central feature of Japanese foreign policy was its alignment with the United States through the Security Treaty of September 1951 and the Treaty of Mutual Cooperation and Security signed in January 1960, many Japanese had felt that this relationship was artificial. Japan's alliance with the United States and its desire to establish its leadership in the Far East in an economic if not a political sense inevitably produced inner tensions. The idea that Japan should cultivate "special relations" with China continued to be strongly espoused. The mainland was still regarded as a natural supplier of raw materials for Japanese industries and as an enormous potential market for their products. Many Japanese, confident that they understood China far better than Americans, did not feel that Peking was a threat. Convinced that Washington's policies were in error, they were inclined to believe, like the British, that a "fat" Chinese Communist was less dangerous than a "lean" one.

Differences between Tokyo and Washington inevitably sharpened. One effect of President de Gaulle's recognition of Communist China was that it emboldened the Japanese to express their opinions more openly and forcefully than had been the case in the past. This was clearly seen at the third meeting of the Joint U.S.-Japan Committee on Trade and Economic Affairs held in Tokyo, January 27–28.[23] Anxious to obtain Japanese cooperation in halting the spreading movement toward diplomatic recognition of Peking, Secretary Rusk gave an unusually candid and critical appraisal of the French decision. He bluntly told the Japanese Cabinet ministers that the French action was irrational and would encourage Communist China's militant and belligerent policies, thereby threatening the entire free world. France was bringing no power to Asia, Mr. Rusk said; nor, he implied, did it have any intention of defending Asia or of sharing in the free world's burdens in the region.

Although Japan tended to favor recognition, it did not wish to endanger its relations with the United States. But the Japanese ministers pulled very few punches in criticizing American economic policies. They attacked a suggested proposal for an equalization tax on overseas investment, which would harm Japan's economic growth since it would hinder the flow of American capital into the country. They were also especially caustic about the "buy-American" policy, delays in customs clearance when it was charged that Japanese goods were being dumped, and restrictions on the import of Japanese steel and cement.

The American delegation discussed these problems frankly and sought to mollify the Japanese. They persuaded some of the Japanese ministers that the interest equalization tax was necessary to keep the dollar strong.[24] Japan was assured that special steps would be taken if it found itself unduly damaged by the measure.

The crux of the problem, however, went deeper than American restrictive economical policies. It lay in a growing conviction that Japan was overly dependent on the United States, and that it should make its own decisions on the basis of its own interests. This was reflected in the Japanese desire to improve relations with mainland China (if not by recognition then by a workable "two Chinas" policy) and to expand its markets in areas other than the United States. As former Ambassador Kennan observed in alluding to this situation, "There is—and Americans may as well face it—a perfectly natural desire among the Japanese to escape at least partially from the cloying exclusiveness of the American tie, from the helpless passivity it seems to imply, from the overtones of 'anything you can do we can do better,' which so often accompanies American friendship, and to throw open a sector of the international horizon where Japan could have a set of relationships and an importance of her own, not dependent on American tutelage. . . ."[25]

During the year, Japan cautiously worked toward a larger role in world affairs. Despite American misgivings, it continued efforts to "normalize" relations with Peking through trade agreements which, though privately conducted, had the support of the Japanese government. Although overtures to South Korea met with serious setbacks, Japan persisted in trying to overcome the heritage of the past. At the same time it sought to work out a new basis of accommodation with Communist China, it continued to cultivate its relations with the Nationalist regime and tried to keep Chiang Kai-shek pacified. Japan was a major purchaser of Formosa's products, its trade with that island being larger than with the Chinese mainland. Significantly, Japan also looked to an expansion of its trade with the Soviet Union.

In May Deputy Premier Anastas I. Mikoyan, heading an

eleven-member delegation, made a surprise visit to Tokyo. He submitted a list of goods totalling $350 million that the Russians wanted to buy from Japan on a deferred-payment basis. The Soviet official told the Japanese that, in addition to the seven-year program for developing the U.S.S.R.'s chemical industry, a new five-year plan was scheduled to begin in 1966 for the development of other industries. One of its purposes was to develop Siberia. Mr. Mikoyan indicated that Japanese cooperation would be warmly welcomed in this venture. Expressing keen interest in doing business with the Soviet Union, Japanese financial and industrial leaders supported the extension of long-term credits. Japan was the first of the free-world allies to break through the "time barrier" of five years on loans to Communist-bloc countries. Two big Japanese firms concluded an agreement with the Soviet Union in September for a $10 million fertilizer plant, 20 per cent to be paid immediately and the balance over eight years.

Japan took a major step to emerge from under America's wing when a final report on a revision of the Japanese constitution was submitted July 3. The government council which had worked on this project for seven years came to the conclusion that the present constitution, imposed on Japan by the United States during the military occupation, had to be replaced by a new one more truly representative of the free will of the Japanese people and more in keeping with their traditions and world realities. Two important recommendations were made, namely, to restore the Emperor as the "head of the state," and to remove the constitutional prohibitions that prevented Japan from building any military establishment.

No action, however, was taken by the Japanese government on these potentially explosive issues. Late in October Premier Hayato Ikeda resigned because of ill-health, and he was succeeded on November 9 by Eisaku Sato, a leader of the ruling Liberal-Democratic party. Mr. Sato told the Japanese Diet that while at the moment he had no intention of seeking changes in the constitution, he would "fully and carefully consider" the opinion presented by the special government council. He also urged the Japanese people to take an active interest in the matter of constitutional revisions.

New uncertainties arose for Japan because of Communist China's detonation of a nuclear device. Although the primary reaction was one of condemnation and a strengthened demand for a universal nuclear test-ban treaty, some conservative quarters were convinced that Japan had to build up its defense capacity—and, perhaps, eventually even produce its own nuclear weapons. Outlining his program early in December, Mr. Sato stressed that he would continue to seek close political, economic, and military ties with the United States, and, at the same time, adopt a "positive" approach toward Peking that would aim at assuring Communist China of his government's desire for friendship. He also emphasized that it was imperative for Japan to play a more important diplomatic role in world affairs, especially in Asia. As Japan looked to the future, a new era appeared to be opening in the nation's history.

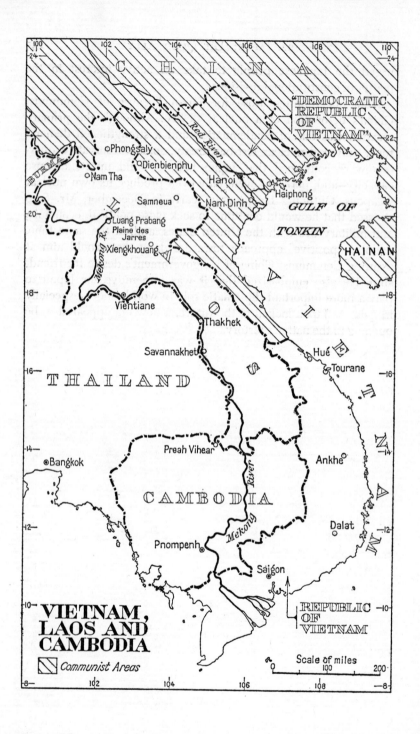

VIETNAM,
LAOS AND
CAMBODIA

Communist Areas

CHAPTER SIX
THE UNITED STATES AND SOUTH VIETNAM

AMERICA'S FOREIGN POLICY faced perhaps the greatest challenge
in Southeast Asia, for here in 1964 the Communists were pursuing their aims with the greatest militancy. Among the nine
countries of this strategic region, Vietnam is of pivotal importance. As Henry Cabot Lodge, the former American ambassador
to South Vietnam has phrased it: "He who holds or has influence
in Vietnam can affect the future of the Philippines and Taiwan
to the east, Thailand and Burma with their huge rice surpluses
to the west, and Malaysia and Indonesia with their rubber, oil
and tin to the south. Japan, Australia and New Zealand would
in turn be deeply concerned by the Communization of South
Vietnam." [1] However important its geographical position, much
more was involved in the struggle over South Vietnam than
"strategic real estate." For the contest tested America's capacity
not only to thwart Communist expansion effected by infiltration,
subversion, terrorism, and guerrilla warfare, but also its ability to
encourage and support the independence of weak nations. A
Communist victory there threatened to jeopardize much more
than the prestige of the United States.

Difficulties in Southeast Asia were indeed formidable. The
slow and painful process of "state-building," especially in the
formerly French-held Indochinese provinces of Vietnam and
Laos, produced considerable domestic conflict and uncertainty.
The involvement of the United States in Southeast Asia had
perforce steadily increased following France's withdrawal in

1954. Despite America's aid, the region failed to become an effective bulwark against Communist encroachment. Following the assassination of President Ngo Dinh Diem and the overthrow of his regime in November 1963, the crisis in South Vietnam grew increasingly grave. The new military junta that acquired political power was unable to establish stability or check the Communist-led Vietcong guerrilla activities. With the situation steadily deteriorating, pressures increased in the United States for stronger measures to prevent a Communist takeover.

23. SOUTH VIETNAM BATTLEGROUND

Early in January 1964 President Johnson tried to bolster South Vietnam's ruling military junta when he assured Major General Duong Van Minh, chairman of the Military Revolutionary Council, that the United States would "continue to furnish you and your people with the fullest measure of support" in the fight against Communist guerrillas. He firmly rejected the "neutralization" of the Indochinese peninsula, based on the withdrawal of both Chinese and American power, such as had been proposed by President de Gaulle.[2] While the United States stepped up its military program, a joint American-Vietnamese report of January 14 warned that the "battle in the crucial Mekong delta could not ever be won" unless South Vietnam's new government carried out reforms at the village level. Detailing accounts of corruption, mismanagement, and neglect by local officials, the report especially criticized the government's failure to hold the loyalty of young people, who were prime targets for the Vietcong.[3]

The worsening of the military situation, combined with de Gaulle's renewed call for neutralization in January, contributed to a sudden, bloodless *coup*. Led by Major General Nguyen Khanh, paratroopers and infantry units from the Saigon area, supported by tanks, toppled General Minh's military regime on January 30. Four military leaders, General Khanh asserted, had plotted with French agents to achieve a neutral settlement in Vietnam, which was to have coincided with President de Gaulle's recognition of Communist China. Washington was clearly embarrassed by the overthrow of the military regime that it had helped bring to power three months earlier. Disclaiming any responsibility for the successful insurrection, the American government further noted that it saw no evidence that France was engaged in any conspiracy to bring down the Saigon regime or that any of the deposed leaders were actually working for a neutralist policy in South Vietnam.

During February the shaky domestic situation led to a buildup in the size, frequency, and intensity of Vietcong attacks throughout the country. The *coup* had badly undercut popular confidence in the South Vietnamese army, hitherto regarded as the one institution that could hold the country together in the war against the Communist guerrillas.

Shaken by the turn of events, the United States reassessed possible courses of action. One choice was a greater American involvement in South Vietnam's affairs. For some time, a minority view in the Johnson administration held that at a minimum the South Vietnamese should be helped to conduct hit-and-run raids on North Vietnam. A few went much further, proposing that the United States assist the South Vietnamese to take and hold part of North Vietnam. The State Department, however, opposed any movement in force into the North, chiefly because it believed that such action—as in Korea—would result in Chinese Communist intervention. A second alternative was to let things stand as they were. A third possibility was withdrawal through some form of face-saving formula such as "neutralization."

The fundamental problem—how to save South Vietnam from eventual conquest by the Chinese Communists—had not changed. To prevent a Communist takeover, the first requisite, Washington believed, was a strong government in Saigon; the second was a firmer military position, to be achieved with American support. Only then could a negotiated settlement be talked about or even considered. President de Gaulle, on the other hand, was convinced that a military solution was impossible—a belief the French leader had expressed to President Kennedy as early as 1961. With the situation heading toward disaster, and with the alternatives rapidly narrowing to a humiliating withdrawal or engagement in a larger war, de Gaulle thought that it was imperative for the West to negotiate while it still held a position of strength. The French President did not propose a plan for the neutralization of Southeast Asia, but rather a line of policy aimed at stimulating political developments to permit diplomatic bargaining.

As conditions continued to deteriorate, Senate majority leader Mike Mansfield urged the Johnson administration to encourage rather than spurn French efforts to negotiate with Peking for a settlement in Southeast Asia. The Montana Democrat said the United States had "teetered for too long on the brink" of turning the guerrilla war in South Vietnam into an American war, and he did not feel the national interest justified such a major commitment of American lives. But President Johnson made it abundantly clear on February 22 that the United States would not accept a Communist conquest of South Vietnam. Although the President declared that the contest had to be won by the South Vietnamese themselves, he warned Hanoi and Peking that "this type of aggression is a deeply dangerous game." Mr. Johnson strongly intimated that the Communists were risking a full-scale conventional war, and perhaps even a limited nuclear war, by pressing for the "liberation" of South Vietnam.[4]

The Soviet Union responded to President Johnson's hints concerning the extension of the war. On February 25 Moscow pointedly told Washington that it would render "necessary assistance and support" to the "national liberation struggle" in South Vietnam.[5] The Kremlin called for a withdrawal of American troops and military equipment, and for an end to U.S. "interference" in the country's internal affairs. France, at the same time, again affirmed that negotiation and neutralization were the only possible courses of action in South Vietnam. Foreign Minister Couve de Murville saw no possibility of a successful military conclusion to the guerrilla conflict—he found it difficult to believe that the United States could win in this struggle with 20,000 military advisors where France had failed with 200,000 troops. However, he neglected to distinguish between the effort to maintain a colonial position and the role of the United States in assisting a Vietnamese government to resist rebellion.

Of America's European allies only Britain and Italy were prepared to support the Johnson administration. West Germany and the Netherlands wanted a military victory for South Vietnam, but they feared any step that might involve Communist China and lead to a global war. Portugal was highly critical of what it termed the United States' "recolonization" of Southeast Asia, while Turkey saw the advantages of neutralism for Vietnam. Despite Europe's generally adverse reaction to American Southeast Asian policies, President Johnson declared on March 7 that the United States would send more men to South Vietnam if they were needed. Meanwhile, Premier Khanh announced a one year program of reforms to rebuild the country's political and administrative structure.

As the United States took steps to enlarge its commitments in South Vietnam, Senator Wayne Morse of Oregon sharply criticized the Johnson administration. "I am completely opposed to increasing the scale of our participation in the Vietnamese war," he said. "I am opposed to it because American involvement in any Asian conflict is going to be nuclear involvement. I am satisfied that there is no other way this country could meet the manpower and geographic advantages that a Chinese-backed force would have. . . . This country would make the gravest mistake of its history by carrying a war, nuclear or otherwise, onto the mainland of Asia." [6] Senator Morse's scathing denunciation of the administration's policies in Southeast Asia found little support in Congress. On the whole, the American public appeared to favor more, rather than less, vigorous action in the region.

On March 8 Secretary McNamara, heading a top-level delegation, including Chairman of the Joint Chiefs of Staff General Maxwell D. Taylor, arrived in Saigon on a five-day mission. An important object of this visit was to build up Premier Khanh's stature as a national leader and strengthen South Vietnam's war effort. Upon his return to Washington, Mr. McNamara recommended to President Johnson a program of increased operations against the Vietcong guerrillas. Though stress was placed on the

importance of eliminating guerrillas in the South, occasional raids
against North Vietnam were not ruled out. Secretary McNamara
and General Taylor concluded that the South Vietnamese government needed and should get additional American military,
economic, and political support, and that this help should be
furnished for as long as it was necessary "to bring Communist
aggression and terrorism under control." [7]

In a speech carefully planned with President Johnson and
Secretary Rusk, Mr. McNamara on March 26 forcefully rejected
"withdrawal," "neutralization," or "peace at any price" in the
war against the Communist insurgents.[8] The Defense Secretary
emphasized that the United States intended to remain in the
struggle against a Communist takeover in South Vietnam until
an "independent and stable" government there made it safe to
withdraw. He reiterated that American objectives were: to help
South Vietnam as a "member of the free-world family" preserve
its independence from Communist attack; to prevent Southeast
Asia, which "has great strategic significance in the forward
defense of the United States," from falling into Communist
hands; and to block Communist aims at aggression in what had
become a "test case for the new Communist strategy." A Communist victory in South Vietnam, Mr. McNamara said, would
place the North Vietnamese regime in control of all Vietnam,
and this "would be only a first step toward eventual Chinese
hegemony."

At the annual Council meeting of the Southeast Asia Treaty
Organization (SEATO), held in Manila on April 13–14, President
de Gaulle's neutralization proposal was rejected. The final communiqué,[9] one of the strongest and most specific in the ten-year
history of the SEATO pact, "expressed grave concern about
continuing Communist aggression against the Republic of Vietnam." It agreed that the "defeat of the Communist campaign is
essential not only to the Republic of South Vietnam, but to
that of South-East Asia. It will also be convincing proof that
Communist expansion by such tactics will not be permitted."
France abstained from endorsing this declaration but subscribed
to the general expression of determination by the Council to

resist overt Communist aggression and subversion in the treaty area.

Immediately following the SEATO conference, Secretary Rusk went to Saigon for a three-day visit—his first trip to South Vietnam since he took office. Like McNamara's mission, its purpose seemed to be to strengthen Premier Khanh's position and to give added momentum to the campaign against the Vietcong guerrillas. "You will have peace . . . when Hanoi and Peiping have been taught to leave their neighbors alone," the Secretary of State said on his arrival. "You and those of us who are at your side must defeat their effort to impose their own misery upon you. That this will be done I have not the slightest doubt, and I am here to make clear once again that we shall help you do it." Mr. Rusk declared himself encouraged by his on-the-spot inspection trip.[10]

But the South Vietnam situation continued to be clouded. To a great extent, the source of the confusion lay in the nature of the conflict. The Vietcong attacks had started early in 1957 with the midnight assassinations of a few South Vietnamese officials by black-garbed "terrorists." These murders were followed by widespread raids until casualties began to run into the thousands each month. From a few scattered armed bands backed by a fairly extensive secret political organization, the Communist Vietcong built up a fighting force estimated at 40,000 men in the mid-1960's. These were organized into 45 battalions throughout the country and armed with modern infantry weapons. They were supported by well over 100,000 less well armed, but still effective, local and regional guerrillas. Roughly 80 per cent of the peasantry in the vital Mekong delta area lived under a Communist shadow government of one form or another, which maintained its own schools and dispensaries and collected taxes like a legitimate political community.

In May Secretary McNamara gave a sober appraisal of the situation. He described conditions as "very serious," and observed that improvements were going to be slow. "It can't be won quickly," Mr. McNamara said, "no guerrilla war ever has been." On May 14 the Defense Secretary submitted a new plan for increased military and economic support for South Vietnam. He recommended, in particular, an increase in the size of the South Vietnamese air force, and modest increases in the number of American training personnel in the country. "This is a war for the confidence of the people and the security of those people," Mr. McNamara emphasized, "and that kind of war is a long, hard war." [11]

Four days later, President Johnson asked Congress to provide an extra $125 million in economic and military aid to South Vietnam.[12] This was in addition to the appropriation of about $500 million that had already been sought by the administration in its foreign aid bill. The increase was necessary, Mr. Johnson said, because of two developments that had taken place: "First, the Viet Cong guerrillas, under orders from their Communist masters in the north, have intensified terrorist actions against the peaceful people of South Vietnam. This increased terrorism requires increased response. Second, a new government under Prime Minister Khanh has come to power, bringing new energy and leadership and new hope for effective action."

At the end of the month the President called a conference of the nation's top diplomatic and military officials to review the critical situation in Southeast Asia. The onset of a pro-Communist Pathet Lao offensive in Laos gave a sense of urgency to the conference, which met in Honolulu on June 1–2. While the emergency atmosphere had been dissipated somewhat by a lull in the fighting in Laos by the time the American officials assembled for the meeting, every effort was made to remove whatever doubts might exist about Washington's commitment to the region—and especially to South Vietnam. But no new dramatic measures came out of the Honolulu meeting.

The United States stressed that the problem in the region was not, as France suggested, to reach a new neutrality agreement with Communist China and North Vietnam, but to see that the Communists lived up to agreements they already had made, particularly at the Geneva conference of 1954, in which neutrality for all of Southeast Asia was pledged, and the Laos accord of 1962, in which the specific neutralization of that country was established.[13] To emphasize that the American commitment to the security of Southeast Asia was "unlimited," Washington asserted at the end of June that North Vietnam and Communist China had to leave their neighbors alone or face a war with the United States. This stiffening of attitude reflected the belief that a compromise could not be negotiated.

The stronger warnings from Washington coincided with a change in the top U.S. diplomatic personnel in South Vietnam. On June 23 President Johnson announced his acceptance of Ambassador Lodge's resignation (Mr. Lodge had wished to return to the United States to participate in pre-convention activities of the Republican party), and the appointment of General Taylor to replace him. To underscore the importance attached to South Vietnam, the President also appointed U. Alexis Johnson, an Under-Secretary of State and prominent career diplomat, to the job of Deputy Ambassador to South Vietnam. The choice of these men assured the South Vietnamese government that Mr. Lodge's departure would not affect Washington's commitment to the fight against the Communist guerrillas or result in any other significant policy changes. Since 1961 General Taylor had been one of the principal architects of American counterinsurgency efforts, which had aimed at building up U.S. military support for waging the kind of war the Communists were fighting in Vietnam while at the same time increasing economic aid to help in coping with the social and economic conditions in which insurgency flourished.

Early in July the tone of Washington's warnings to Communist China and North Vietnam softened. The ultimate objective of American policy, Secretary Rusk said, was to obtain peace, and this "ought to be possible without further extension of the fighting." Military power alone, it was recognized, was not the answer to Southeast Asia's problems. Convinced that military methods would not bring about peace in South Vietnam, U.N. Secretary-General Thant urged on July 8 a reconvening of the 1954 Geneva conference. "The only sensible alternative," he said, "is the political and diplomatic method of negotiation." [14] But Washington responded frigidly to the suggestion. Although the United States recognized that at some point parleys would have to be undertaken, it was concerned about the timing of negotiations, the countries that should participate, and the balance of military advantage between the contending sides. Circumstances were not such during the summer, Washington believed, to encourage talks.

Thus, the impasse persisted. During July both Premier Khanh and President de Gaulle pressed for concrete action, though in opposite directions. The South Vietnamese leader whipped up public excitement by calling for attacks against Communist North Vietnam, shouting "Bac Tien!" ("To the North!") On the other hand, de Gaulle at his news conference on July 23 declared that the best way to end the fighting would be for the United States, the Soviet Union, Communist China, and France to agree to get out and stay out of the Indochinese peninsula. He urged a reconvening of the 1954 Geneva conference to decide upon and organize the necessary guarantees against intervention, and on the maintenance of neutrality. Once peace was established, the French President said, a massive program of economic and technical aid could then be undertaken to help the peoples of North and South Vietnam, Laos, and Cambodia.[15]

President Johnson quickly dismissed de Gaulle's proposal for an international conference. "We do not believe in a conference called to ratify terror," he said. If the Communists honored their previous agreements, Mr. Johnson declared, there could be peace in Southeast Asia "immediately." Until then, the President asserted, the United States would take any action it deemed necessary to support the freedom and independence of South Vietnam and the neutralist government of Laos.[16]

24. GULF OF TONKIN EPISODES

In the midst of conflicting pressures for a solution to the Southeast Asia crisis, North Vietnam suddenly made a bold strike against the United States in the Gulf of Tonkin. Communist China and North Vietnam had come to regard the Gulf of Tonkin—a sizable international body of water, 150 miles wide and 300 miles long—as virtually their private lake. North Vietnam's entire coastline is on the Gulf, which is bounded on the east and north by China's Hainan Island and the Chinese mainland. Premier Chou En-lai had warned on June 28 that foreign vessels not use radar or photographic equipment in the Gulf, stay in the middle of the Hainan Strait, and obey any challenge. Communist countries have often tried to assert their sovereignty over gulfs, bays or seas partly enclosed by their land territories, but Washington viewed these new "regulations" as more than an effort to assert Peking's sovereignty; they seemed to indicate the possibility of a major buildup in the area. The United States had sporadically maintained a destroyer patrol in the Gulf of Tonkin, chiefly to observe and report upon ship movements, particularly suspected shipments of men and materiel from North Vietnam to the Vietcong. Small-scale guerrilla operations across North Vietnam's land and sea frontiers had also been conducted for several years by South Vietnamese forces. With both sides engaged in highly provocative activities in the Gulf, the situation was explosive.

On August 2 three North Vietnamese PT boats attacked the U.S. destroyer *Maddox* while it was on a routine patrol in the Gulf of Tonkin, 30 miles off the coast of North Vietnam. Three torpedoes and some 37 mm. shells were fired; the destroyer and four American planes struck back, damaging the PT vessels and driving them off. Neither the *Maddox* nor the U.S. aircraft sustained casualties or damage. Washington, at first, tried to minimize the incident. "The other side got a sting out of this," said Secretary Rusk. "If they do it again they'll get another sting." Describing the attack as unwelcome, but not especially serious, the Defense Department explained that no effort had been made to sink the PT boats because the fleet was not at war. President Johnson, however, immediately directed the Navy to shoot to destroy attackers in any future incident. A second destroyer as well as a combat air patrol were assigned to the Gulf of Tonkin.

Two days later an undetermined number of North Vietnamese PT boats deliberately attacked the *Maddox* and the *C. Turner*

Joy during the night. Again there were no American casualties, but this time two of the PT boats were sunk. Word of the second attack came an hour before the National Security Council was scheduled to hold a regular meeting at the White House. The immediate reaction of the Council was that this was a clear challenge to the United States, and should not go unpunished.

Within a few hours plans were made for a limited response. Four PT bases along the North Vietnamese coast, from which the attack had come, and an oil depot were singled out; none of these targets was near a population center. The plan was endorsed by the National Security Council at a second meeting at 6 P.M. An hour earlier the Defense Department had publicly disclosed the attack on the destroyers. As tension mounted, President Johnson summoned a large group of congressional leaders to the White House to inform them of the decision that had been made. Mr. Johnson asked them for their support, although he made it clear that the responsibility for whatever action was taken would be his. An announcement was then made that the President would speak to the nation late in the evening on television. At 10:40 P.M., Eastern daylight time, reconnaissance planes took off from carriers in the Gulf of Tonkin to make sure that enemy planes would not intercept the strike bombers.

Shortly before midnight on August 4, President Johnson told the American people that in view of the deliberate renewal of attacks on U.S. naval vessels in the Gulf of Tonkin, he had been compelled "to take action in reply." Repeated acts of violence against America's armed forces could not be ignored, but had to be met by positive action. "That reply," the President declared dramatically, "is being given as I speak to you tonight. Air action is now in execution against gunboats and certain supporting facilities in North Viet-Nam which have been used in these hostile operations." [17] Actually when Mr. Johnson spoke the air attacks had not yet taken place—American planes struck about one hour later. The time lag, Washington later explained, was deliberate, its purpose being to convey to Hanoi and Peking the limited nature of the American retaliatory "reply." Although the United States did not want to give North Vietnam sufficient time to clear its PT patrol bases, it still was anxious to make sure that North Vietnam would understand that the attack would be limited to these bases. At the same time Washington did not want Peking to mistake the American action for an attack on Communist China, for it was presumed that the reconnaissance planes would be spotted by Chinese and North Vietnamese radar.

During a five-hour raid, flying at low level in bad weather, American planes carried on heavy bombing attacks—sixty-four "sorties" were undertaken in all—and demolished the four North Vietnam PT patrol bases, as well as 90 per cent of a major oil storage depot and seven antiaircraft installations. Twenty-five patrol boats—about half of the North Vietnamese gunboat fleet—were caught in their "nests" and destroyed. Two American planes were knocked down by antiaircraft fire, and two others were damaged in the encounter.

The next morning, President Johnson sent a special message to Congress in which he asked for its support of the action that had been taken and requested the adoption of a resolution authorizing the President as Commander-in-Chief to take all necessary measures to repel any armed attack against the forces of the United States and to prevent further aggression. In his message,[18] the President defined American goals by saying "The United States intends no rashness, and seeks no wider war. We must make it clear to all that the United States is united in its determination to bring about the end of Communist subversion and aggression in the area [of Southeast Asia]. We seek the full and effective restoration of the international agreements signed in Geneva in 1954, with respect to South Vietnam, and again at Geneva in 1962, with respect to Laos." Speaking at Syracuse University the same day, the President warned that "there can be no peace by aggression and no immunity from reply."[19]

Although North Vietnam acknowledged that its patrol boats had carried out the first attack on the *Maddox*, claiming that the ship had invited assault by intruding into North Vietnamese waters, it asserted that the second assault was pure fabrication on the part of the United States to conceal its "illegal" acts to aggravate the situation in Southeast Asia. "Their main purpose," said a Hanoi spokesman, "is to save the situation in South Vietnam, which is in a critical phase right now." [20] Peking warned that the American attack meant aggression against the Chinese as well as the North Vietnamese and threatened "grave consequences." It accused the United States of provoking the crisis and asserted that on July 30 American warships had intruded into North Vietnamese waters, shelling the islands of Hon Me and Hon Ngu. On August 1 and 2, the Chinese Communists further said, U.S. planes bombed a North Vietnam border post and a village close to the Laos border. Declaring that the "debt of blood incurred by the United States must be repaid," it demanded that America stop at once "all provocative and sabotaging acts" and called on the signers of the 1954 Geneva agreement on Indochina to "take timely measures to check the the United States warmongers' hands." [21] Although the statement echoed similar Chinese Communist threats of the past, Peking was silent on what action it would take.

Congress quickly moved to approve the resolution supporting President Johnson's action in the Southeast Asian crisis.[22] Principal opposition was voiced by Senator Morse who stingingly denounced the administration and charged that the United States was the "provocateur" of the North Vietnam PT boat attacks on American destroyers. He declared that "the very fact that the [American] ships were in the area where they could have given protection if necessary" to South Vietnamese planes on bombing missions to North Vietnamese islands was evidence of U.S. involvement. "It makes no difference," Senator Morse went on to say, "who says that our objective is peace, even if he be the President of the United States. Our actions speak louder than words; and our actions in Asia today are the actions of warmaking." [23] Senators J. W. Fulbright and Richard B. Russell told the Senate that the North Vietnamese were guilty of military aggression, and the United States had no other course than to fight back. "It should be made equally clear to [the Communist] regimes, if it is not yet sufficiently clear,"

Senator Fulbright asserted, "that their aggressive and expansionist ambitions, wherever advanced, will meet precisely that degree of American opposition which is necessary to frustrate them." [24] On August 7, after a 40-minute debate, the House passed the resolution, 416-0. It was then endorsed by the Senate, 88-2. "The votes," said President Johnson, "prove our determination to defend our forces . . . and to work firmly and steadily for peace and security in the area." [25]

Meanwhile, Ambassador Stevenson told a meeting of the U.N. Security Council that the bombing of North Vietnamese torpedo boats "and their facilities" was an act of self-defense against attacks on American destroyers on the high seas and was authorized by international law and the United Nations Charter. During the debate Mr. Stevenson rejected assertions by the Czechoslovakian delegate that American ships had violated North Vietnamese territorial waters on July 30. No attack or incursion had been made before the retaliatory attack of August 5.[26] The Soviet request that both North and South Vietnam be asked to appear or present pertinent information was approved, but on August 9 Hanoi rejected the invitation. North Vietnam declared, "Only the two co-chairmen [the U.K. and the U.S.S.R.] and the countries that took part in the 1954 Geneva conference have full competence to examine the extremely dangerous acts committed by the United States Government against the Democratic Republic of Vietnam." [27] Rather than have the issue debated in the United Nations, both Communist China and North Vietnam apparently aimed at increasing pressures on Washington for an international conference dealing with Southeast Asia.

There was much speculation on why North Vietnam attacked U.S. destroyers in the Gulf of Tonkin. Although the net effect of the exchange strengthened the American position in the area, the situation remained explosive. With orders to "pursue, attack, and destroy" any Communist unit that committed a "hostile act" against Americans in international waters, U.S. naval forces were put on a wartime alert. On September 18 two American destroyers, the *Richard S. Edward* and the *Morton,* reported sighting four unidentified "shapes"—apparently vessels in attack formation—on their radar screens. They opened fire, and the hostile shapes "disappeared." At a news conference, Secretary Rusk indicated that the destroyers had fired upon and presumably hit what appeared to be four or five hostile vessels.

The impact of the Tonkin incidents immediately made itself felt within South Vietnam. On August 7 Premier Khanh decreed a state of emergency and ordered stringent measures to tighten the government's control over the population. Safeguards were imposed against the threat of large-scale Communist attacks. "The coming weeks will decide the destiny of our entire people," the South Vietnamese leader said. "We will not accept becoming a minor province of Red China."

25. THE STRUGGLE TO ESTABLISH A STABLE GOVERNMENT

It became apparent by the summer that a threefold conflict existed in Vietnam. First, it was evident that Hanoi, directing and supporting a Communist-controlled insurgent movement, was determined on destroying the Saigon regime and taking over South Vietnam. In resisting this aggressive thrust, the South Vietnam government became heavily dependent on American help. Second, the conflict, in a larger sense, embraced Communist China and the United States. Ultimately involved in the struggle was the threat not only of Hanoi's control over South Vietnam, but of Peking's eventual domination over the whole of Southeast Asia. For political, economic, and strategic reasons, the United States was firmly committed to prevent such Communist encroachment. Finally, within South Vietnam itself, a political and social revolution had become manifest, and an internal struggle for political power gained momentum, particularly following the downfall of President Diem.

The turbulence in South Vietnam was a complex of many factors. Among these, the "religious issue" was of considerable significance. Animosities between Catholics and Buddhists that had deep historical roots were, unfortunately, exacerbated during the Diem regime. Although there was little actual religious persecution, the tendency of the Diem government to give preferment to Catholics in civil and military life aroused Buddhist resentment and widespread discontent. As dissatisfaction and protests mounted, tensions increased. They finally reached a climax in the Hué incident of May 8, 1963, when the Ngo family inflicted harsh reprisals against the Buddhists. This action stirred Buddhist wrath, led to a coalescing of the "Buddhist" movement, and contributed significantly to the overthrow of the Diem regime. Much more concerned with political matters than religious doctrine, the "Buddhist" movement became a powerful political force in South Vietnam. Opposed to Catholic dominance, it also reflected nascent nationalist aspirations which looked toward finding a "Vietnamese" solution to South Vietnam's political problems. While Buddhist leaders showed little desire for the responsibilities of political office, they nevertheless were anxious to have a veto over government policies and choices of personnel.

One effect of President Diem's downfall was that it swept away the fragile constitutional system that had been established, without, however, replacing it with another. As a result, South Vietnam found itself in continuing turmoil, with new groups and factions vying for control over the government. Of these, the military establishment emerged as the most potent, but here, too, jealousies and factionalism produced a continuing state of political ferment. Of Diem's political opponents who again emerged on the scene, none succeeded in inspiring any real mass enthusiasm. In the ensuing political vacuum South Vietnamese students, another important group finding emotional identification with the "Buddhist" cause, also searched for new leaders who would offer a Vietnamese solution to their country's problems.

Superimposed on the political crisis in Saigon was the division that existed between the urban and rural regions. For the most part, the Vietnamese peasantry was not involved directly in the urban ferment and had no tradition or sense of identity with a government in Saigon. Regional differences, moreover, were marked and inevitably produced friction. The task of establishing a balance between the urban and outlying areas, between and among the various regions—each of which was concerned with jealously safeguarding its own interests—as well as among the Buddhists, the Catholics, the students, the civilian politicians, and the military establishment was enormously great. It was these divisions and differences which the Communists, of course, sought to exploit, and they effectively played upon the frustration, fatigue, and weariness of the unending civil war. Fundamentally, however, the South Vietnamese people opposed Communist doctrines which were alien to their traditions, and they were especially fearful of Chinese Communist domination. While the turmoil within South Vietnam suggested an inherent incapacity for self-government, actually the struggle going on in 1964 amidst the pressures of civil war was directed toward evolving new balances that would channel or contain political disagreements, and create new institutions that could cope with Vietnamese problems. The major question, however, was whether South Vietnam would be given sufficient time to permit its own revolution to take its course.

On August 16 a fateful move came when the nation's military leaders reasserted their supreme authority. They promulgated a new constitution, patterned after that of the United States, elected Premier Khanh as President, and ousted Major-General Minh as chief of state. Although South Vietnam pledged its faith in democratic ideals and practices, General Khanh, under the constitution, reserved to the presidency virtual dictatorial powers during a temporary state of emergency.

The attempt to impose what appeared to be a "military dictatorship" brought immediate protests from the Buddhists and the students. Seeking to answer their complaints, President Khanh promised that his cabinet would have a majority of civilian ministers and that the emergency measures adopted to fight the Communist insurgency would be relaxed. The United States, like the South Vietnamese people, was perturbed at the enforcement of rigid controls; but it was hopeful that the constitutional changes would lead to a more stable government. Reluctantly, Washington officials accepted the fact that the needs of waging war justified these stringent measures. President Khanh's assurances, however, did not placate either the students or the Buddhists, and antigovernment agitation flared into violence. The Saigon government made no moves to restore order. While the main attack was directed against General Khanh's abrupt assumption of the presidency, his new constitution, and his emergency decrees—as well as against the United States for supporting his attempt to set up a tighter rule—religious disorders between Buddhists and Catholics also spread. Despite the opposition of student and religious groups, Washington reaffirmed its support of the South Vietnamese regime.

This effort to bolster President Khanh failed. On August 25 the Military Revolutionary Council voted to withdraw the new constitution, and President Khanh agreed to step down until a new head of state was elected. But the military rulers were unable to agree on what should be done, and the political crisis deepened. Two days later, provisional agreement was reached on setting up a military triumvirate, including General Khanh and former chief of state Major-General Minh to "lead the nation." Instead of bringing the situation under control, this move brought renewed riots and led to clashes between Catholics and Buddhists that assumed the proportions of open civil conflict. South Vietnam's interim government announced on August 29 that General Khanh had suffered a "breakdown" and would be unable to carry on his duties until he was sufficiently recovered. Troops finally moved in to quell the fighting. Although a new acting Premier was named, the United States indicated that it would have to reconsider its role in the fight against the Communists if General Khanh did not resume his participation in the government. After a brief period of rest, General Khanh returned to Saigon a week later, resumed his premiership, and took steps to reestablish the government as it had been before August 16.

In an effort to build a government acceptable to the Buddhists and other dissatisfied groups, General Khanh pledged that at the end of two months the military leaders would withdraw completely, and all governmental powers would be handed over to civilians. Encouraged by this development, the United States declared that it would continue to strengthen its military mission in South Vietnam. The turmoil within South Vietnam, unfortunately, did not die down; on September 13–14, Saigon was again thrown into confusion when rebellious troops staged a *coup* in a move to overthrow Premier Khanh. Military forces loyal to General Khanh, however, quickly regained control, and the rebellion was quashed.

A High National Council, composed of seventeen civilians, was established on September 26 to prepare a new constitution and political institutions to govern South Vietnam. Membership in the Council embraced rival religious and civic groups, including Buddhists and Catholics. It officially presented on October 20 a charter setting forth a new constitutional basis for civil rule, designed to replace General Khanh's caretaker government. The charter called for the appointment of a chief of state with largely formal functions, a premier, and a national legislature. Four days later, the Council named Phan Khac Suu, a 63-year-old elder statesman, as chief of state; he in turn designated Tran Van Huong, a 61-year-old nationalist politician and Mayor of Saigon, as premier. Trouble arose as soon as the cabinet was installed. Students, Buddhists, and political factions angrily criticized Premier Huong's decision to appoint civil servants to the cabinet rather than active politicians. Street demonstrations and riots again broke out in Saigon. Buddhists were especially incensed at Premier Huong's insistence on separating religion and politics. They, as well as other political factions which had been behind the uprisings against General Khanh's military regime, felt that he had intentionally excluded their leading spokesmen. Charges were also made that the new ministers were followers of the late President Diem.

During the fall the situation in Saigon deteriorated badly. Not only was Washington concerned about the troubled political conditions, but, more immediately, it was disturbed by the stepped-up guerrilla activities of the Vietcong. On November 1 a devastating Vietcong mortar attack on the Bienhoa airbase took the lives of four Americans, destroyed five U.S. B-57 planes, and damaged some fifteen other aircraft. Frustrations steadily multiplied as the internal situation worsened and the American dilemma grew more acute. On the one hand there were pressures for more vigorous military action against the Vietcong, while, on the other, it was realized that such measures would be ineffective unless a stable government could be established. Late in November, Ambassador Taylor returned to Washington to review the problems raised by the growing strength of the Vietcong. From the viewpoint of the United States, the most discouraging aspect was the Saigon government's weakness in exercising control in the capital and in other parts of the country. After consulting with Ambassador Taylor, President Johnson indicated on December 1 that top priority would be given to strengthening Premier Huong's regime and making it more acceptable to opposition factions. At the same time he reaffirmed American support of South Vietnam's "struggle to defeat the externally supported insurgency and aggression being conducted against them." [28] Although consideration was also given to selective American air strikes on Communist supply routes and depots just beyond the South Vietnamese border in North Vietnam and Laos, no firm decisions appeared to have been made.

Signs pointed, however, to a stepped-up program against the infiltration routes into South Vietnam. A communiqué issued in Saigon on December 11 [29] disclosed an American offer of additional military and economic assistance to improve the effectiveness of efforts "to restrain the mounting infiltration of men and equipment by the Hanoi regime in support of the Vietcong." The United States promised to help increase the "numbers of military, para-military and police forces," to strengthen "the air defense of South Vietnam," and to provide "further economic assistance for a variety of forms of industrial urban and rural development." Full support was expressed "for the duly constituted Government of Prime Minister Huong."

Hostility to the new civilian government did not abate, and Buddhist leaders vociferously demanded Mr. Huong's ouster.

As in the period prior to President Diem's overthrow, their verbal attacks built up in ferocity. Unexpectedly, the thrust against the civilian regime came not from the Buddhists but from a group of young South Vietnamese officers, who carried out a swift, bloodless *coup* on December 20. Although these so-called "Young Turks" affirmed their support for the Huong government, they abolished the High National Council, which served as a provisional legislature, arrested some of its members, and reasserted the supreme power of the military that had been relinquished in August.

Caught by surprise, Ambassador Taylor warned the young military officers that unless the "legal government" was promptly restored, the United States might be compelled to reconsider its position in South Vietnam. At the same time Washington made clear that American support was based on the maintenance of a government free of "improper interference" by the military—this being an "essential condition for the successful prosecution of the effort to defeat the Viet Cong." [30] In defiance of the American call to restore constitutional order, General Khanh took full responsibility for the December 20 *coup*. He declared that the armed forces had to help settle disputes if they created situations favorable to the "common enemies," such as "Communism and colonialism." "We make sacrifices for the country's independence and the Vietnamese people's liberty, but not to carry out the policy of any foreign country," he said. "Better to live poor but proud as free citizens of an independent country than in ease and shame as slaves of the foreigners and Communists." [31] There was no doubt that the "foreigners" referred to were the Americans. Shortly after this statement was made, General Khanh, in an interview, accused Ambassador Taylor of meddling in South Vietnam's internal affairs.

The already tense U.S.-South Vietnamese relations were strained still further when a bomb exploded on Christmas eve in Saigon, demolishing a U.S. officers' quarters, killing two Americans, and injuring some hundred people. The incident emphasized the increasing danger from the Vietcong and the evident inability of the South Vietnamese government to counter the growing threat. To underscore its dissatisfaction with the situation, Washington instructed its American advisers on December 26 to withdraw from advance planning of all nonroutine military and civilian operations until the future status of American aid was clarified. Commitments to increase aid, it indicated, would be withdrawn if civilian rule were not restored.

At the end of the year, the situation in Vietnam continued to be precarious. It was clear that the political turmoil, religious discord, military factionalism, and the disrupting effects of regionalism would persist for some time. With South Vietnam buffeted by a social revolution of large dimensions, and subjected to mounting Communist attacks, the burden of resisting Vietcong insurgency could be expected to fall increasingly heavily on the United States. To what extent and for how long the United States would carry this burden could not, at the close of the year, be predicted.

CHAPTER SEVEN
FERMENT IN SOUTHEAST ASIA

PRIMARY OBJECTIVES of the United States in Southeast Asia have centered on the maintenance of the security and independence of the countries in the region, and the promotion of their economic and social well-being. Progress toward these goals was obstructed during the year by Peking's increasing pressures and by the growing discord that developed within, as well as between, the countries in the area. Vietnam, of course, was the arena of direct confrontation between the United States and Asian Communism, but the crisis in Southeast Asia embraced virtually the entire region. Profound political, social, and cultural changes could be observed not only in Vietnam, but in Laos, Cambodia, Burma, Malaysia, Indonesia, and even Thailand. In part, the changes were the heritage of Western colonialism, the impact of which had to a great extent shattered traditional Asian societies. More immediately, they resulted from the dismantling of colonial systems in the post-World War II years, and the acceleration of national revolutions. Directed against Western rule as well as Western influence, these national revolutions stimulated a ferment that was much inspired by a desire to find a new basis for adjusting traditional societies to meet the pressures of the modern world. But the national revolutions also awakened long-slumbering regional rivalries, as well as cultural, racial, religious, and psychological tensions.

For the United States the problems in Southeast Asia were essentially twofold: first, it was faced with the responsibility of helping those countries which desired American military assistance to thwart Communist domination; second, it had to contend with the larger process of revolutionary change. Although the United States could not determine Southeast Asia's future, it was concerned with constructively influencing developments in a manner that would be beneficial both to the countries of the region and to the peace and security of the world. How to attain these goals, especially when Asian attitudes were so hostile to the West, challenged the ingenuity and statesmanship of American leaders.

The complications of dealing with the situation were particularly acute in Cambodia and Laos. Both countries were on the front lines of the "hot" cold war in Southeast Asia. Each was used, Washington charged, as a sanctuary by Vietcong guerrillas for operations in the Vietnam border provinces and as an avenue for the infiltration of men, supplies, and weapons from North Vietnam. Cambodia, squeezed between two hostile neighbors —South Vietnam on its eastern border and Thailand to the west (the most important allies of the United States in the region)—had sought to maintain a position of neutrality. But Prince Norodom Sihanouk became extremely pessimistic about American efforts to force a solution in Southeast Asia by quelling the guerrilla warfare in South Vietnam through counterinsurgency tactics. By 1964 he decided that the best strategy to assure his country's survival would be to accommodate Cambodia to Communist China's leadership. During the year the shaky "coalition" government of Laos was threatened by renewed pro-Communist Pathet Lao attacks, and it was nearly toppled by an abortive right-wing *coup*. Although these thrusts were deflected and Cambodia remained outside Peking's camp, the prospect of maintaining the two countries as a neutral, buffer zone dimmed appreciably.

Nowhere was the national revolution in Southeast Asia more disturbing than in Indonesia where the Communists were numerous and their party extremely powerful. Moreover, to divert attention from domestic difficulties, President Sukarno stepped up his drive to "crush Malaysia." While the United States supported South Vietnamese efforts against the Vietcong, propped up the Laos "coalition" regime, and tried to straighten out its difficulties with Prince Sihanouk, Malaysia and Britain, which was committed to defend the newly created federation, bore the brunt of Indonesia's aggressions. The clear danger that presented itself in the struggle in Vietnam, in the fighting in Laos, and in the bitter quarrel between President Sukarno and Malaysia was that these local conflicts, if unchecked, could widen into a world war.

26. TROUBLES IN LAOS

From the outset, the Laos "coalition experiment" agreed upon by the fourteen-nation conference at Geneva in 1962 [1] had been a risky plan. It will be remembered that this plan had called for the neutralization of Laos, the withdrawal of all foreign military forces, a government of national unity that included the pro-Communist Pathet Lao, and the integration of the armed forces and local administration. Such a government was set up with the neutralist leader, Souvanna Phouma, as Prime Minister. Having signed the agreement to secure the removal of the American military presence in the country, Peking was confident that the Pathet Lao would acquire a dominant position in the coalition government. Laos would thus succumb to a Communist takeover, and there would be no need to attempt a military seizure with the attendant risk of American intervention. Both the United States and the Soviet Union, each for its own reasons, were anxious to create a buffer zone to avoid a military conflict. If the plan worked, moreover, it was thought that the formula might be applied elsewhere; thus providing a way to ease the tensions in the cold war.

Unfortunately, the chances for making the experiment succeed proved to be slim. The leftist Pathet Lao never made more than a pretense of cooperating with the neutralist and right-wing factions in the country. The individual armies of the three groups were neither integrated nor reduced in size. Each faction administered the areas controlled by its army. Although the

International Control Commission, set up at Geneva, had field teams consisting of Canadian, Indian, and Polish officers, it was paralyzed by its inability to travel freely inside Laos. Any of the three factions, moreover, could veto investigations into violations of a cease-fire. The "troika" arrangement, in addition, became unworkable since the Pathet Lao insisted that all decisions taken by neutralist and right-wing ministers were "illegal and void."

When the neutralists failed to bend to its pressures, the Pathet Lao, impatient for power, abandoned the coalition government in April 1963. Apparently encouraged by Communist China, an effort was made to obtain control by military, rather than political, tactics. These moves were undertaken cautiously. Although the Pathet Lao, with Peking's backing, had the military capability to defeat the neutralist and right-wing forces, neither the Pathet Lao nor Communist China wanted to invite full-scale American intervention.

The Pathet Lao's nibbling strategy precipitated a serious political crisis.[2] In February 1964 a Pathet Lao drive in central Laos led to the smashing of key right-wing positions that commanded the gateway to the strategic Plaine des Jarres. Frustrated by repeated military setbacks, a right-wing military junta overthrew the Laotian government on April 19 and formed a new ruling executive committee. The *coup*, which threatened to shatter the Geneva agreement and to create a grave new international crisis, caught the United States completely by surprise. Fearful that the coalition experiment would utterly collapse, Washington swiftly stepped in to reinstate neutralist Premier Prince Souvanna Phouma. London and Paris promptly supported Washington's move. Despite the strong urgings of the Western powers, rightist leaders refused to restore the neutralist coalition regime. But after vigorous prodding, they decided to invite Souvanna Phouma to head a new coalition regime. Washington's threat to withdraw American aid seemed to be decisive. As one Lao colonel who had taken part in the *coup* said, "Without aid, Laos cannot survive."

Although efforts were made by Prince Souvanna Phouma to enlarge and reorganize the coalition government and to unify the national army, they were immediately thwarted by the Pathet Lao, which again opened an attack on a right-wing battalion on the Plaine des Jarres. Hope of unifying the country dwindled. Unable to persuade his half-brother, and leader of the Pathet Lao, Prince Souphanouvong, to leave his headquarters in northern Laos and return to the capital at Vientiane, Prince Souvanna Phouma effected a merger of the neutralist and right-wing factions on May 2 and announced that he was assuming direction of all military affairs. Prince Souphanouvong promptly declared that he would never recognize this merger.

Two weeks later, under a strong Pathet Lao offensive, the neutralist position on the Plaine des Jarres crumbled. Secretary Rusk immediately appealed to a number of Western diplomats and to Soviet Ambassador Anatoly F. Dobrynin for all help possible to preserve Premier Souvanna's government. Washington declared that it was prepared to take any steps short of direct military intervention to stop the fighting. On May 20 President de Gaulle called for an emergency international conference to restore peace and neutrality in Laos, but the United States was cool to the idea, feeling that a conference would not solve the basic problem. The key difficulty, as Secretary Rusk pointed out, was North Vietnam's flagrant violation of the Geneva accord in extending active help to the Pathet Lao. In keeping with the Declaration on the Neutrality of Laos, the United States, he said, "withdrew all 600 of [its] military advisory personnel," but the Pathet Lao "allowed several thousand North Vietnamese military combat men to remain—these are the backbone of almost every Pathet-Lao battalion." Indeed, he asserted, it seemed "to be no more than a puppet subsidiary of Hanoi." Violations of the Laos Declaration, the Secretary added, had been "consistently" supported by Peking, and the International Control Commission had been unable to carry out its responsibilities. "The Soviet Union, while continuing to declare its support for the Geneva accords," Mr. Rusk noted, "has been either unwilling or unable to bring effective weight to bear to support them." [3] Thus Washington believed that the essential task was not to call a new conference—which could merely result in sanctioning Communist gains—but to secure compliance with the Geneva agreements that had already been made.

On May 21 the United States disclosed that unarmed U.S. jet planes piloted by Americans had begun flying reconnaissance missions over the Plaine des Jarres to gather information on Communist forces.[4] Undertaken at the request of the Laotian government, these missions, it said, were necessary because the Pathet Lao and North Vietnamese forces refused to permit the International Control Commission to inspect their areas. While further diplomatic maneuvers ensued, Pathet Lao forces steadily gained ground in the continuing fighting in central Laos. Alarmed at the deteriorating situation, the United States urged Britain and France to use their diplomatic contacts with Peking to try to persuade Communist China to halt the attacks. But this appeal achieved nothing. As Washington debated sending U.S. marines to Thailand (Thailand had already moved troops to the border of Laos), the Pathet Lao advance slowed to a halt.

But just as the United States thought that the dispute was moving back into the diplomatic and political arena, two Navy reconnaissance jets were shot down in central Laos on June 6 and 7.[5] Tension immediately heightened when Washington ordered American pilots to fire back when fired upon. Pressures arose, at the same time, for a more forceful demonstration of the American presence in Laos as much for prestige reasons as for stopping the attacks on unarmed U.S. planes. President Johnson decided to carry out a limited reprisal for the downing of the American planes. On June 9 U.S. Navy jets attacked a Communist gun position in north-central Laos. The small Royal Laotian air force also struck at Pathet Lao bases and troops on the Plaine des Jarres and near the South Vietnamese border. This was followed by thirty-six "sorties" which knocked out a number of Communist posts. Meanwhile, the United States announced that it would continue to fly its reconnaissance missions when necessary and would retaliate against any guns that fired at the planes.[6]

Warning that "peace in Indo-China and Southeast Asia" was "hanging by a thread," Peking said that further expansion of the conflict would be met with a powerful rebuff; but it carefully avoided a specific commitment to intervene with armed forces. The statement was interpreted by Western observers as Chinese pressure for acceptance of an earlier demand to reconvene the fourteen-nation conference.[7] Washington asserted that it would not relax its diplomatic and limited military efforts in Laos until the neutralist government was revitalized. To achieve this goal, Premier Souvanna Phouma appealed to Prince Souphanouvong to meet him in a neutral country to try to settle the crisis. "International tension is mounting," he said, "and it is absolutely necessary for us to meet without delay." [8]

Diplomatic sparring continued during the summer. While Britain pressed for a meeting of the three Laotian factions abroad, the Soviet Union insisted on an immediate, unconditional fourteen-power conference to deal with the Laos problem. Communist China demanded that the meeting be held in August, and it expressed its "approval" of Moscow's support. But London and Washington demurred on the ground that no talks could begin unless (1) agreement was reached on an effective ceasefire, (2) Prince Souvanna Phouma was recognized as Premier rather than head of one of the three factions, and (3) the Pathet Lao forces were withdrawn to the position held in May prior to their offensive against the neutralists.

To break the deadlock, the International Control Commission took steps to arrange a meeting of the leaders of the three factions in Paris. When they met on August 28, they found their views were too far apart to set a date for a formal conference. In preliminary talks held during the next several weeks, each side presented its conditions for ending the strife. Prince Souvanna proposed neutralization of the strategic Plaine des Jarres, occupation of the area by a mixed force of the three factions, and placing it under the International Control Commission. Laotian pro-Communists rejected this plan and offered instead to agree to a cease-fire, to become effective October 1, under which the Pathet Lao forces would yield positions they had taken on the Plaine des Jarres since May 16. In effect, this would have meant a return to the state of affairs that prevailed before June 1962. But Pathet Lao leader Prince Souphanouvong qualified this proposal by insisting on barring the Control Commission from central Laos. This move was interpreted as an attempt by the Pathet Lao to "paper over" the Laotian dispute while preserving its control over the area. Formal meetings started on September 21, and agreement was reached on an agenda to discuss a cease-fire and the peaceful settlement of the military conflict, the reconvening of the fourteen-nation Geneva conference, and the establishment of a coalition government acceptable to the three factions. These talks dragged on without any productive results.

The military situation, meanwhile, showed no signs of improvement. Late in July the Royal Lao army had launched an offensive that had cleared the major north-south road in central Laos of Pathet Lao forces. The Pathet Lao retaliated, but a successful counterattack in September greatly improved the morale of the Royal Lao soldiers. Shortly after Premier Khrushchev's ouster, the United States urged the new Soviet regime to honor the 1962 accords on Laos for restoring the peace and neutrality of the country. Responding on November 24, Moscow expressed its desire for a "peaceful settlement" of the Laotian problem but argued that a solution should be left to the "good will" of the three conflicting factions in the coalition government. As the year drew to a close, it was evident that the military stalemate would continue. While the Royal Lao forces, on the whole, scored a net gain over the Pathet Lao troops in 1964, no significant progress was made in settling the internal conflict. Nevertheless, as the crisis in South Vietnam deepened, signs pointed to increased American support of the Laotian government and to stronger military action to deprive the Vietcong from using Laotian territory as a sanctuary.

27. CAMBODIAN GAMESMANSHIP

The deterioration of the situation in Laos was matched by a worsening of the relations between the United States and Cambodia. After President Diem's downfall in November 1963, Prince Sihanouk had gradually veered toward seeking an alliance with Communist China. As he did so, the points of friction between Washington and Phnom Penh steadily increased. Relations reached a low point during the autumn of 1963 when dissident Cambodians had broadcast violently anti-Sihanouk propaganda from South Vietnam and Thailand. Convinced that the United States was behind this move, Prince Sihanouk had warned Washington that if it did not stop, he would seek an accommodation with the Communist bloc and divest himself of Western aid. At the same time, he launched an economic swing to the left, nationalizing the banks and the largely foreign-controlled import-export companies. On November 19 Prince Sihanouk renounced the American aid program of $30 million annually. Shortly afterwards anti-American feeling was intensified when President Kennedy was assassinated and Field Marshal Sarit Thanarat of Thailand died on December 8. Cambodia declared a holiday to celebrate the death of Sarit, who was considered a hated enemy. Americans had heard derogatory remarks on the official Cambodian radio not only about Sarit but also about President Kennedy. Denying that the Cambodian broadcast had implied joy at President Kennedy's death, Prince Sihanouk demanded an apology from the United States for the allegation. The Philippines tried to mediate the quarrel, and in January hope was expressed for a reconciliation. Washington said that it was prepared to meet Cambodia half-way—but no more than that—to restore friendly relations. Part of the difficulty lay in Prince Sihanouk's insistence on calling a conference to guarantee Cambodia's neutrality. He openly threatened to sign a formal alliance with Communist China unless the West met his demand. Although the United States wanted Cambodian friendship, it hesitated to accept Prince Sihanouk's proposal for an international conference, fearing that it would undermine South Vietnamese morale.

In an effort to resolve the problem, Britain prepared two documents: a draft declaration on Cambodian neutrality, and a protocol suggesting arrangements to supervise any agreement that might be reached at a conference of the fourteen nations that had signed the Geneva Declaration on the Neutrality of Laos in 1962.[9] Prince Sihanouk expressed his approval of the British proposal, and he indicated that "after a conference" differences with the United States would be "solved." Washington believed, however, that a signed declaration, endorsed by the Geneva powers, would be an adequate substitute for a conference. Frankly concerned that a conference which included Communist China and its supporters might extend the discussion of the neutrality of Cambodia to that of all Southeast Asia, the United States delayed its decision. But Prince Sihanouk flatly asserted that a declaration alone would not satisfy his needs, and he fixed May 1 as the deadline for an American agreement to attend a conference. If this was not met, he threatened to sever diplomatic relations, to abandon Cambodia's neutral status, and to sign assistance pacts with "certain great friendly countries."

The situation took an ominous turn on February 4 when South Vietnamese planes bombed the Cambodian village of Mong, killing five Cambodian farmers and seriously wounding six. Declaring that this was the 163rd "aggression" Cambodia had suffered from South Vietnam, Prince Sihanouk again threatened to align his country with Communist China unless the West guaranteed his country's borders and neutrality. He called for a meeting in Phnom Penh by the end of March of representatives of the United States, Thailand, South Vietnam, and Cambodia. In return for a pledge at this conference to guarantee Cambodian neutrality and its territorial integrity "as fixed by present frontiers," he promised "not to permit any foreigners or any rebels to come into our territory to establish themselves or to transport armament," or to allow anyone to establish military bases inside the country.

The United States expressed support for the four-power conference, and South Vietnam also agreed to it in principle. Washington thought that this meeting might result in agreement to establish international supervision of Cambodian borders. Charging that the United States intended to set up a "mixed commission" to outline the frontiers, Prince Sihanouk now rejected the four-power proposal and accused the United States, South Vietnam, and Thailand of seeking to partition his nation. "Cambodia's frontiers," said the Cambodian ruler, "have been clearly defined with Thailand in international treaties and the International Court in The Hague and with South Vietnam by very favorable demarcation lines drawn by the then French Governors of Cochin China." [10] He declared that the American "counterproposals" were "unacceptable and inadmissible," and underscored his rebuff to Washington by sending a Cambodian delegation to Peking and Moscow.

Failure of these diplomatic maneuvers led to a violent riot in the Cambodian capital on March 12 that resulted in the sacking of the American and British embassies. Although the Cambodian government promised to pay for the damages, Prince Sihanouk observed that the riot was "comprehensible," since the Cambodian people had been goaded by "repeated humiliations" inflicted on the country by the "Anglo-Saxon powers." Peking immediately pledged its support of what it called the "just patriotic struggle" of the Cambodian people against "United States imperialist policies of war." Three days after the riot, Cambodia received a shipment of arms aid from Communist China, and Sihanouk proposed to negotiate with North Vietnam for guarantees of his frontiers and to establish friendly relations with the pro-Communist Pathet Lao.

To counter the increasingly dangerous situation, South Vietnam took steps to end its friction with Cambodia and to reestablish normal diplomatic relations with Laos. These moves were abruptly halted on March 20 when a South Vietnamese ground and air attack, with American military advisers participating, hit the Cambodian village of Chantrea. Seventeen persons were reported killed and thirteen injured. Although

South Vietnam and the United States officially expressed their sympathy and said the attack had been an error (Washington denied that American advisers with South Vietnamese forces had "engaged in any firing or directly participated in the military action during the incident"), Cambodia demanded the payment of reparations and the calling of a multinational conference at Geneva to settle disputes over its frontiers.

With no resolution of the issue in sight, Cambodia on May 13 asked for a meeting of the Security Council "as soon as possible" to consider the "repeated acts of aggression" against its territory and civilian population by United States-South Vietnamese forces. The Security Council met from May 19 to 28. Seeking to explain the reasons for the military actions, Ambassador Stevenson stressed three points. First, he said, part of the difficulty lay in the fact that the Cambodian border was not clearly marked. "There are places," Mr. Stevenson indicated, "where one does not know whether he stands on one side of the frontier or the other." Second, evidence indicated that there were collusive arrangements whereby Cambodian border guards granted aid and safehaven to Vietcong insurgents. Third, Ambassador Stevenson noted that the crucial issue was not the question of border disputes but the fact that North Vietnam used Cambodian territory "as a passageway, a source of supply, and a sanctuary for its forces." "It is the people of the Republic of Viet-Nam who are the major victims of armed aggression," he said. "It is they who are fighting for their independence against violence directed from outside their borders. . . . There is fighting in Viet-Nam today only because the political settlement for Viet-Nam reached at Geneva in 1954 had been deliberately and flagrantly and systematically violated." [11]

The United States emphatically rejected Cambodia's suggestion for a new meeting of the fourteen-power Geneva conference. For the first time, however, it indicated that it was prepared to debate the entire Southeast Asian situation in the United Nations, and it tacitly acknowledged that the three-nation commission set up by the 1954 Geneva agreement to supervise the Indochina accords was basically unworkable. Ambassador Stevenson suggested that an immediate solution to the South Vietnam-Cambodia border disputes might be obtained if the United Nations created an international force to watch over the frontier.

Both South Vietnam and Cambodia supported the United States proposal that U.N. inspectors should be stationed along their troubled borders. But Cambodia refused to pay any of the cost of a U.N. presence, and insisted that the task of checking border violations "must" be left to the International Control Commission, which had been established by the 1954 Geneva conference. Nevertheless, Cambodian support of U.N. intervention in its dispute with South Vietnam and the United States was seen as a break in the deadlock. On June 4 the Security Council, by a vote of 9-0-2, adopted a resolution to establish a three-man committee to investigate the friction along the Cambodian-South Vietnamese border and "to consider such measures as may prevent any recurrence of such incidents." [12]

The United Nations mission arrived in Saigon on July 5. In its report to the Security Council at the end of a month, the three-man committee strongly recommended the resumption of political relations between South Vietnam and Cambodia, the sending of U.N. observers to keep the frontier area under surveillance, and the taking of practical steps to delimit and mark the borders. But it concluded that violations of the Cambodian frontier were symptoms rather than causes of the strained relations between the two countries. The difficulties stemmed more fundamentally, the committee said, from Cambodia's avowed policy of neutrality and South Vietnam's unequivocal pro-Western stand. [13]

Although the U.N. inquiry helped reduce the incidents along the Cambodian-South Vietnamese frontier, hostility between the two countries was not eased. Early in September Cambodia rejected the U.N. recommendations to send out an observer team and to take steps to define its borders more clearly. It charged that the three-man committee had erred in concentrating on frontier incidents, and had exceeded its authority in recommending the resumption of diplomatic relations with South Vietnam. Most serious of all, Cambodia felt that the U.N.

mission had taken account only of South Vietnam's territorial claims and not those of Cambodia.

Attempts to remove the friction between the two countries soon reached an impasse. At the same time Prince Sihanouk's drift toward Communist China became more marked. On October 6 the Cambodian Prince announced that Peking had extended "new and most important" economic and military aid to his kingdom. After an eight-day state visit to Communist China, he declared that the relations between Peking and Cambodia had become closer than ever. Describing Communist China as "our No. 1 friend," Prince Sihanouk remarked, "We are indeed not only friends but brothers in arms."

During the following months relations between Cambodia and the United States continued to deteriorate badly. Late in October a new incident occurred when American and South Vietnamese aircraft fired on targets in Cambodia. These attacks were in response to the increase in Vietcong activity from bases in Cambodia. South Vietnam formally apologized for the strafing of a Cambodian village, but Prince Sihanouk angered by these raids turned to Moscow, Peking, and Hanoi for explicit guarantees of their support of Cambodia's territorial integrity. No concrete agreements were concluded, but Communist China and the Soviet Union assured Prince Sihanouk that they would not ignore any acts of aggression that endangered the security of Cambodia.

In mid-November Prince Sihanouk threatened to expel the U.S. Embassy staff from the country, but he had second thoughts about it. Breaking relations with the United States, he decided, might reduce support for Cambodia from the Communist bloc since Communist countries might then take Cambodia's sympathies for granted. In an effort to restore normal relations, Washington proposed on November 16 that talks be held in New Delhi, an overture accepted by Prince Sihanouk. He named two officials to represent him, and President Johnson designated Philip W. Bonsal as his representative. South Vietnam, however, immediately declared that it would not be bound by any agreement that might be reached. Unfortunately, the talks in New

Delhi from December 8 to December 17 did not resolve the
differences between the United States and Cambodia. Prince
Sihanouk's drift toward Peking continued. Convinced that the
Vietcong would ultimately take over in South Vietnam, he
remarked in an interview, "If I wait until the moment when
the Americans are driven out in humiliation and the Viet Cong
are powerful, the Communists will have no reason to offer me
any guarantees of my country's territorial integrity. . . . If I
bargain with them before all is lost by the Americans, I have
something to offer them that is of value." [14]

To the United States, it appeared that Prince Sihanouk was
playing a dangerous game. Though Washington recognized that
the Cambodian leader was not Communist-oriented in his sympathies, the effect of his actions drew him increasingly into Peking's
camp. By the end of the year this trend reached serious proportions; but with the United States heavily committed militarily
in South Vietnam, the chances of effecting a reversal seemed
discouraging.

28. SUKARNO CREATES A "SECOND FRONT" IN MALAYSIA

In addition to the Vietnam "war," in which Laos and Cambodia found themselves deeply embroiled, Southeast Asia was
the scene of yet another conflict that had the potential of en-
dangering world peace. President Sukarno's aggressive ambitions
and his determination to "crush Malaysia" continued to pose a
most frustrating problem to the West. In 1962–63 Sukarno had
successfully invoked the threat of war to bring about the withdrawal of the Dutch from West New Guinea and the transfer
of this territory to Indonesia. The Indonesian government thus
secured sovereignty over the entire territory of the former Dutch
East Indies. After achieving this long-standing goal, Sukarno
then directed his attention to the Federation of Malaysia, established on September 16, 1963. Malaysia had been formed by
a merger of Malaya and Singapore, with the addition of Sarawak
and Sabah; the latter were part of the northern third of the
huge island of Borneo—the bulk of which belonged to Indonesia.

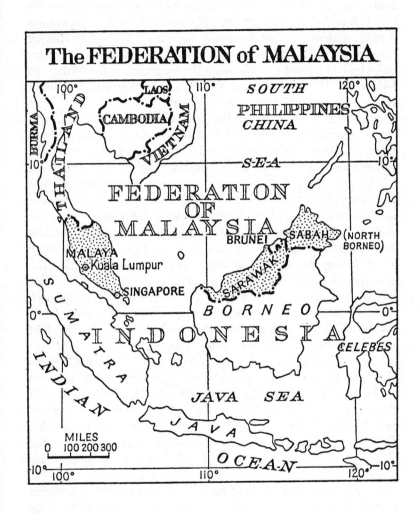

The FEDERATION of MALAYSIA

(The tiny British protectorate of Brunei in Borneo was invited into the federation but refused to join.) Prior to the creation of Malaysia, the United Nations had conducted a survey in Sarawak and Sabah and found that the inhabitants desired incorporation into the federation. But Indonesia disputed this finding. Hoping to extend Indonesian control over all of Borneo, President Sukarno had sought to undermine the formation of the Malaysian federation. When this maneuver failed, he adopted a militant course to destroy the newly created state.

Attacking the new federation, Sukarno charged that it was simply a British satellite that had been conceived primarily to maintain Britain's economic position in Southeast Asia. The Indonesian leader vehemently objected to a U.K.-Malaysian treaty, permitting Britain to retain bases in Singapore and Malaya for the purpose of helping the new federation's defense and preserving peace in Southeast Asia. He insisted that the British presence was a threat to Indonesia, recalling perhaps that Singapore had been a source of smuggled arms to rebel areas during the 1958 insurrection against Sukarno's rule. The assertion that Malaysia's defense arrangements posed a threat was not convincing, particularly since Indonesia had 100,000,000 inhabitants and a well-equipped army of 300,000 men, while Malaysia had 10,000,000 inhabitants and an army of only eight battalions, some of them not up to full strength.

The motivation for Sukarno's objective to "crush" the Malaysian federation was a compound of many factors, but it appeared to be mainly inspired by the Indonesian leader's imperialist dream to create a "pan-Indonesia" in an "Indonesian Ocean," and by his desire to divert the attention of the Indonesian people from their own domestic hardships. Sukarno opposed the British presence in Malaysia not only because it blocked his ambition to absorb the northern Borneo territories, but also because it thwarted his long-range goal of asserting Indonesian domination in general throughout Southeast Asia. Ever since his youth he had believed that it was his mission to lead Indonesia to a place of power among the great nations of the world. This could not happen, Sukarno felt, while Western influence

remained in the Southwest Pacific. Eventually, he was convinced, the day would come when Indonesia would become
sufficiently strong so that the last traces of the West in Southeast
Asia would be swept away.

A more immediate reason seemed to be Indonesia's serious
economic trouble. By staying nonaligned, President Sukarno had
managed to borrow (or be given) almost $2 billion from both
the West and the Communist bloc to sustain his country's economy and maintain its armed forces. But Indonesia continued
to be fiscally bankrupt, and its future remained mortgaged for
the next twenty years. Corruption plagued the government,
and industries produced at only a fraction of their capacities.
The task of transforming an archipelago of 2,500 scattered islands into a nation with a sense of its own identity was indeed
staggering. Sukarno was well aware of the fact that if Malaysia
succeeded in solving its domestic political and ethnic problems
and became a prosperous nation, especially with British aid,
his country would suffer by contrast. Tangible proof would be
offered that the development of newly independent Asian countries could be achieved by maintaining friendly relations with
former colonial powers. By stirring up trouble with Malaysia,
the Indonesian leader aimed not only at ensuring the failure
of the new federation, but also at deflecting opposition to his
own rule. Despite the fact that at least one-third of Indonesia's
exports went to Malaysia, he did not hesitate to cut off trade
with that much-needed market shortly after the federation was
established. The action, however, was far more harmful to Indonesia than it was to Malaysia.

At the beginning of the year, President Sukarno renewed his
attempts to enlist the support of the Philippines in his campaign
against Malaysia. Like Indonesia, the Philippines had broken
diplomatic relations with the new federation. Its quarrel related
to a long-dormant claim to part of Sabah, which it had sought
to reactivate. The dispute was relatively minor, and prospects
were reasonably good for settlement. The Indonesian leader,
nevertheless, was hopeful that the Philippines could be tempted
to join in a "common strategy" against Malaysia. On a visit to

Manila in January, he offered to shift the annual trade volume of some $200 million that formerly went to Malaysians to the Filipinos. But this maneuver did not work. President Diosdado Macapagal refused to join the Indonesian trade boycott or become involved in any way with Sukarno's terrorist raids along the northern Borneo border.

Concerned about Indonesia's deepening quarrel with Malaysia, President Johnson sent Attorney-General Robert F. Kennedy on a thirteen-day mission to see what could be done about finding a peaceful solution to problems. On January 18 Mr. Kennedy met President Sukarno in Tokyo, where the Indonesian leader was vacationing. The Attorney-General argued for a curb on the guerrilla raids into Sarawak and Sabah. Warning that the fighting could develop into a major conflict, he urged that it be halted as a first step toward achieving a peaceful solution to the Malaysian dispute. After his meeting with Sukarno, Mr. Kennedy was encouraged in his belief that Malaysia, Indonesia, and the Philippines would work out their differences around a conference table. "This is an Asian dispute," he declared, "and it must in the last analysis be decided by Asian nations." [15] The major results of Mr. Kennedy's mission were a cease-fire and the agreement of the three nations to hold a foreign ministers' conference in Bangkok the first week in February. This was arranged as a preliminary to a summit meeting. Grave doubts arose that there would be any significant change in the situation, for President Sukarno had already cast a dark shadow on Mr. Kennedy's mediation efforts when on January 23 he vowed continued hostility toward Malaysia. Speaking to 15,000 cheering youths, he declared that his island nation would press its drive to crush Malaysia unless the federation was altered to suit Indonesia's taste. "Onward, never retreat," he cried. "Crush Malaysia."

Although the British welcomed a cease-fire on Borneo and the conference set up by Mr. Kennedy, they were frankly skeptical as to whether the cease-fire would last, and what the conference would accomplish. But Mr. Kennedy remarked sardonically that if the conference was not successful, "then they can all go back into the jungle and shoot at each other again. And all they would have lost is 2 weeks' killing each other." [16]

Trouble over the cease-fire, as British officials feared, developed immediately. Clashes continued virtually without pause. On February 6 the foreign ministers of Malaysia, the Philippines, and Indonesia met in Bangkok. Thailand was formally asked to supervise the cease-fire, and both Indonesia and Malaysia pledged to respect the truce along the Borneo border. Nevertheless, President Sukarno refused to pull his guerrillas out of Malaysian territory. After six days of bargaining, the foreign ministers could only promise to preserve the cease-fire that Mr. Kennedy had secured. But the fighting persisted. At the end of February Malaysia asked Britain to provide air defense against Indonesian attempts to supply guerrilla forces remaining on its territory. Hopes aroused by the Kennedy mission quickly faded.

Tunku Abdul Rahman, Prime Minister of the Malaysian federation, charged early in March that the Indonesians had never carried out their side of the bargain with respect to the cease-fire. "To them," he said, "a cease-fire means that we cease but not they." On April 23 Malaysia released a sixty-four-page white paper declaring that President Sukarno's policy was to attack from the outside and also to "create actively subversive violent communal organizations within Malaysia." Indonesia's aim, it charged, was to pursue an expansionist program in Southeast Asia that was directed toward the eventual absorption of Singapore and the Malay Peninsula into a "Greater Indonesia." Its "confrontation" policy against Malaysia, the document asserted, was "the natural result of the long-term Indonesian policy and not the result of the formation of Malaysia, which is only an excuse made use of by Indonesia to launch her present campaign of aggression." [17]

Both Britain and the United States urged Prince Abdul Rahman during the spring to meet with President Sukarno to try to find out exactly what Indonesia wanted with regard to Malaysia. On May 27 he finally consented, but on the condition that Indonesian guerrillas be withdrawn from Sarawak and Sabah. The following week President Sukarno indicated

that this would be done, and he permitted a border check by
Thailand. As a result, arrangements were made for a summit
meeting of the leaders of Malaysia, the Philippines, and
Indonesia; the conference was held in Tokyo, June 14–21.
Delays occurred before formal discussions started, since Prince
Abdul Rahman insisted on a substantial removal of Indonesian
troops from the northern Borneo area, which had not taken place.
At the meeting the Philippines proposed setting up an African-
Asian conciliation commission to "study" the conflict and recom-
mend a solution. Sukarno agreed to this proposal and said he
would abide by the recommendations of the commission.
Although Malaysia also agreed to it "in principle," Prince Abdul
Rahman declared that the conciliation commission should conduct its study and present its report only after verification that
the last of the guerrillas had left the North Borneo territories.
But President Sukarno replied: "No, No! Withdrawal must be
in conformity with a political settlement." The summit talks
thus ended in failure, and as one Malaysian official said,
"We are clear back to where we started from."

The crux of the problem, as it had been from the outset, was
how to enforce an effective cease-fire. From the time Mr. Kennedy
had arranged a cease-fire until the summit talks, seven major
Indonesian incursions took place into Sarawak and Sabah, and
more than forty other violations occurred. President Sukarno
occasionally threw out hints that he would call off his "crush
Malaysia" campaign if the British quit their Singapore base,
withdrew from Malaysia, and terminated their guarantee of
the federation's independence. The British could not accept
such conditions. The reasons were obvious. As an astute observer pointed out, the Indonesian leader's terms were no compromise "but the opening in a play to annex Sarawak and Sabah
and oil-rich Brunei, after which Sukarno would see how best
to move in on Singapore, one of the world's great ports and then
on Malaya itself." [18]

With the collapse of the Tokyo meeting the situation took
a more dangerous turn. Late in June Deputy Premier Mikoyan
went to Indonesia and pledged Russian help in President Su-

karno's fight to crush Malaysia. Mr. Mikoyan declared Indonesia would receive modern weapons—"far better than the weapons possessed by the British in this area"—and Russian experts would be sent to train troops in the use of the arms. Support of Indonesia, he said, did not contradict the Soviet Union's policy of "peaceful coexistence," because the Indonesian struggle against Malaysia was "just."

Prince Abdul Rahman came to Washington in July. He frankly told President Johnson that he saw no chance of making peace with Indonesia, and asked the United States to sell him planes and ships and to help train his military forces. The President agreed to admit Malaysian personnel into American training schools—the first military link was thus established between the two nations—and the request for additional aid was turned over to the Defense Department for prompt and sympathetic study.[19] In spite of these signs of support for Malaysia the United States expressed hope that American influence could still be retained in Indonesia. Concern existed that some day the large Communist party might seize power. American aid to Indonesia —since 1950 it had totaled $712 million—had been cut back heavily to about $15 million since trouble began over Malaysia, but Washington did not want to stop it completely. Nevertheless, in spite of administration objections, Congress sought to prohibit further aid and to end the training of Indonesian military personnel in this country.

Malaysia's external difficulties were compounded by internal unrest. While Prince Abdul Rahman was visiting the United States, serious communal rioting broke out on July 21 between Malays and Chinese in Singapore (trouble subsequently erupted again early in September), disclosing the fragile nature of the new federation. Conflict between the Chinese and Malay communities was deep-rooted. The long-standing racial, economic, and political rivalry was intensified in the contest between the two groups for a paramount position in Malaysia. The Malays were largely of rural background, and they looked with suspicion on the urban and capitalist Chinese merchants who had managed to gain an overwhelming proportion of the indigenous

wealth in Malaysia. Although under the federation's constitution the Malays were granted special rights and privileges,
and voting in the Federal Parliament was weighted in their
favor, dismay arose that the Chinese were gaining in political
power. Fears were expressed that unless the tensions between
the Malay and Chinese communities were mitigated, the new
federation might not endure.

While Malaysia was occupied with its internal troubles, the
Indonesian campaign entered a new stage. Sukarno, in a three-
hour speech on August 17, harshly denounced the United States
and proclaimed Indonesia's intention to dedicate itself to "A
Year of Living Dangerously." The same day, three groups of
about thirty guerrillas made seaborne landings in Malaya, about
thirty miles northwest of Singapore. Most of the guerrillas were
quickly captured. This first invasion of the Malay Peninsula
itself was seen as an attempt to drive a wedge between the
Chinese community and the Malays and to exploit their animosity by promoting uneasiness and confusion. Indonesia was
confident that some day the Malays would seek its help to
avoid being dominated by the more aggressive and affluent
Chinese. On September 1–2 another thirty paratroopers were
dropped, in the hope that with the support of dissident Malays
and Chinese they could begin a campaign of sabotage and
terror. Virtually all of them, however, were rounded up.

Prince Abdul Rahman immediately accused Indonesia of
"blatant" and "inexcusable aggression" and asked for an urgent
meeting of the Security Council. Evidence indicated, he said,
that Indonesia was preparing a "big offensive" against Malaysia
with saboteurs and agents. A state of emergency was proclaimed.
Indonesia frankly admitted that it was "now on the offensive
to wipe out" enemy military bases. As a new crisis threatened,
Britain airlifted a 500-man antiaircraft regiment from West Germany to Singapore for "emergency operational duties" in the
Far East and announced that four warships from its Mediterranean fleet would follow. London made it emphatically clear
that it would strike back militarily against any new Indonesian
incursions or attacks on Malaya.

On September 9 the Security Council met to consider Malaysia's charges of Indonesian aggression and request that it be condemned. Declaring that the landing of Indonesian paratroopers on the Malay Peninsula was "inadmissible," Ambassador Stevenson urged the United Nations to establish conditions that would make possible negotiations between the two Southeast Asian states.[20] The Indonesian representative made no attempt to refute the accusation. He asserted that the "war," which had been going on for "some time" in the region, was not against Malaysia, but against colonialism. Arguing that the real cause of friction was British "neocolonialism," he claimed that his country was justified in fighting it.

A Norwegian draft resolution[21] deplored Indonesian attacks on Malaysia, called on both sides to halt hostilities and refrain from violating each other's territorial integrity and independence, and suggested that the two powers negotiate on the basis of an African-Asian conciliation commission, as had been proposed at the June Tokyo meetings. Indonesia immediately objected to the appeal to respect Malaysia's territorial integrity and independence. "An independent and sovereign Malaysia has never existed for us," the Indonesian delegate said. "What does exist is a British Malaysia, which we could not and cannot recognize." On September 17 the Soviet Union (joined by Czechoslovakia) cast its 102nd veto to defeat the resolution by a vote of 9 to 2, thereby frustrating any immediate effective action by the United Nations to ease tensions in the area. Malaysia, nevertheless, was gratified that the African and Asian members of the Security Council had supported the resolution. Heretofore many African and Asian nations had often operated on the theory that an attack on a colonial power or on a former colony which had remained allied with its former metropole, as was the case with Malaysia, was not aggression. Despite its defeat, Malaysia believed that something substantial had been won.

Although the African-Asian vote on the Malaysian resolution indicated that perhaps a change of attitude had taken place, Prince Abdul Rahman declared, "The framers of the Charter could not have intended to promote in the same scheme two contradictory doctrines—securing rapid freedom to colonial peoples and leaving almost all of them with redress at the mercy of any predatory power which has arms enough at its elbow to overwhelm a small power, with which it is ready to provoke a quarrel. All protestations of conscious progress toward a peaceful world lose their meaning, when the principal agency to avoid an armed conflict and promote peace is unwilling to act, not because the occasion does not demand it but because to act to meet that demand would hurt a political friend." [22]

During the following weeks, new efforts were made through private diplomatic channels to initiate peace talks between Malaysia and Indonesia, but they failed. Sukarno steadily increased the attacks on the federation. In the course of the year, more than a thousand armed Indonesians infiltrated into Sarawak, Sabah, and Malaya to wreck installations, panic the population, and set up jungle bases to organize subversion and carry on guerrilla warfare. While most of these raiders were killed or captured, many fled back to Indonesia. As the year drew to a close, the situation took a new and ominous turn. Indonesia made a final break with the West, withdrawing from the United Nations in retaliation for the seating of Malaysia as a nonpermanent member for a one-year term on the Security Council. This move was seen not only as an expression of Sukarno's displeasure over Malaysia's seating, but also—and perhaps more importantly—as an indication of Indonesia's growing ties with Peking. Communist China's nuclear explosion in October and improvements in its economic conditions were viewed as key factors in the Indonesian leader's decision to quit the United Nations.

The conflict between Indonesia and Malaysia during the year did not reach the proportions of the struggle that prevailed in Vietnam. With Britain's military support, the Malaysian federation managed to blunt Sukarno's guerrilla raids. Nevertheless, as long as the Indonesian leader persisted in his course of aggression, the threat of a full-scale war remained. The United States, of course, was deeply concerned about the extension of fighting in Southeast Asia; but being heavily committed in South Vietnam, its role in this "second" theater of war was minimal and largely limited to diplomatic efforts to persuade Indonesia, Malaysia, and the Philippines to settle their quarrels.

The problems in individual countries differed substantially when viewed in the whole Southeast Asian context. The Indonesian-Malaysian imbroglio was of a different order from the conflict in Vietnam; so, too, were the special problems of Laos and Cambodia. Although Hanoi's Vietcong-directed guerrilla and terrorist activities in South Vietnam and Sukarno's imperialistic aspirations constituted immediate dangers to the West and to world peace, the causes of turbulence in Southeast Asia encompassed more than these visible disturbances. The spread of Asian Communism was one facet of the problem, and its appeal in Southeast Asia was not purely the result of a conspiracy directed from Peking. In addition to the disruptive element of Asian Communism, the turbulence of the region was compounded by important historic, ethnic, and social cleavages, the lack of a sense of identity or loyalty to a national government, and regional, religious, and cultural rivalries. Hence, it appeared improbable that a solution to the problems of Southeast Asia could be achieved through military means alone. The United States, of course, recognized that this was so; it would have liked nothing better than to see the peoples of the region work out their own problems within the framework of their own societies and traditions, thus permitting the process of change to take its course. As long as Communist aggression persisted, however, the United States was compelled to assume responsibility for helping the countries of Southeast Asia to resist such aggression so that they could be permitted to decide their future without coercion.

CHAPTER EIGHT
POLITICS AND CHANGE IN LATIN AMERICA

MANY ANXIETIES which had formerly perturbed the United States in its relations with Latin America were quieted, though not dispelled, during the year. Disturbances in Panama and troubles with Cuba over Guantánamo Bay and American air reconnaissance, to be sure, created tense situations. But overshadowing these crises was the fact that *Fidelismo* had lost much of its appeal, and the thrust of the Communist offensive on the continent no longer appeared as ominous as it had in earlier years. A hopeful augury was seen in Venezuela. For the first time in that country's 150 years of independent existence, a freely elected president completed his constitutional five-year term, and a peaceful political transfer of power took place with the inauguration of his elected successor. Significantly, the change in Latin America's climate was reflected in the sudden overthrow on April 1 of Brazilian President João Goulart, whose extreme leftist policies and financial mismanagement had been a constant source of apprehension. In July the United States scored a major diplomatic victory when the Organization of American States voted to impose sanctions and isolate Cuba. Secretary Rusk hailed the O.A.S. conference as "the most important ever held in this hemisphere." The defeat of the Popular Action Front, which was sympathetic to Castroism, in Chile's national election in September also marked a major political turn.

In Washington an intensive reappraisal was made of the Alliance for Progress. Disappointment with its specific accomplishments had been expressed both in the United States and in Latin America. Both sides fully recognized the merits of the approach which the Alliance represented, although many Latin American republics were worried about increasing their dependence on the United States. President de Gaulle, well aware of their strong drive to assert themselves, attempted in his visit to Mexico in March and in his unprecedented tour to ten South American countries during late September and early October to encourage a spirit of independence (of the United States) and to foster closer cultural and economic ties with France and Europe.

Although the United States and Latin America were bound together by a broad community of hemispheric interests and extensive economic ties, historically their relations had often been marked by a heritage of suspicion and antagonism. These were in part a product of cultural differences, the striking economic disparities between the two regions, and the predominant power position of the United States in the Western Hemisphere. Traditional Yankeephobia could not be easily erased. But Latin American antipathy toward the United States, especially following World War II, was not solely the result of emotional prejudice. More fundamental was the fact that many Latin American leaders viewed hemispheric problems in far different terms than the United States did. Divergencies in outlook were evident long before the insults and violence that greeted Vice-President Nixon during his trip to Latin America in 1958 awakened Washington to the critical nature of the situation. But even after the United States embarked on a more dynamic policy which culminated in President Kennedy's Alliance for Progress and the signing of the Charter of Punta del Este in August 1961, basic differences remained.

To Latin Americans, the primary motivation behind U.S. sponsorship of the Alliance for Progress seemingly was to bolster the Western Hemisphere's political security against the threat of the spread of the Cuban revolution and Communism. Actually, the United States had come to the conclusion that new economic and social measures were necessary to cope with Latin American problems before Fidel Castro came to power. Unquestionably, however, the Cuban leader's anti-American politics and his espousal of Communism hastened and colored the American response. But many Latin Americans did not look upon Castroism or Communism as paramount issues. Their chief concern centered on internal rather than external problems: to obtain aid for economic development, to attack the staggering problems of poverty, to establish political stability, to keep pace with the tremendous increase in population, and gradually to close the gap between their nations and the more developed ones. Latin American leaders, moreover, felt that the tasks were so vast and the need for improvement so immediate and imperative that the job could only be done by securing public loans and grants, by negotiating liberal trade concessions, and by stabilizing commodity prices. Whereas the United States, though paying heed to these arguments, continually stressed the role to be played by private investment within each country, Latin American leaders were convinced that private capital could be of little more than marginal assistance, especially in providing people with needed housing, a better diet, education, and health services.

The Alliance for Progress in its broad aims, as expressed in the Punta del Este Charter, went far toward meeting the highest aspirations of the Latin American people and establishing a balance between the priorities as seen by both sides. Nevertheless, Latin American misgivings were not completely removed. It was natural to expect that the Alliance would not be welcomed by large landowners and others who felt that their wealth and income would be jeopardized through economic and social reforms. But in addition to the entrenched oligarchy in some countries and the leftist and ardent nationalist groups, whose hostility could be taken for granted, there were many other Latin Americans who tended to regard the Alliance merely as a tool for the advancement of the political and economic objectives of the United States. These goals, it was felt, might not necessarily be in the best interests of Latin America. Complaints were voiced in particular against the implicit downgrading of their relations with Europe and against what they regarded as strings attached to American aid. In general, however, responsible Latin American leaders welcomed the Alliance for Progress.

In the mid-1960's Latin America was experiencing rapid political and economic change, reflected in the social upheaval and reorganization that had been under way for some years. The demand for swift economic development grew more pressing. Politically, many Latin American republics still faced the need for establishing governmental systems that could accommodate social change and contain its more explosive effects. Unfortunately, a serious problem in most of them was the lack of adequate traditions of political responsibility. "Until Latin America's political underdevelopment is corrected," one observer noted, "its economic development will continue to lurch and stumble. For what is retarding development in the major Latin American countries is not so much lack of wealth and technology nor the vested interests of landed or commercial classes; it is the prevalence of corrupt and demagogic leaders, often the legacy of dictators, governing people whose cynicism about politics leads them to alternate between fatalism and violence."[1] The rate of change varied greatly from country to country. On the whole, however, the Latin American republics seemed to be groping for a distinctive and independent way out of their difficulties—a way in keeping with their own traditions and special needs.

Questions that came to the forefront were whether the Alliance for Progress could meet in time the pressing demands of Latin America for economic development and social justice. Change there would be, but what were the chances that it would be peaceful and democratic? Would Latin America take the road to nonviolent transformation or succumb to revolutionary chaos? While some Latin American countries were standing still, others seemed to be moving unevenly down each of these roads, and the future continued to be uncertain.

29. SEARCH FOR A POLICY

Cultivation of close inter-American economic and political cooperation had long been a fundamental goal of United States policies toward Latin America. From the Monroe Doctrine to the Alliance for Progress, the Western Hemisphere's security constituted a vital element of American interest. The Communist movement during the past two decades, no less than the threat of European encroachment in the nineteenth century or Nazi and Fascist penetration in the 1930's, posed a danger that could not be ignored. This was, of course, amply demonstrated in the Cuban missile crisis of 1962; but the danger was continuous and not always posed so dramatically. Subversion and the exploitation of chaotic conditions created the threat of explosive situations. Communists were adept at infiltrating indigenous revolutions and linking *any* revolutionary movement aimed at human betterment with a hatred of the United States. Their propaganda was particularly directed toward showing that the Colossus of the North was somehow responsible for all the ills of the Latin American countries.

While security considerations were an important factor in the relations between the United States and Latin America, other matters also loomed large. Not the least of these was trade. After Europe, Canada, and Japan, Latin America was the largest market for U.S. exports and a principal source of many raw materials.

Through the Alliance for Progress the United States undertook, in a sense, an unprecedented experiment in social engineering. Calling for a "common effort" by the Americas to accelerate economic progress and to achieve "broader social justice within the framework of personal dignity and personal liberty," the Alliance was designed to be a peaceful alternative to violent revolution. Although these goals were to be achieved specifically through systematic social and economic programs, its success also depended on instilling in the Latin American people a sense of *personal* as well as of *national* commitment. A most important ingredient, as Roberto de Oliveira Campos of Brazil suggested, was the creation of a *mystique,* capable of acting "as [a] counter-myth to the Communist ideology which, despite its wanton brutality, has been rather successful in conveying to neglected masses a feeling of participating in the construction of new societies." Unless the Alliance program was capable of reaching men's minds and hearts, he doubted that it would attain its objectives.[2] President Kennedy intuitively recognized this factor. It was largely in attitude and approach that he showed a major departure from traditional American behavior in dealing with Latin Americans, and this struck a responsive chord.

Since Latin Americans regarded the assassination of President Kennedy as a tragic blow to the prospects for the Alliance for Progress, they watched anxiously to see whether President Johnson's commitment would be as deep as his predecessor's. The appointment in December 1963 of Thomas C. Mann as Special Assistant to the President and Assistant Secretary of State for Inter-American Affairs was generally welcomed but created some apprehension. Although the new secretary was a moving spirit behind the Act of Bogotá of 1960 which introduced the principle that social development was indispensable to economic progress, he was known to feel strongly that Latin America's future depended largely on its own efforts. The United States, as he said, could only act as a "catalyst."

Highly pragmatic as President Kennedy's policies had been, they were also imbued with a determination to assert American moral leadership in the Western Hemisphere. In particular, he did not hesitate to make bolder use of foreign aid as leverage for persuading governments to undertake institutional and fiscal reforms, even at the cost of antagonizing important groups in Latin American governments. Mr. Kennedy strongly held that economic and social development under the Alliance for Progress had to move hand-in-hand with the growth of democracy; and unless political democracy was protected and strengthened, no ideological alternative to the inroads of Communism would be possible. In a sense, President Kennedy tried to carry forward Wilsonian precepts with respect both to recognition and to the exercise of diplomatic pressures to advance democratic processes.

When the Johnson administration took over, Mr. Kennedy's pragmatic emphasis was retained, but the moral overtones, for the most part, soon faded. Speaking to a group of high-ranking U.S. officials on March 18, Assistant Secretary Mann intimated, according to the *New York Times*, that the United States should stop trying to distinguish between dictators and democratic regimes in conducting its foreign policy. Efforts should be concentrated instead on fostering Latin American economic growth, protecting the $9 billion American investment in the area, maintaining nonintervention in the internal political affairs of the republics, and opposing Communism. The United States should use its "full power," Mr. Mann was quoted as saying, to help protect any Latin American republic "whose freedom is threatened by forces dictated from beyond the shores of this continent." [3]

Early in June Mr. Mann further elaborated on relations between the United States and Latin America. Citing numerous historical examples, he observed that American attempts to impose democracy on other countries and to force Latin American governments to stay on the path of constitutionality had never been successful, and had merely left a legacy of suspicion and resentment. The bad experience of the United States with its interventionist policies, Mr. Mann remarked, did not mean that Washington would recognize all governments which came to power in an unconstitutional manner. "Each case must be looked at in the light of its own facts. Where the facts warrant it . . . we reserve our freedom to register our indignation by refusing to recognize or to continue our economic cooperation. It does mean that, consistent with our treaty obligations, we cannot put ourselves in a doctrinaire straightjacket of automatic application of sanctions to every unconstitutional regime in the hemisphere with the obvious intention of dictating internal political developments in other countries. . . . Unilateral intervention for the purpose of forcing constitutional changes in an-

other country does not always serve either the cause of democracy or the national security interests of the United States." [4]
Mr. Mann's declaration was censured by liberals, who felt that a short-range pragmatism could hurt the objectives of the Alliance for Progress. Senator Hubert H. Humphrey, agreeing with this critical viewpoint, sharply criticized the Johnson administration's efforts to establish a pragmatic test on recognition. "It would be a mistake to interpret the Alliance program exclusively in terms of a social and economic revolution," he warned, "and to ignore the equally important aim of building political democracy and constitutional government." It was vitally important, he said, to distinguish "between constitutional government pursuing progressive policies and those which shoot their way to power." Where it was necessary to deal temporarily with nonconstitutional government, he argued, the United States should use all of its influence to restore constitutional government at the earliest possible time. Senator Humphrey was especially perturbed by the administration's tendency to downgrade political and ideological considerations in favor of orderly development programs. [5]

Despite President Johnson's efforts, when he met with Mexican President Adolfo López Mateos on February 22, [6] to dispel doubts by reaffirming the pledge to help Latin America and to strengthen the Alliance's program, Latin Americans were disturbed by what seemed to be signs of a lower priority accorded to the Alliance for Progress than had been the case under President Kennedy. Among these supposed signs were the administration's greater stress on enhancing the role of private investment, which appeared to indicate that the United States was reverting to policies it had pursued before the Alliance was established, and the American failure to give firm support to stabilizing world commodity prices.

Early in 1964, however, a long step forward was taken in reshaping the Alliance into a multilateral organization. Latin Americans had long complained that the program was less an alliance than a series of bilateral aid agreements between the United States and the individual hemisphere republics, and there had been much high-level reappraisal of the complaint. To carry out a resolution adopted in 1963 at the second annual meeting of the Alliance for Progress, the Inter-American Committee for the Alliance for Progress (CIAP) was established late in January.[7] Dr. Carlos Sanz de Santamaría, former Minister of Finance in Columbia, was chosen as chairman. Although not given authority over the actual allocation of U.S. funds, the CIAP was assigned the tasks of determining the financial needs of each Latin American country and the adequacy of the self-help development plans it submitted and then recommending to Washington how the program's aid should be distributed. A major objective of the Committee was to improve the coordination of the Alliance for Progress so that it would be a hemispheric program run by all the nations and not just by the United States.

On March 16, speaking to the newly created Committee, President Johnson again pledged full support to the aims of the Alliance. ". . . we will carry forward our Alliance for Progress in such a way that men in all lands will marvel at the power of freedom to achieve the betterment of man." [8] But the President made no reference to Latin American revolutionary pressures or to the relationship between economic development efforts and political realities of the hemisphere. There was thus disappointment among his Latin American listeners who had hoped for a strong reaffirmation of American political and ideological leadership. Early in May, however, Mr. Johnson firmly stressed for the first time that the Alliance program called not only for economic progress and political democracy, but also for a peaceful and democratic social revolution. By emphasizing America's continued support for democratic regimes and social revolution, the President went far toward allaying certain fears that had previously existed concerning the United States' commitment to fulfill the larger purposes of the Alliance.[9]

Nevertheless, the primary focus of the Johnson administration centered not on nurturing a *mystique* to stir Latin Americans psychologically toward a greater personal and national involvement, but rather on practical measures necessary to achieve a greater mobilization and coordination to carry out specific Alliance projects. At the first regular meeting of the CIAP, held in Mexico City in July, an effort was made to identify the obstacles to more rapid progress and to plan methods of eliminating them. Subsequently, in collaboration with the United States, the World Bank, the Inter-American Development Bank, and the International Monetary Fund, the CIAP undertook studies in depth of the economic and social problems in Panama, Ecuador, Mexico, Colombia, Venezuela, and the five Central American republics. Similar investigations for other countries within the Alliance were also planned. Assistant Secretary Mann pointed out on September 17: "Unlike mathematics, the problem of development is not an exact science. There are wide variations in the problems which each country faces and in the steps which each country has taken to meet them. Each country makes its own plan for development, which is presented to the CIAP. . . . All aspects of the country's economy, including monetary and fiscal policy, tax and land reforms, balance of payments and budgetary problems, overall self-help efforts of the country, and estimates of internal resources available and external resources needed, are all considered within the context of a sensible plan for progress. I know of no better way than through the CIAP process of country-by-country study to become acquainted with the problems which other nations face . . ." [10]

Three major problems created uncertainties for the Alliance for Progress. First, in terms of population, Latin America was the fastest growing region in the world. It had to make striking economic advances just to maintain living standards. Although American aid under the Alliance was considerable, it was small in comparison to the needs of the continent. Whether, at existing levels, the Alliance could provide sufficient leverage for decisive change appeared doubtful. After three years, its successes and failures could be seen in somewhat better perspective, but quite evidently foreign assistance alone, even when supplemented by private investment, could not solve Latin

America's economic problems completely. Unless a fresh attack could also be mounted on inflation, trade, and other questions, the risks of continued turbulence in the hemisphere would persist. "Perhaps that is the inescapable pattern," *The Washington Post* commented editorially on March 13. "But better to face the unpalatable truths than pretend that a mouse can move a mountain."

The second difficulty lay in a lack of able, responsible political leaders, capable of mobilizing support for Alliance programs. Whether political institutions and administrative structures could be built and sustained to effect basic modifications in Latin American society was still an open question. The most that could be said was that certain foundations were being laid down which in the long run, it was hoped, would stimulate a full-scale democratic social revolution. Despite some resistance, in eleven countries structural tax reforms were inaugurated. Ten countries passed legislation on land reform, and three others had legislation pending. But accomplishment and enforcement continued to lag far behind declared intentions.

Third, U.S. congressional support was essential to the success of the Alliance. During the year, Latin American leaders became gravely concerned over the delay of the United States in participating in the International Coffee Agreement, over U.S. restrictions on meat imports, and over indications that the share of the subsidized U.S. sugar market assigned to foreign producers would be diminished in favor of domestic growers. Dr. Sanz de Santamaría told President Johnson that Latin Americans found it difficult to understand how the United States expected them to take corrective measures and concentrate on rational development if, in effect, the rug was being pulled from under their economies by congressional actions.

Nevertheless, both the State Department and CIAP, although noting many serious difficulties that had to be dealt with, expressed optimism over the prospects of the Alliance for Progress. On October 30 Assistant Secretary Mann submitted a report to President Johnson which declared that 1964 had been marked "by a new unity of purpose in making the Alliance not just a statement of goals but a reality." For the first time, he said, each of the American republics had begun to discuss in depth its problems and its needs with others. In addition, Mr. Mann stressed the new coordination of economic and political policies within the American government that had made possible a great increase in loans under the Alliance program, and the growth of U.S. private investment.[11] The CIAP, after reviewing the situation at its second meeting held in Washington in November, also concluded that the year had been a "hopeful" one for the Alliance, with Latin American countries experiencing an upturn in their production and trade. Certain republics that had lagged in their economic and social reform now appeared "committed to deal with basic economic and social problems with a new vigor." While the CIAP believed that the Alliance's prospects were generally good, the Committee emphasized the need to deal with the immediate problem of "massive and abnormal" short-term obligations of Latin American countries.[12]

Perhaps the most encouraging development in the Alliance program was that a definite start was made in fields previously ignored. During the year, ten countries exceeded the goal of the 2.5 per cent per capita minimum annual growth rate called for in the Punta del Este Charter, and an increase occurred in intraregional trade, particularly in Central America's common market. At the third annual review conference of the Alliance for Progress held in Lima, December 5–11, Latin Americans especially lauded the fact that the Alliance had become a genuine multilateral effort. For the first time, responsibility in the execution of plans began to match the financial commitments of the United States. Assistant Secretary Mann told the delegates on December 8 that CIAP had completed "the first cycle of country-by-country studies ever made in our hemisphere. . . . [and had] recommended specific and concrete courses of action to countries and international organizations on how to accelerate progress." [13]

The year thus saw the Alliance taking significant forward strides, but the task ahead lay not merely in continuing to improve its machinery so that the program would proceed more smoothly and rapidly. It was also essential to enhance its political appeal so that the restless Latin American people could be mobilized to make Alliance for Progress goals a reality.

30. DE GAULLE VISITS MEXICO AND SOUTH AMERICA

President Charles de Gaulle's four-day state visit to Mexico, March 16–19, and his twenty-seven-day tour of ten South American countries from September 20 to October 16 were among the year's major events. These visits were the first that any Western European head of state had ever officially paid to Latin America. Seeking to assert France's growing importance as an independent world power and as a trustworthy guide for Latin nations, the French leader looked to an expansion of trade, and more especially to the creation of closer cultural and political relations.

Viewing Latin America's appearance "in the foreground of the stage of world affairs" as an important new factor in world relationships, General de Gaulle's broader aim was to seek the reestablishment of European influence in the Western Hemisphere. With Latin America ostensibly faced with the choice between Castroism or Communism, on the one hand, and United States hegemony, on the other, the French President sought to offer a third course that would enable the hemisphere republics to achieve a greater freedom of movement and maneuver. With European cooperation and inspiration, he believed, a new path might be found leading to an important role for Latin America in the Western world. Although Washington was concerned about France's intrusion into hemisphere affairs, it favored any constructive European contributions that could be made toward Latin American development. "We can surely join in extending a warm welcome to friends in Europe," President Johnson said, "who offer help in our progress [in the hemisphere] and markets for our products." [14]

The de Gaulle visits were a personal success. In Mexico, standing on the balcony of the National Palace (the first foreign dignitary ever accorded that honor) and speaking in Spanish, the French President told a wildly cheering crowd: "No doctrine, no quarrel, no divergent interests separate us. Quite to the contrary, we have many reasons that urge us to draw closer to each other. . . . France salutes Mexico with respect. . . . This, then, is what the French people suggest to the Mexican people: Let us walk hand in hand." At the National University, where General de Gaulle received his most enthusiastic reception, exuberant students swept aside security forces and crashed through a glass door to greet the French leader. Throughout the visit, the main theme stressed by de Gaulle was France's mission as a developer of the "third world." Although the French President (as well as President López Mateos) emphasized that France's gesture of friendship should not be regarded as hostile to U.S. policies, a certain sense of skepticism prevailed. Former President Harry Truman bluntly accused the French President of attempting to undermine the American position in the Western Hemisphere. Much to Washington's embarrassment, he advised General de Gaulle to "keep his long nose out of U.S. affairs unless he wants us to cut it off." [15] Secretary Rusk quickly explained that the United States had for some time invited European nations to take a greater interest in the Latin American area.

Despite the warmth of Mexico's response to the French President's visit, there was little that he could offer to further the country's economic growth. In 1963 France had already made available to Mexico about $150 million on a long-term basis for the purchase of French goods and services. The final communiqué issued on March 19 merely asserted that the two countries would work further to explore ways to expand their trade. French assistance, it appeared, would be largely confined to scientific and technical cooperation, particularly in the fields of industry and agriculture.

France did not have and did not claim the capacity to supplant American economic aid in the Western Hemisphere. What President de Gaulle hoped to accomplish was to shake up Latin American thinking and pry it loose from its primary focus on the United States. This goal was even more sharply in evidence on the French President's whirlwind tour to ten South American countries than it was on his Mexican trip. Repeatedly, he urged that the continent's dependence on its northern neighbor should be lessened. He stressed that both France and Latin America shared a common political interest in sustaining the principle of sovereignty and noninterference from other countries. "We cannot admit the right of any state externally to establish the direction of the economic and political affairs around it," he told the Venezuelan Congress. "I believe we agree that all oppression and all hegemony be excluded from our universe." In Colombia the French President softened his implied comments on U.S. domination of Latin America, but President Guillermo León Valencia stirred up a political storm by delivering a strongly pro-American speech that surprised not only General de Gaulle but many Colombians as well. The Colombian President's fervent praise of the United States even included forgiveness for American involvement in the Panama revolution of 1903.

As he traveled from country to country, President de Gaulle increasingly stressed the special educational and cultural contributions which France could make to Latin America. In Ecuador he was hailed as a great French patriot, but Admiral Ramón Jijón, head of the military junta, told him that the country was permanently linked to the United States for peace and liberty. Wherever General de Gaulle went, he was greeted by cheering crowds, but his message of establishing closer links between France and Latin America elicited little enthusiasm. That Latin America's attention was fixed mainly on its own affairs was especially evident in Argentina where the General's visit was marred by violent demonstrations in favor of the exiled dictator Juan D. Perón. Rioting raged for several days, and at one point 3,000 Peronistas closed around the car in which Presidents de Gaulle and Arturo Illia were riding. The situation was politically uncomfortable, although physical danger to the heads of state was averted.

On October 9 President de Gaulle urged Uruguay to join

France in forming a vast group of nations that could stand up to the two world giants—the United States and the Soviet Union. He promised Uruguay a prominent place in this "third force," as well as French economic and technical aid, declaring that "the peace of the world must not depend on the fight between two great champions." In Brazil the French President pledged his support to help combat the country's economic underdevelopment. But President Humberto de Alencar Castello Branco rejected the need for a "third force," which he viewed as a challenge to the inter-American system of political and economic cooperation, as well as an implied attack against the United States.

The French overture brought a measure of sympathy, but no tangible results. The third-bloc idea undeniably had a strong appeal in some Latin American countries. But President de Gaulle's inability to back up this goal with increased trade or aid reduced its attractiveness. Economic development was the key article of Latin American faith, and none of the republics was prepared to undermine it for the sake of a special relationship with France. On the whole, therefore, while the French leader's visits clearly represented a personal triumph, they seemed to have only a rather limited effect on the Western Hemisphere.

31. BRAZIL'S REVOLUTION

"Historically, the events of Easter weekend, 1964, in Brazil, may prove as decisive for Latin America as was the defeat of the Communist attempt to take over Western Europe by strikes and subversion during the winter of 1947–1948," said Adolf A. Berle, former American Ambassador to Brazil. "After a defeat, the Marshall Plan could go forward in Europe. Now, it seems the Alliance for Progress may really go forward in Latin America." [16] Undeniably, the sudden *coup* on April 1 effected a significant change in the hemisphere. Former Brazilian President Goulart's strongly neutralist and far-leftist policies had, indeed, tended to give encouragement to Castroite movements.

By 1964 genuine alarm developed both in Washington and in many Latin American republics over his apparent efforts to steer Brazil sharply to the left. With his ouster, this trend was brought to an abrupt halt. A more cooperative relationship immediately developed between the United States and Brazil, and this situation unquestionably contributed toward a revitalization of the Alliance for Progress.

But the reasons for the Brazilian revolution were less a matter of foreign policy considerations than a question of coping with the country's ever-deepening economic crisis. In the final analysis, it was President Goulart's failure to find a solution to Brazil's financial and economic difficulties that overthrew him. During 1963, a Three-Year Plan for Social and Economic Reform had been launched. Blueprints were drafted for initiating agrarian and other reforms, such as had been urged by the Alliance for Progress; increasing the gross annual product by 7 per cent annually and the per capita growth rate by 4 per cent; and reducing the rate of inflation to 30 per cent in the first year and 10 per cent in the third. When the new year started, however, the growth rate instead of showing improvement actually declined. Inflation raised prices by a staggering 80 per cent, and no brake was applied. Nor did reform proposals reach the Brazilian congress. The foreign debt stood at approximately $3.8 billion, and some $1.3 billion was due in the next eighteen months. President Goulart told the nation in his New Year's message that the $350 million debt payment scheduled to be made would have to be put off. Although the United States tried to help Brazil, Mr. Goulart's unpredictability, demagoguery, and reliance on extremist elements made it virtually impossible to work with his administration. Opposed to budget-cutting, to strict monetary controls, and to a tight-credit policy, the Brazilian leader was convinced that only major social reforms—among which he included a program of land redistribution—could remedy Brazil's "structural" inflation. Meanwhile, Brazil approached the brink of economic chaos, as the country's runaway inflation rapidly accelerated.

Early in the year, as the situation worsened, the Brazilian

leader pressed for an increase of presidential powers. He demanded revisions in the constitution, and immediate, sweeping reforms. Striving to alter the basis of his political power, Mr. Goulart started talking about legalizing the Communist party, and he issued passionate appeals for the loyalty of noncommissioned officers—over the heads of their superiors. He asked that the literacy test on the right to vote be lifted and that noncommissioned army officers and privates be given the same right of the ballot enjoyed only by officers. As he attempted to broaden his executive authority, opposition sharpened not only in Congress (especially among the centrist and conservative groups), but also on the part of state governors and the population as a whole. A series of coups, preventive coups, and counter-coups began to be planned.

President Goulart seemed to be welcoming a showdown. On March 13 he told a crowd of some 100,000 people in Rio de Janeiro that he had signed, on his own initiative, two decrees. The first provided for the nationalization of the five remaining privately owned oil refineries operating in the country; the second authorized the confiscation of all private idle land lying six miles on either side of federal highways, railroads, and waterways. He pleaded for constitutional changes, saying that only thus could his program of basic reforms be completed.

Two days later, at the convening of the congressional session, leaders of the center and rightist parties attacked President Goulart's campaign to "mend or end" the constitution and talked of impeachment. Marches, both for and against Mr. Goulart, took place in the suburbs of Brasilia and in São Paulo as the situation got out of hand. On March 25 a Brazilian marine corporal was arrested for illegally making a vehement speech in favor of the President's constitutional reforms, urging especially the immediate passage of a measure giving enlisted men the right to vote and to run for public office. Charged with violating regulations against political activity by military men on active duty, the corporal's arrest and the issue of the President's "Social Reforms" stirred up a national storm. The following day, a band of about 1,500 sailors and marines barricaded themselves in a union hall in Rio de Janeiro to protest the arrest. Unable to persuade the men to leave, the Brazilian Naval Minister resigned. At first, President Goulart delayed taking any action; but as a major military crisis threatened, he ordered tank-supported army troops to rout them from their stronghold. High-ranking naval officers immediately demanded that the sailors and marines be disciplined and not granted amnesty, charging that the rebellion "was planned and executed by a group interested in general subversion of the nation and with clearly Communist characteristics."

In the midst of the dissension over the punishment of the mutineers, a military revolt broke out on March 31 in Juiz de Fora, eighty miles from Rio de Janeiro. Rebel leaders accused President Goulart of betraying the Brazilian "fatherland," of seeking dictatorial powers, and of permitting Brazil to become "another Cuba," and they denounced his support of "confessed Communists." As their armies marched toward Rio, they demanded his resignation. Unable to rally military forces to his side or to arm the people to resist the rebels, Mr. Goulart, after offering feeble opposition, fled the country. On April 2 Paschoal Ranieri Mazzilli, President of the Chamber of Deputies, assumed the presidency until April 11, when the Brazilian congress elected General Castello Branco by an overwhelming majority as the new interim president until January 31, 1966.

Washington was not unhappy with the developments that had taken place so unexpectedly. On April 2 President Johnson sent his "warmest good wishes" to Mr. Mazzilli.[17] Expressing the American people's admiration at the "resolute will of the Brazilian community" to resolve its difficulties "within a framework of constitutional democracy and without civil strife," he declared that the "friendship and cooperation between our two governments and peoples are . . . a precious asset in the interests of peace and prosperity and liberty in this hemisphere and in the whole world." Because the Brazilian Congress had acted formally to declare the presidency vacant, Washington took the position that the constitutional process was not interrupted, and thus the question of recognition of the new regime did not arise. In contrast to the brief rupture in relations with Argentina when its President Arturo Frondizi was deposed and replaced in 1962, the Johnson administration did not hesitate to express its support for the new Brazilian government even before its character was clearly determined.

On April 7 the military leaders imposed on a hesitant Brazilian Congress an "Institutional Act" which gave the new regime extraconstitutional powers to rule the country until January 31, 1966. This decree stipulated that the democratic constitution would remain in force, except that additional powers would be granted to the president. It gave the interim president sweeping powers to effect a "decommunization" program, and authorized him to oust members of Congress, government officials, military officers, and others found guilty of seditious and pro-Communist activities, as well as to seize their property and wealth. Those removed for extremist connections were given no right to judicial appeal; their political rights, including the right to vote or to hold office, could be suspended for ten years.

The next day, the revolutionary government summarily expelled forty members of Congress on the grounds of pro-Communist or extremist activity and corruption. Political rights of the ousted legislators were suspended for ten years, as were those of sixty other prominent Brazilians. In his inaugural speech on April 15, however, President Castello Branco rejected the "reactionary right-wing" remedies for Communism. He placed his main stress on putting forward an economic program to deal with inflation. "I believe firmly in the compatibility of development with democratic processes, but I do not believe in development in the shadow of an inflationary orgy." General Castello Branco pledged support for private enterprise, calling on the wealthy and managerial classes to cooperate in improving the living standards of the impoverished masses.

Basically, the great change effected by the Brazilian revolution was that internally it ended the country's extreme leftward swing. In foreign affairs it checked Mr. Goulart's efforts to downgrade relations with the United States, to cultivate the Soviet bloc, to coddle Cuba, and to cooperate politically with the nonaligned countries. In contrast, President Castello Branco based his foreign policy on restoring close cooperation with the United States, working with the Alliance for Progress, and attracting the largest possible amount of Western aid and investment for economic development. On May 12 Brazil broke diplomatic relations with Cuba, and three days later President Castello Branco condemned Fidel Castro for his "systematic policy of intervention and aggression" against Venezuela.

On the domestic front, the new regime concentrated on the adoption of urgent economic, social, administrative, and electoral reforms. The Brazilian President pressed for tough measures to deal with the inflation. A plan was put forward which called for ending government subsidies on cheap bread and gasoline, cutting the national budget by 30 per cent, and creating the National Monetary Council to stabilize finance and trade policies. Cutbacks were made in civil service jobs and pay increases, and big landowners were faced with new graduated taxes that penalized them if they failed to make full use of their acreage. But perhaps the most dramatic change in the country was related to foreign investment capital. Under President Goulart it had been virtually impossible to take profits out of the country. To encourage foreign investment, plans were now made to revise the profits remittance law.

During the summer a critical issue arose on setting the date and form of the Brazilian presidential election. On July 22, despite strong opposition, President Castello Branco's term was extended to March 15, 1967. The action indicated the unwillingness of Brazilian military leaders to entrust their power to civilian politicians until there was sufficient evidence that the revolution's program would be continued. Bitterly disgruntled, Governor Carlos Lacerda of Guanabara—an opponent of Mr. Goulart and a leader of the revolution, who had hoped to run for the presidency scheduled for October 1965—acidly commented that "this constitutes the destruction of the revolution."

Within Brazil a struggle developed not only between civilian politicians and military leaders, but also between discontented elements in the armed forces and President Castello Branco. Efforts to undermine the Branco regime, however, were curbed. Although by the end of the year there was much disenchantment with the Brazilian revolution—largely because of resistance to the enforced austerity, the attacks on privilege and corruption, and the agrarian reform proposals—President Castello Branco scored some limited successes in dealing with the country's immense problems. And he obtained impressive outside support. Seeking to help Brazil in its economic recovery, the United States announced in December a projected $1 billion aid package from various U.S. and multilateral sources. "The success of the Brazilian action program [to halt inflation, and to mobilize internal resources for development and instituting reforms]," said David E. Bell, administrator of AID, "is crucially important to the success of the Alliance for Progress throughout the hemisphere." [18]

32. SOUTH AMERICA IN TRANSITION

Political uncertainty prevailed in many Latin American countries during the year. Disillusioned with *Fidelismo*, Latin Americans seemed to be searching for a middle course in line with their own traditions, philosophy and special circumstances. The Alliance for Progress, which had proposed an alternative to Marxism by grappling with economic and social problems, largely failed to stir the imagination of intellectual, labor, and student groups or to take hold effectively among the impoverished people. Hampered by being regarded essentially as a United States program, it did not succeed in becoming a positive political force. By the mid-1960's, signs indicated that the ideological vacuum might be filled by the Christian Socialist or Christian Democratic movement. Rejecting both doctrinaire Marxism and violent revolution and seeking to improve Latin American economic and social standards without destroying individual rights, this movement had won increasing support over the years in a few countries and had become highly organized.

A major test of the movement's political strength took place in

Chile. Though one of the most advanced and democratic nations in the hemisphere, Chile's main problems were similar to those of the rest of the continent. Four per cent of the population owned more than 70 per cent of the land; 10 per cent received more than half the national income; and most of the peasants were landless or worked plots too small to yield more than mere subsistence. Control of the nation's all important copper exports was in the hands of two American companies. Most other large industries were owned by foreigners or dominated by the relatively small non-Spanish minorities. Population was growing rapidly and was especially concentrated in miserable slums around Santiago. For the most part, Chile managed to keep its problems from becoming explosive. President Jorge Alessandri, who headed the Democratic Front—a coalition of Conservative, Liberal, and Radical parties—had succeeded for several years in checking Chile's chronic inflation, in expanding economic growth to about 5 per cent a year, and in cutting unemployment. But as the year 1964 began, the economy took a sharp turn for the worse. The cost of living rose about 50 per cent, and the pace began to accelerate alarmingly. By February it reached crisis proportions.

Since national elections were scheduled for September 4, an intensive political battle loomed. President Alessandri was prohibited by law from seeking a second term. During the spring when the candidate whom he supported as his successor was badly defeated in a congressional by-election, the Democratic Front virtually collapsed. The presidential race narrowed to a contest between Senator Eduardo Frei Montalva, leader of the Christian Democratic party, and Dr. Salvador Allende Gossens, candidate of the Popular Action Front, a group including the Socialist and Communist parties. Both sides called for programs designed to bring about a peaceful social revolution in Chile. Mr. Frei, however, was clearly oriented toward the West and identified himself with the reforms envisioned in the Alliance for Progress. Dr. Allende, on the other hand, favored pushing Chile into closer cooperation with Communist countries and establishing friendly ties with Cuba.

Washington was concerned about the potentially disruptive repercussions that might be produced in inter-American relations if a freely elected Socialist-Communist regime was installed in Chile. Although apprehensive, it remained silent and avoided even the slightest intrusion. Special significance was attached to this election since it was the first held in Latin America in which voters had a clear-cut choice between Christian Democracy and Marxist Communism. After a hard-fought campaign, Mr. Frei, who apparently received the votes of the center and the right, as well as of his own party, emerged as the victor with the biggest plurality in Chile's history. His triumph was one of the most significant changes of government in Latin America since the Cuban revolution. Inaugurated on November 3, President Frei pledged himself to carry out "a profound revolution within liberty and law" to break social barriers and correct the inequitable distribution of wealth, which was the "shame" of the Western Hemisphere. He promptly took steps toward asserting a position of leadership in Latin America by strongly urging, in particular, the strengthening of the Organization of American States and the Latin American Free Trade Association.

Washington was also elated by the election results in British Guiana early in December. Premier Cheddi B. Jagan, whose sympathies with and close links to Communist countries had been a disturbing factor, was finally defeated by the coalition of the two opposition parties, and the new government was formed by Forbes Burnham, head of the People's National Congress party. Racial strife between Negroes and East Indians still deeply divided this British colony and delayed its attainment of independence.

Although the general trend of events appeared encouraging, the sudden overthrow of President Víctor Paz Estenssoro of Bolivia on November 3–4 was a setback to American hopes. Trouble began building up in the Bolivian republic shortly after President Paz Estenssoro won an uncontested election on May 31 for a third four-year term. Opposition parties, which had withdrawn their candidates and urged voters to abstain, immediately labeled the election a fraud. They charged him with seeking to establish a dictatorship and selling out to the United States. American Ambassador Douglas Henderson added fuel to the fire by going along on campaign trips to inaugurate Alliance aid projects. An intense nationalist and founder of the National Revolutionary Movement, the Bolivian leader had been at the storm center of his country's politics for over three decades. He had sparked two revolutions, spent six years in exile, and ousted Bolivia's "tin barons" in 1952. During his first term as president he launched a drastic land reform program, giving new political and social status to the Indian peasants, and nationalized the tin mines which provided 90 per cent of the country's exports. For more than twelve years he had anticipated many of the objectives of the Alliance for Progress by building schools, redistributing wealth, enfranchising illiterates, and he gave Bolivia an unprecedented, if uneasy, political stability. The United States, on the whole, supported these reform efforts. American investment through public aid programs in Bolivian economic and social development became the largest per capita in any of the Latin American republics. By the 1960's Washington was convinced that President Paz Estenssoro was the only political figure capable of curbing partisan strife and preventing anarchy and perhaps civil war.

The political situation deteriorated during September when a plot to overthrow the government and assassinate the president was foiled. A nationwide state of siege was declared, press censorship was invoked, and several opposition leaders were deported. The turmoil had followed months of economic unrest capped by a strike of government teachers and demands by Bolivian tin miners for higher pay. In October, several demonstrations were staged against the regime, in which hundreds of students were arrested, and miners seized a group of militia men as hostages. As tension heightened, the powerful Bolivian Miners' Federation called a twenty-four-hour nationwide strike. Just as it appeared that the disturbances were subsiding, a military rebellion broke out on November 3 and spread swiftly across the country. After a day of bloody clashes, President Paz Estenssoro fled into exile, and the government was taken over by Vice-President René Barrientos Ortuño, a former Bolivian Air Force commander. General Barrientos had broken with President Paz Estenssoro a month earlier and had left the capital in protest against the strong policies adopted to combat the rioting by students and workers. Washington was of course concerned about the overthrow of the Bolivian president and especially feared that chaotic conditions might provide an opportunity for extreme leftists to take over the government. The new military regime, however, proceeded to build up public support, and General Barrientos made known his intention to move toward the reestablishment of a constitutional government. He pledged to continue the work of the Paz government in the economic field, "only with more honesty and efficiency." The Johnson administration made it clear that the military junta could not expect a resumption of diplomatic relations or aid until complete order and political stability had been restored.[19] On December 4 the new regime promised to hold national elections on May 30, 1965. It also affirmed that it would honor all of the country's international obligations. Three days later the United States resumed its diplomatic and economic relations and restored a part of the aid cut off at the time of the *coup*. By the end of the year the military junta was in control of the country, and all active resistance to its regime ended.

The political situation in several other countries in Latin America appeared shaky—most notably in Ecuador where the military junta showed signs of falling apart, and in Colombia where criticism mounted sharply against President León Valencia and tested the stability of his government. Peru, on the other hand, presented a picture of rare tranquillity. Although President Fernando Belaúnde Terry had barely won the 1963 election for a six-year term, he managed to secure the support of opposition leaders Víctor Raul Haya de la Torre, head of the APRA party, and former dictator Manuel Odría for his program of social and economic reform. Some 400 new laws were enacted, among them a major land reform program aimed at resettling one million peasants on undeveloped land. A free education bill to take Peruvian students from elementary school through college was also approved. The nation's gross national product climbed to a record $3 billion during the year, and unemployment declined appreciably.

In Argentina, a vigorous effort was made to deal with the formidable task of economic recuperation, the legacy of years of internal dissension and neglect that followed the downfall of Perón. The attainment of internal peace and stability were the main goals of President Illia, the 63-year-old country doctor who took office for a six-year term in October 1963. He defined his policy as one of protecting democracy and maintaining the principle of government authority without being authoritarian.

During the year grumbling broke out in the ranks of organized labor, more than two million strong. To protest rising living costs and unemployment, a "battle plan" of strikes and temporary occupation of factories was put into effect. Domestic peace was strained by militant Peronistas who clamored for the return of the former dictator. Workers mocked the slow-moving Dr. Illia by turning turtles loose in the streets and chanting "Perón, Perón!" Although business activity and industry improved greatly and exports of wheat, corn, and beef reached the highest volume in years, internal unrest persisted. Not only was it reflected in labor strikes and in the disorders staged by Peronist-directed mobs during the visit of President de Gaulle in October, but also in a nation-wide strike called during the fall by students and teachers demanding the allocation of more money for education. Complaints were voiced that only 10 per cent was allowed for education expenditures, compared with more than 40 per cent for defense. Dr. Illia responded to domestic pressures with characteristic calm.

In December the announcement that Perón had left Spain to return to Argentina caused more than a ripple of excitement. His repeated promises that he would come back sustained his followers, who strongly believed that once the former dictator set foot on Argentine soil the government would topple and they would regain power. For more than a year they had counted on the "retorno," and Perón had given them an "irrevocable" commitment to return before the end of the year. On December 2 his plane landed in Rio de Janeiro. The Brazilian government ordered policemen and air force troops to surround the jetliner, declared him *persona non grata,* and forbade him to stay in Brazil or continue flying south over Brazilian territory. That night he was returned to Madrid on the same plane. The Peronist movement was shaken by the failure of the leader's attempt to return, and it was generally agreed that Dr. Illia's quiet handling of the Peronist challenge won him the biggest political victory of his fourteen months in office.

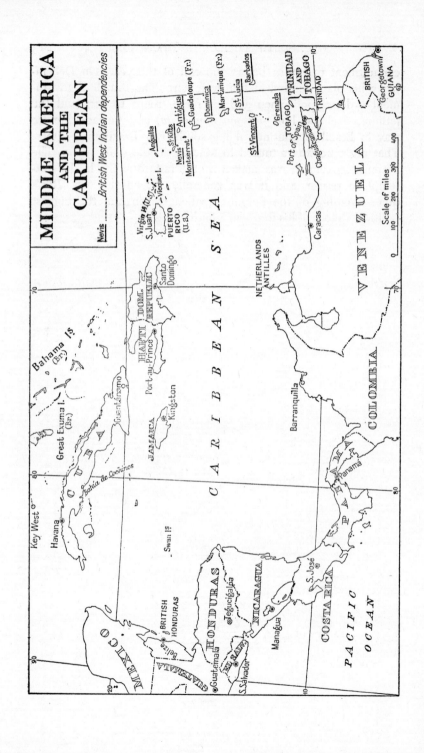

CHAPTER NINE
THE CARIBBEAN AT LOW TIDE

ORDERLY PROGRESS for the states of Middle America and the Caribbean and cooperative relations among themselves and with the United States, the strengthening of the inter-American system, and the prevention of the export of Communism from Cuba to other Latin American countries continued to be prime objectives of American policy in 1964. While the relations of the United States with Mexico showed substantial improvement, and the Central American republics made some headway in their plans to create a common market, the trend in the Caribbean islands was toward ever-increasing unrest both within and between the different countries. The recent or prospective independence of the British colonies added new uncertainties, for the possibilities of a confederation and close cooperation had lost ground. Nationalism, in its various forms and manifestations, seemed to have emerged as the dominant force in the entire area. The Panama incident early in January, triggered by a flag-raising issue, pointed up the nationalist unrest that existed in many other countries.

Cuba continued to be the major concern of the United States in the Caribbean region. Although Castro had failed in his efforts to undermine other Latin American governments—spectacularly in Venezuela in 1963—the island remained the beachhead of Communist penetration in the hemisphere and a base for subversion. With the exception of Mexico, all the Latin American republics which had not already done so broke diplomatic relations with Cuba in accordance with the resolution adopted by the Organization of American States in July. While Castro's influence had steadily declined as his regime became increasingly oppressive, as the Cuban economy grew more shaky, and as the island became tightly linked with and dependent on the Soviet Union, the Cuban leader's survival and his refusal to abandon propaganda and agitation activities or to renounce his intention of spreading political revolts made him a standing menace to the inter-American system.

The Cuban issue brought into focus the key task of how to cope with revolutionary turmoil in the Western Hemisphere. How was the United States to enlist the cooperative efforts of Latin American countries, strengthen their societies, and persuade its European allies that the threat to the security of hemisphere nations required their support and assistance as well?

33. THE CUBAN TRADE ISSUE

By the mid-1960's, Cuba had become a chronic irritant to the United States. Cuban exiles continued to plot and plan invasion of the island; but the United States, embarrassed by the Bay of Pigs invasion and restrained by its general policy of not attempting to overthrow the Castro regime by force, refrained from overtly supporting these activities. Washington, nevertheless, persisted in its efforts to secure the economic and diplomatic isolation of Cuba. Most Latin American countries were far more sympathetic toward the attainment of these goals than they had been formerly. Castro's attempt to precipitate violent revolutionary upheaval in Venezuela to destroy its democratic institutions was partly responsible for the change of attitude. Perhaps more fundamental was the realization after the Cuban missile crisis in 1962 that the island had, in fact, been converted into a Soviet military base which seriously endangered the hemisphere's security. While Latin America generally tended to demonstrate greater hostility toward Cuba, Europe increasingly questioned America's economic embargo policy.

The heated debate on this issue raised the crucial question of how to deal with the Communist world. From the American point of view, the Cuban trade boycott had a specific, fourfold purpose: to disrupt the Cuban economy; to increase the Soviet Union's burden in keeping the island economically afloat; to diminish Cuba's value as a Communist showplace in Latin America; and, above all, to reduce Castro's capacity for subversive mischief-making. The United States believed that Cuba was much more vulnerable than other Communist countries to a policy of economic denial. Before the Castro regime came to power, almost all of Cuba's trade was with the West, and mainly with the United States. From 1959 to 1963, free-world trade with Cuba declined from $1.3 billion to less than $300 million, and Washington convincingly showed that this had contributed greatly to the failures of the Cuban economy. "The Cuban people should not be forced to serve as a vehicle for the intrusion into this hemisphere of an alien way of life that can bring them neither progress nor liberty," Under-Secretary of State Ball said. "We oppose the present Cuban regime not just because its ambitions menace our hemispheric neighbors. We oppose it, above all, because its standards of conduct and its tyrannical practices condemn the people of Cuba to misery and fear." [1]

Despite the sharp drop in trade, Cuba's short-term outlook at the beginning of the year seemed to be more favorable than at any time since 1959. At the end of 1963 the Cuban regime decided to restore the production and export of sugar as the mainstay of the country's economy. Dreams of rapid industrialization and wide agricultural diversification were abandoned. Largely as a result of Soviet prodding, Castro directed his efforts toward raising sugar production. At the same time the Cuban leader took advantage of the high price of sugar—the ironical result of the catastrophic drop in production after 1961 —to buy desperately needed imports from the non-Communist world and to reduce Cuba's staggering commercial debt to the Soviet bloc. With cash in hand, he sought to obtain from Western countries foodstuffs as well as equipment and manufactured goods that Russia found increasingly difficult to provide.

The Soviet Union encouraged Cuba's new trade pattern, and on January 21 the two countries concluded a new long-term trade agreement. Under its terms, the Soviet Union agreed to buy 2.1 million tons of unrefined Cuban sugar in 1965, 3 million in 1966, 4 million in 1967, and 5 million in each of the three following years, at 6 cents a pound. By fixing the price at 6 cents, Moscow hoped to lay a basis for Cuba's long-term development planning by eliminating the influence of world price fluctuations.

Washington's concern over trade relations between its European allies and Cuba steadily increased. The State Department was clearly annoyed that a British firm early in January had negotiated the sale of 450 buses to Cuba to help restore the island's badly deteriorating transportation system. It was equally unhappy with Spain's agreement to exchange fishing trawlers and other goods for 350,000 tons of Cuban sugar, and with the use of Spanish planes and five ships to transport cargo to the island. The Spanish airline *Iberia* provided the only scheduled European air service to Cuba with regular flights. Disturbing also was the fact that on February 7 a French firm negotiated a $10 million sale of heavy trucks and tractors on credit guaranteed by the French government.

Congress had explicitly declared in the Foreign Assistance Act of 1963 that no aid would be given "to any country which failed to take appropriate steps" to prevent the transport of any goods to or from Cuba.[2] Signed by the President on December 16, 1963, this law had to be enforced sixty days after its enactment. Washington warned that defense arrangements with Spain could be jeopardized unless it complied. Spain, however, justified its trade on the ground that the American trade blockade was not complete in excluding the Communist countries, which were helping Castro the most. Neither Madrid, London, nor Paris believed that the Cuban threat to the Western Hemisphere's security was sufficiently dangerous to warrant America's interference with their trade.

On February 18 military aid to Britain, France, and Yugoslavia was terminated, and new commitments to Spain and

Morocco were halted until they took "appropriate steps" to stop their vessels (and in Spain's case, aircraft) from carrying goods to or from Cuba. Fourteen other countries had taken what the State Department determined to be "appropriate steps." The actual military aid to Britain, France, and Yugoslavia proved to be virtually nil; and the proposed sanctions against Spain and Morocco were not applied, since each took what was regarded by Washington as "appropriate steps" within the meaning of the law.

During the following months Washington vigorously defended its position *vis-à-vis* Cuba. On March 13 Secretary Rusk told the Senate Foreign Relations Committee that there would be no retreat in American policy as long as Cuba continued to threaten the security and stability of other nations in the hemisphere.[3] He acknowledged that Cuba had benefited from the abnormally high level of world sugar prices, which had contributed to the "flurry" of Cuban purchases in free-world markets. But he believed that this was temporary and in the long run Cuba was "not likely to be a good customer" and "certainly not a good credit risk." This warning did not deter the French or British from negotiating further trade agreements. Backed by a three-year, $4-million credit guaranteed by the government, a French firm arranged for the sale of twenty French locomotives to Havana late in April, and about two weeks later Britain's Leylands Motor Company announced that it was going to sell another 500 buses to Cuba under an option it had negotiated at the time of signing the original contract. On May 6 President Johnson expressed regret that some of America's allies did not feel they could "cooperate with us all the way." But, he emphasized, "we are going to continue our policy of economic isolation in the hope that we can prevent the spread of Castro's Communism throughout the hemisphere."[4] Despite these breaches in the trade boycott, Washington tightened its own controls. The Department of Commerce issued an order on May 14 requiring export licenses for the sale of food and medical supplies to Cuba—the only items previously exempted from the embargo on humanitarian grounds. This directive, following upon Cuban inquiries to American concerns for bids on selling millions of dollars worth of lard and drugs, sought to emphasize to Western nations that the United States meant business in its embargo campaign. Washington officials suspected that the Cuban inquiries had the purpose of undercutting America's efforts to discourage Britain and France from broadening their trade with Cuba.

Non-Communist nations, nevertheless, continued to trade increasingly with Cuba, with little regard for American feelings. Ships carrying merchandise from Britain, France, Canada, Japan, Italy, Spain, and other countries on both sides of the Iron Curtain docked daily in Havana during the summer. By September, however, a sharp decline in sugar prices—from 11.8 cents in January to 3.5 cents—led to a sharp curtailment of Cuban plans to buy machinery and consumer goods in non-Communist countries. Castro asserted that while credits for Cuban purchases abroad were not being altogether "annulled," certain "adjustments" had to be made. The Cuban trade bonanza, as Secretary Rusk had predicted, soon evaporated, particularly as sugar production, the island's main resource, sank to its lowest level. By the end of the year, the Cuban economy found itself in serious trouble.

34. CONTROVERSIES WITH CUBA OVER GUANTÁNAMO AND AERIAL RECONNAISSANCE

While Cuba faced mounting economic pressures both internally and from Washington, relations between Castro and the United States grew ominous. A critical situation developed on February 2 when the U.S. Coast Guard spotted four Cuban vessels off the Dry Tortugas, fishing inside the three-mile limit. Since the intrusion seemed deliberate and was a violation of a Federal statute, the ships were brought in for investigation. Washington requested that they be released—particularly since the statute contained no sanctions—but Florida officials asked that the boats be turned over to them for prosecution under a recent state law adopted in 1963, which barred fishing in state waters without a license. After consulting Washington, Federal authorities allowed Florida to assume jurisdiction. Castro immediately declared that the seizure of the Cuban boats was "a stupid, provocative act," and he retaliated by cutting off the water supply to the U.S. naval station at Guantánamo Bay until the Cuban crews were released. Shortly afterwards, the Cuban leader announced that he would permit the water to flow for one hour each day.

This action lent credence to Washington's suspicions that Castro had directed the Cuban boats to enter American territorial waters to provoke an incident so that a pretext would be found to eject the United States from Guantánamo. Secretary Rusk declared on February 7 that the "mischievous" attempt to link the seizure of the Cuban boats to Guantánamo would be "unproductive." "We are in Guantánamo," he said, "and will remain there for the forseeable future." [5] Fully prepared for a possible water cutoff, emergency measures were quickly taken to prevent any hardships, and at the same time the Guantánamo base was made self-sufficient in water supply. Two days later, Cuba conceded that the fishing boats may have been in United States waters—a point it had previously denied. However, if the vessels had "inadvertently entered the three-mile limit," they should have been asked to go away. "But once detained," asserted the Havana newspaper, El Mundo, which spoke for the Foreign Ministry, "they should have been set free when it was proved that they engaged only in fishing."

A disturbing feature of this critical affair lay in the fact that through a state law Florida had been able to interfere with the conduct of the nation's foreign policy. No precedent existed for a state assuming jurisdiction over violations of the three-mile limit. Severe punishment for such infractions, the United States recognized, could have repercussions harmful to its relations with other countries. American fishermen, for example, had been involved in such disputes with Mexico, Ecuador, Peru, and other nations. The normal procedure was to assess a fine, whereas the Florida law provided for a maximum penalty of $500 and a year in jail, as well as possible confiscation of the boats and equipment. To avoid serious complications, the State Department urged Florida authorities to deal quickly and leniently with the captured vessels and crewmen. Since the United States had fishermen throughout the world, Washington officials were interested in seeing that the Cuban fishermen would be fairly protected.

Having found the four captains guilty of poaching in state waters, the Florida court freed the Cuban fishermen on February 20 after imposing suspended jail sentences and fines of $500 each. The excitement generated by this incident quickly subsided, but it was evident that Castro intended to press for the recovery of the Guantánamo base through international action whenever he thought the moment opportune.

Another serious problem arose during the spring. In the long-drawn-out aftermath of the 1962 missile crisis, the Soviet Union had gradually pulled out its troops from the island, giving Cubans more and more control over missile installations. Washington became alarmed that the Cuban regime might interfere with American U-2 aerial reconnaissance flights. On April 20, following Castro's belligerent speech the previous day in which he threatened action against the overflights, the United States warned the Cuban leader and the Russians that to launch anti-aircraft missiles against these planes "could create a very dangerous situation." [6] While Soviet crews still controlled and operated the ground-to-air missile sites, it was expected that they would eventually be turned over to the Cubans, who were being trained to replace the Russians.

Cuba told the United Nations on April 24 that American reconnaissance flights over the island were "intolerable" and must be ended. "U-2 aircraft of the Central Intelligence Agency" had flown over Cuban territory 600 times up to "April 20 of this year"; in addition, there had been "1,181 provocations and violations" by American forces at Guantánamo since October 1962. Cuba did not request any specific U.N. action, but it ominously said that the Cuban government would "adopt in self-defense such measures as it deems pertinent." [7] At the same time Premier Khrushchev warned the United States that its policies toward Cuba would "drag the world into the abyss of another world war." He denounced as "evil fabrications" the contention of Washington officials that surveillance flights over Cuba had been in keeping with agreements made between him and President Kennedy in October 1962. At the Moscow May Day celebrations, he flatly said: "There was no such understanding, nor could there have been one. . . . We have always declared and we declare once more that threats against Cuba, continued violations of [Cuban] sovereignty and flights into Cuban airspace may have catastrophic consequences." [8]

Tension built up with speculation over whether Cuba would shoot down any of the U-2 planes, thus precipitating a major crisis. Belligerently, Castro had exclaimed, "We will defend our sovereignty, whatever it may cost and whatever may happen." But the United States continued the overflights. The Cuban leader soon softened his words, declaring his intention to take "all steps of a legal nature" to end the flights. Any attacks against the U-2 planes, he said, would be undertaken only as a last resort.

35. THE O.A.S. APPLIES SANCTIONS

As excitement over the aerial reconnaissance issue subsided, the United States directed its attention toward securing sanctions against Cuba for its subversive and terroristic acts against Venezuela. On February 18 a five-nation inter-American investigating team had submitted a 112-page report to the O.A.S. Council specifically accusing Cuba of shipping a large cache of arms to Venezuela in 1963 for use in subversive operations to overthrow the Venezuelan government.[9] Venezuela had lodged formal charges of aggression against Cuba before the O.A.S. Council in November 1963. The report confirmed Venezuelan claims that the weapons were intended for guerrillas and terrorists of the "Armed Forces of National Liberation," a subversive Communist-led organization that had tried to prevent the holding of Venezuela's 1963 presidential election. The discovery of the arms cache represented the first case of corroborated evidence on an important scale of Cuban subversive activities in Latin America.

While the O.A.S. was prepared to accept as fact Venezuelan charges of Cuban subversion and to condemn this action with a collective warning against the repetition of such revolutionary activity, opinion was divided as to whether sanctions should also be imposed. Generally speaking, the United States and Cuba's nearest neighbors, with the exception of Mexico, favored vigorous action. The more distant South American countries did not feel that Cuba posed a threat to their internal security and were therefore inclined to be less harsh.

During the spring and early summer, Caracas and Washington pressed for a showdown in the O.A.S. In an effort to cushion possible reprisals against Cuba, Castro, in an unusual 18-hour interview with *New York Times* correspondent Richard Eder early in July, indicated that Cuba would withhold material support from Latin American revolutionaries if the United States and its hemisphere allies would cease their material support of subversive activity against his country. The Cuban leader also expressed his desire to "normalize" relations with the United States in the hope of countering the American economic embargo and ending raids and sabotage from abroad.[10] Washington rebuffed this overture, and declared that no negotiations would be possible until Cuba ended its "ties of dependency" on the Soviet Union and ceased to promote subversion in Latin America. Performance rather than words, President Johnson said, would convince the United States of Cuban readiness to end the promotion of subversion.

The Ninth Meeting of Consultation of Ministers of Foreign Affairs of the American States convened in Washington on July 21 to deal with the Venezuelan charge of Cuban aggression. Strongly condemning the Cuban action, Secretary Rusk demanded that sanctions be adopted. "The time has now come," he declared, "to make it abundantly clear to the Castro regime that the American governments in complete solidarity will no longer tolerate its efforts to export revolution" through Communist subversive techniques. Alluding to Castro's July interview, Mr. Rusk sharply remarked that subversion was "not a subject for bargaining. It simply must stop. And when it does, the hemisphere will know it without the need for discussions with the Castro regime." The Secretary of State ended his address with an emotional appeal to the assembled delegates: 'Today it is Venezuela which is under attack. Is there any one of us who can say with assurance, 'It cannot be my country tomorrow'? So let's say to our brothers in Venezuela, its government and its brave people, 'We are with you in full solidarity and will act with you to insure the safety of your democracy. And let's say to the Castro regime, 'Your interference in the affairs of other countries in this hemisphere must stop—must stop and stop now.'" [11]

On July 26, coinciding with the eleventh anniversary of Castro's 26th of July revolutionary movement, the O.A.S. in its Final Act condemned the Cuban government for its "acts of aggression and of intervention against the territorial inviolability, the sovereignty, and the political independence of Venezuela" and imposed economic and diplomatic sanctions.[12] The vote was 15 to 3, with Chile, Mexico, and Uruguay voting against the resolution, and Bolivia abstaining. (As complainant, Venezuela was ineligible to vote.) The ministers reached a final accord when they dropped a proposal to suspend the only airline service between Cuba and other Latin American countries maintained through Mexico, and reworded the diplomatic sanction. The wording was changed so that it ordered O.A.S. members "not to maintain" such ties with Cuba rather than insist that relations be broken. Although sanctions were binding on all members, no deadline was fixed for compliance with them. They called for suspension of all trade with Cuba, except in foods, medicines, and medical equipment; suspension of all sea transportation to Cuba, except for emergency humanitarian reasons; and severance of diplomatic or consular relations with Cuba. Chile, Mexico, Uruguay, and Bolivia were the only O.A.S. members that still maintained diplomatic relations with Cuba.

Actually the psychological and political effects of the resolution were far greater than the economic consequences. Trade between Cuba and O.A.S. nations amounted to less than $15 million—not even 1 per cent of Cuban world trade. Moreover, the bulk of that trade was in foodstuffs, a category not covered by the trade ban. During the next two months the isolation of the Cuban regime in the hemisphere became virtually complete when Chile, Bolivia, and Uruguay broke off their diplomatic ties. Mexico remained the only holdout. While arguing that the resolution contravened Article 96 of the U.N. Charter (a provision prohibiting sanctions by regional organizations without U.N. consent), Mexico's principal objection was that the imposition of sanctions was contrary to the principle of nonintervention.

How much the measures adopted by the O.A.S. would contribute to toppling the Castro regime could not, of course, be determined. In the final analysis, Cuba's fate depended less on a trade boycott or O.A.S. sanctions than it did on the willingness of the Soviet Union to subsidize the Cuban economy. These actions clearly increased the Russian burden; but that they would have any decisive effect was improbable.

36. PANAMA EXPLODES

The Panama crisis that erupted on January 9 over a flag-raising incident had its roots in the Panamanian revolution against Colombia in 1903, in the subsequent treaty relationship with the United States, and in the question of sovereignty over the Canal Zone. The incident unfortunately awakened memories of past American interventionist policies in the Caribbean and Central America. Deep-seated resentments against the United States and the resident Americans or "Zonians" came to focus for both the small, rich oligarchic clique that controlled the Panama Republic and the large majority of Panamanians who lived in poverty. Among Panama's more serious grievances were the unsatisfactory terms of the treaty relationship with the United States, the discriminatory treatment of Panamanians in the Canal Zone, and the inadequate share of the Canal's earnings which Panama received.

Under the terms of the 1903 treaty, in return for the American right to build, operate, and defend an interoceanic canal and to control the Canal Zone "in perpetuity," Panama received a $10-million payment and an annual fee of $250,000 in gold. Subsequently, Panama declared that this was a "shot-gun" treaty, accepted and signed because of fears that Colombia would retake the country and that, in effect, the treaty had made Panama a colony of the United States. Panama objected especially to the creation of a foreign "enclave" in the Canal Zone, to the expropriation of land for defense and other pur-poses, and to the United States monopoly of trans-Isthmian traffic. After years of strained relations, another treaty was signed in 1936 and ratified in 1939 which surrendered the Amer-ican right to intervene and ended the guarantee of Panama's independence. But the United States retained the right of per-petual control over the Canal Zone.

Although Panamanians had complained bitterly about social and economic discrimination in the Canal Zone, many grievances relating to inequality of treatment were removed in a treaty signed in 1955. Resentment nonetheless continued to be voiced over the fact that Panamanian citizens were still being relegated to a second-class category. Panama also insisted on obtaining a larger share of the Canal's earnings. In 1936 the United States had raised its annual rental payment to $430,000 and then to $1.93 million in 1955. While Washington insisted that the Canal was a financial burden, Panama still considered the increased rentals inadequate. Washington claimed that the revenues were insufficient to retire the debt of the Canal, which in recent years had run in excess of $326 million, and pointed out that Panama benefited additionally from the $90 million spent each year in the Zone and also from tourist dollars. Nevertheless, Panama insisted that only if the original treaty were scrapped and re-placed by a new one could relations with the United States be improved. As Senator Fulbright observed, "It is the profound social and economic alienation between Panama and the Canal Zone, and its impact on the national feeling of the Panamanians,

that underlies the periodic crises that arise over the Canal."
Because of this situation, it was "entirely proper and necessary
for the United States to take the initiative in proposing new
arrangements that would redress some of Panama's grievances
against the treaty as it now stands." [13]

During the 1950's the intensified nationalistic feelings con-
verged on the flag issue. Panamanian students had sporadically
demonstrated along the border of the Zone and several times
tried to cross over and plant the Panamanian flag there. In 1959
a number of Panamanians were killed in an attempt to invade
the territory. The following year, in a move aimed at placating
the Panama Republic, President Eisenhower ordered its flag
to be flown in a park in the Canal Zone as evidence of its
titular sovereignty. Several members of Congress sharply criticized this action, calling it a "long-range blunder." They feared
that this would be the first step in ejecting the United States
from the Zone and placing in jeopardy the canal's efficient
operation and American readiness to protect its security. Officials
of the Defense Department consistently stressed the canal's strategic importance. Although conceding that the canal might easily
be destroyed or blocked in an all-out nuclear war, they argued
that as a major transportation artery and a short-cut between
the Atlantic and Pacific it was still of key importance in a cold-
war crisis or any nonnuclear or limited conflict. Political and
psychological effects of the canal's transfer to Panama or its inter-
nationalization could have damaging repercussions on the entire
structure of American bases around the world, and especially
those in the Caribbean and Latin America.

The crisis was precipitated on January 9 when Panamanian
students demanded that their own flag be flown together with
that of the United States at the Balboa High School in the
Canal Zone. Inflamed by Panamanian ultranationalists—and some
suspected Communists and Castroites—violence erupted. Demonstrations against the Zonians and the United States spread rapidly
to the cities at both ends of the canal with riots continuing for
three and a half days, almost without letup. When they finally
subsided, at least twenty-one Panamanians and three American

soldiers had lost their lives. Damage to American property was estimated at more than $2 million.

With the outbreak of the riots, President Roberto F. Chiari broke diplomatic relations with the United States on January 10, citing the "unjustifiable aggression" by American forces.[14] President Johnson telephoned President Chiari and in a personal diplomatic exchange tried to restore calm. Both sides agreed on the need to establish peace promptly, but Mr. Chiari told Mr. Johnson that an "integral revision of treaties" was essential.

President Johnson immediately sent Assistant Secretary Mann and a group of officials to Panama. The Organization of American States, at the same time, promptly dispatched members of the Inter-American Peace Committee, meanwhile deferring action on Panama's charge of American "aggression." Before cordial relations could again be resumed, Panama insisted, it must have sovereignty over the Canal, "just revenues" must be paid to Panama for the use of the Canal, and Panamanian workers must be accorded equal status with Americans.

On January 10 the U.N. Security Council met in emergency session. Panama declared that the prime cause of discord was the status of the Canal Zone and urged that it be changed "either by being nationalized—passing into the property of the state where it actually lies—or being made international." Ambassador Stevenson bluntly denied that the United States had engaged in aggression. "I do know that there is no evidence that either the police of the zone or the United States Army ever went outside the zone, that their only use of firearms was inside of the zone to protect the lives and property of American citizens residing there against an onrushing crowd of several thousand and against snipers." He urged the Security Council to shelve the debate so that the problem could be handled by the O.A.S.[15]

Both the United States and Panama agreed to permit the Inter-American Peace Committee of the O.A.S. to use its good offices to try to settle the dispute. Arriving in Panama on January 11, its members conferred with President Chiari and other Panamanian officials, and their presence temporarily eased the bitterness along the border. But the committee made clear that it had neither the authority nor the desire to assume responsibility for negotiating the status of the Zone. Meanwhile, Assistant Secretary Mann tried to find a basis for negotiation in private meetings with President Chiari. Although Washington stood ready to discuss any points of grievance within the context of the treaties, it would not consider any revision under pressure of Panama's demands. "We have a recognized obligation," a White House statement declared, "to operate the Canal efficiently and securely. And we intend to honor that obligation in the interests of all who depend on it." [16]

Following day-and-night negotiations with the Inter-American Peace Committee, Panama finally agreed on January 15 to resume diplomatic relations on the assumption that future negotiations with the United States would lead to a revision of the treaties. But confusion immediately arose. In the English text of a prepared statement, both the United States and Panama agreed to "formal discussions" of all matters outstanding between them. In the Spanish text, however, they agreed to *"negociaciones formales."* [17] President Chiari promptly declared in a radio broadcast that the United States had accepted his demand to renegotiate the Canal treaty. Washington officials insisted that there was a difference between "negotiate" and "discuss" and that they had never agreed to undertake formal negotiations, but simply to *discuss* the treaty. Angered, President Chiari immediately repudiated the agreement. Domestic politics, national pride, and sensitivity on both sides clearly underlay the semantic misunderstanding. President Chiari had been most anxious to impress on his people the fact that Washington had bowed to his wishes. President Johnson, with an eye on the forthcoming November elections, did not wish to convey the impression that he had made any concessions that would *a priori* sacrifice American interests.

A week later, Mr. Johnson took the initiative and tried to clear the atmosphere by making the American position more flexible. He issued a statement in which he expressed willingness to have a "full and frank review and reconsideration" of all matters outstanding, without limitation. "We have set no preconditions," said the President, "to the resumption of peaceful discussions. We are bound by no preconceptions of what they will produce. . . . We are prepared, 30 days after relations are restored, to sit in conference with Panamanian officials to seek concrete solutions to all problems dividing our countries. Each Government will be free to raise any issue and to take any position. And our Government will consider all practical solutions to practical problems that are offered in good faith." [18] The United States was thus prepared to *discuss* the subject of revision, but it firmly opposed a *renegotiation* of the treaty, especially since it was not certain what Panama wished to change.

President Johnson's offer was not accepted. Panama insisted on invoking the 1947 Rio treaty of reciprocal assistance, declaring its intention of bringing charges of United States "aggression" before the Council of the O.A.S. Washington had no objection to this move, and an emergency session of the O.A.S. Council was held January 31–February 7. The final resolution provided for a five-nation committee to investigate the disorders of January 9 and 10 and to mediate the continuing quarrel.[19] However, all references to charges of U.S. aggression were dropped.

After a week-long inquiry, the O.A.S. committee reported that Communist influence in the riots was minimal and that the firepower used by U.S. troops was "disproportionate" to the threat posed. But, the committee concluded, while American actions were deemed excessive, they did not justify Panama's charges of aggression.[20] A regrettable feature of the incident had been the absence of an American ambassador when it occurred. Both Presidents Kennedy and Johnson had delayed appointing a successor to Ambassador Joseph S. Farland who had resigned in August 1963.

During March further difficulties arose on finding a formula for undertaking the settlement of the dispute. After painstaking efforts to resolve differences in phraseology, the inter-American mediators announced on March 15 that both the United States and Panama had agreed to "designate special ambassadors with sufficient powers to carry out discussions and negotiations with the objective of reaching a fair and just agreement," and to restore diplomatic relations "as soon as possible." However, the next day, President Johnson, in an address to the O.A.S. in Washington, startled the assembled delegates when he declared that there had not yet been "a genuine meeting of minds" between him and President Chiari.[21] Subsequently he explained in a television interview that Panama appeared to want more binding language than the United States was prepared to accept. The effect of the President's statement was the collapse of O.A.S. mediation.

On March 21, however, President Johnson again opened the door to a possible settlement of differences. At a news conference he strongly emphasized American readiness to "review every issue which now divides us, and every problem which the Panama Government wishes to raise." [22] The word "review"— which got around the use of such words as "discuss" or "negotiate" —appeared to imply that the United States would consider a revision of the 1903 treaty. The presidential statement promptly brought a favorable response from Panama. Quite unexpectedly, after secret talks, a joint declaration was signed on April 3 by the United States and Panama which called for the immediate resumption of diplomatic relations and the adoption of procedures for the "prompt elimination of the causes of conflict between the two countries without limitations or preconditions of any kind." Hailing the agreement as a great day for the Western Hemisphere, President Johnson appointed a special ambassador to handle the difficult task of restoring amicable relations with Panama.[23]

In May, Marco A. Robles, who headed the government coalition parties, emerged victorious in Panama's national elections and was inaugurated as President on October 1. His major task was to secure a revision of the Canal Zone treaty, but he also confronted serious economic problems, in part, the result of dislocations caused by the riots in January. Late in November President Robles sent representatives to Washington to discuss the status of the Canal Zone, and preliminary talks were initiated on December 2. Two weeks later, on December 18, President

Johnson announced that he had reached two important decisions: first, to "press forward with Panama and other interested governments" on plans to build a sea-level canal in Central America or Colombia; and second, to negotiate "an entirely new treaty on the existing Panama Canal." Noting that Congress had already authorized $17 million for studies of possible routes, the President indicated four routes that seemed most practical for a sea-level canal—"two in Panama, one in Colombia, and one which goes through Nicaragua and possibly Costa Rica as well." In a new treaty with Panama, Mr. Johnson declared, "we must retain the rights which are necessary for the effective operation and the protection of the canal and the administration of the areas that are necessary for these purposes." He made it clear, however, that the new treaty, which would replace that of 1903, would recognize Panama's sovereignty and provide "for its own termination when a sea-level canal comes into operation." [24] The present treaties, he said, would remain in effect until a new agreement was concluded. For the first time, President Johnson formally linked the questions of the old canal with that of constructing a new canal that would be more adequate for modern shipping needs.

The United States did not indicate which canal route was considered the most feasible. It was expected to take about four years to complete engineering surveys of the four routes. Only then would the technical decision be made on where the new waterway would be situated. Another ten to fifteen years would be required for the actual construction.

The announcement appeared to be welcome in Panama and Latin America, although many saw it as a shrewd step on President Johnson's part to liquidate the long-standing Canal Zone dispute. They were also aware of the President's adroit maneuver in keeping open the selection of the location of a new canal. Since Panama was eager to have the new canal built on its territory, the United States was in a strong bargaining position for negotiating a new treaty. United States officials, moreover, seemed to have little doubt that a new canal in Panama would pose the fewest engineeering problems at the least cost. It was evident that they were prepared to make substantial concessions in any new treaty. Most significantly, however, a new approach had been taken for a reexamination of the canal issue, as well as of America's relations with Panama and Central America.

37. MEXICO . AND . CENTRAL . AMERICA

Relations between the United States and Mexico during the year were generally marked by an effort to further the cooperation and good will nurtured during the Kennedy period. On January 14 the Chamizal Convention, concluded in Mexico City the previous August, was ratified. The Convention settled a long-standing dispute over a tract of land at El Paso, Texas, that had become U.S. territory because of changes in the course of the Rio Grande River. Although the end of the Chamizal controversy indicated the closer ties between the two countries, two other problems aroused concern in Mexico: the salinity of the waters of the Colorado River, and the entry of migrant labor into the United States.

Presidents Johnson and López Mateos met in Los Angeles on February 20 to receive honorary degrees from the University of California, following which they flew to Palm Springs for two days of talks. Mr. Johnson dwelt upon the need to strengthen the O.A.S. and the Alliance for Progress. The Mexican President, on the other hand, emphasized the importance of finding a way to remove excess salt from the Colorado River waters flowing to Mexico, which he regarded as the only really serious problem between the two countries. He was assured that a plan "to find an adequate permanent solution" was being actively considered and would soon be presented to Congress.[25]

During the spring there was much agitation in Mexico over the Colorado waters dispute. Under a 1944 treaty the United States had guaranteed to deliver to Mexico 1.5 million acre-feet of Colorado River water annually. Beginning in 1961, however, Mexicans protested that the waters they were receiving were not acceptable because of their increased salinity—Arizona's

Wellton-Mohawk project, completed in February 1961, was chiefly responsible for markedly changing the quality of the river water, and consequent heavy crop losses. Rich cotton and wheat lands of the Mexicali Valley were slowly being destroyed, and there were demands to take the controversy to the International Court of Justice for arbitration. President López Mateos was greatly disturbed over the failure of the United States to act quickly, since it provided Mexican leftist and Communist groups with a rallying point for their attacks on both the Mexican and American governments and enabled them to stir up anti-American feelings along the northern border.[26] A temporary agreement was reached late in October providing for the diversion of Colorado waters to the Gulf of California for a period of one month. Meanwhile, steps were taken toward a permanent solution involving the construction of a canal to divert the river water to the sea during times of high salinity.

Another source of friction centered around the so-called "bracero" question. In December 1963 Congress decided to end the program under which Mexican migrant laborers were permitted to do farm work in the United States, when it indicated that Public Law 78, due to expire December 31, 1964, would not be renewed. Although President López Mateos said that his country had never considered the program "mandatory," many Mexicans were disturbed that rescinding the law would create hardships and urged the United States to continue to permit entry of migrant farm workers. While Mexico did not consider the problem of "braceros" as acute as the dispute over the Colorado River waters, it nevertheless was hopeful that some alternative to Public Law 78 could be found. During the fall President Johnson asked Secretary of Labor W. Willard Wirtz to undertake a study of how many Americans were available for the agricultural work the "braceros" had done in the past; for if the study revealed a shortage of American labor, the two countries would agree to the continued entry of migrant workers.

But Mexico was primarily occupied with sustaining and advancing its prosperity rather than with any difficulties it might have with the United States. On July 5 the Mexican people turned out in record numbers to elect Gustavo Díaz Ordaz as the nation's new president. It was expected that Mr. Díaz Ordaz, a middle-of-the-roader and advocate of free enterprise, would follow the policies of his predecessor and place economic growth above doctrinaire politics. In his final message to the nation in September, President López Mateos spoke with pride of Mexico's economic growth, which was expected to reach a 7 per cent rate by the end of the year. Observing that Mexico had lifted itself out of the ranks of underdeveloped countries during his six years in office, he pointed to the 52 per cent increase in industrial production since 1958, the advances in agriculture, and the stability of the peso. Although still facing many domestic tasks, Mexico could indeed boast of the fastest-growing, inflation-free economy of any country south of the Rio Grande.

Nevertheless, President Díaz Ordaz cautioned that "the political and economic stability that we enjoy are not gifts. They are the result of a dynamic society that establishes economic development as a fundamental task." In foreign relations the new president pledged to maintain the nation's neutrality with respect to Cuba, in the face of American efforts to rally support in the hemisphere against Castro. Despite differences on Cuba, President Johnson continued his efforts to build up a rapport with Mexico and to remove those obstacles that had marred the friendship between the two countries. This had been strikingly demonstrated in the visit made by President-elect Díaz Ordaz to the LBJ ranch in November when a number of problems were discussed informally, and a personal relationship was established between the two leaders.

In the Central American republics of Guatemala, El Salvador, Honduras, Nicaragua, and Costa Rica, the United States met generally hostile reactions because of the Panama incident. Most Central Americans sided with Panama in its insistence on a renegotiation of the canal treaty and in its demand for sovereignty over the Canal Zone. Although the governments refrained from issuing formal declarations, student demonstrations denouncing American action in the Zone took place in Nicaragua and Costa Rica.

For the most part, however, the countries of Central America were absorbed in their own internal development problems. There was continued progress in the economic integration of the region. On February 25 an agreement was reached to establish a Central American monetary union, a forward step in creating a unified monetary structure. During May President Johnson underlined his support for the Alliance for Progress by signing several long-term, low-credit loans, the largest being the $10 million granted to the Central American Bank for Economic Development. Further steps to encourage the region's economic integration were taken during the third annual review conference of the Alliance for Progress held at Lima in December. The United States announced that it was prepared to contribute $25 million toward the development of the Central American Common Market, if the prospective members would put $5 million into a special fund to be used exclusively for regional projects. Although the advances made in economic integration exceeded the hopes of its backers, politics and internal bickerings continued to cloud the future of Central American unity.

38. THE DOMINICAN REPUBLIC AND HAITI

After the fall of the Trujillo regime in 1961, the United States, it will be recalled, became deeply involved in the Dominican Republic's affairs. An initial period of disorder and chaos followed the dictator's assassination, but once the dust settled, Washington made a valiant attempt to help the Caribbean country achieve a peaceful transition to democracy. Foreign aid assistance was unstintingly extended in an effort to make the Dominican Republic a showplace for the Alliance for Progress. These efforts made a signal contribution to the establishment of a constitutional democracy. In December 1962 remarkably fair elections led to an overwhelming victory for Juan Bosch, a distinguished novelist and political liberal, generally well thought of in Latin America.

President Kennedy had strongly supported Mr. Bosch's goals of achieving agrarian reform, expanded education, full employment, economic development, and political democracy. Unfortunately, the Dominican experiment soon became mired in internal political and economic difficulties. In September 1963 the seven-month-old Bosch administration was overthrown, and a three-man civilian junta representing six right-wing political parties, was installed. President Kennedy at once withheld recognition and suspended economic aid. Not only did this action express the Kennedy administration's disapproval of the Bosch ouster, it also reflected Washington's concern over a trend—the *coup* virtually coincided with military takeovers in Guatemala, Ecuador, and Honduras— that seemed to threaten the foundations of the Alliance for Progress. President Johnson, however, became convinced that the policy of punishing Latin American republics where the military seized power would, in the long run, be detrimental to U.S. interests. On December 14, 1963, the State Department decided to extend diplomatic recognition to the Dominican Republic and Honduras and quietly moved toward restoring some economic and military aid to both countries.[27]

Throughout the year, Washington maintained an attitude of cautious reserve toward the Dominican government. In contrast to the Kennedy administration, President Johnson avoided any involvement in the island's affairs. A measure of anxiety nevertheless persisted, for the United States was worried lest the civilian junta be shunted aside, and an absolute military dictatorship be established in its stead. As a result, Washington tended to support the junta tacitly in spite of the unsatisfactory situation, and hopefully waited for a return to constitutional rule. A possibility that this might take place came during the summer when six political parties ratified a plan for holding two elections—one for a constituent assembly and the other for president and government representatives. Followers of the deposed President Bosch and two other parties withheld their support, however, demanding full political freedom for the exiled leader and more guarantees for a free election. Although September 1, 1965, was the date set by the junta for electing a new president, it appeared unlikely that the plan could go into effect without the agreement of the opposition parties. The civilian junta was faced with the tasks of keeping the economy from collapsing, thwarting threats of violence from Communist and leftist groups, and creating an atmosphere of confidence. Although the junta managed to obtain the support of the business community, other groups in Dominican society were quite discontented. Sabotage, strikes, and underground resistance kept the country in turmoil. Early in June, in a broadcast to the Dominicans from his exile in Puerto Rico, Mr. Bosch predicted that there would be "a revolution soon because of widespread corruption in political and military ranks." [28] Disheartened by the deteriorating situation, Washington intimated that American economic aid might be withdrawn unless the country's financial affairs were put in better order. The various austerity measures adopted were bitterly opposed by the Dominican people. Thus, at the end of the year, economic and political stability still eluded the Dominican Republic.

In Haiti, next door to the Dominican Republic, the United States also had to deal with a difficult situation. Because of the cruel and arbitrary dictatorship of Dr. François Duvalier, the government of this Caribbean country had long been an object of distaste in Washington. American economic and military aid had been cut off in 1962, and in May 1963 diplomatic relations were suspended. For a time a Navy task force had been stationed off Port-au-Prince. But all these actions, much to Washington's embarrassment, had failed to undermine the dictatorial regime. Diplomatic relations were resumed in November 1963, and Benson E. L. Timmons, 3rd, was named ambassador, though he did not take up his duties until February.

The Johnson administration quietly effected a change in the American stance toward Haiti. Although its strong disapproval of the republic's government continued unabated, Washington felt that the impoverished people in the country should not be made to suffer because of the U.S. attitude. The maltreatment of American citizens, the extortionate demands on American business interests, the expulsion without cause of many official

American representatives, and the inhumanity and brutality of
Dr. Duvalier's regime could not be ignored. While it was impossible to consider restoring direct aid, the United States decided to support the extension of indirect assistance in an effort
to ameliorate some of the harsh conditions in the country. Early
in the year, the Inter-American Development Bank, with Washington's blessing, granted a loan of some $2 million to improve
and extend drinking water facilities in Port-au-Prince.

In the spring Dr. Duvalier declared himself president for
life, a move which surprised few Haitians since a year earlier
he had continued himself in the office without benefit of formal
elections. Speaking to a crowd on April 1, he affirmed, "I am
an exceptional man, the kind the country could produce only
once every 50 to 75 years." [29] Three weeks later, the legislature
suspended a series of constitutional guarantees and declared
that Dr. Duvalier would rule by decree. It also discarded Haiti's
1957 constitution and named a fifteen-man committee to write a
new one. On May 25 a new constitution was approved making
Dr. Duvalier president for life; it was confirmed by plebiscite in
June. Two aims seemed to prompt this maneuver: to broaden
Dr. Duvalier's acceptance within the legalistic-minded inter-
American community and to enable him to qualify for long-range
aid under the Alliance for Progress, which required that beneficiaries maintain some semblance of constitutional rule. Late in
May, President Duvalier appealed to the United States for a
better understanding of the special political, cultural, and economic conditions of his country. He defended his form of autocratic
government as the only alternative to chaos and Communism,
and argued that improved relations were necessary to maintain
peace and stability in the Caribbean.

But conditions within Haiti went from bad to worse, and the
government moved steadily toward bankruptcy. In addition
to economic troubles, the Duvalier regime was threatened by
armed invasions of exiled Haitians. Two such invasions occurred,
late in June and early in August. During the summer Dr. Duvalier
tried to buy naval equipment and thirty T-28 trainer aircraft
in the United States to bolster his armed forces, but Wash-

ington blocked the licenses for their export. Although the guerrilla movements were sustained longer than those undertaken in previous years, both were crushed by the fall, and what momentarily appeared to be a major threat to the Duvalier regime ended. While still strongly disapproving of Dr. Duvalier's totalitarian methods, the United States, by the end of the year, reached a point of reluctant acceptance of the Haitian dictator's rule.

CHAPTER TEN
THE MIDDLE EAST AND SOUTH ASIA

LIKE MANY OTHER developing regions, the Middle East and the vast Indian Subcontinent experienced continued turmoil. Although the United States found itself involved both directly and indirectly in disputes that arose between the Arab states and Israel, within the Arab world itself, and between India and Pakistan over Kashmir, it largely sought to avoid any prominent role in the affairs of the several countries.

Undoubtedly, the most difficult problems with which the United States had to contend were the consequences of the rising tide of Arab nationalism. During the year this force made itself especially felt in the continuing Arab campaign against Israel, in opposition to Britain's presence in southern Arabia, in attacks against the retention of American and British bases in Libya, and in Nasser's denunciation of what he described as American-British-Belgian intervention in the Congo.

By the mid-1960's, practically all vestiges of the old colonial systems had been eliminated in the Middle East. Britain still held on to its last foothold in southern Arabia and its protectorates and client states on the Persian Gulf. For a variety of strategic, economic, and political reasons, the British were unwilling to relinquish their base at Aden. It was deemed essential both to Britain's global military position and to the protection of its interests in the Middle East. Of these by far the most important was access to Middle East oil, on which British and Western European economic life was heavily dependent.

Formidable problems continued to plague the Indian Subcontinent where the tasks of coping with the needs of the area's vast population, of stimulating economic development, and of ending religious discord seemed almost intractable. In addition to these chronic ailments, Communist China's explosion of its first nuclear device in October posed a new danger to the region. Its psychological impact inevitably compounded the anxieties occasioned by Prime Minister Jawaharlal Nehru's death in May and the weakening of India's leadership both in Asia and the rest of the world.

39. ARAB-ISRAELI RELATIONS AND THE UNITED STATES

A fever of excitement and apprehension swept through the Arab states—especially in Syria, Jordan, Lebanon, and Iraq at the turn of the year. Israel, after a dozen years of planning and construction, had almost completed the first stage of its National Water Carrier project, the purpose of which was to divert Jordan River waters by a pipeline from Lake Tiberias (the Sea of Galilee) to other parts of Israel and eventually, by 1970, to the arid Negev region in the south. Arabs had long feared that Israel's use of the Jordan to irrigate the Negev would considerably increase its capacity to absorb immigrants and strengthen its military potential. Their spokesmen had created the impression that once the diversion of water began it would be resisted by force.

The problem of water development in the Jordan Valley—like that of boundaries, the Arab refugee question, and the status of Jerusalem—had been a major issue exacerbating relations between the Arab states and Israel. Israeli plans to bring Jordan water to the south had been formulated in the early 1950's. During this period, international plans had also been drawn up for the sharing of the Jordan River waters by Israel and other Arab states. These schemes, notably the comprehensive one proposed in 1955 by Eric Johnston, President Eisenhower's personal representative,[1] were rejected by the Arab states on the ground that their acceptance would amount to a *de facto* rec-

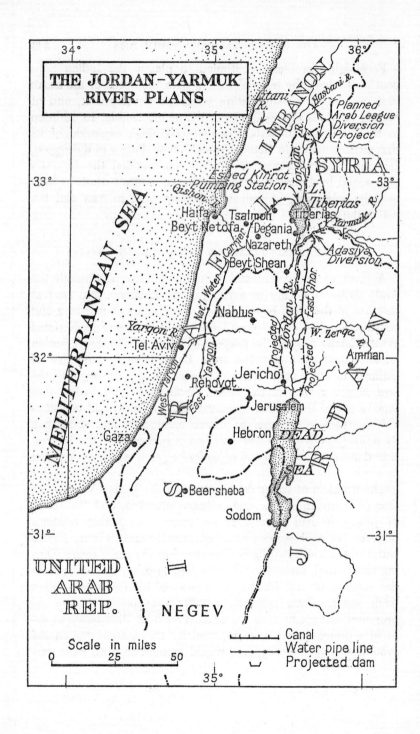

THE JORDAN-YARMUK
RIVER PLANS

LEBANON

Litani R.

Hasbani R.

Planned
Arab League
Diversion
Project

SYRIA

Eshed Kinrot
Pumping Station

Qishon R.

L. Tiberias

Haifa   Tsalmon   Tiberias

Beyt Netofa   Degania   Yarmuk R.

Nazareth   Adasiya Diversion

Beyt Shean

MEDITERRANEAN SEA

Natl Water carrier

Nablus

Projected

W. Zerqa R.

Yarqon R.

Tel Aviv   Yarqon

East

West Yarqon

Jericho

Projected Jordan R.

East Ghor

Amman

Rehovot

Jerusalem

Hebron   DEAD

Gaza

SEA

Beersheba

Sodom

JORDAN

ISRAEL

UNITED
ARAB
REP.

NEGEV

Canal
Water pipe line
Projected dam

Scale in miles

0   25   50

ognition of Israel, and also because the plan would benefit Israel. In the view of Arab leaders, anything that helped Israel in any way was a threat to their nationalist cause. Nevertheless, Israel decided to develop its share of the river system within the general scheme of allocation specified in the Johnston plan. Jordan meanwhile formulated its own project, partly financed with aid from the United States, to divert waters from the Yarmuk River, a tributary of the Jordan. The Yarmuk project began operations in 1961 when the first stage of the east Ghor Canal was completed. Washington supported both the Jordan and Israel ventures, but it constantly sought to keep open the possibility of a regional approach to the development of Middle East water resources.

As pressures built up for Arab action against the Israeli Jordan River plan, the Arab states were startled in December 1963 when President Nasser announced that he had no intention of involving Egypt in a war with Israel on this count. His statement was taken as a blunt warning to Syria and Jordan that they could not depend on the U.A.R. to intervene if they clashed with Israel "The mistakes of 1948 must not be repeated," Nasser asserted. "If I cannot make war I shall say so. Because to wage war without being ready to do so would mean catastrophe." The Egyptian leader made it clear that before joint Arab action could be undertaken, the bitter feuds that divided the Arab states and dissipated their energies had to be ended. On December 23, 1963, he called for a summit conference of the heads of state of all Arab countries to meet in Cairo to deal with the problem. Nasser grasped the opportunity for a renewed drive toward Arab leadership, and also sought to shift the ground in the struggle against Israel from a basically military to a political approach.

A great assembly of Arab kings and presidents representing thirteen nations met in Cairo, January 13-17. Nothing like this gathering had been seen since the Arab League was founded in March 1945. Although the Cairo meeting's basic purpose was to plan a counterattack on the Israeli water project, steps were also taken to foster Arab political unity. Arab leaders, some of whom had been at each others' throats, suddenly enveloped each other in warm embraces. Perhaps most astonishing was to see President Nasser handsomely greeting King Saud of Saudi Arabia, whom he had once accused of plotting his assassination. Both Jordan's King Hussein, who also bitterly opposed Nasser, and King Saud reopened diplomatic relations with Egypt. At the Cairo meeting a declaration was unanimously endorsed by the Arab leaders to end their differences, cease propaganda attacks on one another, and forge closer relations. Similar declarations and agreements in the past had, however, foundered.

The thirteen-nation conference decided upon a threefold program of action. First, agreement was reached on a joint Arab project to divert large quantities of water from the headwaters of the Jordan River. Waters of three tributaries—the Hasbani, the Banias, and the Yarmuk—were to be siphoned off by dams and irrigation networks in Lebanon, Syria, and Jordan. The cost of the project was estimated at about $200 million, most of which was expected to be financed by Arab oil revenues from Saudi Arabia, Kuwait, Iraq and perhaps Libya. As a start, though, the Cairo meeting undertook only to try to effect a simple diversion of the Jordan River headwaters that would require $17.5 million and eighteen months to complete, and it sought to accelerate and expand a diversion project being constructed by the Jordanian government on the Yarmuk River. Although ostensibly the plans aimed at greater Arab use of the Jordan River, their primary purpose appeared to be to reduce drastically the volume available in its lower reaches and thus deprive Israel of essential water.

Second, the Arab leaders decided to establish a unified Military Command, under Egypt's Lieutenant-General Aly Amer, and to strengthen the armies of Syria, Lebanon, and Jordan, enabling them to back up the Arab diversion plan against an Israeli attack. The summit conference, however, rejected Syria's demand for immediate resort to arms, if necessary, to block Israel's project.

Third, the Arab summit meeting agreed on the creation of a "Palestine entity" or "personality" that would represent Palestinians in the Arab League. The proposal, though vague, aimed at the formation of a representative body which would seek to rally all Palestinian Arabs, no matter where they might be located, into a single movement—its object being to give force and direction to their yearning to recover their "lost homeland."

Generally speaking, in view of the past belligerent stance taken by the Arab leaders against Israel's Jordan River plan, the results of the Cairo meeting were moderate. Nevertheless, although the situation was not immediately dangerous, Israel could not help but be concerned that the Arab states were embarking on a program of thorough preparation for a trial of strength. Even if Israel could manage without the Jordan River waters, which it claimed it could not, the project had gone too far to turn back. The $150 million spent on the scheme was the largest sum which Israel had allocated for a single project in its sixteen-year history. But more fundamental was the thought that its national sovereignty and independence were at stake. There was little question that in a showdown Israel would fight to assure its existence.[2] Water, in the arid lands of the Middle East, was as inflammable as oil.

The United States declared that its intention, as in the past was to try to promote regional stability and to be friends with *all* parties in the Middle East. Evidently responding to the Cairo conference, Deputy Under-Secretary U. Alexis Johnson, in a formal statement on American policy, warned the Middle Eastern nations on January 20 that "any intended victim of any would-be aggression can count on our support." He stressed that the United States did not want to take sides in any regional dispute, but "this does not mean that we will stand idly by if aggression is committed." The United States, Mr. Johnson said, was pledged not only to take a hand in any Arab-Israeli conflict, but he implied that it was also ready to defend one Arab state against another. "We have an interest in the independence and well-being of all the states of the Near East," the Under-Secretary explained. "Instability, uncertainty, and insecurity in one Near Eastern state may quickly spread into the region as a whole." Reiterating President Kennedy's statement of May 8, 1963, he reaffirmed the administration's policy to support the security of both Israel and its neighbors, to oppose the use of force or the threat of force in the Middle East, and to seek to limit the spread of Communism in the region.[3]

Cairo angrily charged that the United States could not play a neutral role in the Middle East since "Israel was born on the doorstep of the White House." Washington promptly assured the Arab states that Under-Secretary Johnson's statement was not meant as a reply to the Cairo summit meeting resolutions; but the Arabs, nevertheless, took it as a warning to them. President Johnson, speaking in New York at the annual dinner of the Weizmann Institute on February 6, further offended the Arabs when he managed in one sentence to touch on three subjects on which they were extraordinarily sensitive—cooperation with Israel, nuclear power, and water. The United States, said the President, "has begun discussions with the representatives of Israel on cooperative research in using nuclear energy to turn salt water into fresh water." He quickly added that the American offer of cooperation with Israel was also open to "other countries," presumably Israel's neighbors. "Water should never be a cause of war; it should always be a force for peace." [4] The Arab world, however, immediately saw sinister implications in the announcement.

King Hussein of Jordan, on an official visit to the White House in mid-April, ruled out the possibility of any international compromise on the Arab-Israeli dispute over Israel's water plan. Reaffirming the stand taken by Arab leaders at Cairo, he said at a news conference on April 14 that the decision was not to oppose Israel's project by force, but simply to dam two of the Jordan's tributaries rising in Arab lands to prevent Israel from ever getting the water. Declaring that Israel was a "real and ever-present danger" to the survival of Arab nations, King Hussein urged the United States to take a "new look" at its Middle East policy.[5] Without any fanfare, about three weeks later, on May 5, water began to flow through the first sections of Israel's pipeline; full operation did not start until the summer. When completed, the pipeline was expected to stretch a hundred miles from the western Galilee to the northern reaches of the Negev Desert. Israel assured the United States that withdrawals would not exceed its share as originally proposed under the Johnston plan.

In the meantime Premier Khrushchev, on his first trip to Africa, arrived in Egypt on May 9 for a sixteen-day visit in connection with ceremonies marking the completion of the first stage of the billion-dollar Aswan High Dam. Greeted by thousands of cheering Egyptians and warmly embraced by Nasser, the Soviet Premier declared that the Soviet Union was carrying out the great task—which he later called the "eighth wonder of the world"—"for the sake of liberating nations and consolidating peace all over the world." Standing on a granite bluff high over the site of the Aswan Dam on May 14, Khrushchev and Nasser together pressed the button setting off a dynamite charge that opened a channel to divert the waters of the Nile. It would take four more years to complete the project, which was expected to increase tillable acreage along the Nile from six to eight million acres. By contrast, Mr. Khrushchev did not hesitate to endorse strongly the Arab stand against Israel's diversion of the Jordan River waters. He told applauding Egyptians that Israel had "robbed Arabs of their own sources of water" and condemned it as a "stooge of imperialists."

Before departing, the Soviet Premier announced that a $277 million loan had been granted to the U.A.R. to help finance roughly 10 per cent of Egypt's second five-year plan that was to start in 1965. Partly to counter the Soviet Union and to preserve its own links with the Nasser regime, the United States urged the International Monetary Fund to extend a $40 million loan to Egypt that was unprecedented in its liberal terms.

About a week later, on June 1, Premier Levi Eshkol of Israel visited the White House. Although former Premier David Ben-Gurion had been in the United States several times, most recently in 1961, this was the first official visit of an Israeli Premier since the founding of Israel in 1948. He told President Johnson that it was "not only possible but imperative" for Israel and its Arab neighbors "to resolve their disputes peacefully." In a joint communiqué,[6] Premier Eshkol was reassured of American "support for the territorial integrity and political independence of all countries in the Near East," and "the firm opposition of the U.S. to aggression and the use of force or the threat of force against any country."

On September 5 the Arab chiefs of state met for a second time at Alexandria for the purpose of implementing the January decisions. Although they had agreed on projects to cut off the Jordan headwaters, no actual construction had taken place. Difficulties steadily mounted in achieving cooperative action. Lebanon, Jordan, Syria, and Saudi Arabia, in particular, refused to give blanket permission to joint Arab forces—which presumably would be mainly Egyptian—to enter their territories. Since the Arabs expected Israel to attack their water works once construction began, this intransigence threatened not only the establishment of a united Arab military command, but also the start on the river projects.

General Amer presented a grim report to the summit meeting on the relative strengths of the Israeli and Arab forces. He bluntly declared that Lebanon, Jordan, and Syria—upon whom the main burden of controlling the headwaters and tributaries of the Jordan would fall—were incapable of defending themselves against a possible Israeli attack. Pledges of $14 million a year for the next five years were made to strengthen the armed forces of these countries. However, Syria, Jordan, Lebanon, and Saudi Arabia rejected a demand by General Amer for authority to move his troops from one Arab country to another in peacetime to meet any anticipated threat. Lebanon further insisted that no other Arab toops would be permitted to cross its borders under any circumstances without the Lebanese Parliament's prior approval. Disheartened by these reservations, General Amer argued that unless the Arab states supported a strong unified force, there was little hope of carrying out the proposed political decisions.

Although the Arab leaders were unable to agree on military arrangements, they decided to order an immediate start on construction projects in Syria and Jordan. As a first step, plans were pushed forward for the building of a large storage dam at Makheiba on the Yarmuk River in Jordan at a cost of $28.7 million. The Arab chiefs of state also endorsed a new Palestine Liberation Organization as the legal representative of the Palestine refugees and approved the formation of a Palestine army which would be recruited from among the refugees in Arab lands. The latter decision was potentially the most explosive action taken at the Alexandria conference. It envisioned the creation of a new commando force, to be trained in guerrilla and conventional warfare and operating under the unified Military Command; its primary task would be the "liberation of Palestine." Despite the efforts to develop mechanisms for cooperative action, the summit meeting disclosed that it was far easier for Arab leaders to agree on opposition to Israel than on the means to implement it.

As Israel moved ahead with its National Water Carrier project and as the Arab states took steps to strengthen the unified Military Command, tensions increased. They came to a head on November 13 in a clash between Israel and Syria along the northeastern border near the headwaters of the River Dan. A two-hour battle, in which Israeli jet fighters attacked Syrian entrenched positions after three Israeli villages had been bombarded, was one of the worst outbursts of Israeli-Arab violence since the 1956 Sinai-Suez crisis. Fighting started when a mobile Israeli patrol came under Syrian fire along a road being repaired in the area of Tel Dan. This section was particularly sensitive, partly because both parties differed over the location of the armistice demarcation line where the work was being done, but mainly because at Tel Dan one of the three sources—and by far the largest—of the Jordan River rises. Control of the Dan source was vital to Israel's water program, since it supplied about half the total volume of the Jordan River waters.

On November 16, the U.N. Security Council was called into urgent session at the request of Syria and Israel. Both parties accused each other of provoking the incident. The Syrian delegate charged that the Israeli patrol had been some fifty yards inside the Syrian border when it was fired upon, but the Israeli ambassador denied this assertion and declared that, according to a 1962 survey, the road was definitely within Israeli territory, seven yards from the border. It was evident, however, that the real issue was not the road, but the question of sovereignty over the area, especially with respect to Tel Dan and its immediate vicinity, and the fact that the Arabs had threatened to divert the headwaters of the Jordan to deny the water to Israel. Well aware that Syria had called for immediate military action at the Alexandria conference, Israel suspected that the Syrian aim was to force other Arab states into more active support of Syria. Syrians, however, were convinced that Israelis had precipitated the incident to test the effectiveness of the unified Military Command. Arabs also felt that the air attacks might have been a prelude to a "preventive war," which they claimed was advocated by certain Israeli circles.[7]

A U.N. investigation found that the firing on November 13 had begun from the Syrian side, though both sides, it said, had obviously been prepared for an intensive bombardment. To avoid future friction in the area, it recommended that an independent land survey of this section of the Syrian-Israeli border be undertaken. On December 17 a Moroccan-sponsored resolution blaming Israel alone for the incident failed of adoption.[8] Four days later the Soviet Union vetoed a United States-British resolution calling upon Israel and Syria to cooperate to prevent future clashes in the disputed area; it had sought to obtain the agreement of both parties to a survey and demarcation of the armistice line, as suggested by U.N. investigators.[9]

The tensions between the Arab world and Israel over water were ominous, but it was evident that they were a symptom rather than a cause of hostilities which developed during the year. No less than in previous years, the fundamental problems were how to achieve an accommodation that would make it possible for the Arabs to accept the existence of the Israeli state, and how to temper the emotional hatreds in the region so that attention could be concentrated on necessary constructive tasks to develop the resources of the Middle East for the benefit of all its inhabitants. While the chances were dim that these goals could be obtained, the United States was hopeful that in time it could be realized, provided the sources of conflict could be contained and regional cooperation could somehow be encouraged.

40. NASSER, THE ARAB WORLD, AND THE WEST

Nasser worked assiduously through the year to extend Egypt's influence in the Arab world. He showed vigorous leadership at the two Arab summit conferences. With a view to reestablishing on a new basis the United Arab Republic (Syria's defection in 1961 had broken up the earlier union), he took steps to coordinate Egyptian policies with those of Iraq and Yemen. By various maneuvers he tried to patch relations with Jordan, Morocco, and Saudi Arabia; he took a new approach to the Yemeni war; and with his fulminations against American and British bases in Libya and the British presence in Aden and southern Arabia, he renewed pressures on the West and reiterated the identification of Nasserism with Arab nationalism.

Within the Arab world, an immediate goal of Egyptian policy was a political union with Iraq and Syria. But a major obstacle to union was the Baath party. In opposition to those who wanted to see the Arab world united around Cairo, the Baathists, strong in both Syria and Iraq, espoused a more polycentric arrangement among the Arab states with several foci of local influence and power, cooperating closely with each other but nevertheless maintaining autonomy. With the overthrow of the Baathists in Iraq in November 1963, the Iraqi government was taken over by men who were basically friendly toward Nasser. Earlier, in the summer of 1963, a similar pro-Nasser plot in Syria had been crushed by the Baathist leader General Amin al-Hafez, and twenty-seven Nasserites were shot. The Baath regime in Syria sharply contested Nasser's thesis that the Egyptian revolution and its ideas should be the sole model for all Arab states. It strongly argued that each revolutionary experiment in the Arab world had something unique to contribute and should be given equal status with the others. At the January Cairo conference General al-Hafez was the only Arab leader Nasser refused to see privately. It soon became clear that the Egyptian President was determined to isolate and, if possible, to destroy the Baath, thus removing a roadblock to the restoration of the union with Syria. To further this isolation, Nasser turned his attention toward securing the support of Iraq, Jordan, and Saudi Arabia.

Both during and after the Cairo meeting, the Egyptian leader pressed President Abdel Salam Arif of Iraq to recognize Kurdish national rights, in order to end the strife that had wracked the country with intermittent warfare for nearly two and one-half years. Largely as a result of Nasser's personal intervention, early in February, a cease-fire was announced, and a four-man Kurdish delegation went to Baghdad to negotiate with Iraqi officials on their demands for autonomy. Although the Iraqi government refused to grant autonomy, it promised to respect the "national rights of Kurds within one Iraqi national union," and to incorporate this right in the country's provisional constitution. The truce, welcomed by all factions in the Arab world except by the Baathists in Syria, was hailed by Nasser as an important step toward "strengthening Iraqi national solidarity." Actually, no solution was achieved, since the Iraq government did not accept Kurdish proposals for settling the dispute.

As Iraq tried to stabilize its internal situation, difficulties piled up in Syria. A steady deterioration in the domestic economy led to growing unrest. With a declining volume of business, unemployment increased in Damascus. Shopkeepers protested against the government's nationalization policies, and landowners became worried about the Baathist socialist program of land reform. Early in February clashes occurred, and a number of Nasserites were arrested. Syrians were convinced that Presidents Arif and Nasser together were abetting the disturbances to topple the Baathist regime. A strike was called in Homs on February 22 on the sixth anniversary of the unification of Syria and Egypt. In an ensuing riot, twenty-five persons were killed and about one hundred were wounded, for, even though the Egypt-Syria union of 1958 had failed, it still had a symbolic importance that stirred the Arab people.

Trouble erupted again in mid-April when another short-lived rebellion was crushed in Hama. General al-Hafez bluntly declared that the insurrection had been "inspired and financed by certain foreign powers in cooperation with feudalists and reactionaries" who opposed his land reform and socialist measures. On April 28 Syria's Revolutionary Council abrogated a treaty of military union with Iraq concluded in October 1963. Actually, it had never been put into effect, since President Arif had overthrown the Baath regime in Baghdad the following month. But the Syrian action made the break official and, more significantly, it emphasized the growing tension between the two countries.

Outside pressures continued to build up against Syria. Encouraged by Nasser's efforts at the January Cairo meeting to launch a new policy of friendly coexistence with traditional regimes in the Middle East, King Hussein sought to effect a reconciliation with the U.A.R. In March he discussed with President Nasser the possibility of replacing with Arab subsidies the West's subsidies to the Jordanian economy. (Since 1957 the United States had provided $35–$50 million annually in economic and military aid, and Britain had also contributed several million dollars yearly.) Although Jordan had previously sought financial support from the U.A.R., Saudi Arabia, and Syria without much success, King Hussein was apparently optimistic that the situation had changed since the late 1950's. No definite financial commitments were forthcoming, but Nasser clearly encouraged the establishment of closer bonds between Jordan and Egypt.

Nasser further tightened the ring around Syria by concluding an agreement with Iraq on May 26 for a joint military command and for the eventual coordination of policies. Both countries saw this accord as the "first step toward full Arab unity" and as a possible means of reestablishing the union of Egypt, Iraq, and Syria. At the signing ceremony, Nasser opened the door to the "Syrian people," without mentioning the bitter fight he had been having with their Baathist leaders.

While Nasser took steps to strengthen the Iraqi regime, a group of Cairo-sponsored Syrian exiles met in Beirut from July 14–18 to set up a political and military organization dedicated to the destruction of the Baath movement. Calling their movement the Arab Socialist Union for the Syrian region, they adopted a resolution which declared that their first task was to seek "the restoration of the United Arab Republic (the union of Syria and Egypt) by removing the secessionist Baathist regime." The conference also affirmed that the Egyptian revolution had to be accepted as the "base and vanguard" of the Arab revolutionary struggle everywhere, and that Nasser's uncontested leadership of the movement had to be recognized.[10]

As the Egyptian President exerted pressures on Syria, he stepped up his opposition against the presence of the United States and Britain in the Middle East. Demanding the evacuation of foreign bases in Cyprus and Libya, Nasser declared on February 22 that "No country can claim independence unless the military bases on its territories are liquidated. What guarantees are there for us that American and British bases in Libya will not be used against the Arabs in the event of a clash with Israel?"[11] The next day, responding to the Egyptian leader's pressure, Libya announced that it did not intend to renew the treaties whereby the United States and Britain maintained bases on its soil. These agreements, however, did not run out until 1971 and 1973. Under its treaty with Libya the United States maintained the Wheelus Air Force base near Tripoli—the largest American air base outside the United States. Britain kept two and one-half battalions in Libya; its base was used as a staging post and for training purposes for the Royal Air Force. In return, Britain paid Libya an annual subsidy of $9.8 million; American aid ran about $12 million yearly in economic help, and about $1 million in military aid. Early in March both the United States and Britain agreed to Libya's request to review their military and financial agreements, and during the summer Washington indicated that a decision would probably be made in 1965 as to when the Wheelus Air Force base would be discontinued.

Another objective of Nasser was the restoration of Yemen's union with Egypt. The Yemeni kingdom, it will be recalled, had been loosely federated with the Egyptian-Syrian United Arab Republic in March 1958. But four months after Syria's secession in September 1961, Yemen had severed its ties. When Cairo encouraged a revolt against the Imam, Muhammad al-Badr, army officers and civilian leaders who had long opposed the Imamate seized power and proclaimed Yemen a republic in September 1962. Restoration of a formal union seemed certain, but the Imam refused to acknowledge defeat. Supported by Saudi Arabia and, in the early stages by Jordan, he and tribesmen loyal to the monarchy resisted the republican forces, and fighting has persisted without any conclusive decision. In the course of the conflict Egypt deployed as many as 40,000 troops in Yemen, and became heavily bogged down militarily and financially in campaigns to crush the royalists. In April 1963 the United States had helped, with U.N. mediation, to negotiate an agreement for the withdrawal of Egyptian troops and the withholding of material support by Saudi Arabia.[12] Despite the presence of a U.N. supervisory mission in Yemen, the civil war continued. The Saudis, in the main, kept their part of the bargain, but Egyptian troops were only slightly reduced. Then in 1964, instead of pulling out its forces, Egypt actually increased them.

On March 28 a significant development took place in conservative, traditionalist Saudi Arabia. Crown Prince Faisal, with the support of members of the royal family and of religious and tribal leaders representing a consensus in the country, stripped King Saud of his political powers and reduced his role to that of figurehead. Three days later Prince Faisal named himself Viceroy and conferred upon himself all the powers of the Saudi monarchy. Subsequently, on November 2, King Saud was dethroned, and the highest political and religious authorities in the land proclaimed Crown Prince Faisal the new king.

The Yemeni dispute meanwhile broadened in scope. Following an R.A.F. retaliatory raid on a Yemen fort in March, Nasser announced his intention of expelling the British from the Federation of South Arabia, which the United Kingdom had created from Aden and thirteen of the nineteen sheikdoms of the Aden Protectorate. The Federation had largely been set up for the dual purpose of withstanding pressures from Yemen and of enabling Britain to retain its military base at Aden. As the crisis deepened in Yemen, dissident tribesmen in the rugged, sun-baked and mountainous Radfan area, about fifty miles from the Yemeni frontier, rebelled against the South Arabian Federation. The British claimed that they were trained, armed, and paid by Nasser to stir up trouble. London was also convinced that the Egyptian leader was eyeing Aden as a steppingstone to the Persian Gulf oil. When Yemen-based planes strafed a hillside in the Federation on March 28, the British struck back the next day in a raid on Fort Harib, killing a number of Yemenis.

Yemen immediately complained to the United Nations about the British action, and the Security Council debated the incident, April 2–9. The Yemen delegate charged that the British raid was a premeditated, "flagrant act of aggression" directed against the "progressive" Yemeni Republic whose presence "endangered their own . . . interests in the region." The British delegate countered that if any country had been a victim of aggression it was the Federation of South Arabia. Peaceful conditions, the U.K. delegate said, could be quickly restored if Yemen stopped its "unprovoked and senseless attacks across the border." Ambassador Stevenson, noting that there had been incursions and attacks across the border in both directions, put forward the U.S. view that all delegations would wish to join in expressing disapproval of the use of force by either side as a means of solving disputes. But the Security Council was less even-handed, adopting on April 9 a resolution by a vote of 9-0-2 (United States and United Kingdom abstaining) condemning reprisals as incompatible with the purposes and principles of the United Nations, and deploring the British military action. It held that Britain's retaliatory raid was wrong and exaggerated in size,[13] thus agreeing in part with Britain's Labor party and some Conservative critics who had said the raid was like using a "sledge hammer against a nut."

On April 23 Nasser made a surprise visit to Sana, the capital of Yemen. In an impassioned speech before thousands of Yemenis, the Egyptian leader said that the people in Aden and in the neighboring British protectorates were suffering from the "harshest form of tyranny, oppression, and torture at the hands of

British colonialism," and vowed to expel Britain "from all parts of the Arab world, because Arab land belongs to Arabs." These belligerent remarks reinforced the British conviction that President Nasser was seeking to drive the British out of Aden, destroy the South Arabian Federation, and secure control of the Persian Gulf. Once this goal was attained, he would then be in a position to cement his hold on Yemen and force Saudi Arabia to come to terms with him. Unification of the Arab states under Nasser's domination would thus be advanced, and so too would his projected confrontation with Israel, for which Arab unification was proclaimed a primary condition.

Britain strongly urged the United States to help counter Nasser's ambitions and to stop his drive against the British in Aden. But Washington believed that rash action—either in the form of military or economic reprisals—would only unite a divided Arab world more strongly behind Nasser. Some British critics warned against the possibility of being drawn into a war that could go on endlessly, despite temporary successes. They indicated that the conflict in the Middle East might have been avoided if Britain had followed the lead of the United States and recognized the pro-Nasser Yemen government when it came to power in 1962. America, they also pointed out, had demonstrated that oil could readily be purchased at a reasonable price without maintaining a colonial or semicolonial relationship with oil-producing sheikdoms. There were enough alternative sources of oil to prevent the Arabs from using their supplies for political blackmail. Those in Britain who opposed Britain's "war" with Nasser argued, moreover, that a base in Aden, held against the wishes of the local population, could be more of a liability than an asset, and they urged coming to terms with the Arab nationalists. In this way, they said, there might be a chance that an independent Aden would agree voluntarily to rent a base to Britain, as Singapore had done.

Prime Minister Sir Alec Douglas-Home rejected these views. On May 7 he told the House of Commons that Britain would not abandon its treaty obligations to defend its friends in the Middle East. Meanwhile, a joint operational force of about 3,000

British and Federation troops was built up, and continued probes and reconnaissance in strength were made to determine the positions of tribesmen and intruding Yemenis near the border area around Radfan. As activities moved threateningly close to the Aden base itself, reinforcements were flown in from Britain's strategic reserve in Kenya, and other units in Britain were kept on the alert. At the same time, London warned Nasser that continued infiltration by Yemenis into the South Arabian Federation might lead it to abandon its policy of nonintervention in the struggle between the republicans and royalists within Yemen.

To make its position more secure against the pressures of Nasser's followers, Britain on May 7 called for a constitutional conference in London to set a time limit for the independence of Aden and the Federation. Early in July, at the end of this conference, London announced that it would grant the Federation independence not later than 1968, and that the colony of Aden would be given the same status as the other Federation members "as soon as practicable." But Britain also declared that it would continue to assist in the defense of the Federation, and to maintain its military base in Aden. Although a change in the British attitude had been expected when the Labor party took over the government in October, Labor party leaders firmly insisted on maintaining Britain's position in the Persian Gulf despite Arab objections. They suggested the possibility, however, of creating two or three small floating bases in the Indian Ocean. After these were set up, it was felt that in time the bases in Aden and Singapore could be given up. "A sovereign base in someone else's country is never secure," observed Patrick Gordon Walker, who was in charge of foreign affairs in Labor's "shadow-cabinet." "We would far prefer to hire dry-docking and other facilities." [14]

Nasser meanwhile took steps to consolidate his relations with the Republic of Yemen. On July 13 the U.A.R. and Yemen signed an agreement for full coordination of their policies "as a step toward complete unity." They declared that "any attack or threat against either country" would be considered "as directed against the other." A coordinating council, similar to the joint council set up in May with Iraq, was established, with headquarters in

Cairo, its purpose being to work for the unity of the two countries. As royalist prospects for dislodging republican forces grew increasingly slim, Jordan recognized the Yemen Republic on July 22.

During the summer Nasser greatly strengthened his military position as Egyptian and republican forces extended their area of control in a brisk, twelve-week campaign. With these successes, President Nasser sought to get Saudi Arabia to join Jordan in official recognition of the Yemen republican regime. Private meetings between himself and Prince Faisal following the Alexandria meeting had pointed to a possible settlement of the Yemeni dispute. A joint communiqué of September 14 declared that "full cooperation" had been reached, and steps would be taken to establish "necessary contacts with [the] parties involved for [the] peaceful settlement" of the two-year-old civil war.[15] Details were not disclosed. But it was believed that the settlement would proceed in three stages: (1) agreeing on a formal cease-fire; (2) setting forth the terms for a phased withdrawal of Egyptian troops; and (3) finding a formula for creating a coalition regime that would allow for some representation of the royalist tribes.

When a cease-fire was declared on November 8, the republican regime granted amnesty to tribal leaders and others who opposed the government. Plans, meanwhile, were made for calling a "national congress" of 169 religious, military, and tribal leaders that was expected to organize a new coalition government in Yemen. But the royalists insisted that before the conference met on its scheduled date, November 23, the Egyptians be committed to withdraw at a set time, and that the chief of state be an Imam. "It is no use trying to settle anything else," said a Yemeni royalist leader, "until we know when and how the Egyptians are going to leave."

Expectations that the Yemeni war might soon be ended died. Quarrels arose over the location of the site of the conference, and over the selection of delegates. Two days before the National Reconciliation Congress was scheduled to meet, its postponement was announced. Royalists accused Egyptians of making more

than 100 air raids since the cease-fire went into effect. Meanwhile, the Imam's forces had regained much of the northern territory taken by Egyptian and republican troops in their push during August and September. The difficulty of maintaining mechanized equipment in rough terrain and the ineffectiveness of
Egyptian air support made it virtually impossible to hold the new
positions. While the Imam declared that he was ready "at any
moment" to discuss peace terms with the republicans, he insisted
that the Egyptians had set intolerable conditions and demanded
the withdrawal of Egyptian troops from Yemen. "The world
should know," he said, "that we cannot negotiate with an Egyptian pistol at our heads and Ilyushins in our sky." Since Nasser
was determined to maintain Egypt's influence in Yemen and
assure republican control, the prospect of liquidating the Yemeni
war dimmed appreciably at the close of the year.

41. INDIA AND PAKISTAN: THE KASHMIR DISPUTE

While the Middle East grappled with its internal problems,
India and Pakistan continued their bitter quarrels. Locked in the
perennial Kashmir dispute, and torn by profound religious discord, both countries eyed each other with distrust and hatred.
These two issues again came to the forefront during 1964 and
virtually overshadowed all other matters.

Tragedy struck on December 27, 1963, when a strand of hair
said to be from the head of the Prophet Muhammad, a relic kept
in a silver-capped glass vial, was stolen from a mosque outside
Srinagar in Kashmir. The city went into mourning, and as strikes
and riots ensued Kashmir's economic life became practically
paralyzed. Religious passions quickly mixed with political unrest
over India's control over largely Moslem Kashmir. Hundreds of
thousands of people marched through the cobbled streets of
Srinagar, and demanded that the relic be returned to its shrine.
Fortunately, on January 4, the relic hair, undamaged and still in
its original glass container, was returned to the shrine. Three
Moslems—one of whom was caught as he tried to run away after

surreptitiously replacing the stolen relic—were arrested for the theft.

Despite the recovery, a wave of arson and murder spread to Calcutta, and mob fighting broke out in East Pakistan and West Bengal. Religious clashes between the Hindus and Moslems produced tensions that were unparalleled in the region since the riots that had preceded the partition of India and Pakistan in 1947. On January 7, in the midst of these disturbances, Prime Minister Nehru after months of failing health suffered a stroke that left him bedridden and partially paralyzed.

As the new year began, the United States was greatly distressed by the instability on the Indian Subcontinent. Concern arose over the continuing bloodshed between the Hindus and Moslems in both India and Pakistan, over the severe difficulties India had encountered in its economic development program, and most especially, over the uncertainty about Nehru's successor. Although Prime Minister Nehru's health improved and he gradually returned to public life, it was evident that he could no longer bear the heavy burdens of political responsibility. Late in January some of his duties were delegated to Lal Bahadur Shastri, who joined the cabinet as a Minister without Portfolio. Shastri, a Hindi-speaking Indian, now 59 years old, was himself in frail health because of a heart attack. For years he had worked closely with Nehru and was regarded as one of the nation's ablest politicians. Indian moderates and conservatives supported him as a candidate to succeed to the post of Prime Minister. Although a colorless figure, Shastri had gained a reputation as an architect of compromise, a conciliator of factions, and a faithful follower of Nehru.

Problems on the Indian Subcontinent were, of course, not only internal but external as well. The Communist Chinese invasion of Indian territory in 1962, which had led to Peking's occupation of 12,000 square miles in Ladakh along the northwest border, had had a shattering impact. Although Nehru had been inclined to be sympathetic to the Chinese before the attack and had held tenaciously to a policy of nonalignment, he began to turn increasingly to the United States for support. Washington responded unhesitatingly. Over recent years, America had poured a half billion dollars annually into Indian economic development, and had sent about $50 million a year to rebuild its armed forces, that had been badly shaken by Communist China's offensive. It was this military buildup which greatly perturbed Pakistan, and edged it toward Peking. During 1963 Pakistan and Communist China concluded a trade agreement (January), a border agreement (March), and a civil air transport agreement which provided, among other things, for regularly scheduled service to Pakistan by Chinese aircraft (August). To Pakistan, the real threat was India, not China, and any strengthening of India was viewed as endangering Pakistan's security. It derived little consolation from repeated assurances of the United States and its allies that such aid was designed to bolster India against China, not against Pakistan. More particularly, Pakistan, as in the past, saw a direct relationship between the buildup of India's defenses and India's moves to absorb Kashmir.

The Kashmir region was one of the most sensitive trouble spots in Asia. Its borders touched not only on India, Pakistan, and Afghanistan, but on Communist China's Sinkiang Province and Chinese-occupied Tibet. Although it was predominantly Moslem, Nehru had refused in 1947 to agree to its incorporation into Pakistan, and open war almost developed over the region during 1947–48. Clashes were halted when the United Nations negotiated a cease-fire agreement, arranged a truce line—India secured control of the richer two-thirds of Kashmir—and induced India and Pakistan to consent to a plebiscite. But this plebiscite had never been held.

On February 3 the Security Council met again on the perennial Kashmir issue. Pakistan had called for an "immediate meeting" to deal with the "grave situation" that had arisen as a result of the riots of early January; they were attributed to India's "unlawful steps" in seeking to destroy Kashmir's special status. Specifically, Pakistan accused India of deliberately "integrating" the Indian-occupied part of Jammu and Kashmir with the Indian Union. Under a special status provision, the Indian constitution had given Kashmir more autonomy than other states of India.

Late in 1963, Indian leaders had indicated that this status would gradually be abolished so that Kashmir could be put on the same footing as other Indian states. The move stirred the wrath of the Pakistanis. By "trampling underfoot" the basic rights of the Kashmir people, and seeking to annex the state, Pakistan told the United Nations, India had created a "vicious climate" which made possible "such criminal acts of sacrilege and vandalism as the recent theft of the sacred hair of the Holy Prophet." [16] Denial of the right of self-determination in Kashmir, the Pakistan delegate declared, poisoned the relations between India and Pakistan, and harmony in the Subcontinent could be achieved only if the dispute were resolved.

India maintained that legally and constitutionally Jammu and Kashmir were Indian territory. The Indian representative charged Pakistan with instigating the rebellion in Kashmir and inciting the religious riots to weaken India and cripple its defenses against Communist China. He warned the Security Council that Pakistan was "playing the Chinese game." Again rejecting Pakistan's demand that Kashmir's status be determined by a plebiscite, as provided in past Council resolutions, India held that the plebiscite was contingent on Pakistan's withdrawal from the disputed territory—a condition it had never fulfilled. The fundamental point made by the Indian representative was that the quarrel over Kashmir was rooted primarily in the fact that India based its state on secularism, whereas Pakistan was a theocratic state. While India had accepted the partition of the Subcontinent, it repudiated a division in which religion was the sole criterion. "If the Hindus and Muslims constitute two nations then the inevitable result must follow that the fifty million Muslims in India are aliens in their homes," said the Indian delegate. "We refuse to subscribe to the theory that religion can be the sole basis of nationality. We believe in multi-racial, multi-communal, and multi-linguistic society and, according to us, peace and goodwill in this world depend upon the success of such a society." [17] He sharply rebutted Pakistan's characterization of India's presence in Kashmir as "colonial," saying it was a gross insult to the people of Kashmir who were Indians and had been Indians "ever since one can remember."

Ambassador Stevenson suggested that if India and Pakistan were genuinely interested in solving their differences, a fresh start might be made by the United Nations—in the light of present realities—to try and achieve a political settlement. He urged the two countries to consider the possibility of third-party mediation in which Secretary-General Thant might be of assistance.[18] But the Security Council made no formal recommendation on the Kashmir dispute. On February 17, the Pakistan delegate requested a postponement of the debate for a few days so that Pakistan would have "more time for reflection." Although the Indian delegate protested this delay, the debate was temporarily shelved.

Pakistan apparently called a halt to discussions because its U.N. representative had to return to Karachi for the arrival on February 18 of Premier Chou En-lai for an eight-day visit. Indian apprehension was reflected in Mr. Shastri's remark that he feared Pakistan and Peking "might hatch up something against us." Speaking to the Indian Parliament, he called for "a realistic and practical view" in regard to Communist China: "We have to ask ourselves whether we want war or peace. In human affairs one cannot always take a rigid or fixed view." Reacting to Pakistan's growing hostility and renewed world pressures for a Kashmir settlement, India began to move cautiously toward negotiating the Himalayan border dispute with Communist China. A major result of Chou En-lai's visit was that China fully endorsed Pakistan's demand for a plebiscite in Kashmir, and abandoned its previous "neutral" position.[19]

Early in March Mr. Phillips Talbot, the U.S. Assistant Secretary of State for Near Eastern and South Asian Affairs, visited New Delhi and Karachi. Although the trip was described as routine, one of its purposes appeared to be to allay Indian resentment against the American and British stand on the Kashmir debate in the Security Council. Both powers had opposed the Indian contention that Kashmir was an internal problem and that its accession to India was final. Mr. Talbot evidently sought to convince both India and Pakistan that the United States would continue its policy on the Kashmir question of doing nothing to alienate either of the two rivals. He also tried to persuade both countries that it was in their own long-term interests to settle the dispute and cooperate in a joint defense of the Subcontinent. Pakistan indicated, however, that the best way that this goal could be achieved was for the United States to force a settlement.

A major source of difficulty was the problem of refugees that moved between India and Pakistan. Unfortunately, the hope that the Moslem and Hindu religious communities would settle down after the bloodshed that accompanied the 1947 partition was never fulfilled. There was a constant flow across the frontiers of dispossessed, embittered Moslem and Hindu refugees, who stirred up unrest wherever they settled. Although Indian secularism bade the Hindus to regard the Moslems as co-citizens, many looked upon them as some kind of extension of Pakistan into India, and pressed for their eviction. Pakistan would then retaliate by driving out the Hindus from its soil. During the year the exodus of Hindus from East Pakistan ran into scores of thousands. Wherever their convoys rested, riots invariably broke out and bloodshed occurred.

Addressing the Indian people for the first time since his stroke, Prime Minister Nehru appealed on March 26 for an end to religious strife. "This communal trouble is entirely opposed to our policy and to our future," he asserted. "India is a country of many communities and unless we can live in harmony, respecting each other's beliefs and habits, we cannot build up a great and united nation." Early in April, high-level discussions were undertaken by India and Pakistan on the problem. Although the two countries agreed on the principle of protecting minority communities, they disagreed on what should be done. Pakistan wanted to create an international tribunal to investigate the mass eviction of Moslems from the Indian state of Assam, but India insisted that priority should be given to a consideration of the Hindu influx from East Pakistan. India flatly rejected the proposal for an international tribunal as an infringement of its sovereignty. Although India acknowledged that thousands of Moslem "infiltrators" from East Pakistan had been evicted, it insisted that this had been done only after a thorough judicial screening had disclosed that they lacked proper immigration papers and were not Indian citizens. While declaring that a country's "very basis" of sovereignty was its right to identify aliens in its midst, India expressed a willingness to give Pakistan a voice in devising screening procedures for the evictions, and to suspend further deportations for two months. However, Pakistan turned down this offer. In spite of the impasse, the fact that the problem was discussed as a mutual matter gave some hope that a future understanding might be attained.

A further indication of possible betterment in the relations of the two countries came on April 8 when India finally freed Sheik Muhammad Abdullah, the "Lion of Kashmir." A popular figure, Sheik Abdullah had been Prime Minister of Kashmir from 1947 to 1953. Arrested in August 1953 for his advocacy of a plebiscite, he was charged with conspiracy against the state and collusion with Pakistan. Sheik Abdullah had been imprisoned since that time except for a brief period of freedom in 1958. Early in April the conspiracy charge against him and thirteen other defendants was withdrawn, and they were "acquitted." Disturbances in Kashmir, the outbreak of Hindu-Moslem killings, and India's growing isolation from African and other nations in U.N. discussions of the Kashmir problem were some of the reasons for Sheik Abdullah's release. Although India was still fearful that in any plebiscite the big Moslem majority in Kashmir would vote to join Pakistan, it hoped that the "Lion of Kashmir" might find some less drastic solution to the problem and thus ease other tensions.

During the next several weeks, Sheik Abdullah directed his efforts toward this end. India indicated its readiness to make certain concessions, but insisted on the fundamental point that the Indian-controlled two-thirds of Jammu and Kashmir had to remain a part of India. To reconcile the conflicting positions of India and Pakistan, Sheik Abdullah tried to advance a formula to establish an Indian-Pakistani condominium, which involved (1) a sharing of sovereignty over the whole state of Jammu and Kashmir, (2) joint responsibility for its defense and integrity, and (3) agreement on a definition of its boundaries. The proposal brought to the forefront a number of problems, not the least of them being Pakistan's border agreement with Communist China, delimiting Pakistan-controlled Kashmir. Indian agreement to the condominium would presumably necessitate approval of that border settlement—a step India was not prepared to accept. But those in favor of the condominium were convinced that its adoption would pave the way for cooperation between India and Pakistan. Once this was achieved, the problem of the Hindu-Moslem minorities could move toward solution. Another advantage to the condominium was that it would avoid the plebiscite to which India had repeatedly objected.

The Security Council resumed its discussion of the issue, May 5–18.[20] Despite the hopes raised by Sheik Abdullah's release and his attempts at reconciliation, neither India nor Pakistan budged from its previously held position. However, the Indian delegate noted that a hopeful sign lay in the talks held on restoring communal harmony, and stressed the need for restraint in order not to spoil the atmosphere for their resumption. Differences between the two countries, the Indian representative emphasized, could only be solved by direct negotiation. "No superimposed solution [by the United Nations]," he said, "will do any good." When Pakistan realized that Kashmir was not a "political shuttlecock," that India had no designs on Pakistan's independence, and that the prosperity of the whole Subcontinent was based on the prosperity of their two countries, then, declared the Indian delegate, the Kashmir question would be solved.

The U.S. representative, Mr. Francis T. P. Plimpton, called for a "fresh look" at the dispute, and urged that a renewed effort be made at conciliation. Both the United States and Britain were encouraged by Indian-Pakistani talks on the religious minority issue and by the release of Sheik Abdullah, and they urged that every effort be made to reduce tensions on the Subcontinent. The U.S.S.R. agreed, saying that bilateral talks were "the most promising and effective way of proceeding." The consensus in the Council was that time was required for developments to yield constructive results, and hope was expressed that the dispute could be settled by direct negotiations. Meanwhile, the Security Council appealed to both countries to exercise utmost restraint to avoid more violence, which seemed to be the most that the Council could do. It was clear that any attempt to play a more positive role by reaffirming past demands for a plebiscite or effecting any mediation would be doomed by the opposition of either India or the Soviet Union.

Shortly after the Security Council debate, word came on May 27 that Prime Minister Nehru was dead. At 2 P.M., the Indian Parliament was told "The light is out"—the same words used to announce Gandhi's death in 1948. An epoch in Indian history had come to a close. Many shared President Johnson's sentiments when he said: "History has already recorded his monumental contribution to the molding of a strong and independent India. And yet, it is not just as a leader of India that he has served humanity. Perhaps more than any other world leader he has given expression to man's yearning for peace." [21]

Nehru was gone. He had held the nation together by the force of his personality, his character, and his leadership, in the face of problems that were monumental in scope. He had not found the answers to them in his lifetime. But he had tried to guide India along a democratic path, keeping it aloof from the world's power conflicts, moving it into the modern age, and easing its wretchedness and despair. "Within his own society he was a revolutionary, constantly haranguing his own people about their own superstitions and encrustments," commented the New York Times. "He was a revolutionary in international councils, and a successful one, in that he was the first to prove that a nation without military might could and would be heard by the militarily mighty."

As an immediate consequence of Nehru's death, hopes that Sheik Abdullah could mediate a solution of the Kashmir problem were suspended—and possibly killed. Just a day before the tragic news, the "Lion of Kashmir" announced that he had succeeded in arranging a meeting between Nehru and President Ayub Khan, to be held the following month. Throughout his six-

teen years as Indian Prime Minister, one of Nehru's chief pre-
occupations had been to find a solution to the problems with
Pakistan. In his last address to the Congress party on May 16, he
denounced the killings of Moslems in eastern India as "horrible,"
and assured Pakistan it had nothing to fear from India unless it
attacked the Indian nation. "I hope it may be possible," he said,
"for the two countries to develop closer and more intimate relations to the advantage of both."

On June 1, after four days of bitter argument, leaders of the
Congress party unanimously agreed to endorse Mr. Shastri as
Prime Minister. President Ayub Khan extended "a warm hand
of friendship," expressing hope that the new government would
adopt a forward-looking, moderate approach toward settling the
dispute over Kashmir. The time had come, he said, for a "change
of heart" on both sides of the border. The Pakistani leader urged
his people to put aside the bitterness and recriminations of the
past, the only accomplishment of which had been to cause "human misery and suffering apart from the incalculable loss in material terms." Mr. Shastri warmly responded to this plea and
agreed that the tide of "unfortunate relations" between India
and Pakistan had to be reversed.

Although signs pointed to somewhat less rigidity on the Kashmir dispute, Pakistan continued to draw more closely to Communist China during the summer. On July 11, while attending
the Commonwealth Prime Ministers' conference in London,
President Ayub Khan announced that he had accepted Mr.
Shastri's invitation to discuss the future of Kashmir and other
differences between their countries. But progress on negotiations
was delayed, chiefly because of a recurrence of Mr. Shastri's
heart ailment. Matters thus proceeded at a snail's pace. In the
meantime, at the end of the month, Pakistan accepted a $60 mil-
lion long-term, interest-free loan from China—the first loan
offered by Peking to Pakistan. A Pakistani official felt sure that
the Chinese were "sincerely interested" in assisting developing
countries, and that they had no territorial ambitions and no
aggressive designs against any country.

It was not until October that President Ayub Khan met Prime

Minister Shastri in an informal visit at Karachi when the latter was returning home from the conference of nonaligned nations in Cairo. After nearly five hours of talks, the two leaders issued a joint statement saying merely that relations between their countries "needed to be improved." To achieve this, it was necessary to promote a better understanding and settlement of their disputes "on an honorable and equitable basis." Although little of a concrete nature came out of the meeting, steps were taken for officials of the two governments to get together soon to explore their problems more fully. Expressing cautious optimism, Mr. Shastri indicated that both countries were eager to ease tensions in South Asia, and "to show a spirit of conciliation."

On the whole, prospects during the latter part of the year pointed to a favorable turn in relations between the two countries. Encouraging in this regard was President Ayub Khan's suggestion for a joint effort to harness the annual floods of the Ganges and Brahmaputra rivers. The Kashmir issue still remained the key to the solution of many problems in the Subcontinent. "Once this has been resolved," the Pakistani leader said, "it should be possible to usher in an era of mutual collaboration, assistance, and friendship." But at the end of the year, the chances for a reconciliation were as slim as they had ever been. In December the Indian government announced that it was taking further steps to absorb the part of Jammu and Kashmir that was under Indian control. It proposed to empower the president of India to take over administration in case the government there failed. A move was also contemplated to change the title of the head of state to governor and that of the prime minister to chief minister to bring Kashmir in line with other Indian states. There was no indication that India intended to change its position or to consider any compromise with Pakistan.

CHAPTER ELEVEN
UNDER AFRICA'S VOLCANO

OVER THE PAST two decades, the region of the world which experienced the greatest and most profound changes was the continent of Africa. Following World War II, Africa's transformation from a passive into an active force in world politics occurred swiftly. The change appeared to be due chiefly to the impact of four developments. First, the crumbling of the Western European colonial system in Asia and the Middle East gave impetus to the rapid rise of African nationalism. After a slow start, nationalist demands for self-government asserted themselves quickly and aggressively, particularly during the latter part of the 1950's. The year 1960 marked a high point with the withdrawal of Western European control and the creation of seventeen new African states, which became members of the United Nations.

A second major development contributing to Africa's transformation arose from the shift in the centers of world power away from Western Europe to the United States and the Soviet Union. America's relations with Africa illustrate one effect of this development. Before 1960 the United States had looked upon Africa as a region primarily of European responsibility, although it did what it could to help European powers and nationalist movements work out their problems peacefully. With the vacuum created by Western European withdrawal and the threat of Communist encroachment, American involvement increased greatly.

Racial hostility between whites and blacks—epitomized in

South Africa's *apartheid* policy and the reaction against colonialism—was a third factor. As black African states became independent, they increased the pressure on areas of the continent still under white rule. While the whites in southern Africa were intent on preserving their control, their culture, and investments, built up over many decades (most notably in South Africa and Southern Rhodesia), powerful forces were undermining the white man's rule. Memories of white racialism stirred the passions of black Africans, stimulated their attack on the continued presence of European control on the continent, and contributed to a volcanic undercurrent of violence in a number of countries. "The personal humiliations suffered by colored people at the hands of arrogant or thoughtless whites were often so vivid that it would be difficult to exaggerate their significance," said a noted authority on Africa. "The racial superiority complex of Westerners was perhaps more responsible than any other factor for the ground-swell of anti-Westernism . . ." [1]

Finally, leaders of independent black states were acutely aware of the profound disparities between the living standards of the relatively well-to-do industrial peoples and those of the poorer peoples of the predominantly agricultural countries. Swept by the "revolution of rising expectations," black Africans were eager to push toward modernization. Unfortunately, many African leaders had the illusion that independence would automatically lead to peaceful, stable, and prosperous societies. When this did not occur, the "let-down" was severe, and the reaction intensified the revolt against the West. Charges of "neocolonialism" alternated with pleas for Western support in trade and aid.

African efforts to establish a firm political and economic base for each nation were, of course, hampered by many difficulties. For one thing, tribal cultures and other traditional patterns made it hard to create national cohesion and political stability. For another, there was a conspicuous lack of indigenous capital and of technical, managerial, and administrative know-how. Instability was also aggravated by the exodus—both voluntary and involuntary—of Western Europeans who had a practical monopoly of these requisites for progress. In the nineteenth century,

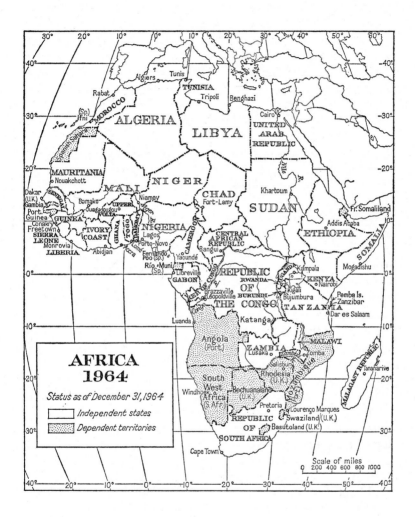

AFRICA
1964

Status as of December 31, 1964

☐ Independent states
▦ Dependent territories

moreover, the European powers had carved out their colonies with little regard for ethnic or geographic considerations. During the 1960's, the continent found itself buffeted and torn by pressures of African states to develop regional groupings, on the one hand, and, on the other, to safeguard jealously their territorial sovereignty. Border wars inevitably erupted as attempts were made to reclaim areas that contained inhabitants of similar ethnic origins. In addition, tribal warfare and internal struggles for political power greatly complicated the task of achieving national unity within individual countries. Although the movement toward African union made some headway with the establishment of the Organization of African Unity, it continued to face the obstacles of diverse regional groupings, of personal rivalry among African leaders, and of the reluctance of individual states to surrender their sovereignty to supranational authorities.

With the continued turbulence on the continent early in 1964, many Americans became somewhat skeptical about the nation's involvement in Africa. The ominous turn of events in East Africa, irrational attacks against the United States in Ghana, the massacre of thousands of Watusi tribesmen in Rwanda, and the renewed eruption of the Congo crisis were disturbing. Because of the unstable and precarious nature of most African states, the tendency of the United States, on the whole, was to limit rather than increase its commitments. This trend was reflected in the projected decrease of foreign aid assistance to Africa for the fiscal year 1965. Only $237 million was allocated for economic and military aid by the Agency for International Development and the Defense Department—far less than for any other major underdeveloped region. To be sure, another consideration was the feeling that Britain, France, and other European powers had an obligation to assist their former colonies.

Problems in Africa were vast in scope, and foreign aid alone could not solve them. Although most African leaders were hopeful that overcoming the continent's poverty and backwardness could be achieved with Western cooperation, many were prepared to turn for assistance to any quarter willing to help them. But it was evident that the continent could not grow strong economically or politically under the conditions of Balkanization characterizing the post-independence period. This dilemma was further compounded by the fact that Africa would soon contain about fifty states with a population of approximately 250 million people. Thus, while some would face added troubles brought on by overpopulation, others would still have no remedy for their enfeebling smallness.

42. EAST AFRICA TURMOIL

The volatile nature of the situation in Africa is sharply revealed in a few figures. Since the end of World War II, of the thirty-three African states that had achieved independence (twenty-seven were established in 1960–64), more than half had been wracked by severe political and economic convulsions. During 1963 alone, three regimes were toppled in French-speaking West Africa, two attempts were made to overthrow the Ivory Coast government, and plots were uncovered against the ruling regimes in Senegal, Chad, Cameroon, Tunisia, and Morocco. A revolt by non-Arab tribes in southern Sudan, which had flared up in 1955 and continued sporadically down to 1964, increased in intensity during the year. Acknowledging that the "southern problem" was his nation's most critical issue, General Ibrahim Abboud, the Sudanese Premier, promised the south equal rights, a part in national elections, and an end to martial law. However, a point appeared to be reached in 1964 where nothing would satisfy the tribes in the south short of separation from the north.

Ironically, it was East Africa that seemed to give the greatest hope of advancing toward stability. As the vestiges of British colonial rule disappeared with the granting of independence to Kenya and Zanzibar in December 1963, prospects looked favorable for the transformation of the loose economic union of Tanganyika, Uganda, Kenya, and Zanzibar into a full political federation—the East African Federation. This merger would have resulted in the creation of a single political unit larger than all of Western Europe. In addition, the move was expected to have wide-ranging repercussions, for Ethiopia, Somalia, Rwanda,

Burundi, Malawi (Nyasaland), and Zambia (Northern Rhodesia) had expressed their interest in allying themselves with
the federation to form a common market for greater East Africa.
But trouble arose on a number of problems, especially in determining what prerogatives each country would be willing to give
up for the larger advantage of political union. The hope that
economic union would naturally lead to political union failed
to materialize. President Julius K. Nyerere of Tanganyika declared that the "greatest disappointment" in Africa in 1963 had
been the lack of agreement on an East African Federation. "One
of the hard facts we have to face on our way to African unity,"
he said, "is that this unity means, on the part of the countries,
surrender of sovereignty, and on the part of the individual leaders, surrender of high positions. We must face squarely the fact
that so far there has been no such surrender in the name of
African unity."

As the new year opened, the tenuous stability of the region
completely disintegrated. On January 12 African rebels on the
island of Zanzibar overthrew the predominantly Arab government. Striking before dawn, they captured the island's capital,
seizing the cable office, airstrip, and radio station, and swept the
prime minister and his cabinet from power. Proclaiming Zanzibar
a republic, they formed a revolutionary government. The U.S.
destroyer *Manley*, which had been on a goodwill visit to Kenya,
raced to the island to evacuate most of the sixty Americans who
were based at a Project Mercury space-tracking station.

Although Abaid Karume, a former trade union leader and head
of the Afro-Shirazi party—Zanzibar's black nationalist movement
—took over as president, the real power of the revolutionary
regime seemed to be concentrated in the hands of its vice-president, Kassim Hanga—a bitter foe of the West who had studied
in Moscow and had a Russian wife—and the Minister of External
Affairs and Defense, Sheik Abdul Rahman Muhammad, leader
of Zanzibar's militant leftist Umma or People's party, who was
trained by Chinese Communists and had been the representative
of a Chinese press agency on the island. Secretary Rusk told
the Senate Foreign Relations Committee that the uprising de-

finitely seemed to have been conducted by Zanzibaris who were trained in Communist China and Cuba. Recognition was quickly accorded the new regime by the Soviet Union, Communist China, Cuba, and North Korea.

Tension flared up momentarily on January 16 when the United States Consul, Frederick P. Picard, 3rd, was marched out of a Zanzibar hotel with a gun at his back. An argument had taken place between the American consul and the President, during which the latter heatedly denounced the United States for its failure to recognize his government and berated Mr. Picard for helping evacuate Americans from the island. The American consul was placed under house arrest and the next day he was flown to nearby Tanganyika. Four American newsmen, accused of having sent out distorted messages concerning the rebellion, were also expelled from the country.

On January 20, in the midst of this confusion, Tanganyikan troops mutinied against their British officers, who were in the country by agreement with the Tanganyikan government. Two weeks earlier, President Nyerere had abandoned the principle of "Africanization" of the administration, saying that skill and experience, not race, would be the criterion for hiring and promotion. "The skin in which this skill is encased is completely irrelevant," he asserted. Soldiers who were restive about their pay and resented the fact that British officers still commanded their units some three years after independence, reacted with hostility to this pronouncement. President Nyerere's remarks were interpreted to mean that the white officers would remain. When 300 Tanganyikan policemen were sent to Zanzibar at President Karume's request to help restore order on the island, the African enlisted men of the Tanganyika Rifles arrested their British officers and demanded that their own pay be increased. The mutiny touched off a wave of nationalism that sent mobs on a rampage of destruction. Caught up in a fervor of revolt, crowds shouted, "Colonialists go home!" Nyerere went into hiding, at the same time requesting military help from Britain to restore order. As a result of the disturbance, at least twenty Tanganyikans were dead, whole blocks in the Arab and Indian quarters lay

in ruins, and the Nyerere government—once considered the most
stable in East Africa—was seriously undermined. With Zanzibar
falling into leftist hands, British officials became worried that an
outbreak of rebellion would engulf all of East Africa and were
quick to respond to Tanganyika's request. About sixty British
commandos with one bazooka, an antitank rocket, some fireworks
and a bogus barrage from two warships offshore disarmed the
mutineers in about forty minutes. Returning to the capital, President Nyerere condemned the mutiny as a "disgrace" and announced that both battalions of the Tanganyika Rifles would be
disbanded and reorganized.

No sooner had the Tanganyika mutiny been quelled when a
barracks revolt broke out in the Kenyan army and disturbances
flared up in Uganda. As in the case of Tanganyika, the troops
demanded more pay as well as the dismissal of their British
officers. At the request of Kenya and Uganda, British forces
again moved in and subdued the mutineers. The decision of
East African leaders to use a show of British force had been
risky. The fact that they had to call on their former colonial
"master" for help was both embarrassing and humiliating, and
Britain unintentionally added to their loss of face by the ease
with which its tiny contingents put down the insurgents. On
January 27 President Nyerere took the initiative and called for
an emergency meeting of the Organization of African Unity to
discuss the "grave danger" that had been created by the army
revolts in East Africa.

At the Organization's emergency session held on February 12
at Dar es Salaam, Nyerere intimated that his country's position
could be compromised by further reliance on British commandos.
He appealed for the creation of a joint African military force
to replace the British troops in his troubled land, and urged that
"Africa . . . find from Africa a means of assisting Tanganyika in
the task of maintaining law and order." Formation of an African brigade under the direction of a supranational high command
was rejected, however, and great pains were taken to avoid suggesting that whenever an African state had internal difficulties
it could call on the O.A.U. for military help. Nevertheless, all

members of the Organization gave tacit approval to Nyerere's decision to call on British troops to quell the mutiny, and gave him a vote of confidence. While they agreed that Africans should replace British officers as soon as possible, it was left to Tanganyika to decide how this should be done. It was suggested that troops might perhaps be drawn from Algeria, Ethiopia, and Nigeria. But the problem of paying for these forces and their transportation to Tanganyika was not settled.

Meanwhile, conditions in Zanzibar gradually improved and, on February 12, West Germany recognized the revolutionary regime. Two weeks later, the United States jointly with Britain and six other Commonwealth countries also extended recognition.[2] This action aimed largely at restoring the Western presence on the island and at discouraging, if possible, the trend toward a Communist alignment. But Communists from abroad and extremists on the island rapidly began to expand their influence. Both the Soviet Union and Communist China sent top-level ambassadors to the island, and Chinese and East German technicians began to arrive in growing numbers. At the same time, pressures were exerted against Britain and the United States. British subjects were ordered to leave the island by the end of April, and the United States was asked to close its space-tracking station. Signs indicated that the Communists intended to concentrate their efforts on making Zanzibar a "showcase" of economic development, establishing it as a base for political penetration into the continent, and using it as a training center for guerrilla activities in East Africa. In the three months following the Zanzibar *coup,* agriculture was nationalized, and East Germans increasingly took over governmental posts in economic planning, finance, and housing. At the end of March Soviet arms began to arrive, including light artillery.

The strong drift toward a Communist takeover was suddenly deflected on April 23 when Presidents Nyerere and Karume signed an agreement to merge their two countries into one nation. President Nyerere appeared anxious to check the possibility of Zanzibar becoming a potential Cuba of Africa, and he hopefully thought that union would revive the prospects for the eventual creation of the East African Federation. Two days later, the two countries were merged into a single sovereign state as the United Republic of Tanganyika and Zanzibar. (In late October, the country officially changed its name to the United Republic of Tanzania.) Early in May President Nyerere declared that he was "fully committed" to an immediate federation with Kenya and Uganda, but Uganda replied that it would not be "pushed into federation."

The union of the two countries did not end the Communist threat. Actually, under the terms of the agreement, Zanzibar still retained its own separate identity, had its own parliament and government, and remained under the direct authority of its former president, Abaid Amani Karume. Communist China and East Germany continued to be Zanzibar's chief economic supporters, with a growing influx of Chinese "technicians"; and the Soviet Union continued training and building up Zanzibar's armed forces.

President Nyerere sought to neutralize the Communist penetration and Marxist influence. He edged three pro-Communists out of politically sensitive posts on the island and replaced them with African nationalists. At the same time, the Tanganyikan leader took steps to strengthen Karume's position, to integrate the police, and to lay the groundwork for the merger of armies of the two countries. Preparations were also made for the drafting of the United Republic's first constitution, and agreement was reached on a flag for the new nation.

Although the extension of Communist control was partially checked, the situation was still serious. By the summer, Communists managed all the vital services on Zanzibar as though the merger with Tanganyika had not occurred. They appeared to have more experts, advisers, and technicians in the island's government than the British had before the January revolution. A *New York Times* correspondent reported that "the Russians run the port and harbor; the Chinese the agriculture; and the East Germans the Finance, Education and Information Departments as well as the official radio station." [3] Peking extended to Zanzibar some $14 million in credits, and in August it became the first African country to receive a Chinese military mission to help train its army. President Nyerere, however, also pointed out that the United Republic had been negotiating with West Germany and expected to conclude a five-year agreement to train the Republic's army air wing. "Why," he asked, "should people say we should be afraid of being unduly influenced by the Chinese, but not by West Germany? Yet our agreement with the Chinese is for only six months, whereas our agreement with West Germany is for five years." He stressed that his position remained what it had always been. "We are trying to be non-aligned," said President Nyerere. "We live in a complex world in which, try as we will, we are not going to be left alone." [4] On August 30 the Soviet Union, Poland, and Czechoslovakia announced their intention to extend $42 million in credits for Tanganyika's five-year development program.

From the point of view of the West, the future of East Africa was decidedly cloudy, and prospects remained that the island of Zanzibar might still become a stepping-off point for a Communist thrust into the heart of the continent.

43. BORDER, TRIBAL, AND RACIAL CONFLICTS

"Emergence from colonial status is naturally and inescapably a difficult process," U.N. Secretary-General U Thant told the Algerian National Assembly on February 4 during his first visit to Africa. "There are many obstacles, political, economic, administrative, institutional and psychological to be overcome before a normal state of equilibrium and activity can be reached." [5] While Africa desperately tried to cope with the many problems of freedom, it was clear that in the mid-1960's the continent's vulnerability lay in widespread disorders that threatened almost every country. These threats were manifested not only in the East African mutinies, but in border wars, tribal massacres, and racial conflicts, and they inevitably created political instability. Chaotic conditions, in addition, invited Communist encroachments, as well as Western intervention.

Unquestionably, a significant factor on the African scene during the year was the intrusion of Sino-Soviet competition. Premier Chou En-lai's visit to ten African states from mid-December 1963 to February 1964 had aimed at establishing an identity of interest between Communist China and the newly independent African states. Although the personal impact of the Chinese leader could not be effectively measured, his appeal against imperialism, colonialism and neocolonialism, and his references to the common struggle shared by Africans and Chinese against backwardness and for economic development tended to produce a favorable response in some quarters. Premier Khrushchev, on his first visit to Egypt in May, had also anxiously sought to cultivate the affections of the Africans. In the duel between Moscow and Peking, the Soviet Union had certain important advantages, not the least of which was its ability to furnish much greater aid to the African nations. Nevertheless, it was evident that the Chinese Communists were determined to make Africa a major target, and they intended to involve themselves directly or indirectly in every active revolution on the continent. They intruded not only in Zanzibar, but also in the Congo, Burundi, Rwanda, and Southern Rhodesia, as well as in Portuguese Angola and Mozambique. Peking's inroads in Africa were as yet relatively minor, but their cumulative effect in time, it was recognized, could become dangerous both to the West and to the Soviet Union.

Neither the Soviet Union nor Communist China was responsible for African turbulence, but both powers did not hesitate to exploit the existing disorders to their advantage. One of the serious situations that came to the forefront early in the year was the border war between Somalia and Ethiopia. The area in contention was the Ogaden Province, inhabited by some one million Somalis, which was incorporated into Ethiopia. Following World War II, Ogaden Somali leaders vigorously put forward demands for self-determination, but their request was ignored by both Ethiopia and the United Nations. As a result, an underground resistance movement began to build up, and in June 1963 it flared into open rebellion. From this time on, guerrilla warfare was waged against the Emperor's troops. The

Somali Republic (created in July 1960 from the merger of former British and Italian Somaliland) had insisted not only on a revision of boundaries with Ethiopia, but also with Kenya. In 1963 it accused Britain of betraying its interests by handing over the Northern Frontier District to Kenya in disregard of the findings of an independent commission that had pronounced the area as being predominantly inhabited by Somalis.

Somalia did not have the power to seize the contested areas or to negotiate from strength with its two more powerful neighbors. A defense pact concluded between Ethiopia and Kenya, moreover, increased its sense of isolation and vulnerability. Unable to secure a satisfactory arms arrangement with the West—the Somalis were convinced that the United States and Britain preferred to back Ethiopia and Kenya—Somalia turned to the Soviet Union in October 1963 and obtained a pledge of some $30 million in arms assistance and other aid. During the following months, tension mounted as terrorist attacks in the Ogaden Province became more widespread. They finally reached a climax early in February in full-scale clashes between the armies of Ethiopia and Somalia. On February 9 Secretary-General Thant sent an urgent appeal to Ethiopia and Somalia to end hostilities. Emperor Haile Selassie replied that his forces had taken action to meet Somalia's flagrant violations of the principles of the United Nations and the Organization of African Unity. "We have exercised the utmost restraint in the face of the unbearable provocation and shall continue to do so," he said. "We are desirous of putting an end to clashes entailing bloodshed and loss of life, but Somalia leaders must abandon their reckless policy of territorial expansion at our expense." [6]

Evidence indicated that the border conflict was not instigated by the Somali government, but by the "liberation movement" of Somali inhabitants within Ogaden. It caught the Somalis wholly unprepared for any large-scale engagement. The emergency caused by the renewal of border violence pushed Somalia toward even heavier reliance on Russian arms. Somalia pressed Moscow to speed up its arms deliveries and training program for Somali cadets. On February 12 the Somali government, declaring that Ethiopian planes had strafed and bombed its villages in defiance of the U.N. cease-fire appeal, told U Thant that it was "determined not to suffer such aggressions passively," but that it would try "to keep them from erupting into general conflict." Three days later, the Organization of African Unity, which had been meeting at Dar es Salaam to deal with the East Africa crisis, called on Ethiopia and Somalia to end the shooting along their borders, and it also urged a peaceful settlement of the frontier dispute between Somalia and Kenya. Although a truce was declared on February 16, fighting continued and Somalia refused to relinquish its claims to the Ogaden region.

On March 18 Somalia and Ethiopia finally agreed to open negotiations at Khartoum in the Sudan to resolve the border dispute. After about two weeks of discussion, the two countries agreed to a cease-fire but no effective compromise was reached on the frontier quarrel. Although Ethiopia was prepared to consider an exact demarcation of its southern border, Somalia was not interested in boundary revisions only. Its main concern was the unification of all Somali-inhabited areas, including not only the Ogaden Province, but also much of northern Kenya as well as all of French Somaliland.

As the Somali-Ethiopian dispute smoldered, a wave of massacres erupted in Rwanda. For more than four centuries the Watusi, an "aristocratic" tribe, most of whose members were over six feet tall, had been the overlords in this small country, dominating the Bahutu, a tribe of shorter people who were their vassals. In a violent revolution of November 1959 the Bahutu serfs overthrew the traditional Watusi monarchy. Thousands of Watusis were killed and about 130,000 fled from Rwanda into Tanganyika, Burundi, Uganda, and the neighboring Kivu Province of the Congo. In December 1963 an armed guerrilla band of Watusi exiles invaded Rwanda from Burundi and nearly seized the capital before they were routed. Fearing a counterrevolution, the Bahutus clubbed, beat, and hacked the Watusis to death in a wave of terror. The invasion set off mass killings early in the year in Rwanda that threatened the virtual extinction of the Watusi in the country. Savage reprisals, as one investigator said, approached genocide. The Rwanda government apparently did nothing to prevent the slaughter.

In addition to border conflicts and tribal warfare, racial tensions continued to be acute in Africa, especially in Southern Rhodesia and South Africa. On the eve of the new year, the Federation of Rhodesia and Nyasaland was dissolved. The Federation, which had been established by the British ten years earlier as a major experiment in multiracialism, ended in failure. On July 6 Nyasaland was granted independence, and became known as Malawi—the thirty-fifth African state to achieve independence. On October 24 Northern Rhodesia secured its independence as the Republic of Zambia.

Most critical was the situation in Southern Rhodesia where the white population of some 200,000 exercised political power over a 3.7 million African majority. Since 1923 the Southern Rhodesian whites had been self-governing in all internal matters, though no important legislation, particularly that touching non-Europeans, was ever passed without consulting London. Largely responsible for the economic development of the country, they insisted on keeping the government in what they called "civilized hands," which meant, of course, blocking African participation. Both the whites and Africans wanted independence. The former wished to continue governing the country under the existing system of restricted voting; the latter demanded that the constitution of the new independent state be based on universal adult suffrage. Despite the sharp divergence, it was galling to both groups, but most especially to the whites, to see their less developed, black-ruled neighbors in Nyasaland and Northern Rhodesia achieving independence while such status was stubbornly withheld from them by Britain. But London was adamant that before independence would be granted the whites had to agree to greater African representation.

The great danger in Southern Rhodesia stemmed from the fact that white extremists, whose party had won the elections of 1962 and had the support of most of the white community, threatened to establish independence unilaterally if Britain persisted in its refusal to agree to this step. Such action, it was feared, would lead to a devastating collision between the races that would have far-reaching repercussions throughout the continent. Late in March the U.N. Special Committee on ending colonialism drew the Security Council's attention to "the explosive situation in Southern Rhodesia," warning that it constituted "a serious threat to international peace and security." On March 25 the Committee adopted a resolution calling on the United Kingdom "once more" to hold a constitutional conference as a preliminary to granting independence with the guarantee of universal adult suffrage. The Committee also urged Britain to make clear to "the minority settler government" the consequences of a unilateral declaration of independence, and to take measures to prevent such action.[7]

During the spring the impasse seemed to point to a showdown. On April 13 Prime Minister Winston Field was ousted and replaced by Ian Douglas Smith, a former Minister of the Treasury, who strongly supported a scheme for "community development" which did not differ greatly from South Africa's policy of *apartheid*. An-out-and-out white supremacist, the new Prime Minister expressed his determination to get independence for Southern Rhodesia as soon as possible. London quickly warned Mr. Smith that if he proclaimed independence unilaterally, Southern Rhodesia would be expelled from the Commonwealth and its sterling assets of some $120 million would be frozen. Britain also hinted at other retaliatory measures. At the same time, the United States indicated that it would refuse to recognize the country.

To head off a collision, Britain agreed at the Commonwealth Prime Ministers' conference in July—to which Southern Rhodesia was not invited, a break with a thirty-year old tradition—to call a meeting of both white and black Southern Rhodesians to discuss terms on which the self-governing colony would achieve independence. Prime Minister Jomo Kenyatta of Kenya, spokesman for the African delegations, appealed to Britain to use its influence to secure the release of African nationalists who had been imprisoned in Southern Rhodesia, and to arrange for a constitutional conference to revamp the complicated electoral laws which kept the white minority in political power. A new constitution, he said, should be drawn up based on the principle of "one man, one vote" to eliminate the weighted-voting system.

At the talks held early in September in London, Prime Minister Smith seemingly intended to show that negotiations for independence were impossible, and that southern Rhodesia's only choice was rebellion. Expecting the discussions to collapse, Mr. Smith apparently planned to stalk home angrily and demand a unilateral declaration of independence. But Prime Minister Douglas-Home forestalled this maneuver by promising independence, *provided* Southern Rhodesia could prove to London's satisfaction that a majority of the people, both black and white, desired independence under the existing constitution and restricted franchise. Expressing confidence that he could get a mandate, the Southern Rhodesian leader told a news conference that a unilateral declaration "for the time being" had been "chucked out of the window." "We are not wild men. We seek only to expand and maintain the standards of civilization built up during 50 years of European settlement. . . . We are convinced that a majority of the whole population supports our request for independence on the basis of the present constitution and franchise." [8]

Prime Minister Smith intended to decide the issue by a referendum of all registered voters—which meant the white population—and by *consultation* with Africans "within the tribal structure." This meant that the wishes of the majority of Africans who were ineligible to vote would be made known by the decision of the tribal chiefs, who were paid officials of the government. The Southern Rhodesian leader's hand was strengthened when a prominent former Prime Minister, Sir Roy Welensky, who had opposed the extremist government policies, was defeated in a by-election on October 2 by a pro-Smith candidate. Three weeks later, the tribal chiefs gave their unqualified approval of independence under white rule.

Upon taking office in October, the British Labor party adopted an even tougher policy toward Southern Rhodesia than the Tory government had. Prime Minister Wilson appealed to the voters of Rhodesia to repudiate Ian Douglas Smith and force him to resign. He warned the colony's white population against proclaiming independence without the consent of the black population. Any unilateral declaration of independence, Mr. Wilson declared, would be "an open act of defiance and rebellion" that would invite a series of political and economic reprisals." [9] The United States firmly backed the British Labor government in its stand. Nevertheless, the white electorate on November 5 strongly voted in favor of independence under continued white rule. As Southern Rhodesia edged toward a possible decisive break with England, the prospects of a racial explosion grew ominous. "I give the Republic of Iansmithia, if it comes, three months," the head of a local diplomatic mission said. "African government will come in next year." [10] Without determined British intervention, the chances, however, of a peaceful transition to majority rule seemed slight.

As the time bomb ticked on in Southern Rhodesia, Britain announced on July 30 that the Gambia, a tiny, peanut-growing enclave and its last remaining colony on Africa's west coast, would be given independence on February 18, 1965. During the summer Britain also agreed to early independence for Malta, the strategic island in the Mediterranean, and this was granted in September.

Although there were no signs of imminent crises in the Republic of South Africa or in the Portuguese colonies of Angola and Mozambique, African pressures continued to build up during the year for an end to *apartheid* and Portuguese colonialism. On April 20 a United Nations panel of experts submitted a report to the Secretary-General in which it advocated a national convention of all South African racial groups to be held under U.N. auspices. The panel's report said that this would be "the last chance to avoid a vast tragedy." Only a national convention, the experts believed, could save all the people of South Africa from "catastrophe," and "the world from a conflagration of incalculable consequences." [11]

On May 29 South Africa charged that the U.N. panel of

experts had been guilty of bias and distortion of facts. It rejected its call for a national convention, and declared that its
policy of racial segregation was a domestic matter for which
South Africa was not accountable to the Security Council. The
U.N. Special Committee on the Policies of *Apartheid*, set up
in 1962,[12] urged the Security Council to take mandatory steps to
make the South African government comply with United Nations
decisions. It again underlined the gravity of the situation, and
expressed alarm over the continued persecution of opponents
of *apartheid*, as well as the passage of new discriminatory legislation which deprived the non-white population of its few remaining rights. The Committee called attention to the trials of leading
opponents of South African racial policies who were held "under
arbitrary laws" that provided for the death penalty.[13] On June 8
the Security Council resumed its consideration of the South African situation and adopted two resolutions: the first on June 9,
urged the South African government to renounce the execution
of persons sentenced to death for anti-*apartheid* actions; the
second, on June 18, endorsed the main conclusions of the panel
of experts that "all people of South Africa should be brought into consultation and should thus be enabled to decide the future
of their country at the national level." [14]

The struggle to end Portuguese colonial rule in Angola persisted. At the start of the year, Holden Roberto, who headed
the Angolan government-in-exile, agreed to accept aid from
Communist China and "other Communist countries." Criticizing
the Western powers for their hypocrisy in paying lip service to
self-determination while supporting its NATO ally, Portugal,
"with arms that are used to kill us," he went on to say: "Only
the Communists can give us what we need. None of the African
countries produces arms; they have to buy them themselves. It
would be a betrayal of the suffering Angolan people not to turn
to those who can help." [15]

By summer it appeared, however, that the nationalist guerrilla rebellion, which had broken out in February 1961, had been
virtually quelled. At the Cairo meeting of African chiefs of
state, Angolan nationalist leaders acknowledged that serious

setbacks had occurred. They attributed this to insufficient military equipment and to the more effective control which Portuguese forces were exercising over the 1,000-mile Angolan border with the Congo. Portugal steadily increased its military strength, so that by 1964 it had 85,000 troops in Africa, the largest defense force on the continent below the Sahara. Besides Angola, troops were deployed in Mozambique to meet threats of guerrilla invasions by rebel groups from neighboring Tanzania, and in Portuguese Guinea, where fighting was also going on to break Lisbon's shaky toehold in West Africa.

44. THE CONTINENT GROPES FOR UNITY

Beneath Africa's upheavals the desire to achieve cohesion persisted both within individual states and on the continent as a whole. Because of the danger of the independence movement foundering on conflicting ambitions and ideologies, the fostering of a sense of individual and group identity was seen as the immediate task. African leaders talked about union, the liberation of territories still under colonial rule, and the abolition of *apartheid,* but the fact remained that African peoples did not know each other, and each country was largely absorbed with its own internal problems. Land routes from one country to another were extremely primitive. Whatever railroads had been built ran only to the sea. Africa's commercial patterns had been formed in the nineteenth century largely to suit the purposes of the colonial powers. Few of the African states that emerged after 1957 had viable economies, none was wholly self-sustaining, and some were all but helpless economically. Ethiopia and the Sudan, with their favorable climate and large areas of fertile land, were better off than most. The Congo had the potential of becoming economically independent. But most of the rest of the African nations were fortunate if they had one or two raw materials or crops to exchange for the necessities of life. Burundi, Mali, and Somalia were typical of the majority that could not really develop on their own.

African leaders were well aware that the continent's problems would not be resolved unless greater cooperation and unity were attained. Two schools of thought prevailed on how this goal could be achieved. President Kwame Nkrumah of Ghana was the most vocal spokesman for a United States of Africa and "union now." He argued fervently that none of the independent states would lose its sovereignty in such a political federation. But most African leaders feared Nkrumah's driving ambition and egotism, and they did not discount the possibility that he might become the first, and perhaps permanent, "president" of such a federation. Emperor Haile Selassie represented the second school of thought which propounded a pragmatic approach. No scheme, however noble and farseeing, he felt, was good if it would not work. The Emperor believed that the African states had to move step-by-step toward union because "tradition cannot be abandoned at once." Largely as a result of his sponsorship and inspiration, African leaders at a "summit conference" in Addis Ababa in May 1963 agreed to set up the Organization of African Unity. Like the Organization of American States in the Western Hemisphere, it was a grouping of wholly independent and sovereign states. With permanent headquarters established in Addis Ababa, the O.A.U. in July named Diallo Telli of Guinea as its first Secretary-General. Progress in developing intra-African relations was slow and a "spirit of unity" was not especially noticeable, but it was clear that the creation of the organization was a notable step forward. By providing a forum and a mechanism for the resolution of some of the continent's problems, the O.A.U. offered the promise of cushioning the crises that erupted. But the euphoria that accompanied the establishment of the O.A.U. all but vanished in 1964.

Ghana came into the spotlight at the start of the year when an attempt was made to assassinate President Nkrumah on January 2. As the Ghanian leader was walking toward his car outside his office, five shots were fired at him from close range. Although he was unhurt, a security guard was fatally wounded. Some Ghanians who distrusted the government thought that the incident was stage-managed to evoke support for Nkrumah. The whole assassination story, they thought, may have been a "ruse" to get the people to "rubber stamp" Nkrumah's one-party constitution. Foreign diplomats also were inclined to believe that the government version of the incident did not match several known facts. No further violence broke out, but the atmosphere became charged with strain. One Ghana official said that things were so quiet, all one could hear were "whispers."

Early in February a chanting crowd of Ghanians attacked the American embassy. This came after a referendum was held—which Western newsmen said had been marked by widespread fraud and intimidation—giving President Nkrumah virtually unbridled dictatorial powers. Washington temporarily recalled its ambassador to emphasize its protest against the anti-American campaign. The United States suspected that the Ghanian President, encountering serious internal opposition, was seeking to ascribe this condition to American intervention. The barrage of anti-American propaganda did not cease until late in April. Since President Nkrumah needed large amounts of foreign capital to restore his country's deteriorating economy, he evidently decided to change his attitude. His new seven-year development plan called for $280 million in foreign investment, and he relied heavily on American support for a $196 million Volta River hydroelectric project that was expected to reach completion in two years.

In tiny Gabon, with a population of 450,000, President "Papa" Léon M'Ba had been regarded as one of Africa's most secure and popular leaders. But M'Ba began to reach out for dictatorial control. When he dissolved the sixty-seven-member National Assembly on January 20, calling for new elections to be held in February for a smaller, forty-seven-member assembly, political opposition quickly crystallized. The problem in Gabon was, in some respects, similar to that in Ghana. Both countries were increasingly subjected to authoritarian rule. Whereas Nkrumah maintained tight control, M'Ba encountered unexpected resistance. Cut loose from their ancient tribal, patriarchal, and hierarchical moorings, Africans appeared torn between conflicting loyalties and rival concepts of modern democracy and the old chieftancy system. In both Ghana and Gabon, the chieftancy pattern seemed to be reemerging in a new authoritarian form. This problem, of course, was not unique to these two countries; it existed in many other African states.

On February 17 a handful of junior officers of Gabon's 400-man army, together with a number of police, effected a bloodless *coup*. President M'Ba was seized in the presidential palace; he announced his resignation; and the rebels quickly formed a revolutionary council to govern the West African republic. For twenty-four hours, the *coup* appeared to have been a complete success. The next day, however, President de Gaulle, invoking a mutual defense agreement signed in 1960, intervened to restore the toppled regime. At M'Ba's request, French troops were rushed in the next day from Senegal and the former French Congo. Gabon was one of the biggest producers of uranium in the franc zone, and had some of the world's highest grade manganese, as well as untapped deposits of iron ore. It supplied President de Gaulle with most of the uranium for the French nuclear program. French paratroopers took the capital with little resistance, and France served notice that it was prepared to intervene with military force at any time to maintain political stability in French-influenced areas of Africa.

Although President M'Ba regained power, the situation remained explosive. Less than a month later, several thousand Gabonese, spearheaded by students, rioted against the French and M'Ba. After four days of violence, order was again finally restored by French soldiers.

The French armed intervention gave rise to a serious problem, for it posed the question of how free a country was if a foreign power could decide when a *coup* was popular and when it was not. President de Gaulle had claimed that the Gabon revolt did not have popular support, and it was partly for this reason that French action was taken. Evidence indicated, nevertheless, that the revolt did have the backing of much of the army and police and at least the tacit approval of Gabon's opposition party, the Democratic and Social Union. To many Gabonese who sided with the rebels, the French intervention was a flagrant violation of the nation's sovereignty. But the dilemma remained. Political instability endangered the nation's vital interests, invited chaos, and created hardships. Western powers could not be indifferent when their own interests were involved, and the possibility of Communist encroachment existed. For Africa, unfortunately, instability appeared to be the price of freedom.

45. THE CONGO AGONY

The most serious problem in Africa was the threat of the disintegration of the Democratic Republic of the Congo (Leopoldville). Like the peoples of many other African countries, the Congolese had little sense of nationhood. About three hundred tribes existed in the former Belgian colony—in each of which tribal loyalty was very strong. Conflict was frequent among the tribes and with the central government. While the task of dealing with clashing tribalism and threats of secession proved to be inordinately great, difficulties also arose from the presence of tribal groups whose homelands were on both sides of the borders between the Congo and neighboring African states, for, as elsewhere, the existing frontiers had been drawn without reference to ethnic lines.

Since the establishment of the Congo's independence in July 1960, the United States had been deeply concerned with the preservation of the new state's territorial integrity, and the prevention of its "Balkanization." Washington feared that the breaking up of the Congo would simply give rise to the creation of additional scores of small, economically unstable states that would decline into chaos or fall prey to Communist and other intrigues. Partly to arrest this development, and to enable the Congo to gain time to establish some degree of political stability, the United States had firmly supported the United Nations' efforts to force mineral-rich Katanga Province to rejoin the Congo. Although the United Nations successfully accomplished this mission, the Congo regime failed to build up sufficient strength to cope with renewed threats of disorder and guerrilla warfare after the U.N. troops and other officials departed.

Three contributory factors to the Congo crisis that erupted during 1964 should be noted. First, a group of about a hundred exiled Congolese had organized in 1963 a Committee for National Liberation (C.N.L.), whose leader, Pierre Mulele, had been ambassador to Egypt in the deposed leftist secessionist government of Antoine Gizenga. After a year and a half of exile in Cairo and Communist China, he returned to the Congo secretly in the summer of 1963. Soon after his reappearance the C.N.L. was formed early in October, and headquarters were set up in Brazzaville, capital of the Republic of Congo, just across the river from Leopoldville. In January a branch office was opened in Bujumbura, the capital of Burundi. The Committee for National Liberation did not appear to have any program beyond the desire to overthrow the central government by force. Second, Communist China began to intrude in the Congolese situation. In December the Kingdom of Burundi recognized Peking, and Brazzaville followed suit two months later. Soon it became evident that the Chinese had decided to help the rebels. Third, the determination of the United Nations to withdraw its military forces from the Congo in June 1964 would remove one restraining element.

Early in January, terrorist attacks spread through the Kwilu Province, a rich agricultural area 250 miles east of Leopoldville. Here the Bapende and Babunda tribes had long and bitterly opposed the provincial government, and the C.N.L. seized the opportunity of using this tribal resistance to start a full-scale revolt. Although it had been known for several months that Mulele had been recruiting and training rebel bands, it was not until January 11 that the first national troops were sent to Kwilu to replace the local police. By then, most of the police in the area had either deserted to the rebels or run away, and Mulele soon controlled an area the size of New England. The response of the Congolese regime was frighteningly inept. A *New York Times* correspondent observed, "For weeks, as the revolt built up, the top Congolese leaders toured European capitals. Premier [Cyrille] Adoula made state visits to Paris and Rome. Gen. Joseph Mobutu, the army commander, took a leisurely swing through Britain, Belgium and West Germany, despite urgent appeals for him to return." [16]

During March, as the situation continued to deteriorate, President Joseph Kasavubu suspended the Congolese Parliament, and steps were taken to draft a new Congolese constitution that was intended to provide a strong presidential form of government. This move, it was hoped, would lead to promoting the nation's political stability. To bolster the Congolese regime further, Foreign Minister Spaak (the first Belgian official to be welcomed in Leopoldville since the Congo became independent) concluded a series of agreements on March 20 that resulted in the settlement of the four-year financial dispute, and laid the groundwork for a period of cooperation. Besides resolving financial problems, Belgium also agreed to cede its military bases in the Congo to the Congolese government. The United States, on its part, offered its help to improve the Congo's security before the U.N. troops left on June 30. The situation was particularly acute not only because of the upsurge of terrorist activities, but because no progress had been made in the military training program which was supposed to prepare Congolese troops to take over the U.N. peace-keeping task.

Late in March President Johnson sent Under-Secretary of State Harriman to Leopoldville for a first-hand look at the Congo's problems. There were serious doubts that the ill-disciplined and meagerly trained Congolese army would be able to cope with the spreading unrest. U Thant expressed his concern about new threats in Katanga and the possibility of revolt in the eastern Congo and a half dozen other widely separated spots. Mr. Harriman's visit seemed to be directed toward reaffirming American support of Premier Adoula and considering limited means of assisting the Congolese army to meet attacks against the central government. In particular, it was expected that the United States would provide substantial air and ground transport to improve the army's mobility so that troops could be sent to trouble spots. Washington, however, made it clear that no American forces or arms would be sent to the Congo for combat.

In the spring a rebellion, resembling the one in the Kwilu region, broke out in the north of Kivu Province. Once again the C.N.L. exploited the tribal conflicts to push its revolutionary movement. On May 19 the rebels gained control of an important main road connecting the Kivu Province with Burundi. As the fighting spread, evidence continued to accumulate that the Liberation Committee was being actively supported by the Chinese embassy in Bujumbura. In June Washington acknowledged that several single-engine, propeller-driven T-28 training planes had been adapted as fighters and sent to the Congo. While some were flown by American "civilian" pilots under contract to the Congolese government, most of the pilots were Cuban exiles. The United States also expanded its military aid mission with several experts in counterinsurgency warfare. But this increase in American support had little effect in halting the rebel drive. On June 19 Albertville, the capital of north Katanga, fell to the rebels. Although there was no apparent direct connection between the rebellions in Kwilu, Kivu, and Katanga, it was nevertheless suspected that they were abetted by the Committee for National Liberation, behind which stood the Chinese Communists.

With the retreat of the Congolese army on all fronts, pressures arose for the creation of a government of "national reconciliation." It was at this moment that Moïse Tshombé, former President of Katanga Province, returned to Leopoldville on June 26. "The evolution of the country's situation," he declared, had compelled him to return "suddenly." He asserted that only a "sincere and total reconciliation between all Congolese" could save the country "from misery and anarchy."

On June 30, the fourth anniversary of the Congo's independence, the last of 143 Nigerian and Canadian soldiers under U.N. command withdrew from the country—the rear guard of a force once numbering 20,000. Not a single Congolese official went to the airport to pay his respects. Yet it was mainly through the efforts of the U.N. peace-keeping operation that the government had been able to maintain its authority. Three hours later, President Kasavubu announced Premier Adoula's resignation.

This action was expected since a provisional government would have to rule pending the holding of a national referendum to approve a new constitution and new parliamentary elections. The next day Tshombé was asked to form a transition government. He announced his intention of forming a government of national unity, and on July 9 was named Premier. Although Tshombé tried to appease the C.N.L. and other left-wing leaders and evinced a desire for a political settlement, violence did not abate. On July 24 President Johnson, ignoring past quarrels with the Katangese leader, told a news conference, "We are going to be as cooperative and as helpful as we can and attempt to see that the people of that area have as good a government as is possible and we have every intention of being understanding and cooperative." [17]

During the summer the situation went from bad to worse. On August 5 Stanleyville fell to rebel forces, and its loss threatened to cut off the entire northern Congo from Leopoldville's control. The Congolese army was falling apart, for it seemed utterly incapable of suppressing or even confining the rebellions in the country. The next day, President Johnson sent Under-Secretary Harriman to Brussels. With the withdrawal of U.N. troops, responsibility for stemming the growing chaos was increasingly assumed by the United States and Belgium. As a result of Mr. Harriman's conversations with Belgian officials, agreement was reached on August 7 to augment technical aid for the purpose of shoring up the Tshombé government, although both countries made it clear that they would not provide military personnel for combat. The United States was to supply transport planes, trucks, and communications equipment, and Belgium its military and technical experts to train Congolese troops in their use. At the same time, Tshombé indicated his intention to recruit the Katanga gendarmerie—a force he had organized during the unsuccessful Katangese secession attempt —and to hire mercenaries to reinforce the 30,000-man army. Although the Congolese Premier preferred to obtain help from other African nations, the availability of such aid was considered doubtful, chiefly because Tshombé was identified with European interests and looked upon as a "tool" of the white man, and also because he was held responsible for Lumumba's murder. Moreover, he seemed unable to rally the tribal and other Congolese leaders to his government. Tshombé concluded that a substantial force of foreign mercenaries would have to be recruited to put down the rebellions. Both the United States and Belgium seemed ready to equip, transport, and help the Congo bear the cost of such a force; but they firmly believed that "Africanization" of the struggle was the most desirable long-range solution.

In the meantime, the commander of the rebel force in Stanleyville demanded that the United States withdraw its consul and three other consular officials from the city. When this was not done, they were imprisoned or kept under heavy guard until their rescue three and one-half months later. Following Stanleyville's capture by the rebels, the United States sent four C-130 transport planes to the Congo along with approximately 100 army and air force personnel, including some forty paratroopers, to guard the planes at their temporary base near Leopoldville. Washington frankly acknowledged that the situation had become "extremely serious" and that the rebellion-torn country was "coming apart at the seams." Early in July the United States had already sent sixty-eight officers and men to Leopoldville to advise the Congolese army. This group, members of the U.S. Congo mission, represented a minor version of the American military mission in South Vietnam.

Disturbed by the buildup of American forces, Senator John Stennis of Mississippi, on August 14, called for the "full facts" about the administration's intentions in the Congo. He asked whether the sending of planes and men was but the first in a series of steps that would ultimately lead to a heavy commitment of men and material. "I strongly oppose letting the Congo become our African Vietnam," Senator Stennis said. He warned that the situation was "fraught with potential danger and the possibility of serious involvement." [18]

In mid-August Assistant Secretary of State for African Affairs G. Mennen Williams went to Leopoldville. As a result of his visit, the United States agreed to provide Premier Tshombé with several "long-range" reconnaissance planes as well as a few B-26 light bombers. It was emphasized that American pilots would not fly the planes and that the Congo would be responsible for finding its own pilots. Mr. Williams strongly urged the Congolese leader to obtain help from other African countries, indicating that the United States would assist such troops financially. Although Premier Tshombé asked for help from Senegal, Liberia, Nigeria, Ethiopia, and Malagasy, none of these countries responded to his appeal.

As the crisis deepened at the end of August, Senator Mansfield added his warning against unilateral American involvement. "Our entanglement may well lead to unsatisfactory consequences for the United States." Stressing that "the mess in Africa" was not "our doing," and recognizing that dissociation was difficult, he nevertheless felt that it would be "most unfortunate" if the United States were drawn into the "internecine warfare of the Congolese." "Responsibility must be taken by the Congolese themselves, who now have the independence which they have sought," he said. "To the extent that there is an outside responsibility, it rests, first with the Europeans and, in the case of the Congo, more specifically with the Belgians. . . . We must resist the urge to try to solve every problem where it crops out." [19]

Unable to obtain help from other African states, Premier Tshombé recruited mercenaries from South Africa and Southern Rhodesia. With the mercenaries formed into a "shock brigade," a turn in the fighting against the rebels took place. By early September, Albertville was recaptured. Congolese columns with white officers, and the protective air cover of U.S. planes piloted by anti-Castro Cubans, advanced into rebel-held territory. On September 3 the rebel commander at Stanleyville told the United Nations that the city's entire white population, numbering about 800, would be held as hostages against any air raids carried out by the Congolese government.

With the situation becoming increasingly tense, the foreign ministers of the member states of the Organization of African Unity gathered in Addis Ababa on September 5 to deal with the crisis. In the meantime, on September 7, the pro-Communist rebels at Stanleyville announced the formation of the "Congolese People's Republic Government" headed by Christophe Gbenye, a founder of the C.N.L.

On September 10, by a vote of 27 to 0, the O.A.U. approved a six-point resolution calling for (1) the ending of recruitment of mercenaries and the expulsion of those already in the Congo; (2) an immediate cease-fire; (3) an appeal to all political parties for a government of national reconciliation to insure order and free elections; (4) the creation of a committee to help political leaders achieve national reconciliation and restore normal relations between the Congo and its neighboring states; (5) a mission to visit the countries accused of interfering in the Congo and to ask them to stop their activities; and (6) a request to O.A.U. states to cease any actions that might aggravate the situation.[20] As a result of the resolution a ten-nation Congo Conciliation Commission, headed by Prime Minister Kenyatta, was appointed to help restore order. Premier Tshombé promptly said that he would carry out the resolution, but he stressed that it would have to be implemented "in the light of our sovereignty, our territorial integrity and our inalienable right to national independence." However, the Congolese leader refused to accept a "cease-fire" since it put the government and the rebels on an equal footing.

Shortly after the O.A.U. meeting, the Conciliation Commission declared its intention to establish contact with the rebel forces. It also indicated its desire to visit the Republic of Congo and Burundi in an attempt to resolve their dispute with the Congolese regime. Premier Tshombé firmly opposed the committee's decision to meet the rebels officially but raised no objection to unofficial contacts, and insisted that the rebels lay down their arms before their case was heard. "It cannot be disputed," he said, "that they are anything else but rebels and bandits who bring chaos to the country." The O.A.U. nevertheless affirmed that the Commission would meet with the rebels officially "as the commission and not as individuals." On September 22 the Conciliation Commission called on the United States to end immediately its military support of the Tshombé regime as an essential first step toward the restoration of peace. It also named a special delegation, the representatives of five African countries, to fly to Washington to appeal directly to President Johnson. The State Department had tried to dissuade the delegation from undertaking this visit, which it deemed inappropriate at the moment. While expressing support for O.A.U. efforts to solve the Congo problem, it stressed that the limited American military assistance was given at the request of the Congolese government "to assist it in maintaining law and order." Washington indicated that if the Congo was willing, it would "be prepared to meet with representatives of the Government of the Congo and the O.A.U. Commission at a mutually agreed time and place and on the basis of a previously agreed agenda."

Nevertheless the *ad hoc* O.A.U. Commission came to Washington on September 25 "on a good-will mission." After talking with Secretary Rusk and Assistant Secretary Williams, the Africans bowed to the American position that U.S. military aid could not be discussed without the participation of the Congo government. The United States, in turn, acknowledged that the Conciliation Commission was "engaged in a most significant undertaking in the service of Africa," to the success of which it attached "great importance," and expressed its desire "to cooperate with the Commission in every appropriate way in carrying out the mission entrusted to it by the O.A.U." [21]

During October, African hostility toward Premier Tshombé was demonstrated when he was barred from the conference of nonaligned nations in Cairo and held under house arrest for four days by order of President Nasser. The affront to the Congolese leader, designed in part to lower his prestige in Leopoldville, backfired. Upon Tshombé's return to his homeland he was wildly cheered by more than a quarter million Congolese who turned out to greet him. At the same time, Congolese forces began slowly but surely to close in on the rebels. By early November the drive had turned into a major offensive. The rebel retreat in the northeast and the west soon approached a rout. The main force from the south began to converge on Stanleyville. Led by a Belgian colonel and 250 mercenaries, a mechanized Congolese brigade pushed toward the rebel-held city. Food supplies started to run out, and the rebels pillaged the city almost unchecked. In desperation, rebel leader Gbenye threatened to massacre white hostages unless the advance on Stanleyville was halted, and declared, "We can no longer guarantee the lives and property of Belgian and American citizens."

On November 19 the United States accepted a Congolese rebel offer to negotiate for the safety of some sixty Americans, including Dr. Paul Carlson, a missionary under a death sentence. With Premier Tshombé's consent, the United States agreed to meet with a rebel emissary in Nairobi, Kenya. Talks collapsed when the rebel "Foreign Minister" demanded that a government spearhead column, which was a day's march from Stanleyville, be turned back. Meanwhile, both the United States and Belgium faced an agonizing decision. About 600 Belgian paratroopers were poised on Ascension Island in the South Atlantic Ocean ready to fly into Stanleyville to prevent the massacre of hostages. A battalion had been sent to the island earlier in the week in U.S. Air Force planes as a precautionary measure. When their presence was prematurely disclosed, a Belgian official announced that the paratroopers would be used only on request by the central government and if developments within the next twenty-four hours warranted the intervention. Fearing a lightning swoop, the rebels announced that the American and Belgian hostages were being moved out of the city into the jungle "while awaiting the end of negotiations" on their fate.

When hope faded that the hostages would be spared, the United States and Belgium arranged to land the Belgian paratroopers to undertake a humanitarian rescue operation. Foreign Minister Spaak said it was the "gravest decision" of his career— one that was "even more difficult than the decision to go to war in 1940 because then the train of events forced this decision on us." [22] At 5 A.M. on November 24 nearly 400 troops were dropped over the Stanleyville airport, capturing it in five minutes.

Within an hour the rest of the forces landed and began moving toward the city. Later that morning Congolese troops, led by white mercenaries, entered Stanleyville from the south. Meanwhile, about 250 hostages were herded into the main square. At the sound of U.S. planes circling overhead, and only minutes before the Belgians fought their way to the square, rebel troops guarding the foreigners opened fire and massacred an estimated thirty to thirty-five white hostages, including Dr. Carlson. They then fled to the jungle. Many foreigners were shot as they ran toward the airport when they heard about the arrival of the paratroopers. Survivors reported that during the period of rebel occupation, thousands of executions, mostly of fellow Congolese, had been carried out.

The Soviet Union and Communist China immediately denounced the seizure of Stanleyville, and scorned the rescue aspects of the airdrop. *Izvestia* asserted that the fate of the hostages had merely been a pretext to camouflage "criminal actions" against the rebels by "the imperialists and their puppets." Peking charged that the operation was a "flagrant aggression . . . to suppress the surging armed struggle of the Congolese people." Palpably staged assaults were made on American, Belgian, British, and Congolese embassies in Communist and even in neutralist capitals. Most African states also attacked the rescue action as an "imperialist" intervention in Congolese internal affairs. In Cairo, mobs not only shattered scores of windows at the American embassy, but they burned and gutted the 27,000-volume John F. Kennedy Library in the embassy compound. The State Department, however, emphatically rejected "any suggestion that the mission was military intervention in the Congo."

Despite mounting repercussions, Belgian paratroopers on November 26 undertook a second rescue operation, capturing the rebel town of Paulis. But, tragically, the troops were unable to prevent a last-minute massacre in which at least twenty-one hostages were slain in a mass killing. They managed nevertheless to evacuate over 200 foreigners. With the completion of the two rescue missions, Foreign Minister Spaak announced plans for the departure of the paratroopers, which began the next day.

About 1,000 Europeans and Asians were still left in rebel territory in the northwestern Congo, in areas inaccessible for air rescue. During the four-day operation it was estimated that about 2,000 foreigners had been rescued. State Department officials explained that the ending of the mission before all foreign hostages had been rescued had been dictated by military and diplomatic considerations. To try to save the remaining hostages would have meant extended military operations which might have raised doubts about the humanitarian purpose of the mission. But it was evident that the decision was also influenced by concern over possibly more hostile international reaction to the continued presence of Belgian forces. Anxiety was also expressed that further operations might provoke the rebel forces into killing more hostages. Hope of rescuing the remaining foreigners was therefore placed largely on the mercenary-led Congolese troops. President Johnson assumed "full responsibility" for the United States role in the decision to transport the Belgian paratroopers in American planes. "In this humanitarian venture," he told a news conference, "we had to act and act promptly in order to keep hundreds and even thousands of people from being massacred, and we did act in time." [23]

While steps were being taken for the Belgian troop withdrawal, the Congo Conciliation Commission met in emergency session at Nairobi. Many members declared that the rescue operation was "international banditry" masquerading under the "lofty banner of humanitarianism." The Ethiopian delegate went so far as to urge the rest of the African states to consider "collective reprisals and sanctions" against the United States and Belgium as an expression of moral indignation over the airlift. Only the Nigerian Foreign Minister expressed approval of the rescue of the hostages. The African reaction was so intensely hostile because the rescue operation touched on the raw issues of racial relations and the fear of lingering colonialism. Apprehension, in part, sprang from concern that the mission to save whites in the Congo would set the precedent for intervention elsewhere. As one correspondent put it, "What would happen, they [the Africans] ask, if there were spontaneous nationalist revolts in white-ruled Southern Rhodesia, Angola and Mozambique? Would the U.S. intervene on the side of the Portuguese and the white Rhodesians under the veil of a 'humanitarian' mission to save whites? And what about South Africa?" [24]

At the request of twenty-two member states, including eighteen African countries, the Security Council met on December 9 to consider the Congo situation. Permission was granted to fifteen African nonmembers of the Council to participate in the meetings. Practically all the African states again condemned the rescue operation. Their emotional attacks largely centered on three points: that the intervention was mainly intended to bolster Tshombé's regime and crush the rebel opposition; that the humanitarian purpose for the rescue of hostages was merely a pretext on the part of the "colonialists" to regain control of the Congo; and that the recruitment of "white racist mercenaries" from South Africa and Southern Rhodesia must be stopped immediately, and all interference in Congolese internal affairs ended. Representatives of the African states urged that full cooperation should be given the O.A.U. Commission on the Congo in its efforts to obtain national reconciliation and the restoration of order in the Congo.

Foreign Minister Spaak categorically denied that the Stanleyville operation was in any way a "military intervention" to help the Congolese national army against the rebels or to hold any territory. The primary question, he declared, was simply that of saving the lives of some 2,000 persons. Appeals to the United Nations, to the Organization of African Unity, and to the Congolese rebels at Stanleyville, Mr. Spaak asserted, had all been in vain. He said that in talks with the rebels at Nairobi, political conditions—such as a cease-fire—had been the price set for saving the lives of the hostages. Since the Leopoldville government was opposed to a cease-fire, there was no way for the United States and Belgium to obtain it. The rescue operation, Foreign Minister Spaak made clear, had been decided upon only as a last resort when great danger arose as the Congolese army approached Stanleyville. All of the hostages liberated, he told the Security Council, said that they would have been massacred if the operation had not been undertaken. Mr. Spaak flatly denied that it was a "racist" operation; he pointed out that at least 400 Indians and Pakistanis and more than 200 Congolese were among those evacuated from Stanleyville.

Rebuking African delegates for their "irrational, irresponsible, insulting, and repugnant language," Ambassador Stevenson declared on December 14, "We have no apologies to make to any state appearing before this Council. We are proud of our part in saving human lives imperiled by the civil war in the Congo." He warned that "if every internal rivalry is to become a Spanish Civil War, with each faction drawing in other Africans and great powers from other continents, the history of independent Africa in this century will be bloody and shameful and the aspirations of Africa's wonderful peoples will be cruelly postponed." [25] Among the African countries supplying arms to the Congolese rebels, Mr. Stevenson listed Algeria, Ghana, the Sudan, the Congo Republic (the former French Congo), and Burundi. In addition, he said, the rebels were being aided by the Soviet Union and Communist China.

On December 30 the Security Council adopted a compromise resolution by a vote of 10 to 0, with France abstaining, which called for an end to all foreign intervention in the Congo, a cease-fire, and the withdrawal of foreign mercenaries. It also asked the O.A.U. to continue its efforts to achieve a "national reconciliation" in the Congo, and for all countries to assist the organization in securing this objective.[26]

The task of finding a solution to the Congo problem was not easy. Although rebel forces were driven out of Stanleyville, the rebellion against the Congolese government was not crushed. By the end of the year, the rebels still controlled an estimated one-fifth of the country. Congolese troops managed to hold some key towns with the help of mercenaries, but they were unable to occupy the countryside. Both the United States and Belgium urged Premier Tshombé to strengthen the Congolese government by broadening his cabinet to include ministers that would be more acceptable to other African countries; by granting an amnesty to all rebels not accused of acts punishable under the Congolese criminal code; by extending guarantees to opposition parties, enabling them to participate in the election campaign which was tentatively scheduled for February 1965; and by taking steps to secure a cease-fire in the fighting against the rebels. Tshombé resisted these suggestions and flatly refused to consider a cease-fire. He was convinced that it would merely give the rebels time to rebuild and rearm their forces, and would also constitute an unacceptable partition of the Congo. As evidence accumulated that the rebels were receiving increasing aid from Algeria, the United Arab Republic, Ghana, the U.S.S.R., and other states, and that Premier Tshombé was building up—instead of halting—the recruitment of mercenary forces, the prospects for ending the Congolese civil war faded.

CHAPTER TWELVE

THE UNITED NATIONS AT A CROSSROAD

WITHIN THE SPAN of its relatively brief nineteen years of existence, the United Nations has helped to deter or end warfare in Iran and Greece, in Kashmir and Korea, in the Middle East, the Congo, in the Caribbean, the Western Pacific, and the Mediterranean. "It is not fanciful to speculate that any or all of us," said Secretary Rusk, "may owe our lives to the fact that these dangers were contained with the active and persistent help of the processes of the United Nations." [1]

Few could deny the important role played by the United Nations in preserving world peace and in helping newly independent countries to grapple with their complex problems. That the United States was fully responsive to these efforts could be seen in its participation and general support of the United Nations, its specialized agencies, and other international organizations. To speak only of the volume and variety of that participation, the United States belonged to fifty-three such organizations. It contributed more than a third of a billion dollars to these organizations and to twenty-two international programs sponsored, for the most part, by them. During 1964 the United States participated in some 550 international intergovernmental conferences. As Harlan Cleveland, Assistant Secretary of State for International Organization Affairs, pointed out, in 1964 and the preceding year the United States had attended more international conferences than it did in its "entire history from the founding of the Republic to the beginning of World War II." [2]

Revolutionary advances in scientific discovery and technology, pressures for change and modernization on the part of developing countries, combined with startling improvements in communications and transportation, were in part responsible for insistent demands to build international institutions. "While nations may cling to national values and ideas and ambitions and prerogatives," Mr. Rusk commented, "science has created a functional international society, whether we like it or not. And that society, like any other, must be organized." [3]

Unquestionably, the formidable task of organization lay at the heart of the crisis in which the United Nations found itself during the 1960's. From the outset it had never been clear whether the member nations, particularly the great powers, wanted the United Nations to be essentially a forum and negotiating site or an active force with executive capacity to intervene effectively in the conduct of international relations. As the late Secretary-General Dag Hammarskjold observed in the introduction to his last annual report on the organization's work, the United Nations had been torn between two concepts of the proper role of the organization: that of functioning as a "static conference machinery," or that of serving as a "dynamic instrument of governments," carrying out executive actions. [4] The United States tended to view the U.N. Charter as a kind of constitution capable of organic growth; the Soviet Union, however, generally regarded the United Nations restrictively as a contract between states. Moscow appeared primarily concerned with using the organization for its own purposes and particularly with preventing it from damaging its own interests.

Despite the limitations implicit in the structure of the United Nations, the range of activities of the world organization and its specialized agencies had grown greatly, especially in the economic, social, and humanitarian fields. The varied nature of the organization's interests could be seen in the numerous studies and reports that were regularly brought to the attention of the Economic and Social Council. These included, for example, important investigations on population projections, the applications of science and technology, the relation of health to economic progress, the social and human aspects of industrialization, the international flow of capital and its effect on the world economy, the organization of technical assistance and its impact on developing countries. The United Nations was also constantly concerned with international law and its application to achieve peaceful solutions to international controversies. In addition, on the political level the world organization continued to be occupied with the specific questions relating to disarmament, to the peaceful uses of outer space, and to problems relating to decolonization.

Advances made in these areas were sporadic, but they were by no means negligible. Most disappointing in 1964 was the fact that the hopes raised by the limited nuclear test-ban treaty, the establishment of a direct communications link between Moscow and Washington, and the General Assembly resolutions to ban nuclear and other weapons of mass destruction from outer space were not fulfilled. No substantive progress was made by the Eighteen-Nation Disarmament Committee in 1964, but as Secretary-General Thant commented in the introduction to the annual report, "the intensive discussions at the Conference once again served to clarify positions and to indicate in what areas and in what ways progress might be possible." [5] That the desire to stop the arms race persisted was indicated in the mutual cutbacks in the production of fissionable material for military purposes by the United States, the Soviet Union, and the United Kingdom. (Section 16.) To create a climate for peace, the United Nations continued to press for an agreement to ban underground tests, to halt the spread of nuclear and nonnuclear weapons, and to reduce and eliminate vehicles for the delivery of nuclear weapons. At the same time, it sought to encourage international cooperation in the peaceful uses of outer space, and it urged countries to work together to develop a law of space to meet the needs of the international community as a whole. Indicating their willingness to advance cooperation in space, the United States and the Soviet Union concluded a preliminary agreement in June for a joint review of achievements in space biology and medicine. To encourage this development, the U.N. Committee on the Peaceful Uses of Outer Space recommended that consideration be given to convening an international conference in 1967 to examine the whole range of space problems.

The question of decolonization continued to take up much of the time and attention of the United Nations. In 1964 special anxiety was caused by the situation in Southern Rhodesia. (Section 43.) Alarming also was the fact that no improvement was discernible in the racial problem in South Africa. "Taking account of the composition of the population of South Africa and the present international context," remarked Mr. Thant, "there is a great danger that a continuation of the efforts to impose policies decided by one racial group in South Africa and the closing up of possibilities for a peaceful change may increasingly lead to violence which is likely to have widespread international repercussions." [6] In its resolutions, the Security Council again urged the need for developing racial harmony based on equal rights and fundamental freedoms for all the people of South Africa. (Section 43.)

As we have seen in several preceding sections, the major concern of the United Nations was the task of maintaining peace. During the year it was especially occupied with the situation in Cyprus. Here, the U.N. forces helped to contain the fighting between local Greek and Turkish Cypriotes, although the efforts to find a solution to long-range problems proved to be elusive. In other areas the United Nations had to curtail its peace-keeping operations. While the United Nations forces in the Congo were withdrawn on June 30, about 2,000 U.N. personnel remained and continued to provide technical assistance and to help in public administration, as well as in the rehabilitation of areas that were seriously disrupted by the fighting that persisted in the country. On September 4 the United Nations Yemen Observation Mission, set up in mid-1963, came to an end. Both Saudi Arabia and the United Arab Republic had reported to the Secretary-General that they were not prepared to continue to meet the costs of the operation, and the Security Council did not extend the mandate of the Observation Mission. Disturbances in Yemen, nevertheless, remained troublesome. Other major disputes brought before the Security Council included the anti-

American riots in Panama, Pakistan's complaints against India over Kashmir, U.S. bombings of North Vietnam in retaliation for the Gulf of Tonkin episodes, Cambodia's border disputes and complaints of "aggression" committed by South Vietnam and the United States, Malaysia's charges of Indonesia's violations of its territorial integrity, the Syrian-Israeli dispute, and the Belgium-U.S.-U.K. "intervention" in the Congo for the rescue of hostages held by rebels at Stanleyville.

For the United Nations in general, however, three problems were highlighted during the year. The first touched on the question of adjusting the United Nations to the realities of the political world. Since its establishment in 1945, its internal structure had changed radically, with its membership more than doubling from 51 to 115. Most significant was the fact that African membership had grown from 3 to 37, and Asian from 9 to 24. As a result of this increase, the Afro-Asian countries became a powerful "bloc" in the General Assembly, though in practice they did not act monolithically except on colonial issues. The United States believed that because of this rapid expansion, a grave disparity had occurred between formal voting power, on the one hand, and responsibility and capacity for carrying out decisions, on the other. An adaptation of procedures seemed necessary if the United Nations was to remain relevant and effective in the world. "Theoretically," Mr. Rusk declared in his historic Dag Hammarskjold Memorial Lecture, "a two-thirds majority of the General Assembly could now be formed by nations with only 10 percent of the world's population, or who contribute, altogether, 5 percent of the assessed budget. In practice, of course, this does not happen, and I do not share the dread expressed by some that the General Assembly will be taken over by its 'swirling majorities.'

"But even the theoretical possibility that a two-thirds majority, made up primarily of smaller states, could recommend a course of action for which other nations would bear the primary responsibility and burden is one that requires thoughtful attention." [7]

Directly related to the General Assembly's role in the United

Nations was a second issue that concerned the authorization
and financing of peace-keeping operations. In an effort to overcome the "paralysis" of the organization brought on by the Soviet
veto in the Security Council, the United Nations had adopted
a "Uniting for Peace" resolution in 1950.[8] It facilitated rapid
Assembly action should the Council fail to reach a decision due
to a lack of unanimity on the part of the permanent members
when a threat to the peace or breach of the peace existed. This
resolution had made it possible for the General Assembly to
authorize the organization to engage directly in peace-keeping
activities. The purpose of this move was not to create a U.N.
force that would be capable of imposing peace on the great
powers; rather, its object was to permit the United Nations to
deal with threats to the peace that might arise from smaller
powers, and then only in special circumstances and with limitations. Unwilling to tolerate U.N. operational policies that it
opposed, the Soviet Union—especially after the United Nations
intervention in the Congo of which it did not approve—adamantly insisted that the Security Council was the only organ
that had the right to decide on peace-keeping activities as well
as to determine their necessary expenditures. Despite the fact
that Article 17 of the U.N. Charter gave the General Assembly
authority to levy assessments for peace-keeping operations, the
U.S.S.R. flatly refused to pay for activities it considered "illegal."

Moscow's exercise of a "financial veto" on the U.N. peace-
keeping role not only imposed a severe financial strain on the
organization, but also affected basic political and constitutional
issues. The only sanction that the United Nations had on member
states which refused—or were unable—to pay assessments levied
by the organization was to deprive them of their vote in the
General Assembly, if they owed the equivalent of two years'
assessed contributions (Article 19 of the Charter). The United
States insisted that this sanction had to be applied; but Moscow
repeatedly warned that to do so would wreck the United Nations.

During the year the prospect of a showdown between the
United States and the Soviet Union over the United Nations—

particularly how it should be managed and what ends it should serve—was indeed ominous. At issue was not so much the question of the organization's survival—although this possibility could not be completely ruled out. Rather, the issues were whether the United Nations would be able to preserve its capacity to undertake peace-keeping tasks on a "collective" basis, expand the scope of its activities, enlarge its responsibilities, and meet the demands of an increasingly complex world; or, whether it would be confined in its operations to what Mr. Hammarskjold had called a "static conference machinery." It was in this sense that the United Nations in the mid-1960's found itself at a crossroad.

The immediate concern of the United Nations centered on its future effectiveness in political and security affairs. But a third problem also occupied its attention, namely, economic and social development. Part of the great drama of the nuclear age was the massive effort by the advanced industrial nations to transfer capital and adapt modern technology to underdeveloped countries. The significance of this task was underscored by the fact that the 1960's had been proclaimed as the United Nations Development Decade. With the United Nations Conference on Trade and Development, held at Geneva from March 23 to June 16, the year 1964 witnessed the culmination of many years of effort by the United Nations to formulate sound economic strategies on the national and international levels so that growth and change could be accelerated. The twelve-week session led to the recommendation for action by the General Assembly to attain two principal goals: (1) an enlarged role for the United Nations in the field of international trade and development, and (2) improved and more effective negotiation and conciliation procedures so that decisions essential for modifying world trade relations could be reached.

In contrast to the peace-keeping activities, no significant opposition, in principle, existed toward the promotion of economic growth in the developing countries. Basically, the issue was not whether but how this should be done and what part the United Nations should have in it. Division here was not one between East and West, but rather between North and South, between the developing states seeking international and stable markets for their exports and the industrially advanced nations, Western and Communist, which were primary suppliers of economic aid. For the underdeveloped countries the problem was one of overcoming the caution of the great powers and breaking down the economic barriers to their own rapid progress. They favored protectionism for themselves. Mainly, they wanted a privileged position that would guarantee them high and stable prices for their own goods—plus plenty of capital on easy terms. "The United Nations is and seems certain to continue to be," a Brookings Institution study pointed out, "the major setting for the confrontation of the political demand of the developing states and the political reluctance of the highly developed ones." [9]

It was clear that the next few years would be a critical period for the United Nations, though the international organization had weathered many bad storms in the past. Since the great powers believed that it served a vital function and was useful for their respective national purposes, it was doubtful that they would seek to destroy it. What was uncertain was whether the United Nations would be provided with the means to assume the increasingly greater responsibilities which it has been called upon to fulfill. In other words, the test of the immediate future appeared to be whether the United Nations would be permitted and equipped to do the larger job.

46. THE UNITED NATIONS AND WORLD POLITICAL REALITIES

Born in the crucible of World War II, the United Nations was based on the assumption that the victorious powers—the United States, the Soviet Union, Britain, France, and China—would continue their wartime cooperation and join together in maintaining world peace. This illusory hope was quickly shattered. The Security Council became an arena of the cold war, and its capacity for dealing with threats to the peace and breaches of the peace through "collective security" had eroded.

To guard against immobility in cases where the veto was employed or threatened to block action in the Security Council,

the United Nations had drawn in 1950 on the Charter's authority
to call on the General Assembly's reserve capacity to deal with
peace and security. By the mid-1960's, however, fear was expressed by some that the power center in the organization was
shifting not only to the Assembly, but more particularly into
the hands of the smaller states. It seemed that an imbalance
in the structure of the United Nations needed correction, since
the new majority did not accurately reflect existing power realities in the world. At the same time, the newer and smaller
nations felt underrepresented on the Security Council and the
Economic and Social Council, where membership was based
on the initial size and composition of the United Nations, and
pressed for organizational changes. On December 17, 1963, the
General Assembly adopted a resolution which called for increasing the Security Council's members from 11 to 15 by adding
four nonpermanent members, and enlarging the Economic and
Social Council from 18 to 27. All member states were requested
to ratify amendments to the Charter to affect this change not
later than September 1, 1965.[10]

The demand on the part of the Afro-Asian states for a revision
of the internal structure of the United Nations to provide them
with more representation in the Councils while retaining the
ability to muster a numerical majority in the Assembly raised a
number of questions. Secretary Rusk was especially concerned
with the problem of enabling the expanded General Assembly
to work with reasonable proficiency and establishing a proper
balance between the power of large and small nations. "With
more than twice as many voices to be heard, views to be reconciled, and votes to be cast and counted, on a swelling agenda
of business," Mr. Rusk said, "there is obvious danger that the
General Assembly will be swamped." Noting that it was the only
parliamentary body in the world that tried to do most of its
business in committees-of-the-whole, the Secretary asserted that
some ways had to be found to delegate some of the work "to
units less cumbersome than committees of 113 members." Although the Assembly had established several subcommittees,
he suggested that a number of others would be necessary.

Secretary Rusk chiefly directed his attention to the problem
of reconciling the role of the big powers and smaller nations
in the United Nations. On the one hand, he pointed out, there
were those who believed that no action should be taken by
the United Nations without the unanimous approval of the
Security Council. On the other hand, there were those who
insisted that action must be based on the formula "one nation,
one vote" that prevailed in the General Assembly. Neither position, Mr. Rusk believed, was in accord with the realities of the
situation. The notion "that what a majority wants done must be
done regardless of what states make up the majority" flew in
"the face of common sense." "The plain fact of the matter," he
continued, "is that the United Nations simply cannot take significant action without the support of the members who supply it
with resources and have the capacity to act." Although Mr. Rusk
noted the difficulties raised by suggestions to weight the vote
of members in the General Assembly—whether by population
or wealth or level of contribution or some combination of these
factors—he did not make any concrete proposal to solve the
problem. He urged, however, that new approaches be found to
safeguard the United Nations against irresponsible acts of the
small powers, and that all members give the organization their
proper financial support. "I hope," the Secretary remarked, "that
the discussions which lie ahead will not only strengthen the
financial underpinnings of the U.N., but among other things,
develop an acceptable way for the General Assembly to take
account of capacity to act, of responsibility for the consequences,
and of actual contributions to the work of the U.N. Such a way
must be found if the United Nations machinery is to be relevant
to the tasks that lie ahead—in peacekeeping, in nation building,
and in the expansion of human rights." [11]

The likelihood of any fundamental reorganization of the United
Nations appeared highly doubtful, since a proposed amendment
of the Charter requires ratification by two-thirds of the members, including the five permanent members of the Security
Council. Many proposals to change the world organization have
been suggested since 1946. But the first ever put forward for

ratification were the two proposed amendments to expand the Security Council and the Economic and Social Council—the resolution which the General Assembly had adopted in 1963. Before a reorganization could be effected, it was clear that many divisive problems that plagued the United Nations would have to be resolved. Not the least of these related to the question of peace-keeping functions, and finding a solution to the "financial crisis."

47. THE PEACE-KEEPING "BATTLE"

Three important issues have been involved in the peace-keeping battle. First, the Soviet Union and France, as well as a number of other countries, have raised serious constitutional and legal problems. Over half a billion dollars had been appropriated by the General Assembly for the U.N. Emergency Force in the Middle East and the operation in the Congo; but the Soviet Union, France, the U.A.R., and other nations refused to pay assessments levied by the United Nations on the grounds that the operations had not been properly authorized, and that the General Assembly was without power to assess contributions in support of such operations. (France did contribute to the U.N. Middle East Emergency Force on a "voluntary" basis, though it refused to do so for the Congo operation.) The legal question involved was referred to the International Court for an advisory opinion. In July 1962 the Court by a vote of 9 to 5 ruled that the expenditures authorized by the Assembly for the Middle East and the Congo were "expenses of the organization" within the meaning of Article 17 of the Charter, and that the assessments levied were therefore binding on the member states. The states which had refused to pay were unimpressed by the Court's advisory opinion. They continued to insist that the Charter contained no direct provision for the use of forces not engaged in enforcement action and that the financing of the Middle East and Congo operations had not been approved by the Security Council, thus making the peace-keeping activities "illegal."

By early 1964 seventeen members, including the U.S.S.R., were in arrears by an amount in excess of the equivalent of two years of their regular assessment. The Soviet position on peace-keeping operations, however, was no mere legalism. It was designed, as a State Department official cogently remarked, "to vitiate the power of the General Assembly, as its use of the veto vitiates the power of the Security Council and as the troika proposal would have vitiated the power of the Secretary-General." Thus the impact of nullifying the Assembly's capacity to act "would be primarily on those newer and smaller states whose voice in world affairs is heard mainly through the Assembly." [12]

Fundamentally connected with the constitutional and legal issues was a second problem concerning past, present, and future financing of peace-keeping activities. On September 30 arrears for the Middle East and Congo operations totaled $112.3 million, the United Nation's cash resources amounted to $24.8 million, and it's deficit was $113.3 million. Over $90 million of the arrears was owed by members who did not allege *inability* to pay, but claimed instead that they had no *obligation* to pay. "I am convinced by the experience of the past three years that a policy of drift, of improvisation, of *ad hoc* solutions, of reliance on the generosity of the few rather than the collective responsibility of all, cannot much longer endure," Secretary-General Thant said. "In fact, time, if I may say so, is rapidly running out." [13] Complicating the situation was the fact that the peace-keeping responsibilities of the United Nations were, if anything, increasing. That they were growing more critical than ever was pointed up during the year by the organization's role in Cyprus, in Southeast Asia, and in Yemen. Without financial resources, and with the multiplication of crises throughout the world, the ability of the United Nations to exercise a restraining influence, it was clear, would be drastically reduced.

The only sanction that the General Assembly had against member states refusing to pay their assessments was the application of Article 19, which denied such states the right to vote. Even with the application of Article 19, the financial problem still would not be solved. Nor would the basic political problem. Nevertheless, failure to invoke this sanction, Washington feared, would impair the prospects for U.N. peace-keeping activities since the financial authority of the General Assembly would have been undermined and the United Nations would have to rely almost exclusively on voluntary contributions.

Not only did the United Nations have to worry about where to get money, it also had to confront a third problem bearing on any future peace-keeping activities: how and where to get forces to carry them out. The seriousness of this situation was seen in Cyprus. Following the adoption of the Security Council's resolution on March 4,[14] it took three weeks to organize a force and land the first contingents on the island. Had British troops not been present, fighting between Greek and Turkish Cypriotes might have gone beyond control, and an armed conflict might have broken out between two NATO members, Greece and Turkey. Fortunately, Secretary-General Thant obtained the agreement of Canada, Finland, Ireland, and Sweden to furnish troops to supplement the British forces. Speaking at Princeton University on March 23, Ambassador Stevenson pointedly noted that Cyprus had exposed the "frailties" of existing U.N. peace-keeping arrangements, particularly in the delays that had occurred. "When time is of the essence, there is a dangerous vacuum during the interval while military forces are being assembled on a hit-or-miss basis." [15] U Thant not only had to persuade member states to submit their forces to the hazards of duty in Cyprus, but he also had to go hat in hand for needed funds. The United States came forward with $2 million of the estimated $6 million cost for the first three months of operation, and Britain contributed an additional $1 million. It was with some degree of difficulty that Mr. Thant managed to collect the remaining $3 million to transport the U.N. force to Cyprus.

In an effort to find a solution to the financial crisis the United States and Britain submitted a joint proposal to the U.S.S.R. in March suggesting that future peace-keeping operations be dealt with in the Security Council first. In the event the Security

Council was unable to act, the General Assembly could then step into the picture. As for financing, a special committee would recommend plans to the General Assembly, which would undertake to vote financing, but only on the recommendation of the committee. Major contributors to international actions would have a larger voice in the committee but no veto. The committee would be authorized to propose methods of financing peacekeeping efforts and, where necessary, recommend a new scale of assessment. The joint British-American proposal hinged on the satisfactory settlement of arrears by the Soviet Union, Soviet bloc countries, and other members who had failed to pay their assessments. To avoid the application of Article 19 of the Charter, the U.S.S.R. would be required in 1964 to pay about $8 million of its $52.5 million indebtedness.

While efforts were made to deal with the financial problem, steps were taken by a number of states to create stand-by forces that could be placed at the disposal of the Secretary-General for use on short notice in peace-keeping activities. Ever since Norway, Denmark, and Sweden had been called upon to furnish troops for the Congo in 1960, the three Scandinavian countries had considered taking the initiative to provide an operational stand-by force. Since the Congo experience they had conducted negotiations on the creation of such a force. In 1963 Finland joined the negotiations, and during 1964 concrete proposals were formulated and ratified by the parliaments of the four countries to establish separate voluntary contingents to give men special training for peace-keeping operations.[16] Other countries like Canada and the Netherlands had either earmarked units or announced their intention to do so. Prime Minister Pearson warmly endorsed these moves. "If the UN assembly . . . refuses to take [the] initiative—if it is unable to agree on permanent arrangements for a 'stand-by' peace force— then why should a group of members who feel that this should be done not do something about it themselves? Why should they not discharge their own responsibilities individually and collectively by organizing a force for this purpose, one formally outside the United Nations but ready to be used on its request?"[17]

The United States firmly believed that it was necessary to improve the peace-keeping machinery of the United Nations. It had supported steps taken by member states to earmark troops for U.N. service, which could be trained specifically for the task of keeping the peace. The need for such troops clearly had grown inexorably out of the facts of international life. Washington supported this flexible call-up system in which nations voluntarily specified troops that would be available at the request of the United Nations. In addition, the United States encouraged the idea of increasing the United Nations' military and planning staff so that peace-keeping operations, as Ambassador Stevenson said, could be "set in motion with the utmost speed and effectiveness." [18]

On July 7 the Soviet Union countered the U.S.-British proposals with a memorandum addressed to the Japanese government and then distributed to other U.N. members as a United Nations Security Council document on July 10.[19] In it Moscow called for the establishment of a permanent United Nations force, and set four conditions: First, the Security Council was to be the only U.N. body authorized to take action in the maintenance or restoration of international peace and security. Second, no other body, including the General Assembly, was to have the right to decide on matters relating to the establishment of peace-keeping forces, the definition of their duties, their composition and strength, the direction of their operations, the structure of their command and the duration of their stay in the area of operation, or to deal with matters of financing. Third, the composition of U.N. armed forces was in the future to include, together with contingents from Western or neutral countries, contingents from "socialist" countries; this meant participation of representatives of the "socialist" countries in the command structure of peace-keeping forces as well. (The Soviets made clear, however, that they did not believe it advisable for peace-keeping forces to include contingents from nations that are permanent members of the Security Council.) Finally, military action should only be taken when economic sanctions proved ineffective in deterring aggression. In the event that the Security

Council was required to use U.N. forces, the Soviet Union said that the "necessary expenses" should be paid by the aggressors; but it expressed its willingness "to share expenses necessary to maintain and operate the United Nations force in an emergency."

Although Washington's initial reaction was that the Soviet proposals had put the two sides "within negotiating distance," it quickly expressed its disappointment over the key provisions. In particular, the United States saw in the Russian maneuver another attempt to introduce the "troika" principle into the United Nations, as was evident in the Soviet demand that Communist, neutralist, and Western contingents must be a part of any international military force established by the Security Council. In essence, the Soviet plan was viewed as a dual attack on the jurisdiction of the General Assembly and on the Secretary-General, and thus as a restatement of Russia's long-standing position. Suspicion was also voiced that it was an effort to becloud the issue of Moscow's refusal to pay its peace-keeping assessments. Nevertheless, on July 24, Britain responded to the Soviet proposals and invited Moscow to decide "how and when" talks should begin. In its note it also put on record for the first time the major principles contained in the U.S.-British joint proposal of March.[20] But the Soviet Union gave no sign of agreeing to negotiations.

In the meantime, a decision was made to postpone the opening of the General Assembly, which usually took place in September. Twenty countries requested on May 1 that it be put off until after the heads-of-state meeting of nonaligned nations scheduled for Cairo in October. Secretary-General Thant agreed to the delay, and the opening date was scheduled for December 1. In an effort to break the deadlock on the financial "crisis," a group of Latin American delegates early in July suggested the possibility of a new approach that would divide into two categories the countries which were behind in their assessments by more than two years. For those nations genuinely unable to pay because of conditions beyond their control, they recommended a waiver of Article 19's sanctions; but all other nations would be subject to its application. A major purpose behind this move was to isolate the U.S.S.R. from the poor countries and to increase the pressure on Moscow to induce it to make a partial payment on its arrears so that the question of loss of voting rights would not cause a crisis.

Later in the month, Secretary-General Thant visited France and the Soviet Union. When he conferred with President de Gaulle on Jully 21, he was told that France still felt that the establishment of peace-keeping forces was beyond the powers conferred by the Charter. Nor was he able to persuade Moscow to modify its stand. Mr. Thant, however, was permitted to make a television address—it was said he reached an estimated forty million viewers—in which he appealed directly to the Soviet people, explaining the serious financial plight of the organization. Declaring that the United Nations was the only hope for mankind "in the second half of the 20th century, in the shadow of the hydrogen bomb," he recalled that the League of Nations had died after 19 years because it had been an exclusive European club with financial difficulties similar to those confronting the United Nations. The Secretary-General urged all nations to give the "closest attention to this aspect of the problem and come up with some solution." Upon returning from Moscow and Paris, he termed the situation "very critical" for the United Nations.

During the following months, the positions of both the United States and the Soviet Union stiffened. On September 14 Washington officially presented the proposals for financing peace-keeping operations that had been embodied in the joint U.S.-British plan of the previous March.[21] But Moscow declared that the Western scheme was unacceptable because it was merely a disguise for usurping the functions of the Security Council. The Soviet Union insisted that the use of armed forces under the U.N. flag required unanimity of the Council's five permanent members, and that the veto was a protection against misuse and could not be bypassed. Francis T. P. Plimpton, the deputy American representative to the United Nations, firmly declared that giving the Council an absolute monopoly over peace-keeping

efforts was against the Charter, and against "every instinct of
those among us who are for a democratically controlled United
Nations." [22]

The United States maintained that there was no alternative
to the application of Article 19. It did not see how it could agree
that the article not be applied against a great power, simply
because it was a great power, without violating the Charter.
Washington, however, was prepared to be flexible regarding
the method of payment; but it indicated that the "essential
ingredient in any solution" had to be that the funds be made
available to the United Nations. [23] The Soviet delegate adamantly asserted that it would pay "not one kopeck, not one
cent" toward the "illegal" peace-keeping operations in the Middle East and the Congo.

On November 13 Ambassador Stevenson suggested that the
Soviet Union and other countries could avoid losing their votes
in the Assembly by paying their debts in any form. "Voluntary
payments," he said, "could be made without prejudice to the
Soviet's, or anyone else's legal views," and arrangements acceptable to the Secretary-General would be satisfactory to the United
States if they were consistent with the Charter. [24] To show that
the United States meant business, Washington served official
notice four days later that it would withhold its pledge of aid
to United Nations technical assistance programs for developing
countries—these were supported by voluntary pledges, and the
United States had always been a major contributor—until the
world organization's financial and constitutional crisis was resolved. [25]

As the days ticked away toward the opening of the Assembly
session on December 1, it appeared that the long-threatened
showdown between the U.S. and U.S.S.R. would not be prevented. Apprehension steadily built up. By some last minute
maneuvering, Secretary-General Thant managed to win a breath-
ing spell. Just before the session convened, he obtained an agreement from American, Russian, British, French, and other delegates that no formal votes would be taken until the Assembly
concluded its general debate, in which heads of delegations

stated general views on U.N. issues. Since this was expected to take at least two or three weeks, the dispute concerning the application of Article 19 could thus be put off until after the Christmas recess. With the collision temporarily averted, the General Assembly opened its session in a subdued but uneasy atmosphere. Alex Quaison-Sackey of Ghana was elected President of the Nineteenth Session "by acclamation" on December 1, and no objections were voiced to the admission of the three newly independent states of Malawi, Malta, and Zambia.

The next day, Soviet Foreign Minister Gromyko agreed to negotiate on all aspects of peace-keeping problems, including the question of financing. As a result of discussions between Secretary Rusk and Mr. Gromyko, a dual set of negotiations was decided upon—one dealing with the issue of unpaid assessments and the other with the complex constitutional problems produced by peace-keeping interventions. The United States suggested that U Thant assume the responsibility of handling the arrears problem, since this was a matter that involved the entire organization and should not be left to negotiations between the United States and the Soviet Union. Washington believed these discussions should proceed independently from the parleys that would be concerned with the long-range problems relating to the authorization, composition, direction, and financing of future peace-keeping forces. Moscow's agreement to separate talks on these issues was viewed as a hopeful element in the situation.

As the year drew to a close, the future outcome on the United Nations crisis could not, of course, be predicted. The one thing perhaps that could be said was that neither the United States nor the Soviet Union wanted the United Nations to collapse, and both major powers were under strong pressures from the smaller countries to seek a mutually acceptable solution to the financial and peace-keeping difficulties so that the dark shadows that had hovered for so long over the United Nations could be cleared away.

48. THE U.N. CONFERENCE ON TRADE AND DEVELOPMENT

"Ranking in importance with arms control, peacekeeping, and human rights," remarked Assistant Secretary Cleveland, "is that rich and colorful variety of problems and prospects which we sum up in a bureaucratic-sounding phrase: economic and social development." [26] As a result of the convening at Geneva in March of the United Nations Conference on Trade and Development—or UNCTAD as it became known—the world's attention sharply focused on this problem during the year. Attended by some 2,000 delegates representing 119 countries, UNCTAD was the biggest trade conference ever assembled.

The idea of holding a world trade conference had initially been pressed in the late 1950's by the Soviet bloc in the United Nations primarily as a means of attacking the Western (chiefly the United States) policy with respect to trade with Communist countries. At that time, the proposal made little headway. But in 1961 developing nations enthusiastically embraced the idea as an opportunity to underscore their own trade and development problems. Reluctantly the United States and other industrialized countries agreed in 1962 to support the project, and both the Economic and Social Council and the General Assembly gave it official sanction. A thirty-two-nation preparatory committee was appointed to draft a provisional agenda and to make recommendations on administrative arrangements. As careful and extensive preparations were undertaken, developing nations anticipated that UNCTAD would be as important as the San Francisco Conference of 1945 that had produced the United Nations Charter.[27]

At a news conference on January 21, Secretary-General Thant succinctly posed the problem presented by world trade relations. "The developing countries have been losing ground steadily in world trade for ten years or more. The United Nations cannot remain content with a situation in which the growth of developing countries continues to be inhibited by the difficulties they face in export markets." Dr. Raúl Prebisch, the Argentinian

Secretary-General of the conference, declared that the central purpose of UNCTAD was to find a way to close the "trade gap" between the advanced and developing nations. In a preliminary report, he predicted that if prevailing trends continued, by 1970 this "gap" would widen to $20 billion a year, and underdeveloped countries would be forced to slash their imports drastically.[28]

During the weeks preceding the conference, it was clear that the developing nations were in an impatient mood. They did not disguise the fact that their aim was nothing less than rewriting the rules of world trade and reshaping international economic relations to secure for themselves a much better position. Dr. Prebisch was deeply worried that unless this was done, unless steps were taken to improve the export earnings of poorer countries, and a new institution created to provide the machinery for dealing with the problems of trade relations between developing and developed nations, the former would remain prey to totalitarian demagogues, and the hope of democratic growth would be blunted, if not destroyed.

Most Western governments were tolerant of Dr. Prebisch's ideas, but they were frankly nervous about them being applied too rapidly. Although they acknowledged that the "trade gap" problem was serious, they were skeptical about certain assumptions made by the Argentine economist, and they disagreed with developing countries on what could and should be done. Leaders of the latter maintained that as they were already doing everything they could on their own behalf, it was necessary for the advanced industrial countries to help them, not simply through aid, but, more particularly, through fostering the increase of their trade. They strongly urged the need for commodity agreements to support prices, plans to guarantee markets, schemes to compensate them for declines in their terms of trade, and special preferential arrangements for the export of their manufactured products in the markets of industrial countries. Nor did they feel that aid was being given to less developed nations in a way and under terms that were most satisfactory and desirable. Advanced industrial countries, on the other hand, argued that the lack of economic growth stemmed not so much from external as from internal obstacles in the developing nations. The United States definitely frowned on schemes to fix world prices, and questioned whether it was wise to grant greater subsidies to countries run by inept and sometimes corrupt bureaucracies. Western developed nations, on the whole, took the position that the crucial factor in economic development was self-help, and that greater attention should be focused on the responsibilities of the developing countries themselves, as well as on the external situation.

This task was defined by Mr. G. Griffith Johnson, Assistant Secretary for Economic Affairs, when he observed: "The external trading environment of the developing countries is only part of the problem. In fact, economic history shows that an expansion of trade is largely a consequence rather than a precondition of industrialization. Perhaps the central issue in economic development is what the less developed countries can or will do for themselves. The less developed countries have talked about the need to reduce the disparities in individual incomes in the richer and poorer countries; it is also important to reduce the disparities within the less developed countries in order to develop the domestic markets without which sound industrialization is not possible. The less developed countries have talked about the need for restructuring all world trade in order to give them a greater role; but they must also act to restructure their own domestic economies so that they have the basis on which this greater role can be exercised. The less developed countries have cited the importance to them of improving the terms of trade in the relationships between their exports and their imports; but perhaps even more urgent is the need to improve the interchange between the rural and urban areas within their domestic economies." [29]

The developing countries disagreed with this diagnosis. Shortly before the opening of UNCTAD, an eighteen-nation Latin American political and economic conference was held at Alta Gracia, Argentina. On March 6 it promulgated a unanimous declaration which charged that the industrial nations had an imperative moral responsibility to establish a whole new structure of world trade so that the inequities hobbling the underdeveloped countries could be removed. The meeting's formal documents clearly reflected the conviction in Latin America that the region's problems stemmed primarily from unfair treatment by the world's developed countries.

This theme was forcefully stressed in a 150-page report prepared by Dr. Prebisch for UNCTAD.[30] Blaming the protectionism of advanced nations for the insufficient growth of the trade of the developing countries both in primary commodities and in manufactured goods, the report outlined a plan for new international agreements, new financing arrangements, new development programs, and a new institutional framework. "It is no good," Dr. Prebisch declared, "to preach the need for the developing countries to develop their own efforts, and at the same time to limit their possibilities of giving practical expression to that effort in the international field through the expansion of their exports."

When UNCTAD began its sessions on March 23, the industrial nations generally tended to feel that the large, unwieldy conference would become entangled in a long and sterile debate. Little expectation existed that it would produce positive gains. Warning the world's poorer nations against embracing vague and visionary schemes, Under-Secretary Ball told the Trade Conference, "We must be wary of approaches that do not closely reflect the economic or political realities—approaches that begin and end in discussion and thus obscure the actions really needed for progress." [31]

During the next 12 weeks heated controversies arose between the developing and developed nations on the elimination of all forms of protection by industrial countries on farm products and raw materials, on the granting of tariff preferences to underdeveloped countries for their exports of manufactures and semimanufactures, on commodity policy and how to deal with deterioration in the terms of trade of the developing countries, on compensatory financing, and on the creation of a new institution to deal with trade and related development problems facing the less developed countries.

As the debates unfolded, the political implications of UNCTAD soon overshadowed the economic issues. Strikingly discernible was the unity of the world's less developed countries. At the conference, these countries worked closely together in a group called "the 75"–later expanded to "the 77"–and emerged as a new and major force on the world economic scene. Conscious of their individual weakness, "the 75" made great efforts to advance their claims on a common front. Careful not to expose publicly their differences (which were often great), the developing nations operated virtually as a cohesive bloc throughout the conference. At the final plenary session on June 16 a joint declaration was read–it was later incorporated in full in the *Final Act* of the conference [32]–which affirmed that the unity of "the 77" was, in the view of the developing countries, "the outstanding feature of the entire conference and an event of historic significance." UNCTAD was the first major conference in which a North-South, rather than East-West, confrontation predominated.

Since UNCTAD was not intended to be a conference for negotiating binding commitments, but rather an occasion to discuss issues and their possible solution and to make recommendations for future joint action, the most sensitive question that arose concerned the creation of new organizational machinery to deal with trade and related problems of development. From the outset, the United States and other developed countries agreed that some organ should be set up. While many developing nations wanted a new world trade organization as a separate institution that would supersede GATT, the United States insisted that the new machinery be established within the United Nations structure. The conference finally recommended the establishment of UNCTAD as an organ of the General Assembly, to be convened at intervals of not more than three years (the next conference was scheduled for 1966); the formation of a fifty-five-member Trade and Development Board that would meet semiannually; and the appointment of a small, permanent secretariat within the United Nations Secretariat, the members of which would be selected by the Secretary-General and confirmed by the General Assembly.

A major sticking point over the "continuing machinery" concerned the procedures by which resolutions would be adopted in future conferences and subordinate bodies. Developing countries wanted to continue the United Nations principle of "one nation, one vote." The industrially advanced nations insisted that there was no point in paper majorities demanding action which the world's great trading nations generally opposed, and that appropriate procedures were necessary to assure that recommendations of the conference represented a consensus. In the final conference hours, agreement was reached on a resolution which sidestepped the problem. Delegates requested that the Secretary-General be asked to appoint a special committee to report to the General Assembly. The committee's job was "to prepare proposals for procedures . . . designed to establish a process of conciliation to take place before voting, and to provide an adequate basis for the adoption of recommendations . . . affecting the economic or financial interests of particular countries."

The issue over voting procedures struck deeply, for it underlined the basic struggle between the larger and smaller nations in the United Nations. Although it was doubtful that this conflict would be easily or quickly resolved, an encouraging result of UNCTAD was that it raised the possibility of finding a conciliation formula—one that would be effected *before* voting took place—and which promised, as Dr. Prebisch indicated, the promotion and consolidation of "wider and wider agreement without which international cooperation in the field of trade and development as in other fields, cannot be really effective." [33] As Richard N. Gardner, Deputy Assistant Secretary of State for International Organization, put it: "The process of persuasion is assisted when delegates seek a consensus through conciliation and express that consensus in resolutions. It is not assisted—it may even be set back—by the passage of self-serving resolutions by automatic majorities. Public opinion in the industrial countries cannot fail to react adversely to recommendations that are passed over the opposition of the industrial countries but call for action by them. It is therefore in the interest of all nations—less developed as well as developed—to substitute conciliation for voting on the difficult issues that divide the two groups." [34]

The major concrete result of UNCTAD was its decision to create a U.N. body to continue debating unresolved problems. Its *Final Act*, a massive 80,000-word document, set forth all conference recommendations, and reservations on them by individual delegations. It included a statement of "general" and "special" principles, specific proposals to stimulate economic and social development, and a strong call for new institutional arrangements. Developing nations, however, stressed that UNCTAD was just an "initial step." Their joint declaration expressed the belief that there still had not been an adequate appreciation of the "trade gap" problem, and that only the "most limited approaches" had been made regarding trade in primary commodities and preferences for exports of manufactures. Although the industrial nations promised in the *Final Act* to give support to widespread actions to help the developing nations further their economic growth, they emphasized that substantial progress would be possible—and UNCTAD's success assured—only if there was a general recognition of the need for shared responsibility. [35]

The significance of the United Nations Conference on Trade and Development lay not so much in its immediate accomplishments as in its future promise. What it did, above all, was to reveal clearly the aspirations of the developing nations, the methods and programs these countries believed were essential to fulfill them, and their strong conviction that urgent and great changes were necessary in international economic policy. More immediately, by seeking to establish a "continuing machinery" within the U.N. structure, UNCTAD gave renewed evidence of the importance which both developing and developed countries attached to the United Nations role in the international community.

How effective and dynamic a role the United Nations would be able to play in matters of economic and social development—as well as in the area of political security—remained uncertain in the mid-1960's. Much depended on how its financial and constitutional "crises" would be resolved.

NOTES

Following is a list of periodical and serial publications cited in the notes:

"Bulletin": *Department of State Bulletin* (Washington: G.P.O.)
Congressional Record (Washington: G.P.O.)
Current Soviet Documents (New York: Crosscurrents Press)
Disarmament and Arms Control (New York: Pergamon Press)
"Documents": Documents on American Foreign Relations (New York and Evanston: Harper & Row, for the Council on Foreign Relations). Documents cited by number, and without yearly date, will appear in the volume for 1964.
East Europe (New York: The Free Europe Committee, Inc.)
Foreign Affairs (New York: Council on Foreign Relations)
Hispanic American Report (Palo Alto, California: Hispanic American Society, Stanford University)
Maclean's Magazine (Toronto, Canada: MacLean-Hunter Publishing Co., Ltd.)
NEWSWEEK (New York: Weekly Publications, Inc.)
New York Times (New York: The New York Times Company)
Pacific Affairs (Vancouver, Canada: University of British Columbia)
Peking Review (Peking: Foreign Language Press)
Soviet News (London: Press Department of the Soviet Embassy)
Speeches and Press Conferences (New York: French Press and Information Service)
Survey of Current Business (U.S. Dept. of Commerce, Washington: G.P.O.)
The Evening Star (Washington, D.C., The Evening Star Newspaper Co.)
The Nation (New York: The Nation Company)
The New Republic (New York: The New Republic Company)
The Reporter (New York: The Reporter Magazine Company)
The United States in World Affairs (New York and Evanston: Harper & Row, for the Council on Foreign Relations)
The Washington Post (Washington, D.C.: The Washington Post Company)

TIME (New York: Time Inc.)

"U.N. Review": United Nations Review (New York: U. N. Office of Public Information)

UN Monthly Chronicle (New York: U.N. Office of Public Information)

Full texts of presidential news conferences are published in *The New York Times* of the following day.

All dates refer to the year 1964 unless otherwise indicated.

I. The Torch Is Passed

1. *Documents, 1963,* p. 87.
2. *Documents,* no. 6.
3. Roberto Ducci, "The World Order in the Sixties," *Foreign Affairs,* Apr., p. 386.
4. *Bulletin,* Feb. 24, p. 288.
5. See Louis Harris public opinion poll in *The Washington Post,* Dec. 28.
6. Excerpts in *Documents,* no. 1.
7. White House Press Release, May 22.
8. *New York Times,* Aug. 20.
9. Public Law 88-352.
10. *Bulletin,* Apr. 20, p. 621.
11. *Documents,* no. 4.
12. Public Law 88-633, approved Oct. 7.
13. Excerpts from President Johnson's Economic Report to Congress, Jan. 20, in *Documents,* no. 3; figures from *Survey of Current Business,* March 1965.
14. Text of Republican platform in *New York Times,* July 12 and 13. Text of Democratic platform in same, Aug. 23, 24 and 25.
15. Excerpts in *Documents,* no. 7.
16. *New York Times,* Aug. 18.
17. Cf. Sen. Goldwater's speech in *Documents,* no. 9a.
18. Excerpts in *Documents,* no. 9b; *Bulletin,* Oct. 5, p. 459.

II. The Atlantic Alliance in the Mid-Sixties

1. Excerpts in *Documents,* no. 93; *Bulletin,* Jan. 27, p. 116.
2. Excerpts in *Documents, 1962,* pp. 168–80.
3. Press conference, Jan. 31, *Speeches and Press Conferences,* no. 201.
4. *Documents,* no. 10.
5. *Bulletin,* Feb. 24, p. 290.
6. Same, Feb. 10, p. 192.
7. *Documents,* no. 14.
8. Excerpts in *Documents,* no. 12; *Bulletin,* May 25, p. 828.
9. W. W. Rostow, "The Atlantic Agenda," in *Bulletin,* Apr. 13, pp. 578–87.

10. *Documents, 1957,* p. 113.
11. Same, *1960,* p. 325; see also *The United States in World Affairs, 1960,* pp. 149–51.
12. *Documents, 1961,* p. 276.
13. President Johnson's message to Congress of June 30 in *Bulletin,* July 20, p. 93.
14. Text of agreement of May 18 in *Documents,* no. 16; for text of 1955 agreement see *Documents, 1955,* pp. 86–9.
15. Henry Kissinger, "NATO's Nuclear Dilemma," in David M. Abshire and Richard V. Allen (eds.), *National Security: Political, Military, and Economic Strategies in the Decade Ahead* (New York: Frederick A. Praeger, 1963), p. 308.
16. *New York Times,* Sept. 11.
17. Drew Middleton in the *New York Times,* Mar. 8.
18. Same as note 3.
19. Excerpts in *Documents,* no. 17. Press conference, July 23, *Speeches and Press Conferences,* no. 208.
20. Texts of U.S.-Soviet memorandum on establishing a direct communications link and of the limited nuclear test-ban treaty in *Documents, 1963,* pp. 115–16 and 130–2 respectively.
21. *The Washington Post,* May 19.
22. Same as note 7.
23. *Documents,* no. 18.
24. *Documents,* no. 20.
25. *Documents,* no. 21.
26. *New York Times,* July 11.
27. Same, Nov. 6.
28. Same, Nov. 15.
29. Same, Nov. 29.
30. Excerpt in *Documents,* no. 13; *Bulletin,* Dec. 21, 866–8.
31. *Documents,* no. 22.
32. *The Washington Post,* Dec. 10.
33. Statement of Dec. 13 in *Bulletin,* Jan. 4, 1965, p. 2.
34. Excerpts in *New York Times,* Dec. 17.
35. Text of communiqué in *Documents,* no. 15.
36. *New York Times,* Dec. 21.

III. Conflict and Tensions Within the Western Community

1. *Bulletin,* May 11, p. 750.
2. Texts in *Documents, 1959,* pp. 381–92.
3. *Soviet News,* Feb. 10.
4. *Documents,* no. 23a; details in the *U.N. Review,* Apr., pp. 5–15.
5. *Documents,* no. 23b.
6. *Documents,* no. 24a.
7. *Documents,* no. 24b.
8. *Documents,* no. 25b; details in *UN Monthly Chronicle,* Aug.-Sept., pp. 3–18.

9. *The Washington Post*, Sept. 9.

10. U.N. Document S/5987.

11. *New York Times*, Oct. 2.

12. U.N. Document S/6121.

13. Joint statement in *Documents*, no. 26a; related material in *Bulletin*, Feb. 10, pp. 199–208.

14. President Johnson's Proclamation in *Documents*, no. 26b; see also *Bulletin*, Oct. 12, pp. 504–16 for related material.

15. Cf. William E. Griffith, "Quebec in Revolt," *Foreign Affairs*, Oct., pp. 29–36.

16. *New York Times*, Oct. 11.

17. Same, Oct. 15.

18. Cf. *The United States in World Affairs, 1963*, p. 129.

19. *Bulletin*, May 18, pp. 770–4.

20. An analysis of the survey appears in *The Nation*, Aug. 10, pp. 51–3.

21. Lester B. Pearson, "Good Neighborhood," *Foreign Affairs*, Jan. 1965, p. 256.

22. For official summary see *Documents, 1962*, pp. 496–508.

23. *Bulletin*, Nov. 30, p. 771.

24. Resolution of May 21, 1963, in *Documents, 1963*, pp. 196–9.

25. *Bulletin*, May 11, p. 750.

26. Same, Nov. 16, p. 714.

27. Herter statement and Declaration of the GATT Trade Negotiations Committee in *Documents*, no. 28.

IV. A Pause in the Cold War

1. Excerpts in *Documents*, no. 33; *Bulletin*, Mar. 16, p. 393.

2. *Documents, 1963*, p. 117.

3. Excerpts in *Documents*, no. 5; see also J. W. Fulbright, *Old Myths and New Realities* (New York: Random House, 1964).

4. Exchange of New Year's messages in *Bulletin*, Jan. 27, p. 121.

5. Excerpts from the Soviet message, released Jan. 2 in *Documents*, no. 35a.

6. *Documents*, no. 35b.

7. *New York Times*, Jan. 30.

8. Same, Mar. 12.

9. *TIME*, Mar. 20, p. 32.

10. *Bulletin*, Aug. 3, pp. 145–6.

11. State Department statement on signing the agreement of Feb. 22 in *Bulletin*, Mar. 23, p. 451.

12. *Documents*, no. 30.

13. *Documents*, no. 31.

14. *Documents*, no. 32a and b.

15. *Documents*, no. 32c.

16. *The Washington Post*, Oct. 18.

17. *New York Times*, Oct. 30.

18. *Bulletin*, Mar. 2, pp. 336–7.

19. *New York Times,* Mar. 11.
20. *Bulletin,* Mar. 30, pp. 474–85; see also U.S. Senate Committee on Foreign Relations, 88th Cong., 2d sess., *East-West Trade: Hearings, Part I* (Washington: G.P.O., 1964).
21. News conference statement, *New York Times,* Apr. 26.
22. Excerpts in *East Europe,* June 1964, pp. 25–30.
23. *Bulletin,* Mar. 30, p. 487.
24. *Documents,* no. 34.
25. *Bulletin,* June 15, p. 923.
26. For discussion of this issue see George F. Kennan, *On Dealing with the Communist World* (New York and Evanston: Harper & Row, for the Council on Foreign Relations, 1964), pp. 37–51.
27. Excerpts in *Documents,* no. 1.
28. *Documents,* no. 36. For further documentation see *Report of the Conference of the Eighteen-Nation Committee on Disarmament* (U.N. Document A/5731 (DC 209), Sept. 22); also *Further Documents Relating to the Conference of the Eighteen-Nation Committee on Disarmament (Session January 21 to April 28, 1964)* (Miscellaneous No. 20 [1964]; Cmnd. 2486; London: H.M.S.O., 1964).
29. *Documents,* no. 37.
30. *Documents, 1962,* pp. 115–47.
31. *Soviet News,* Mar. 3.
32. Conference Document ENDC/144, Sept. 14 (annex to U.N. Document A/5731, cited in note 28).
33. Conference Documents ENDC/131, and ENDC/132, respectively (annexes to U.N. Document A/5731, cited in note 28).
34. *Documents,* no. 38.
35. For a detailed discussion of this problem see Karol D. Lapter, "Nuclear Freeze in Central Europe," *Disarmament and Arms Control,* Summer 1964, pp. 299–309.
36. *Bulletin,* June 29, p. 1005.
37. *New York Times,* Sept. 4.
38. *Bulletin,* Oct. 12, pp. 524–5.

V. Sino-Soviet Conflict and the Far East

1. Press conference, Jan. 31, cited, p. 14.
2. *Documents, 1963,* pp. 304 and 311.
3. *Peking Review,* Feb. 28, pp. 9–12.
4. *Documents,* no. 6; also *Bulletin,* May 11, p. 730.
5. For Chinese letter of Feb. 4 see *Peking Review,* Feb. 7, pp. 5–21; text of Soviet letter of July 14, 1963, in *Current Soviet Documents,* Aug. 5, 1963.
6. Text in *Soviet News,* Apr. 3 and 6.
7. *New York Times,* May 9.
8. Same, Aug. 31.
9. *Documents,* no. 41a.
10. *Documents,* no. 41b; also *Peking Review,* Oct. 16, Supplement.

11. *Documents,* no. 41c.
12. *Bulletin,* Nov. 2, p. 615.
13. *Soviet News,* Sept. 7.
14. *New York Times,* Feb. 3.
15. Same, Sept. 6.
16. Same.
17. Same as note 2.
18. Excerpts in *Documents,* no. 5.
19. *New York Times,* Apr. 5.
20. Secretary Rusk's statement in *Documents,* no. 42.
21. For a perceptive analysis of South Korea's domestic problems see William A. Douglas, "South Korea's Search for Leadership," *Pacific Affairs,* Spring 1964, pp. 20–36.
22. *Documents,* no. 44.
23. *Documents,* no. 45.
24. Public Law 88-563, approved Sept. 2.
25. George F. Kennan, "Japanese Security and American Policy," *Foreign Affairs,* Oct. 1964, p. 22.

VI. The United States and South Vietnam

1. *New York Times Magazine,* Jan. 17, 1965, p. 15.
2. *Bulletin,* Jan. 27, pp. 121–2.
3. *New York Times,* Jan. 15.
4. News conference statement in *New York Times,* Feb. 23.
5. *TASS* statement in *Soviet News,* Feb. 28.
6. *Congressional Record,* Mar. 4, p. 4205.
7. White House statement of Mar. 17 in *Bulletin,* Apr. 6, pp. 522–3.
8. Excerpts in *Documents,* no. 47.
9. *Documents,* no. 46.
10. Secretary Rusk's arrival statement of Apr. 17 in *Bulletin,* May 4, p. 694; for statement on his return see same, pp. 695–7.
11. *New York Times,* May 15.
12. Text of President Johnson's message to Congress in *Documents,* no. 48; see also *Bulletin,* June 8, pp. 891–3.
13. For text of 1954 agreements see *Documents, 1954,* pp. 283–301. Text of the 1962 accords in same, *1962,* pp. 284–94.
14. *New York Times,* July 9.
15. Press Conference, July 23, cited, pp. 11–12. Excerpts in *Documents,* no. 17.
16. *New York Times,* July 25.
17. *Documents,* no. 49a; *Bulletin,* Aug. 24, p. 259.
18. Text of President Johnson's message in *Documents,* no. 49b.
19. *Bulletin,* Aug. 24, p. 261.
20. *New York Times,* Aug. 6 and 7.
21. Text in same, Aug. 7; also *Peking Review,* Aug. 7, Special Supplement.
22. *Documents,* no. 49c.

23. *Congressional Record,* Aug. 5, pp. 17548–54.
24. Same, Aug. 6, pp. 17815–18.
25. *New York Times,* Aug. 8.
26. *Bulletin,* Aug. 24, pp. 272–4; details in *UN Monthly Chronicle,* Aug.–Sept., pp. 18–24.
27. *New York Times,* Aug. 10.
28. *Documents,* no. 50; *Bulletin,* Dec. 21, p. 870.
29. *New York Times,* Dec. 12.
30. *Bulletin,* Jan. 11, 1965, p. 39.
31. *New York Times,* Dec. 27.

VII. Ferment in Southeast Asia

1. *Documents, 1962,* pp. 284–94.
2. See Eric Pace, "Laos: Continuing Crisis," *Foreign Affairs,* Oct. 1964, pp. 64–74.
3. *Bulletin,* June 8, p. 889.
4. Same, June 29, footnote p. 994.
5. State Department statements of June 6 and 7 in *Documents,* no. 51a and b.
6. State Department statement of June 11 in *Documents,* no. 51c.
7. Text of Chinese statement of June 15, together with Peking's notes of June 13 to the co-chairmen of the 1962 Geneva conference, in *Peking Review,* June 19, pp. 8–10.
8. *New York Times,* June 17.
9. Same, Jan. 16.
10. Same, Mar. 10.
11. Excerpts in *Documents,* no. 55a; details in *UN Monthly Chronicle,* June, pp. 12–17.
12. *Documents,* no. 55b; details in *UN Monthly Chronicle,* July, pp. 25–30.
13. U.N. Document S/5832, July 27; details in *UN Monthly Chronicle,* Aug.-Sept., pp. 24–28.
14. Interview with Marguerite Higgins in *The Evening Star,* Dec. 4.
15. *Bulletin,* Feb. 17, p. 240.
16. Same, p. 242.
17. *New York Times,* Apr. 23.
18. Hamilton Fish Armstrong, "This Was in Borneo: Whose Side Are We On?" *The Reporter,* June 4, pp. 16–20.
19. *Documents,* no. 58.
20. Statement of Sept. 10 in *Documents,* no. 59.
21. *Documents,* no. 60; details in *UN Monthly Chronicle,* Oct., pp. 25–34.
22. *New York Times,* Sept. 20.

VIII. Politics and Change in Latin America

1. Philip W. Quigg, "Latin America: A Broad Brush Appraisal," *Foreign Affairs*, Apr., p. 409.
2. Quoted in Mildred Adams (ed.), *Evolution or Explosion* (New York: Dodd, Mead & Co., 1963), p. 55.
3. *New York Times*, Mar. 19.
4. Excerpts in *Documents*, no. 63; *Bulletin*, June 29, p. 999.
5. Hubert H. Humphrey, "U.S. Policy in Latin America," *Foreign Affairs*, July, pp. 585–601.
6. Joint communiqué in *Documents*, no. 76.
7. *Documents, 1963*, pp. 407–13.
8. *Documents*, no. 61.
9. President Johnson's remarks of May 11 in *Documents*, no. 62.
10. *Bulletin*, Oct. 5, p. 481.
11. *Documents*, no. 65.
12. *New York Times*, Nov. 15.
13. *Documents*, no. 66.
14. *Bulletin*, Mar. 16, p. 400.
15. *Hispanic American Report*, May, p. 210.
16. A. A. Berle, "As the Dust Settles in Brazil," *The Reporter*, Apr. 23, pp. 27–8.
17. *Documents*, no. 77.
18. *New York Times*, Dec. 15.
19. *Documents*, no. 78.

IX. The Caribbean at Low Tide

1. Excerpts in *Documents*, no. 67; *Bulletin*, May 11, p. 744.
2. *Documents, 1963*, p. 50.
3. *Bulletin*, Mar. 30, pp. 480–3.
4. News conference remarks in *New York Times*, May 7.
5. *Bulletin*, Feb. 24, p. 277.
6. *Documents*, no. 69a.
7. *New York Times*, Apr. 25.
8. Same, May 2.
9. O.A.S. Document OEA/Ser. G/IV, Feb. 18.
10. *New York Times*, July 6.
11. Excerpts in *Documents*, no. 70a; *Bulletin*, Aug. 10, p. 179.
12. *Documents*, no. 70b.
13. *Old Myths and New Realities*, cited, p. 21.
14. *Documents*, no. 71.
15. *Bulletin*, Feb. 3, p. 154; details in *U.N. Review*, Feb., pp. 6–8 and 43–4.
16. *Documents*, no. 72a.
17. *Documents*, no. 72b.
18. *Documents*, no. 72c.

19. *Documents,* no. 73b.
20. *New York Times,* Feb. 17.
21. Statement of Mar. 15 in *New York Times,* Mar. 16. President Johnson's address in *Documents,* no. 61.
22. *Documents,* no. 73c; *Bulletin,* Apr. 6, p. 539.
23. Joint declaration in *Documents,* no. 74. President Johnson's statement in *Bulletin,* Apr. 27, pp. 655–6.
24. *Documents,* no. 75.
25. *Documents,* no. 76.
26. See Norris Hundley, Jr., "The Colorado Waters Dispute," *Foreign Affairs,* Apr., pp. 495–500.
27. *Documents, 1963,* pp. 396–7.
28. *Hispanic American Report,* Aug., p. 522.
29. Same, Apr., p. 324.

X. The Middle East and South Asia

1. For discussion see *The United States in World Affairs, 1955,* pp. 171–3.
2. William Mehlman, "Jordan's Troubled Waters," *The Reporter,* Jan. 30, pp. 29–33.
3. *Documents,* no. 79. President Kennedy's statement of May 8, 1963, in *Documents, 1963,* p. 268.
4. *Bulletin,* Feb. 24, p. 285; see *Documents,* no. 83 for text of U.S.-Israeli agreement on desalting.
5. Joint communiqué of President Johnson and King Hussein in *Documents,* no. 81. King Hussein's news conference in *New York Times,* Apr. 15.
6. *Documents,* no. 82.
7. Summary of debate on the Israeli-Syrian dispute in *UN Monthly Chronicle,* Dec., pp. 3–8; same, Jan. 1965, pp. 28–32.
8. U.N. Document S/6085/Rev. 1. The Moroccan draft resolution of Dec. 5 failed of adoption by a vote of 3 to 0, with 8 abstentions.
9. *Documents,* no. 84.
10. *The Washington Post,* Aug. 1.
11. *New York Times,* Feb. 24.
12. U.N. Document S/5331, June 11, 1963, in *Documents, 1963,* pp. 263–4.
13. *Documents,* no. 80; details in *UN Monthly Chronicle,* May, pp. 14–20.
14. Patrick Gordon Walker, "Labor's Defense and Foreign Policy," *Foreign Affairs,* Apr., p. 396.
15. *New York Times,* Sept. 15.
16. *U.N. Review,* Mar., p. 5.
17. Same, p. 8.
18. *Documents,* no. 85.
19. Chinese-Pakistan joint communiqué in *Peking Review,* Feb. 28, pp. 8–9.

20. Details in *UN Monthly Chronicle,* June, pp. 3–12.
21. *Bulletin,* June 15, p. 926.

XI. Under Africa's Volcano

1. Vernon McKay, *Africa in World Politics* (New York and Evanston: Harper & Row, 1963), p. 11.
2. *Documents,* no. 87.
3. Robert Conley in *New York Times,* June 28.
4. Interview with Colin Legum in *The Washington Post,* Aug. 30.
5. *U.N. Review,* Mar., p. 14.
6. *The Washington Post,* Feb. 11.
7. *U.N. Review,* Apr., pp. 16–20 and 36–7. Further resolutions in *UN Monthly Chronicle,* May, pp. 33–4; same, June, p. 30.
8. *NEWSWEEK,* Sept. 21.
9. *New York Times,* Oct. 28.
10. Quoted in Russell Warren Howe, "Rebellion in Rhodesia?" *The New Republic,* Nov. 14, p. 14.
11. *UN Monthly Chronicle,* May, p. 40.
12. *Documents, 1962,* pp. 326–8.
13. *UN Monthly Chronicle,* May, pp. 43–4.
14. U.N. Documents S/5761 and S/5773, respectively; details in *UN Monthly Chronicle,* July, pp. 16–17; *Documents,* no. 92b for June 18 resolution.
15. *New York Times,* Jan. 4.
16. J. Anthony Lukas in same, June 7.
17. Same, July 25.
18. Same, Aug. 15.
19. Same, Aug. 22.
20. *Documents,* no. 88.
21. *Documents,* no. 89.
22. *New York Times,* Nov. 24; see also *Documents,* no. 90. Further details in *Bulletin,* Dec. 14, pp. 838–44.
23. *Documents,* no. 90e.
24. Donald H. Loucheim in *The Washington Post,* Nov. 29.
25. *Documents,* no. 91a.
26. *Documents,* no. 91b; details in *UN Monthly Chronicle,* Jan. 1965, pp. 7–23.

XII. The United Nations at a Crossroad

1. Excerpts in *Documents,* no. 93; also *Bulletin,* Jan. 27, pp. 112–19.
2. Introduction to Richard N. Gardner, *In Pursuit of World Order* (New York: Praeger, 1964).
3. Same as note 1.
4. *U.N. Review,* Sept. 1961, pp. 12–17 and 34–5.

5. Excerpts in *Documents*, no. 94. Complete text in General Assembly *Official Records*, Nineteenth Session, Supplement No. 1A (A/5801/Add.1).

6. Same as note 5.

7. Same as note 1.

8. *Documents, 1950*, pp. 182–6.

9. John G. Stoessinger and Associates, *Financing the United Nations System* (Washington, D.C.: The Brookings Institution, 1964), p. 17.

10. Resolution 1991 (XVIII) in *Documents, 1963*, pp. 471–3.

11. Same as note 1.

12. *Bulletin*, June 8, p. 905.

13. Same as note 5.

14. *Documents*, no. 23b.

15. Excerpts in *New York Times*, Mar. 24.

16. See Per Haekkerup, "Scandinavia's Peace-Keeping Force for U.N.," *Foreign Affairs*, July, pp. 675–81.

17. Lester B. Pearson, "A New Kind of Peace Force?" *Maclean's*, May 2 issue.

18. Same as note 15. For a more extended discussion see Gardner, cited, Chap. 4.

19. U.N. Document S/5811.

20. U.N. Document S/5853, Aug. 5.

21. *Documents*, no. 95a.

22. *New York Times*, Sept. 24.

23. See *Documents*, no. 95b for the U.S. position on this issue.

24. *Bulletin*, Dec. 7, p. 827.

25. Same, pp. 827–8.

26. Same, Aug. 17, p. 241.

27. Isaiah Frank, "Aid, Trade and Economic Development: Issues Before the U.N. Conference," *Foreign Affairs*, Jan., pp. 210–26.

28. U.N. Document E/Conf. 46/3, Feb. 12.

29. *Bulletin*, Mar. 16, p. 414.

30. Same as note 28.

31. Excerpts in *Documents*, no. 96; *Bulletin*, Apr. 20, p. 635.

32. See *Proceedings of the United Nations Conference on Trade and Development*, E/Conf. 46/141, Vol. I, pp. 66–9 for "Joint Declaration of the Seventy-Seven Developing Countries." Excerpts from the *Final Act* in *Documents*, no. 97.

33. Raúl Prebisch, "Spirit of Conciliation," in *UN Monthly Chronicle*, July, p. 76.

34. Gardner, cited, p. 169.

35. For further discussion see Sidney Weintraub, "After the U.N. Trade Conference: Lessons and Portents," *Foreign Affairs*, Oct., pp. 37–50.

CHRONOLOGY OF MAJOR EVENTS

JANUARY 1–DECEMBER 31, 1964

N.B. Italicized references are to sections of the text which provide additional information or background data.

An asterisk (*) opposite the name of a country indicates that one or more high-level conferences with the President of the United States will be found listed under "The United States: Presidential Visitors."

A dagger (†) indicates that additional entries will be found under "The United Nations."

I. THE UNITED STATES

Major Treaties and Agreements

Entered into force:

Jan. 14—Convention with Mexico for the solution of the problem of Chamizal (signed Mexico City, Aug. 29, 1963). *Sec. 37.*

Sept. 16—Treaty with Canada Relating to Cooperative Development of Water Resources of Columbia River Basin (signed Washington, Jan. 17, 1961). *Sec. 11.*

Nov. 17—Extradition treaty with Brazil (signed Washington, Jan. 13, 1961).

Signed:

Feb. 22—Agreement with the U.S.S.R. on Exchanges in the Scientific, Technical, Educational, Cultural, and Other Fields for 1965–66 (signed in Moscow). *Sec. 13.*

June 1—Consular Convention, the first bilateral treaty between the U.S. and U.S.S.R. (signed in Moscow). *Sec. 13.*

July 24—Agreement on international management and ownership of a global communications satellite system (signed in Washington).

Nov. 18—Agreement with the U.S.S.R. on Cooperation in Desalination of Sea Water (signed in Moscow). *Sec. 13.*

The Presidency

Nov. 3—Lyndon B. Johnson is elected 36th President of the U.S. for a 4-year term beginning Jan. 20, 1965. Senator Hubert H. Humphrey is elected Vice-President. Democrats retain control of both houses in the 89th Congress. *Sec. 4.*

Presidential Visitors

Following is a list of formal conferences held by President Johnson with visiting heads of state or government (in Washington unless otherwise noted).

Jan. 14–15—President Antonio Segni, Italy.
Jan. 21–23—Prime Minister Lester B. Pearson, Canada. *Sec. 11.*
Feb. 12–14—Prime Minister Sir Alec Douglas-Home, United Kingdom. *Sec. 14.*
Feb. 21–22—President Adolfo López Mateos, Mexico (Palm Springs, Cal.). *Sec. 37.*
Apr. 14–16—King Hussein, Jordan. *Sec. 39.*
Apr. 27—Prime Minister Eric E. Williams, Trinidad and Tobago.
May 27–29—President Eamon de Valera, Ireland.
June 1–2—Prime Minister Levi Eshkol, Israel. *Sec. 39.*
June 9—Premier Jens Otto Krag, Denmark.
June 12—Chancellor Ludwig Erhard, Federal Republic of Germany. *Sec. 8.*
June 22–23—Prime Minister Ismet Inönü, Turkey. *Sec. 10.*
June 24–25—Prime Minister George Papandreou, Greece. *Sec. 10.*
July 1—President Francisco J. Orlich, Costa Rica.
July 20—Prime Minister Keith J. Holyoake, New Zealand.
July 22–23—Prime Minister Tunku Abdul Rahman, Malaysia. *Sec. 28.*
July 27–28—President Philibert Tsiranana, Malagasy (Madagascar).
Oct. 5–6—President Diosdado Macapagal, Philippines.
Nov. 12–13—President-elect Gustavo Díaz Ordaz, Mexico (LBJ ranch, Johnson City, Texas). *Sec. 37.*
Dec. 7–8—Prime Minister Harold Wilson, United Kingdom. *Sec. 9.*

The Congress

Jan. 7–Oct. 3. The 88th Congress holds its Second Session and adopts the following major enactments affecting foreign affairs (with Public Law numbers and dates of presidential approval):

P.L. 88-272, Feb. 26—Revenue Act of 1964 (H.R. 8363).
P.L. 88-277, Mar. 7—Presidential Transition Act of 1964 (H.R. 4638).
P.L. 88-285, Mar. 17—Authorizing funds for Peace Corps operations, fiscal year 1965 (S. 2455).
P.L. 88-288, Mar. 20—Authorizing funds for procurement of aircraft, missiles, and naval vessels, and research and development for the armed forces (H.R. 9637).
P.L. 88-300, Apr. 29—Proposed American-Mexican Chamizal Convention Act of 1964 (S. 2394). *Sec. 37.*

P.L. 88-308, May 20—Prohibiting fishing in territorial waters of the United States, and certain other areas by persons other than U.S. nationals or inhabitants (S. 1988). *Sec. 34.*

P.L. 88-310, May 26—Authorizing U.S. participation in an increase in the resources of the International Development Association (S. 2214).

P.L. 88-352, July 2—Civil Rights Act of 1964 (H.R. 7152). *Sec. 2.*

P.L. 88-408, Aug. 10—Joint Resolution to promote the maintenance of international peace and security in Southeast Asia (H.J. Res. 1145). *Sec. 24.*

P.L. 88-411, Aug. 10—Authorizing conclusion of agreements with Mexico for construction of flood control works on the lower Colorado River (H.R. 7419). *Sec. 37.*

P.L. 88-446, Aug. 19—Department of Defense appropriations, fiscal year 1965 (H.R. 10939).

P.L. 88-468, Aug. 20—U.S. contributions to the International Commission for Supervision and Control in Laos (S. 1627).

P.L. 88-487, Aug. 22—To promote economic and social development of Pacific Island Trust Territories (H.R. 3198).

P.L. 88-527, Aug. 31—Department of State and other appropriations, fiscal year 1965 (H.R. 11134).

P.L. 88-563, Sept. 2—Interest Equalization Tax Act of 1964 (H.R. 8000).

P.L. 88-609, Sept. 22—To provide for study to determine a site for construction of a sea-level canal between the Atlantic and Pacific Oceans (S. 2701). *Sec. 36.*

P.L. 88-633, Oct. 7—Authorizing funds for the foreign aid program for fiscal year 1965 (H.R. 11380). *Sec. 2.*

P.L. 88-634, Oct. 7—Foreign Assistance Appropriations Act, 1965 (H.R. 11812).

P.L. 88-638, Oct. 8—Extending for two years the Agricultural Trade Development and Assistance Act of 1954 (S. 2687).

Other Developments

Jan. 8. President Johnson announces cutback in nuclear materials production. *Sec. 1.*

July 15–16. Senator Barry M. Goldwater and Representative William E. Miller are nominated as Republican candidates for President and Vice-President, respectively. *Sec. 4.*

July 28. Ranger 7 is launched on a scheduled 68-hour flight to the moon, crashing into the moon on July 31, after transmitting the first U.S. close-up lunar pictures.

Aug. 26. President Johnson and Senator Humphrey are nominated as Democratic candidates for President and Vice-President, respectively.

Sept. 28. The Warren Commission, investigating President Kennedy's assassination, unanimously finds that Lee Harvey Oswald, acting alone, was the assassin.

II. THE WESTERN COMMUNITY

The North Atlantic Treaty Organization

Apr. 13. Vice-Admiral Ernesto de Pellegrini dai Coi (Italy) succeeds Vice-Admiral Stefano Pugliese (Italy) as Commander, Central Mediterranean area.

Apr. 28. French naval officers are withdrawn from commands in the Mediterranean and the English Channel. *Sec. 5.*

May 13. Manlio Brosio (Italy) is elected Secretary-General of NATO, and succeeds Dirk U. Stikker (Netherlands) on Aug. 1.

May 12–14. The North Atlantic Council holds its spring ministerial session at The Hague. *Sec. 5.*

June 4. Maj. Gen. Ernst Gerber (West Germany) is appointed head of the new strategic planning staff.

Dec. 15–17. The Council holds its regular ministerial session in Paris. *Sec. 9.*

The European Economic Community (E.E.C.) (Sec. 12)

Jan. 8. The European Parliamentary Assembly endorses (59–9) the Mansholt plan to unify cereal grains prices in E.E.C. countries.

Nov. 16. Exceptions lists are submitted, and the Kennedy Round resumes its negotiations.

Dec. 15. Uniform prices for wholesale grain purchases are adopted, ending a year-long deadlock.

European Free Trade Association (EFTA)

Feb. 13–14. The Ministerial Council meets in Geneva.

July 9. EFTA holds its 23rd ministerial meeting in Edinburgh.

Organization for Economic Cooperation and Development

Apr. 28. Japan becomes the 21st member and first Asian nation to join O.E.C.D.

Dec. 2–3. The O.E.C.D. holds its 4th session in Paris.

United Kingdom *

Oct. 15. General elections give the Labor party 317 seats in the House of Commons to 304 for the Conservatives and 9 for the Liberals. With a slim 4-seat margin, Harold Wilson becomes Prime Minister succeeding Sir Alec Douglas-Home (Conservative; assumed office Oct. 19, 1963). *Sec. 9.*

Nov. 25. Eleven nations extend $3 billion in credits to support the British pound. *Sec. 9.*

France

Jan. 27. France and Communist China announce the establishment of diplomatic relations. *Secs. 7, 20, 22, 23.*

Jan. 31, July 23. President Charles de Gaulle enunciates French foreign policy at semiannual press conferences. *Sec. 7.*

Mar. 15–24. President de Gaulle visits Mexico and French territories in the Western Hemisphere. *Secs. 7, 30.*

Sept. 20–Oct. 16. President de Gaulle visits ten South American countries. *Sec. 30.*

German Federal Republic *

July 1. President Heinrich Luebke (inaugurated Sept. 15, 1959) is re-elected for a second 5-year term by the Federal Assembly in elections held in West Berlin.

Nov. 14. A military cooperation agreement between the U.S. and West Germany is signed in Washington. *Sec. 8.*

Berlin

Sept. 23. The German Federal Republic approves an agreement with the "German Democratic Republic" permitting West Berliners to visit relatives in East Berlin. *Sec. 8.*

Italy *

Aug. 23. Premier Aldo Moro's new cabinet, virtually identical with his four-party coalition government (resigned June 26), is sworn in.

Dec. 28. Giuseppe Saragat (Democratic Socialist) is elected on the 21st ballot by the Italian National Assembly to succeed Antonio Segni (Christian Democrat; inaugurated May 11, 1962; resigned Dec. 6, 1964, after suffering a cerebral hemorrhage Aug. 7) for a 7-year term as President.

The Vatican

Jan. 4–6. Pope Paul visits the Holy Land.

Sept. 14–Nov. 21. The 21st Ecumenical Council (Vatican II) holds its 3rd session in Rome.

Sept. 15. An agreement is signed with Hungary restoring the Church's right to form a hierarchy and to communicate freely with it.

Dec. 2–5. Pope Paul VI attends the international Eucharistic Congress in Bombay, India.

Greece *

Feb. 16. The Center Union Party wins in general elections. George Papandreou sworn in as Premier on Feb. 19 replacing the caretaker government of Ioannis Paraskevopoulos, formed on Dec. 31, 1963.

Mar. 6. King Constantine succeeds to the throne upon the death of his father, King Paul I.

Cyprus (Sec. 10) †

Jan. 15. Delegates from Turkey, Greece, the Greek and Turkish Cypriote communities, and the U.K. open talks in London.

Jan. 31. The U.S. and Britain jointly propose an international 10,000-man force to keep order on Cyprus. President Makarios rejects this proposal and also a new revised Anglo-U.S. plan on Feb. 14.

Mar. 25. Secretary-General Thant names Sakari Severi Tuomioja of Finland as U.N. mediator in Cyprus.

Mar. 27. The U.N. Force in Cyprus formally undertakes its peace-keeping operations.

Apr. 4. Archbishop Makarios abrogates the treaties with Britain, Greece, and Turkey, which guarantee the island's constitution and its territorial integrity.

Aug. 8–9. Turkish Air Force jets attack the northern coast of Cyprus. The U.N. Security Council calls for a cease-fire, which is accepted by Turkey and Cyprus on Aug. 10.

Aug. 25. President Makarios rejects the compromise plan devised at talks held in Geneva in July and August by U.N. mediator Tuomioja and demands that the Cyprus question be placed before the U.N. General Assembly in November.

Aug. 27. President Makarios refuses to permit the rotation of Turkish troops on Cyprus. U.N. officials negotiate an agreement that takes effect Oct. 26.

Sept. 9. U.N. mediator Tuomioja dies; Secretary-General Thant appoints Galo Plaza Lasso of Ecuador as his successor on Sept. 16.

Sept. 30. Cyprus and the U.S.S.R. sign a military and economic aid agreement in Moscow.

Malta (Sec. 43) †

Sept. 21. The British colony of Malta becomes independent within the Commonwealth, with Giorgio Borg Olivier as Prime Minister.

Luxembourg

Nov. 12. After 45 years as reigning monarch, Grand Duchess Charlotte abdicates in favor of her son the Crown Prince Jean.

Austria

Feb. 25. Chancellor Alfons Gorbach (People's party; assumed office Mar. 27, 1963) resigns and is replaced Apr. 2 by Josef Kraus (same party).

Denmark *

Sept. 25. As a result of general elections on Sept. 22, the Social Democratic-Social Liberal coalition government (formed Nov. 18, 1960) is replaced by a Social Democratic minority government with Jens Otto Krag continuing as Prime Minister.

Finland

Sept. 11. Johannes Virolainen (Agrarian party) forms a nonsocialist majority coalition cabinet to replace the nonpolitical caretaker government of civil servants (appointed Dec. 18, 1963).

Sweden

Sept. 20. Though not winning an absolute majority in elections to the lower chamber of the Riksdag, the Social Democrats continue their 32 years of unbroken rule.

Ireland *

Canada (Sec. 11) *

Apr. 29–30. The 9th meeting of the Joint United States-Canadian Committee on Trade and Economic Affairs is held at Ottawa.

III. EAST-WEST RELATIONS AND THE COMMUNIST WORLD

Disarmament (Sec. 16)

Jan. 21–Apr. 28; June 9–Sept. 17. The Conference of the Eighteen-Nation Committee on Disarmament meets in Geneva.

Apr. 20. The U.S. and the U.S.S.R. announce unilateral pledges to reduce the production of fissionable materials for nuclear weapons.

The U.S.S.R.

Apr. 2. U.S.S.R. announces launching of Zond-1, an automatic space station, on a Venus probe.

July 14–16. The U.S. and the Soviet Union hold talks in Washington on cooperation in developing methods for desalting sea water. *Sec. 13.*

July 15. Anastas I. Mikoyan is unanimously elected Chairman of the Presidium of the Supreme Soviet to succeed Leonid I. Brezhnev (elected May 7, 1960), who becomes Premier Nikita S. Khrushchev's deputy in the Secretariat of the Communist party Central Committee.

Oct. 12–13. The Soviet Union orbits a three-man crew in *Voskhod,* the world's first multiman spaceship. It returns to earth after 16 circuits lasting 24 hours and 17 minutes.

Oct. 15. A communiqué announces that Premier Nikita S. Khrushchev is removed (Oct. 14–15) from his government post as Chairman of the Council of Ministers (elected Mar. 27, 1958), and from his party posts as First Secretary of the Communist party Central Committee (named Sept. 12, 1953) and member of its Presidium. He is replaced by Aleksei N. Kosygin as Premier, and by Leonid I. Brezhnev as First Secretary. *Sec. 13.*

"German Democratic Republic"

June 12. The U.S.S.R. and East Germany sign a 20-year treaty of friendship and cooperation. *Sec. 8.*

Sept. 21. Premier Otto Grotewhol (named Oct. 7, 1949) dies. Willi Stoph, Acting Premier since 1960, is named Premier on September 24.

Poland

June 20. Wladyslaw Gomulka (installed Oct. 19–21, 1956) is reelected First Secretary of the United Workers' (Communist) party.

Aug. 12. Edward Ochab is elected Chairman of the Council of State, succeeding Aleksander Zawadzki (named in 1952) who died on Aug. 7.

Czechoslovakia

June 14. A new National Assembly and the Slovak National Council are elected from a single list of candidates approved by the National Front.

Nov. 12. President Antonín Novotný is reelected by the National Assembly for a second 5-year term; he continues as First Secretary of the Czechoslovak Communist party.

Rumania

May 18–June 1. The U.S. and Rumania discuss economic and trade matters in Washington. *Sec. 15.*

Dec. 23. The U.S. and Rumania extend the 1961 cultural agreement for two years.

Yugoslavia

Dec. 7–13. The long-delayed 8th Congress of the Yugoslav League of Communists is held and Marshal Josip Broz Tito is reelected as its Secretary-General and head of the Executive Secretariat of its Central Committee.

IV. THE FAR EAST AND SOUTHEAST ASIA

Communist China and Sino-Soviet Relations

Feb. 4. Premier Chou En-lai completes a tour (begun Dec. 14, 1963) to Albania and ten African states. Feb. 13–Mar. 1, he visits Pakistan, Burma, and Ceylon. *Secs. 17, 41, 43.*

Mar. 7. The U.S.S.R. proposes a series of Communist conferences to prepare for a meeting of the world's Communist parties in the fall. On May 8 Communist China rejects the Soviet call. *Sec. 17.*

Oct. 16. Communist China announces the explosion of a nuclear device. *Sec. 18.*

Nov. 5–12. Chou En-lai visits Moscow with other Communist bloc leaders for talks with the new Soviet leadership. *Sec. 18.*

Dec. 12. The meeting of 26 Communist parties in Moscow (announced Aug. 10 and scheduled for Dec. 15) to prepare the world congress if postponed until Mar. 1, 1965. *Secs. 17, 18.*

Dec. 20–Jan. 4, 1965. The 3rd National People's Congress meets in Peking; Liu Shao-chi is reelected chief of state.

Japan (Sec. 22)

Jan. 27–28. The third meeting of the Joint U.S.-Japanese Committee on Trade and Economic Affairs is held in Tokyo.

Nov. 9. Eisaku Sato (Liberal Democratic party) is elected Premier by the Diet. He succeeds Hayato Ikeda (same party; assumed office July 19, 1960) who resigned Oct. 25 because of ill health.

Republic of China (Sec. 20)

Feb. 10. Nationalist China breaks off diplomatic relations with France because of the latter's recognition of Communist China.

May 28. The U.S. State Department announces termination of economic aid to Nationalist China by June 30, 1965, because of its successful economic growth.

The Colombo Plan

Feb. 19. Konthi Suphamongkhol of Thailand named Secretary-General to succeed Pote Sarasin (resigned Dec. 13, 1963).

Nov. 9–20. The Colombo Plan Consultative Committee holds its 16th ministerial session in London.

The ANZUS Treaty

July 17–18. The ANZUS Council meets in Washington.

New Zealand *

Southeast Asia Treaty Organization (Sec. 23)

Apr. 13–15. The Council of Ministers holds its 10th annual meeting in Manila.

South Vietnam (Secs. 23, 24, 25)

Jan. 30. Maj. Gen. Nguyen Khanh, in a bloodless coup, proclaims himself Chief of State, replacing Maj. Gen. Duong Van Minh (assumed power Nov. 2, 1963).

Feb. 8. Gen. Khanh forms a new government, naming himself Premier and Gen. Minh titular Chief of State.

Aug. 2. The U.S.S. Maddox is attacked in international waters off the coast of North Vietnam by North Vietnamese torpedo boats, followed by a second attack on Aug. 4. In retaliation, U.S. planes bomb North Vietnamese torpedo boat bases and an oil storage depot on Aug. 5.

Aug. 7. Congress adopts a joint resolution supporting President Johnson in taking all necessary measures to repel any armed attacks against U.S. forces in Southeast Asia.

Aug. 16. Gen Khanh is elected President by the Military Revolutionary Council under a new constitution, which abolishes the offices of premier and chief of state and provides for a strong presidential system.

Aug. 25. Because of continuing riots against repressive measures under the state of emergency (declared Aug. 7) and against Gen. Khanh's assumption of wider powers, the government resigns.

Aug. 27. The constitution is withdrawn. The Military Revolutionary Council disbands and is replaced by a military triumvirate of Generals Khanh, Minh, and Tran Thien Khiem, who, as the National Provisional Steering Committee, are to form an interim government until a national convention selects a new leader.

Aug. 29. Nguyen Xuan Oanh is designated Acting Premier.

Sept. 3. Gen. Khanh resumes the premiership. The military triumvirate is dissolved, then reinstated the next day with Gen. Minh as Chairman of the National Provisional Steering Committee with the powers of chief of state.

Sept. 13. An attempted coup led by deposed Minister of Interior Brig. Gen. Lam Van Phat fails.

Sept. 26. A High National Council of 17 civilian members is appointed to prepare a new provisional constitution.

Oct. 20. The new draft constitution for a civilian government is presented. On Oct. 24 the Council elects Phan Khac Suu as chief of state (installed Oct. 26), who accepts the resignation of Gen. Khanh as premier and Gen. Minh as chairman of the ruling triumvirate. On Oct. 31 the Council approves Tran Van Huong as premier; his cabinet is installed Nov. 4, and Gen. Khanh is appointed commander-in-chief of the armed forces.

Dec. 19. Dissident army officers (members of the Armed Forces Council) intervene in the government to dissolve the High National Council, which had been functioning as a provisional legislature, and arrest many political leaders.

Laos (Sec. 26)

Apr. 19. A right-wing military junta overthrows the coalition government of Prince Souvanna Phouma. On Apr. 23 Prince Souvanna is asked to remain as Premier and form an enlarged and reorganized government.

May 21. The United States announces that U.S. jets are flying reconnaissance missions at the request of the Laotian government.

Cambodia (Sec. 27) †

Feb. 19. Prince Norodom Sihanouk proposes a 4-nation conference of Cambodia, South Vietnam, Thailand, and the United States to guarantee Cambodia's neutrality and territorial integrity but Thailand declines to participate.
Dec. 8–17. The United States and Cambodia hold talks in New Delhi in an effort to improve relations.

Federation of Malaysia (Sec. 28) *†

Jan. 17–26. Attorney General Robert F. Kennedy confers with leaders of Indonesia, the Philippines, Malaysia, Japan, Korea, Thailand, and the United Kingdom. He mediates a short-lived cease-fire in the Indonesian-Malaysian dispute Jan. 23.
Apr. 25. Prime Minister Abdul Rahman's Alliance party wins 125 of the 159 seats in general elections for the federal Parliament.
June 20. The third summit conference of the heads of government of Malaysia, Indonesia, and the Philippines, held in Tokyo, collapses on the first day over the issue of withdrawing Indonesian troops and guerrillas from Malaysian territory.

Indonesia (Sec. 28) †

Dec. 31. Indonesia announces that it will withdraw from the United Nations if Malaysia takes its seat on the Security Council in 1965.

The Philippines *

V. INTER-AMERICAN AFFAIRS

General

Feb. 7. The O.A.S. Council votes 15–0–2 to establish a 5-nation committee to investigate the January riots in Panama and to assist in finding a solution. Sec. 36.
July 13–21. The Inter-American Committee for the Alliance for Progress (CIAP) holds its first meeting in Mexico City to coordinate and improve the implementation of Alliance projects. Sec. 29.
July 21–26. The American Ministers of Foreign Affairs hold their 9th Meeting of Consultation in Washington, and resolve 15–3–1 to impose economic sanctions on Cuba and to urge all members not to maintain diplomatic relations with Cuba. Sec. 35.
Dec. 5–11. The Inter-American Economic and Social Council holds its third annual meeting in Lima, Peru, to review the Alliance for Progress. Sec. 29.
Dec. 16–18. The O.A.S. Council approves a resolution, the Act of Washington, setting up procedures for the admission of new members.

Bolivia (Sec. 32)

May 31. President Víctor Paz Estenssoro is reelected for a third 4-year term, beginning Aug. 6.

Nov. 3–4. A military junta headed by Alfredo Obando Candia ousts President Paz; Gen. René Barrientos Ortuño, the Vice-President, is sworn in as President on Nov. 5.

Brazil (Sec. 31)

Apr. 1. President João Goulart (sworn in Sept. 7, 1961, upon the resignation of President Jânio Quadros) is deposed following an army revolt on Mar. 31. Ranieri Mazzili is declared interim President Apr. 2.

Apr. 11. The Brazilian Congress elects army chief of staff Humberto Castello Branco as President. He is inaugurated on Apr. 15 to serve until Jan. 31, 1966.

July 22. Congress extends President Castello Branco's term for 14 months to Mar. 15, 1967, and postpones to Nov. 1966 the presidential election scheduled for 1965.

Dec. 14. The United States announces a $1 billion aid loan.

British Guiana (Sec. 32)

Dec. 14. Forbes Burnhan is sworn in as Prime Minister (succeeding Cheddi B. Jagan; People's Progressive party), after the People's National Congress and the United Force win a combined majority in national elections on Dec. 7.

Chile (Sec. 32)

Sept. 4. Senator Eduardo Frei Montalva (Christian Democrat) is elected to succeed President Jorge Alessandri Rodríguez (Conservative-Liberal; elected Sept. 4, 1958) for a 6-year term, beginning Nov. 3.

Costa Rica *

Cuba

Jan. 7. The United Kingdom announces a multimillion dollar sale of 450 buses. Sec. 33.

Jan. 13–21. Premier Fidel Castro pays an official visit to the U.S.S.R. and concludes an agreement calling for increased Soviet purchases of Cuban sugar. Sec. 33.

Feb. 3. The U.S. Coast Guard seizes 4 Cuban fishing boats within U.S. territorial waters; Castro cuts off water supply for the U.S. naval base at Guantanamo in retaliation on Feb. 6. Sec. 34.

Haiti

Apr. 1. Dr. François Duvalier installs himself as President for life. *Sec. 38.*

Mexico (Sec. 37) *

July 5. Gustavo Díaz Ordaz (Institutional Revolutionary party) is elected President, succeeding Adolfo López Mateos (same party; elected July 6, 1958). President Díaz is inaugurated Dec. 1 for a 6-year term.

Panama (Sec. 36)

Jan. 9. Three days of anti-American riots break out in the Canal Zone over flag issue.

Jan. 10. Panama suspends diplomatic relations with the United States and denounces the Canal Zone treaties; the diplomatic break is completed on Jan. 17.

Jan. 11–29. The Inter-American Peace Committee unsuccessfully attempts to negotiate the resumption of diplomatic relations between Panama and the U.S.

Apr. 3. The U.S. and Panama resume diplomatic relations.

May 10. Marco A. Robles is elected President; assumes office on Oct. 1 for 4-year term, succeeding Roberto F. Chiari (assumed office Oct. 1, 1960).

Peru

July 27. President Fernando Belaúnde Terry forms a new cabinet ending a 4-day government crisis.

Trinidad and Tobago *

Venezuela

Mar. 11. Dr. Raúl Leoni (Democratic Action party; elected Dec. 1, 1963) is inaugurated President for 5-year term, succeeding Rómulo Betancourt.

VI. THE MIDDLE EAST AND SOUTH ASIA

The Central Treaty Organization

Apr. 28–29. The 12th session of the Ministerial Council meets in Washington.

July 5. Turkey, Iran, and Pakistan announce decision to establish a regional planning committee and increased economic, technical, and cultural ties.

Turkey *

Aug. 27–29. Large-scale anti-U.S. demonstrations in Ankara, Istanbul, and Izmir over supposed U.S. role in Cyprus crisis.

Arab Countries, General

Jan. 13–17. Thirteen Arab nations hold a summit conference in Cairo to discuss action against Israel's use of Jordan River waters. *Sec. 39.*

Aug. 13. An agreement to create an Arab common market, effective Jan. 1, 1965, is signed in Cairo by Iraq, Jordan, Kuwait, Syria, and the U.A.R.

Sept. 5–11. The Arab chiefs of state meet in Alexandria to implement agreements of their January conference. *Sec. 39.*

The United Arab Republic

Mar. 23. President Gamal Abdel Nasser submits a draft constitution to be in effect until a new National Assembly adopts a permanent charter.

Mar. 24. Ali Sabry is appointed Premier, and Abdel Hakim Amer First Vice-President on Mar. 26.

May 9–24. Premier Khrushchev visits Egypt to mark the completion of the first stage of the Aswan Dam project on May 14. *Sec. 39.*

Iraq

May 3. A provisional constitution is promulgated, providing that Abdel Salam Arif would be President for three years and that the National Council of the Revolutionary Command would retain legislative powers. Prime Minister Taher Yahya reorganizes the Cabinet on June 18.

May 26. President Arif and President Nasser of the U.A.R. sign an agreement in Cairo to set up a joint military command in war time and for exploratory talks on unifying the two governments. *Sec. 40.*

Jordan *

Jan. 15. Jordan resumes diplomatic ties with the U.A.R. broken off in 1961. *Sec. 40.*

July 6. Bahjat al-Talhouni succeeds Premier Sherif Hussein ibn Nasser (appointed Apr. 20, 1963), who resigned because of ill health.

Kuwait

Dec. 6. Sheik Abdullah al-Salim al-Sabah forms a new government, after having resigned on Nov. 30.

Lebanon

Aug. 18. A new Parliament elects Charles Helou as President for a 6-year term beginning Sept. 23. He succeeds Fuad Chehab.

Nov. 18. Hajj Hussein Oueini is appointed Premier.

Syria †

Apr. 25. A provisional constitution is promulgated.

Apr. 28. The treaty of military union with Iraq is officially abrogated. *Sec. 40.*

May 9. Maj. Gen. Amin al-Hafez, chairman of the ruling Revolutionary Council, relinquishes the premiership (assumed Nov. 12, 1963) to Salah al-Bitar (Baath Party) and is named President on May 13.

Oct. 3. President al-Hafez again takes over the premiership from al-Bitar and forms a new cabinet.

Saudi Arabia

Mar. 3. Saudi Arabia and the U.A.R. announce the resumption of diplomatic relations. *Sec. 39.*

Mar. 28. Crown Prince Faisal, the Premier, assumes all powers formerly held by King Saud. *Sec. 40.*

Nov. 2. King Saud is dethroned and Crown Prince Faisal is proclaimed King; he abolishes the post of premier Nov. 18 and makes himself the absolute ruler. *Sec. 40.*

Yemen †

Mar. 28. British planes destroy a Yemeni fort in retaliation for an attack on the Federation of South Arabia. *Sec. 40.*

Apr. 28. Yemen adopts a permanent constitution. Major-General Hamud al-Jaifi is appointed Prime Minister, and Shaikh Ahman Muhammad Numan named head of a Consultative Council, which has legislative authority.

July 13. The U.A.R. and Yemen sign an agreement to coordinate their policies, "as a step toward complete unity." *Sec. 40.*

Israel *†

May 5. The National Water Carrier project, to carry water from the Sea of Galilee to the Negev, becomes partially operational. *Sec. 39.*

The Palestine Problem †

May 28–29. In the Jordanian sector of Jerusalem the Palestine National Congress, holding its first meeting since 1948, forms a Palestine Liberation Organization.

Nov. 13. Israeli and Syrian forces battle on the northeastern frontier. *Sec. 39.*

Iran

Mar. 7. Hasan Ali Mansur is named Prime Minister to succeed Amir Assadollah Alam (appointed Oct. 22, 1963).

Afghanistan

Sept. 19. The Loe Jirga (Grand Assembly) approves a new constitution providing for a bicameral elected parliament, an independent judiciary and limiting the powers of the king and his family. The Loe Jirga is dissolved on Oct. 2.

India

May 27. Prime Minister Jawaharlal Nehru dies and is succeeded by Lal Bahadur Shastri, who assumes office June 9. *Sec. 41.*

Kashmir (Sec. 41)

Feb. 3. Pakistan charges in the U.N. Security Council that India is threatening the special status of Kashmir; 15 meetings by May 18 produce no decision.

Apr. 8. Sheik Muhammad Abdullah, political leader in Kashmir, is released from prison after 10 years.

Ceylon

Dec. 4. The Parliament is dissolved by Prime Minister Sirimavo Bandaranaike after the House of Representatives rejects the 4-year-old coalition government's legislative program on Dec. 3.

Tibet

Dec. 30. The Panchen Lama is deposed.

VII. AFRICA

Organization of African Unity

Feb. 12–14. The Council of Ministers of the O.A.U. meets in emergency session in Dar es Salaam to discuss troop mutinies in East Africa and to appeal for a truce agreement in the Ethiopia-Somalia dispute. *Sec. 42.*

Feb. 24–Mar. 1. The foreign ministers of the O.A.U. meet in Lagos, Nigeria.

July 17–21. The heads of state and government of the O.A.U. meet in Cairo and elect Diallo Telli of Guinea as Secretary-General of a permanent secretariat. *Sec. 44.*

Sept. 5–10. A special session of the O.A.U. meets in Addis Ababa to discuss the situation in the Democratic Republic of the Congo. It establishes a 10-nation Congo Conciliation Commission headed by Premier Jomo Kenyatta. *Sec. 45.*

Nov. 27–28. The Congo Conciliation Commission meets in emergency session in Nairobi, Kenya to discuss the U.S.-Belgian mission for the rescue of hostages. *Sec. 45.*

North Africa

Nov. 29. The Economic Ministers of Algeria, Libya, Morocco, and Tunisia, meeting in Tangiers, Morocco, sign an agreement to form the Maghreb Economic Community.

Algeria

Feb. 20. Algeria and Morocco sign a cease-fire agreement terminating their border war.

Apr. 16–21. The National Liberation Front holds its first Congress and elects Ahmed Ben Bella Secretary-General.

Sept. 20. The National Assembly of 138 deputies is elected for a 4-year term from a single list of candidates designated by the National Liberation Front.

The Democratic Republic of the Congo (*Sec. 45*) †

Mar. 20. Belgian Foreign Minister Paul-Henri Spaak and Premier Cyrille Adoula announce agreement on the settlement of a 4-year financial dispute and other matters.

June 30. The U.N. Operation in the Congo (ONUC) completed the withdrawal of its forces from the Congo.

July 6. President Joseph Kasavubu asks Moïse Tshombé to form a transitional government following the resignation of Prime Minister Adoula on June 30; Tshombé is sworn in on July 10.

Sept. 7. Rebels establish the "Congolese People's Republic Government" in Stanleyville with Christophe Gbenye as President.

Nov. 24–Nov. 28. Belgian paratroopers with U.S. planes rescue about 2,000 foreign hostages from Stanleyville and neighboring towns.

Dahomey

Jan. 19. Justin Sourou-Migan Apithy, the only candidate, is elected President, replacing the provisional regime that overthrew the government of President Hubert Maga on Oct. 27, 1963.

Gabon (*Sec. 44*)

Feb. 19. French troops oust the rebel government, which had deposed President Léon M'ba on Feb. 17, and restore M'ba as President on Feb. 20.

Ghana (*Sec. 44*)

Feb. 21. A constitutional amendment, approved by popular referendum, makes Ghana a one-party state.

Kenya

Jan. 24. A mutiny by native troops is quelled by British troops on the following day. *Sec. 42.*

Dec. 12. Kenya becomes a republic within the British Commonwealth with Jomo Kenyatta as President.

Liberia

Jan. 6. President William V. S. Tubman (elected May 7, 1963) is inaugurated for a fifth 4-year term.

Libya

Jan. 22. Mahmud Muntasser is appointed Premier to succeed Muhyiddin Fekini (designated Mar. 18, 1963), who resigned on the same day.

Malagasy *

Malawi (Sec. 42) †

July 6. Nyasaland becomes the independent state of Malawi within the British Commonwealth with H. Kamuzu Banda as Prime Minister.

Nigeria

Dec. 30. National elections, boycotted by the United Progressive Grand Alliance, are held, with the Nigeria National Alliance winning an apparent majority. Sir Abubakar Tafawa Balewa continues as Prime Minister.

Sierra Leone

Apr. 29. Albert M. Margai is appointed as Prime Minister, succeeding Sir Milton Margai, who died Apr. 28.

South Africa (Sec. 43) †

Southern Rhodesia (Sec. 43)

Apr. 13. Prime Minister Winston Field resigns and is succeeded by Finance Minister Ian Douglas Smith.

The Sudan

Oct. 30. General Ibrahim Abboud resigns as president and prime minister and becomes head of state; Sir el-Khatim el-Khalifa forms a civilian coalition cabinet to prepare for free elections and a permanent constitution.

Nov. 15. General Abboud resigns as chief of state and head of the armed forces.

Tanzania (Sec. 42)

Jan. 12. The Arab government of Premier Sheik Muhammad Shamte Hamadi is overthrown in Zanzibar; Abeid Amani Karume becomes President.

Jan. 20. African troops mutiny in Tanganyika. British forces, called in by President Nyerere, quell the mutiny on Jan. 25.

Apr. 26. Tanganyika and Zanzibar merged as the United Republic of Tanganyika and Zanzibar; the name is changed to Tanzania on Oct. 29.

Tunisia

Nov. 8. President Habib Bourguiba is reelected for a second 7-year term.

Uganda (Sec. 42)

Jan. 23. Mutiny breaks out and is put down on Jan. 25 by British troops, called in by Prime Minister Milton Obote.

Republic of Zambia (Sec. 43) †

Oct. 24. Northern Rhodesia becomes the independent Republic of Zambia within the British Commonwealth, with Kenneth D. Kaunda as its first President.

VIII. THE UNITED NATIONS

General Assembly (Sec. 47)

Dec. 1–30. The Assembly holds the first part of its Nineteenth Regular Session in New York under the presidency of Alex Quaison-Sackey of Ghana.

On the issue of the loss of voting rights because of unpaid assessments, a compromise agreement provided that no formal votes be taken until the conclusion and that items be approved "by acclamation."

Dec. 29. The Netherlands and Uruguay are elected members of the Security Council for 1965–66, and Malaysia for 1965.

Dec. 30. Under a compromise agreement Jordan and Mali split a 2-year term on the Security Council in 1965 and 1966, respectively.

Dec. 30. Authorizes the Secretary-General to use temporary funds to meet the 1965 expenses.

Dec. 30. Establishes UNCTAD as a permanent body of the General Assembly, setting up the Trade and Development Board and a secretariat.

Membership

U.N. membership is increased to 115 with the admission of Malta, Malawi, and Zambia on Dec. 1.

Security Council

Following is a list of major Security Council actions and decisions, with votes:

Mar. 4. Establishing the U.N. Force in Cyprus for peace-keeping operations and authorizing the Secretary-General to appoint a mediator (unanimous). *Sec. 10.*

Apr. 9. Condemning British bombing of a Yemeni fort (9–0–2). *Sec. 40.*

June 4. Deploring the border clashes between Cambodia and Vietnam and sending a 3-man committee to investigate them (unanimous). *Sec. 27.*

June 9. Urging South Africa to renounce the death penalty for anti-*apartheid* leaders in South Africa (7–0–4). *Sec. 43.*

June 18. Condemning *apartheid* and requesting a study of legal and practical aspects of economic sanctions against South Africa (8–0–2).

June 20. Extending the United Nations peace-keeping operations in Cyprus for another three months until Sept. 26 (unanimous). *Sec. 10.*

Aug. 9. Calling for an immediate cease-fire in Cyprus (9–0–2). *Sec. 10.*

Sept. 17. The U.S.S.R. casts its 102nd veto to defeat a resolution deploring Indonesian attacks on Malaysia and calling upon the two countries to reopen negotiations (9–2). *Sec. 28.*

Sept. 25. Extending the mandate of the United Nations Forces in Cyprus until Dec. 26 (unanimous). *Sec. 10.*

Oct. 9. Recommending Malawi (Nyasaland) for United Nations membership (unanimous).

Oct. 30. Recommending Zambia (Northern Rhodesia) and Malta for United Nations membership (unanimous).

Dec. 18. Extending the United Nations peace-keeping operations in Cyprus until Mar. 26, 1965 (unanimous).

Dec. 21. The U.S.S.R. casts its 103rd veto to defeat a resolution calling for Israeli-Syrian cooperation to prevent future clashes in the Sea of Galilee area (8–3). *Sec. 39.*

Dec. 30. Calling for an end to all foreign intervention in the Congo, a cease-fire, and withdrawal of foreign mercenaries (10–0–1). *Sec. 45.*

Other Activities

Aug. 31–Sept. 9. The third U.N. International Conference on the Peaceful Uses of Atomic Energy is held in Geneva.

Mar. 23–June 16. The U.N. Conference on Trade and Development meets in Geneva. (*Sec. 48.*)

Specialized Agencies

International Bank and Fund:

Aug. 31–Sept. 9. The Boards of Governors of the International Bank for Reconstruction and Development, the International Monetary Fund, and the International Finance Corporation hold their 19th annual meeting in Tokyo.

Intergovernmental Maritime Consultative Organization:
October. The 4th I.M.C.O. Assembly is held in London.

International Labor Organization:
June 17–July 9. The 48th International Labor Conference is held in Geneva.

International Law Commission:
May 11–July 24. The I.L.C. holds its 16th session in Geneva.

UNESCO:
Oct. 20–Nov. 20. The 13th General Conference is held in Paris.

World Health Organization:
Mar. 3–21. The 17th World Health Assembly meets in Geneva.

General Agreement on Tariffs and Trade (GATT)

May 4–6. The sixth round of GATT trade negotiations, the Kennedy Round, meets in Geneva. *Sec. 12.*

The Cairo Conference

Oct. 5–11. A second conference of heads of state or government of 47 nonaligned countries is held in Cairo. *Sec. 45.*

INDEX

Abdullah, Sheik Muhammad, 268–70
Acheson, Dean, 26; and Cyprus, 60, 63–4, 65
Addis Ababa, 293, 302
Aden, 242, 258, 259
Adenauer, Konrad, 32, 47
Adoula, Cyrille, 297
Africa, difficulties of independence, 274–6, 283; economic backwardness, 276–7; nationalism in, 273; "neocolonialism," 274; racial hostilities, 274; political instability, 274–6; relations with U.S., 273, 276; U.N. membership, 273, 315; Western European withdrawal from, 273, 274; see also individual countries
Africa, East, army revolts in Kenya, 280; Zanzibar and the Communist threat, 281–2; East African federation (proposed), 277–8, 282; Tanganyika revolts against British, 279–80; O.A.U. and Tanganyika, 280–1; revolution in Zanzibar, 278–9, 281; Tanganyika and Zanzibar merge (Tanzania), 281–2; see also individual countries
Africa, Portuguese, 284, 308; Angolan rebellion, 291–2
Africa, South, apartheid, 274, 290
Agency for International Development (AID), 10, 207, 276
Aid, foreign, 9–11, 318; see also individual countries
al-Badr, Muhammad, 257
Albania, 114
Alessandri, Jorge, 208
Algeria, 281, 309, 310

al-Hafez, Amin, 253–4
Allende Gossens, Salvador, 208
Alliance for Progress, accomplishments, 196–8; and Dominican Republic, 237; and economic development, 189, 194–8, 237; and Haiti, 240; Inter-American Committee for the Alliance for Progress (CIAP), 194, 195; purposes, 187–9, 190–1, 193–4, 195; reappraisal of, 186–7; support of, 196, 207
Amer, Aly, 250
Angola, 284, 308; rebellion in, 291–2
Apartheid, 274, 290, 292
Arab-Israeli relations, U.S. warns against Arab aggression, 247–8; Palestine Liberation organization, 250–1
Jordan River dispute, background, 243–5; Cairo meeting of Arab leaders, 246–7
Arab states, 242; Alexandria meeting of leaders, 250–1; Cairo meeting of leaders, 245–7; see also individual countries; Nasser; United Arab Republic
Argentina, 212–13
Australia, 113, 137

Ball, George W., 4, 9, 22, 24, 71, 91, 333
Barghoorn, Frederick C., 87
Barrientos Ortuño, René, 211
Belaúnde Terry, Fernando, 211
Belgium, and the M.L.F., 28, 49; aid to Tshombé government, 300–301; rescue operations in Congo, 305–6

plan, 63–5; *enosis*, 54, 56, 59, 61, 63–4; military buildup, 58, 60–1; Treaties of Guarantee and Alliance, 54; see also Turkey, Cyprus crisis

Grivas, George, 60–1

Gromyko, Andrei A., 105, 329

Guantánamo Bay, 186, 221

Guatemala, 236, 238

Haiti, Duvalier becomes president for life, 240; internal conflict in, 238; U.S. economic aid to, 239–40

Halleck, Charles A., 6

Hammarskjold, Dag, 312, 317

Hanga, Kassim, 277

Harriman, W. Averell, 100, 298, 300

Haya de la Torre, Víctor Raúl, 211

Heeney, Arnold, 70

Henderson, Douglas, 210

Herter, Christian A., 26, 36, 77

Hilsman, Roger, 112, 123

Hodges, Luther H., 93

Home, Lord, see Douglas-Home, Sir Alec

Honduras, 236, 238

Humphrey, Hubert H., 193

Hungary, 36, 95, 98

Hungarian Revolution, 36

Huong, Tran Van, 156

Hussein I, 246, 255; and Jordan River dispute, 248; requests aid from U.A.R., 255

Illía, Arturo, 212, 213

India, Chinese invasion of (1962), 263; death of Nehru, 270–1; and disarmament, 105–6; Hindu-Moslem relations, 262–3, 265, 267–8, 269; Shastri becomes Prime Minister, 271; U.S. foreign aid to, 264

Kashmir dispute with Pakistan, 242, 271–2; Sheik Abdullah attempts settlement, 268–9, 270; U.N. mediations on, 264–7, 269–70

Indonesia, 137, 160; economic position of, 177; and U.S.S.R., 180–1; U.S. aid to, 181; withdraws from U.N., 184

dispute with Malaysia, 161–2; causes of, 176–7; cease-fire mediations, 178–80; invades Malay peninsula, 182–3; see also Sukarno

Inönü, Ismet, 59, 60, 61

Inter-American Committee for the Alliance for Progress (CIAP), 194, 195

Inter-American Development Bank, 195, 240

International Bank for Reconstruction and Development (I.B.R.D.), 12, 195

International Coffee Agreement, 196

International Monetary Fund (I.M.F.), 12, 195, 249

Iran, 311

Iraq, 243, 246; possible merger with Syria, 253–4

Ireland, 323

Israel, Jordan River dispute, 243–5; U.S. warns U.A.R. about aggression against, 247–8; Levi Eshkol visits Johnson, 250–1

Italy, 12, 50, 117; and the M.L.F., 28, 48; and South Vietnam, 141; trade with Cuba, 220

Jagan, Cheddi B., 209

Japan, 111, 117; defense capacity, 135; economic growth of, 131–2; Joint U.S.-Japan Committee on Trade and Economic Affairs, 132; relations with "People's Republic of" China, 131–2, 134, 135; relations with U.S., 132–3, 135; trade, development of, 132–3; with Cuba, 220; with U.S.S.R., 92, 133–4; Treaty of Mutual Cooperation and Security, 131

Jijon, Ramón, 200

Johnson, Alexis, 145, 247

Johnson, G. Griffith, 76, 332

Johnson, Lyndon B., 2, 39, 40, 52, 70; assumes presidency, 1, 7; and

peace-keeping activities, assembling forces, 323–6; financial difficulties, 321–3, 324, 326, 327, 328; U.S.S.R. proposals, 325–6, 327, 328; U.S-U.K. proposals, 323, 325–6, 327

Cambodia-South Vietnam border dispute, 171, 172–3, 315; and the Congo, 296, 299, 300, 308–9, 314, 316, 321, 322, 324; and Cyprus, 57–9, 60, 62–3, 64, 65, 66, 314, 323; and Israeli-Syrian conflict, 251–2; Kashmir dispute, 264–7, 269–70; and Malaysia, 183–4; and Middle East, 321, 322; and Panama, 229, 315; and South Africa, 290–1, 314; and Southern Rhodesia, 288, 314; and Syria-Israel dispute, 252; and Yemen, 258, 259–61, 314

Committee on the Peaceful Uses of Outer Space, 313; Conference on Trade and Development (UNCTAD), 2, 76, 317, 330–7; Economic and Social Council, 312, 319; Emergency Force in the Middle East, 321; Special Committee on the Policies of *Apartheid*, 291

U.S., and agricultural trade, 75–8; balance-of-payments deficit, 2, 11–12; Canal route proposals, 233; civil rights, 9; and disarmament, 104, 105–7, 108–9; and foreign aid, 8, 9–11; gold losses, 12; presidential control of nuclear weapons, 16–17; tax cut, 8–9; presidential elections, 13–17; see also Johnson, Lyndon B.

Uruguay, 225

Valencia, Guillermo León, 200, 211
Venezuela, 186, 195, 215, 216, 223; Cuban intervention, 216, 223–5
Vietnam, 123, 160
Vietnam, Republic of (South), 1, 7, 33, 34, 113, 137, 161; border dispute with Cambodia, 172–4; communization of, 137, 139–40, 153–

4; proposed neutralization of, 138, 139–40, 142, 146; U.S.S.R. involvement, 140; Vietcong military strength, 143

internal political unrest; friction between religious and political factions, 155–9; overthrow of Diem regime, 138, 152–3; overthrow of Duong Van Minh regime, 138–9; opposition to Khanh government, 154–6; Tran Van Huong becomes Premier, 156, 157

U.S. involvement, enlarges its commitments, 139–41; McNamara assesses situation, 142, 143–4; offers additional military and economic assistance, 157; warns Communist China and North Vietnam, 145–6

Vietnam, "Democratic Republic of" (North), 161; and Communist China, 146–7, 150; and Laos, 164–5; Vietcong attacks, 156–7; U.S. warns against aggression in South Vietnam, 145–6

Gulf of Tonkin, attack on U.S. PT boats, 147–50; Congress supports Johnson's action, 150–51; discussion at U.N., 151; U.S. retaliatory attacks, 148–9

Welensky, Sir Roy, 289
Wilson, Harold, and the M.L.F., 43, 46; and Rhodesia, 290
Wilson, Woodrow, 24
Wirtz, Willard W., 235

Yemen, 253, 314; and Nasser, 256–8, 259–62; union with U.A.R., 256–7; U.K. retaliates, 257–60; U.N. debate on, 258
Yugoslavia, 82, 94, 219

Zambia (Northern Rhodesia), 278, 287
Zanzibar, 277, 281, 282; Communist aid to, 281–3; revolution in, 278–9
Zorin, Valerian A., 108–9

COUNCIL ON FOREIGN RELATIONS

PUBLICATIONS

FOREIGN AFFAIRS (quarterly), edited by Hamilton Fish Armstrong.

THE UNITED STATES IN WORLD AFFAIRS (annual). Volumes for 1931, 1932 and 1933, by Walter Lippmann and William O. Scroggs; for 1934-1935, 1936, 1937, 1938, 1939 and 1940, by Whitney H. Shepardson and William O. Scroggs; for 1945-1947, 1947-1948 and 1948-1949, by John C. Campbell; for 1949, 1950, 1951, 1952, 1953 and 1954, by Richard P. Stebbins; for 1955, by Hollis W. Barber; for 1956, 1957, 1958, 1959, 1960, 1961, 1962 and 1963, by Richard P. Stebbins.

DOCUMENTS ON AMERICAN FOREIGN RELATIONS (annual). Volume for 1952 edited by Clarence W. Baier and Richard P. Stebbins; for 1953 and 1954, edited by Peter V. Curl; for 1955, 1956, 1957, 1958 and 1959, edited by Paul E. Zinner; for 1960, 1961, 1962 and 1963, edited by Richard P. Stebbins.

POLITICAL HANDBOOK AND ATLAS OF THE WORLD (annual), edited by Walter H. Mallory.

AFRICAN BATTLELINE: American Policy Choices in Southern Africa, by Waldemar A. Nielsen (1965).

NATO IN TRANSITION: The Future of the Atlantic Alliance, by Timothy W. Stanley (1965).

ALTERNATIVE TO PARTITION: For a Broader Conception of America's Role in Europe, by Zbigniew Brzezinski (1965).

THE TROUBLED PARTNERSHIP: A Re-Appraisal of the Atlantic Alliance, by Henry A. Kissinger (1965).

REMNANTS OF EMPIRE: The United Nations and the End of Colonialism, by David W. Wainhouse (1965).

THE EUROPEAN COMMUNITY AND AMERICAN TRADE: A Study in Atlantic Economics and Policy, by Randall Hinshaw (1964).

THE FOURTH DIMENSION OF FOREIGN POLICY: Educational and Cultural Affairs, by Philip H. Coombs (1964).

AMERICAN AGENCIES INTERESTED IN INTERNATIONAL AFFAIRS (Fifth Edition), compiled by Donald Wasson (1964).

JAPAN AND THE UNITED STATES IN WORLD TRADE, by Warren S. Hunsberger (1964).

FOREIGN AFFAIRS BIBLIOGRAPHY, 1952-1962, by Henry L. Roberts (1964).

THE DOLLAR IN WORLD AFFAIRS: An Essay in International Financial Policy, by Henry G. Aubrey (1964).

ON DEALING WITH THE COMMUNIST WORLD, by George F. Kennan (1964).

FOREIGN AID AND FOREIGN POLICY, by Edward S. Mason (1964).

THE SCIENTIFIC REVOLUTION AND WORLD POLITICS, by Caryl P. Haskins (1964).

AFRICA: A Foreign Affairs Reader, edited by Philip W. Quigg (1964).

THE PHILIPPINES AND THE UNITED STATES: Problems of Partnership, by George E. Taylor (1964).

SOUTHEAST ASIA IN UNITED STATES POLICY, by Russell H. Fifield (1963).

UNESCO: ASSESSMENT AND PROMISE, by George N. Shuster (1963).

THE PEACEFUL ATOM IN FOREIGN POLICY, by Arnold Kramish (1963).

THE ARABS AND THE WORLD: Nasser's Arab Nationalist Policy, by Charles D. Cremeans (1963).

TOWARD AN ATLANTIC COMMUNITY, by Christian A. Herter (1963).

THE SOVIET UNION, 1922-1962: A Foreign Affairs Reader, edited by Philip E. Mosely (1963).

THE POLITICS OF FOREIGN AID: American Experience in Southeast Asia, by John D. Montgomery (1962).

SPEARHEADS OF DEMOCRACY: Labor in the Developing Countries, by George C. Lodge (1962).

LATIN AMERICA: Diplomacy and Reality, by Adolf A. Berle (1962).

THE ORGANIZATION OF AMERICAN STATES AND THE HEMISPHERE CRISIS, by John C. Dreier (1962).

THE UNITED NATIONS: Structure for Peace, by Ernest A. Gross (1962).

THE LONG POLAR WATCH: Canada and the Defense of North America, by Melvin Conant (1962).

d Edition), by

itical Implica-
Edition), by

ity, by Arthur

nplications for
ohn P. Gillin,
V. Patch, and

vised Edition),

an Policy (Re-

can Policy, by

and Prospects,

beration, 1950-

olicy in Under-
1958).
Percy W. Bid-

bore (1958).
nce (1958).
, by Phillips

A. Kissinger

vard L. Boor-
nd Benjamin

enry L. Rob-